AIRCRAFT WORKSHOP: Learn to make models that

by Kelvin
Shacklock

NEXUS
SPECIAL INTERESTS

Nexus Special Interests
Nexus House
Swanley
Kent BR8 8HU
United Kingdom

First published 2000

© Kelvin C Shacklock 2000

ISBN 1-85486-216-2

Printed and bound in Great Britain

Contents

Before we begin

Some people enjoy seeing a couple of ducks hurtle through a gap in the willows, bank hard onto finals, drop flaps, undercarriage down, flare, reverse thrust and slice a pair of silver shards across the ink black pond . . . gazing at a hawk lazily riding a thermal till lost in the infinite blue . . . watching for hours as a scatter of gulls rehearses its ballet sequence along some rocky cliff.

Designing, building and controlling model aircraft seem to sharpen this enjoyment. Modelling is not competing with the birds but joining their fun. We are not attempting to fly but we are revelling in seeing our creation fly, apparently so effortlessly, with grace, speed and at some risk. And we don't underrate the importance of risk, for this is the salt that brings us back again and again, trying to do better, to overcome some greater challenge. Above all, model planes are not a poor substitute for the real thing. While they are constrained by the same natural laws as full size aircraft there is the fundamental difference that the pilot inside the cockpit cannot also watch the performance.

Over the years modellers can accumulate a very broad spectrum of experience, especially if they have good friends who share their interests, discuss their questions and participate actively in their sport. I have been extremely lucky in the people I have known, the friends I have and the knowledge they have shared without condition. In writing this book I'd like to think that I am passing on some of the enthusiasm, encouragement and support I've enjoyed.

In particular I should name those directly involved in preparing some of the material such as Mark Halliday, my radio guru; Alastair Rivers, on camera for those crucial maiden flight photos; Helen Barr of the eagle eye that can spot a glitch at forty yards and most of all, my wife Helen who amongst her other attributes has had a blind eye for the real costs to us of preparing this material. May you be just as fortunate as you become a builder of model aircraft.

4

Practice	*Why?*	Because

■ This book is written for people of all ages; people who have a love of things that fly; people who dream a little and want to explore for themselves the pure pleasure of making beautiful things that fly beautifully.

The structure of the book is designed to raise questions; questions which will challenge you to think about the reasons why rather than to go for the quick fix that overlooks the understanding.

We learn best by doing. By working through a structured progression of projects you will quickly gain the skills and background knowledge which will eventually set you free to design our own models, follow your own path, build your own dreams.

■ The subject is confined to learning to build radio controlled scale models of powered aircraft.

Making all sorts of flying models would be a hugely complicated process. We settle for one area.

The fastest growing and probably most popular area is reproducing the impression of a real aircraft in flight.

■ The method used is to assume you don't just want to be told, but would also like to be shown.

Proper understanding often involves seeing, doing and reading. That's why there are lots of building photos.

Since each of us learns by our own preferred method, visual, practical and written information is included.

■ The layout of the text is in three columns. This column contains practical instructions on what to do next.

This column poses questions which are likely to arise as you follow instructions on the left.

Explanations of what is happening and background information will be printed in this column.

You may choose to read progressively down the left-hand column, through to completion of a project, or read across the page as you go, to learn more on the subject.

These may be practical hands-on problems you encounter, or theory which you could need to know more about, so you can learn as much as possible while you go along.

There will be no attempt to go deeply into definitive technical theory, but rather to consider common sense reasons for what's happening at a level that's helpful and easily understood.

■ We go right to the beginning and build a hand launch glider or two, quickly progress to more complex models until eventually you graduate with your own 'scratch' built, 1/5 scale, radio controlled masterpiece.

If all I really want to know is how to build and fly a big, high-powered warbird, why should I go through all this kid's stuff with chuckies and such?

We all want to start 'cutting wood' on that plane we dream of building. Please believe it, if you don't already have lots of model aircraft experience you'll break your heart if you start at the wrong end of the model spectrum.

We discuss plans, enlarging them, drawing up your own designs, and consider their structures and stresses.

Lots of people start out with a 4-channel radio controlled trainer so why not cut out all this glider business?

Look upon it as learning your scales before you can perform as a concert pianist. If this approach is not for you, consider the options of buying ARF kitsets. They are quick to assemble and are generally sound aerodynamically, but for us, they are not the stuff dreams are made of.

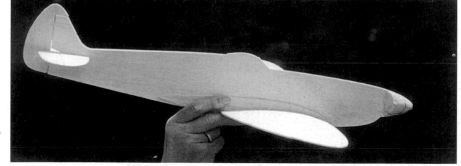

Photo 0:3 *The hand launch glider with adjustable control surfaces helps you to turn aerodynamic theory into practical experience.*

Practice

We are going to practice building and flying all at the same time so you test and fly the models as you make them. In the process we will gradually look more deeply into aerodynamics, stability and flight characteristics, flying techniques and flight line safety.

■ The projects go like this:
We build:
- a glider or two
- a rubber powered Piper Cub
- a large training model that starts out as a glider, gets radio control, then an engine and wheels (there are plans for you to eventually adapt this into a photo plane)
- a sports-scale trainer
- a 1/4 scale vintage racer
- a Schneider sport float plane

Photo 0:4 *The Schneider sport float plane adds lots of fun*

- a 60" scale warbird
- a 1/5 scale Spitfire

With each model we will, wherever practical, try to use a different form of construction and various materials. You will experience the pros and cons of the different methods so you can judge which is best for you.

■ We will also see how to work with various materials like fibreglass, expanded polystyrene and acetate sheet as we mould engine cowlings, covers and a bubble canopy.

■ There are special techniques for getting an accurate fit between wings and fuselage. There are sections on wing stitching, building floats, making your own scale pilot, and a scale exhaust system that really works, all in addition to learning more about working with balsa.

Why?

Most model aircraft books are broken into chapters, each covering an aspect of modelling such as 'The Principles of Flight', 'Choosing a Model', 'Engines', 'Radio Gear' and so on. Why is this book different?

Photo 0:5 *Micro T, a trainer which takes your through four easy steps, shown here completed to stage 4 with an engine, 4-channel radio and steerable undercarriage.*

I thought you bought components like fibreglass cowlings, cockpit canopies and so on.

Photo 0:7 *Rib stitching adds authenticity to scale models of fabric covered aircraft. And it's easy this way.*

Because

Rather than reading a whole book before putting what you have read into practice, you will 'learn as you do it'. You don't need to know all about engines until you start using them. Work your way up to those things gradually once you have ventured into all three fields of design, construction and flight.

Photo 0:6 *The Hawker Fury incorporates your own custom-built fibreglass cowling, pilot and bubble canopy.*

Sure, you can get a lot of components off the hobby shop shelf but, when you can't get exactly what you want, or they don't stock the size you need, isn't it nice to be able to make your own!

6

Practice

■ Materials and equipment you will need to start out with are very basic. Things like a small workbench with a suitable cutting area, a good craft knife, a steel rule, some sandpaper, pins, glue, a sheet of typist's carbon paper and some assorted sheets of balsa are enough to start with. You'll soon need a small carpenter's square and a razor saw so you could also get them now.

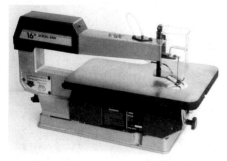

Photo 0:8 *Don't feel you have to jump in and buy 'all the tools'! This scroll saw would be great but only after you know you're going to use it often.*

Once you become totally committed, a power scroll saw and a sanding wheel will be the greatest help to speed your work along. After that you'll probably want a power drill, preferably with a drill press stand. Then, possibly a Dremel power tool.

It will help if you have access to a good photocopier, especially if it is one which can enlarge.

■ In the future you will probably use parts of this book as a reference source. See the first pages of the back Appendices for a quick guide to the contents.

Photo 0:12 *Use the 'Summary of Contents' to quickly find that handy tip you read about.*

Why?

The workshops that the gun builders have are crowded with tools, materials and a whole raft of model components. Can I really start out with such a modest budget?

Photo 0:9 *Unless you already have access to a comprehensive workshop, start out simply with only the basic tools you know you'll need. Later, when you have decided on the level of your commitment it will be time spend more on tools.*

I had never thought of a photocopier as helpful with model making.

Photo 0:10 *This large disc sander is extremely helpful, especially for truing square cuts and angles.*

What do we do now?

Because

Remember not to rush things. If you keep it simple right from the beginning you will gradually accumulate the things you find you really need. This will help you keep within a sensible budget and make sure you don't get carried away by your initial enthusiasm.

Copying plans and drawings will be central to gaining skills for designing your own planes. Try hard to get access to a copier that enlarges.

Photo 0:11 *The Dremel power tool is a high-revving, all-purpose crafting device that's really useful.*

Why not quickly read through the Summary of Contents (pages 241–245) For an overall picture, read in earnest the first couple of chapters, then come on into the workshop.

Chapter 1: Our first 'chuckie'

Practice

■ The first project is to build a simple Spitfire chuckie.

■ The Spitfire makes an interesting model because it features an elliptical wing plan form. Though this was a difficult shape to manufacture, the designer, R.J. Mitchell, chose it for its aerodynamic qualities.

We selected the Spitfire Mk XII-B for its enlarged rudder, which helps with a model's stability and, being powered by the Griffon engine, it has a longer nose than the Merlin-powered Marks. This extra overhang allows the model to be correctly balanced using less weight in the nose. And weight is something we will always work hard to avoid.

■ To begin you will need:

> **Facilities:**
>   Flat work area
>   Cutting surface
> **Tools:**
>   Fine bladed craft knife
>   Steel straightedge rule
>   Pins
> **Materials:**
>   Balsa cement
>   1 sheet $^1/_{16}$" soft balsa
>   Typist's carbon paper
>   Fine sandpaper
>   Plasticine
>   Photocopy pages 9 and 11

■ First, make photocopies of pages 9 and 11, place them over the carbon paper and, using a ballpoint pen, draw over the outline of each part onto the balsa (get the carbon right way up or you'll be very frustrated!).

Why?

Why call it a 'chuckie'?

What can I do if I have no access to a photocopier?

Is this the only way to transfer the outline onto the wood and if there are other ways, why did you choose this way?

Because

A 'chuckie' is a simple hand launch glider which you 'chuck' (throw) into the air. It is intended to loop up over your head, perhaps roll out, then settle into a glide and land.

Photos 1:1 and 1:2   *Compare the difference between the short nose of the Merlin Spitfire (top) with the Griffin Spitfire (below).*

An alternative is to trace the outlines of the wing, fuselage, tailplane, wing fillets and three assembly jigs.
Use these tracings just as you would have used the photocopies.

There are lots of ways to get the plan onto the wood. Some are quick, some tedious. We will use four or five different methods and then you can decide which you like best.

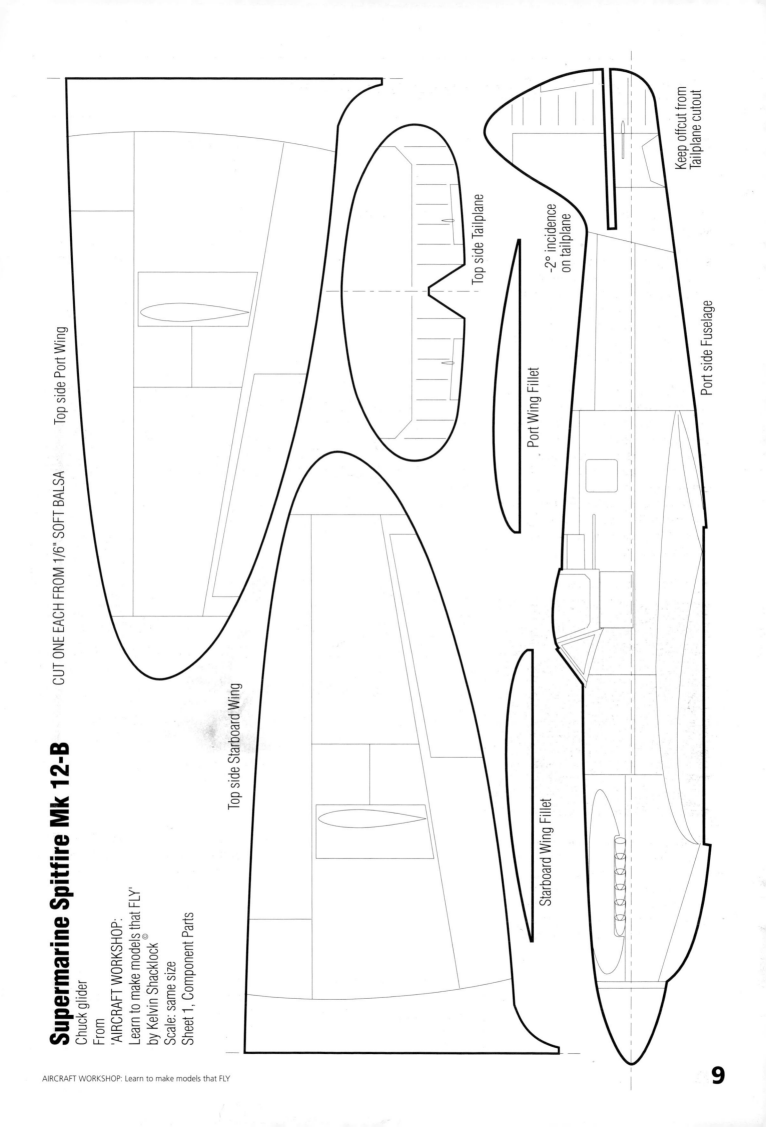

Supermarine Spitfire Mk 12-B

Chuck glider

From

'AIRCRAFT WORKSHOP:
Learn to make models that FLY'
by Kelvin Shacklock ©
Scale: same size
Sheet 1, Component Parts

CUT ONE EACH FROM 1/6" SOFT BALSA

Top side Port Wing

Top side Tailplane

Port Wing Fillet

-2° incidence on tailplane

Port side Fuselage

Keep offcut from Tailplane cutout

Top side Starboard Wing

Starboard Wing Fillet

Practice

When you position the copy on the balsa, take care that the grain of the wood runs along, not across, each major part. One exception to this is the rudder, but there's no alternative if it is to be part of the fuselage cutout.

■ When you are happy with the outlines start cutting!

Don't cut on the dining room table. It could ruin your whole hobby future.

Take care of your fingers. Always hold down on the wood at a place where you can cut away from your fingers.

Use a steel straightedge for the straight cuts.

Make the longer, easier cuts first and don't hesitate to start out well away from the line. You can always make a second or third cut, getting closer to the line each time.

Allow a little clearance for sanding the edges smooth, especially over the long, sweeping curves like the leading and trailing edges of the wings.

■ Sandpaper the edges of all the parts so they are smooth along the line and rounded, except for the under edge of the fuselage where the wings fit, along the square cutoff ends of each wing where they join one another, the tailplane slot, and the underside of the wing fillets where they touch the wings.
Leave all jigs square-edged.

■ Pin down through each wing into its wing jig so that the thin end of the jig just misses the squared off end of the wing while the thick end is about in line with the wing tip (see photo 1:3).

Why?

Why is grain direction important?

What's likely to happen because the grain is wrong way across the rudder?

The knife keeps cutting in towards the line, even when I angle it away.

The cut is in the right place on the top side of the wood, but it has gone further in on the underside.

Every now and then the knife bites out a piece of balsa instead of cutting it cleanly.

I've split a piece right through the middle! Must I throw it away and start again?

Shouldn't I sand the trailing edges of the wings, tail plane and rudder thinner so they're more like an aerofoil?

What's the purpose of leaving some edges square?

Why are we using 'jigs'?

Because

The strength of balsa is very grain dependent, especially when dealing with thin sheets. Cut a 2″ square and feel how it bends and finally breaks. On this sort of model, the rudder is probably the first thing that is broken off by rough handling or crashing. However, it's easy enough to fix.

The grain of the wood can deflect the knife blade out of line. Always cut with the flow of the grain leading away from the part you are cutting out.
There's a knack to keeping the cutting blade vertical. If you've noticed the problem, practise until you can get it right. Meantime, cut slightly oversize and sand it square later.

Is the blade really sharp? It could be that you are pushing the knife through the wood. Use less pressure and just stroke the wood, several times if necessary.

Don't panic. Continue cutting out the piece until it is finished ready for sanding. Spread out a piece of cling wrap or waxed paper. Run a little glue along the split edges, press them together, lay them on the cling wrap and weigh them down flat while the glue dries. And don't glue the weight to the job!

Yes, you should but, so you can proceed quickly and because it won't make too much difference to the way the chuckie will fly, just leave them rounded and move on.

Where surfaces meet and are to be glued, the more surface that can come into contact with the part it's joining, the stronger it will make the joint.

If you've ever tried to hold various pieces of a model together while you wait for the glue to harden, you'll like this process of using jigs. These are supports which are intended to align and hold everything right in a way your hands could never do.

Supermarine Spitfire Mk 12-B

Chuck glider
From
'AIRCRAFT WORKSHOP:
Learn to make models that FLY'
by Kelvin Shacklock©
Scale: same size
Sheet 2: Jigs and Assembly

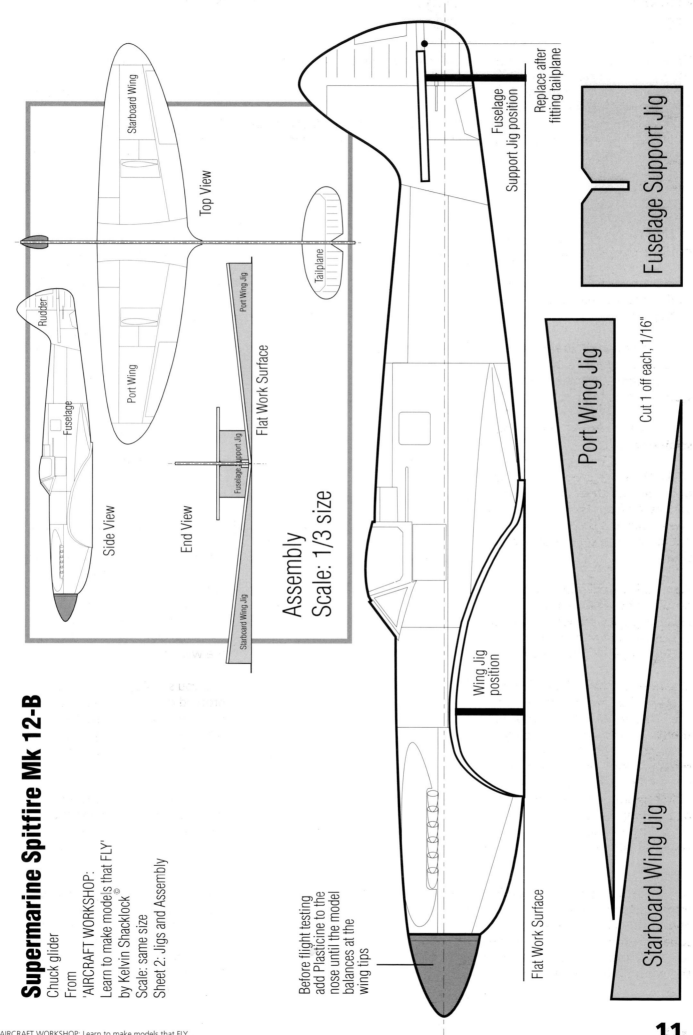

Top View

Starboard Wing

Port Wing

Tailplane

Side View

Rudder

Fuselage

End View

Fuselage Support Jig

Flat Work Surface

Port Wing Jig

Starboard Wing Jig

Assembly
Scale: 1/3 size

Replace after fitting tailplane

Fuselage Support Jig position

Wing Jig position

Flat Work Surface

Before flight testing add Plasticine to the nose until the model balances at the wing tips

Fuselage Support Jig

Port Wing Jig

Cut 1 off each, 1/16"

Starboard Wing Jig

The wings can now be put on a flat surface and moved together. If they are absolutely in line with each other and their jigs are holding them up nicely to form the correct angle (dihedral), glue them together. Waxed paper or cling film will make sure you don't glue them to the bench.

■ Slide the tailplane into its slot and test fit the fuselage support jig. Now place the fuselage over the wings and see that everything fits nicely.
Take apart again and this time glue the tail and wing joints to the fuselage, using the jigs to hold everything while the glue hardens.
Fill the slot behind the tailplane with the offcut.

■ We describe changes in an aircraft's attitude as being on one or more of three axes—

X: 'roll', when a wing tip rises or falls
Y: 'pitch', when the nose moves up or down
and Z: 'yaw' when the nose moves to the side.

We don't use the words 'climb', 'dive' and 'turn' because these terms describe changes in *direction*, which can be very different from changes in *attitude* (an aircraft can fly level while it is in a pitched-up attitude or straight when it is 'yawed' to one side such as in a cross wind).

Why do the wings have to slope up like that?

Most aircraft use 'dihedral' to give stability on the 'roll' axis (see opposite).

Photo 1:3   *Your chuckie model taking shape on the assembly jigs.*

Terms used to describe changes in the attitude of an aircraft.

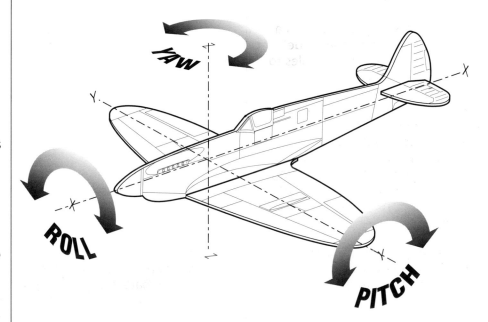

Practice

■ A 'stable' aircraft is one which, if the controls are set to neutral, will continually correct itself on all three axes to maintain straight and level flight (or a predetermined glide angle). Your chuckie is designed to maintain a stable glide. We shall soon trim the model to establish stability.

Stability on the roll axis is generally provided by dihedral. If a gust of wind lifts one wing the plane will tend to automatically come back to level. On a model you will notice it also turns into the roll as part of the correcting action. This comes from pressure on the rudder as the model slides sideways away from the raised wing.

Too much dihedral makes a plane very prone to roll away from even small crosswind gusts.

■ When the glue is hard you are ready to roughly balance the model. Add Plasticine to the nose until it balances while you gently support it at the wing tips.

Begin air tests by standing on a chair and dropping the model. Let it go from all different angles to see how it behaves.

■ The next exercise is to throw the model into a glide. Just behind the wings, take the fuselage between your first finger and thumb and, without letting go, make some practice moves, just like a golfer preparing his swing.

When you feel the model is moving freely along the direction you want it to go, give it a bit extra and let go.

Try to throw it level or even slightly downward. Give it three or four more tries.

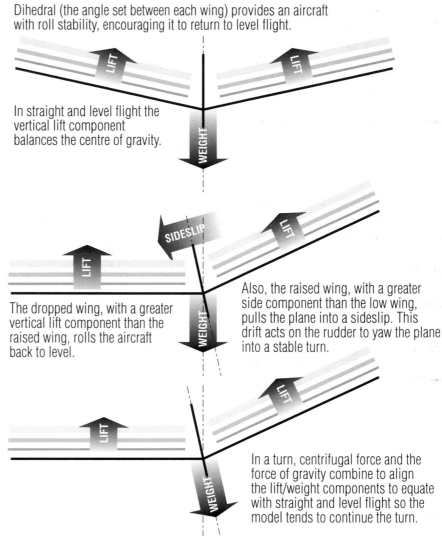

Dihedral (the angle set between each wing) provides an aircraft with roll stability, encouraging it to return to level flight.

In straight and level flight the vertical lift component balances the centre of gravity.

The dropped wing, with a greater vertical lift component than the raised wing, rolls the aircraft back to level.

Also, the raised wing, with a greater side component than the low wing, pulls the plane into a sideslip. This drift acts on the rudder to yaw the plane into a stable turn.

In a turn, centrifugal force and the force of gravity combine to align the lift/weight components to equate with straight and level flight so the model tends to continue the turn.

It doesn't seem to matter how I drop it, as long as it has enough height, the model always goes into an almost vertical dive. Is this what's supposed to happen?

Yes. It is the first fundamental of aerodynamic stability for a fixed wing plane that, if its speed through the air is below flying speed, it should automatically pitch into a dive to restore safe speed.
A correctly trimmed model will do this (and regardless of how close it is to the ground).

Important lesson No 1: keep up your flying speed, especially at low altitude!

Each time I throw the model it turns the same way and one wing hits the ground first. What's wrong?

You may have a twist in the wings. One is trying to climb more than the other. Correct the faulty wing by gently squeezing, sliding and twisting it between your thumb and fingers until it flies straight.

Practice   *Why?*   Because

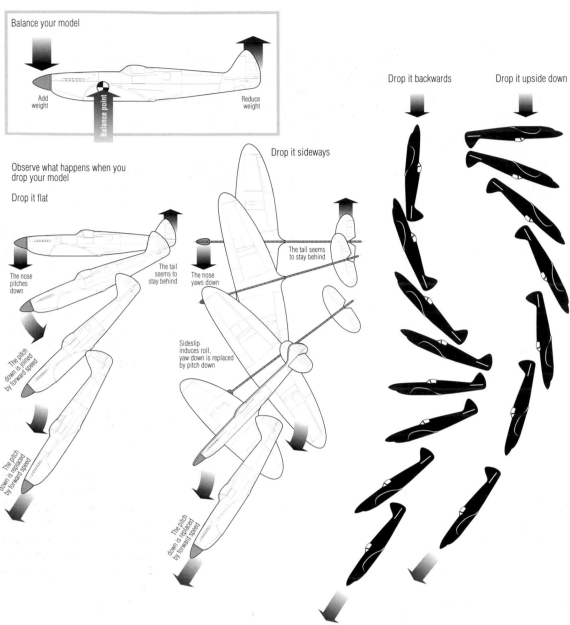

Balance your model

Add weight   Balance point   Reduce weight

Drop it backwards   Drop it upside down

Observe what happens when you drop your model

Drop it flat

Drop it sideways

The nose pitches down

The tail seems to stay behind

The nose yaws down

The tail seems to stay behind

The pitch down is joined by forward speed

Sideslip induces roll, yaw down is replaced by pitch down

The pitch is replaced by forward speed

The pitch is replaced by forward speed

If it's doing more or less the same thing each time you throw it, your throw is not too bad.

■ Now let's study what the model is really doing.

The strength of your throw will produce the first effect you will observe.
Too fast and the model will climb then probably 'stall'.
Too slow and the model will drop, either hitting the ground or, if it just misses, it will build up too much speed and climb, then probably stall.

Just right and the plane should glide at an even angle all the way to the ground.

When I throw mine, it goes into a steeper and steeper dive until it hits the ground.

My model flies quite straight. At first it climbs then gradually pitches forward and glides along until it lands.

Mine climbs almost straight up then stops, pitches forward and dives into the ground.

The one I've made goes a bit like that but it climbs up, slows, pitches forward into a dive and, as it gets faster goes into another climb, then does it all over again.

Surely, the harder I throw my model, the further it should go?

Your's probably has too much Plasticine on the nose. Try it with less.

That's a good start. Meantime do nothing!

One of two possibilities. You are either throwing it too hard or you need more Plasticine on the nose.

Your's definitely needs more Plasticine.

Sorry, it doesn't work that way. In the diagram you will see the relationship between the weight on the nose of

14

Practice ⬇	*Why?* ⬇	Because ⬇

The effect of speed on the tailplane of your model.

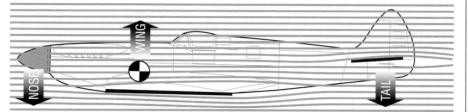

Notice the tailplane of your model is set with the front edge downward while the front edge of the wing is raised slightly. This angle from the centreline is called the angle of 'incidence'. In very simplified terms, the faster the air travels over your model the more the tail is pressed down and the wing is lifted up. This counteracts the weight in the nose, pitching the nose up. The faster the model travels, the greater this pressure, so the greater the pitching effect. Slow down and the opposite happens.

Pitching up into a typical over-speed 'stall'

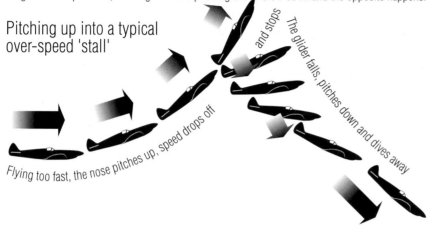

Flying too fast, the nose pitches up, speed drops off — and stops — The glider falls, pitches down and dives away

---

Column 1 (Practice):

■ The amount of weight on the nose and the incidence on the tailplane relative to the wing, work together to set the speed at which your model should stabilise.

Put more weight on the nose or reduce the incidence (angle) of the tailplane and the model will fly faster.
Reduce the weight and/or increase the incidence of the tailplane and the model will fly slower.

■ The faster you want your model to fly, the steeper it will go down.

Only up to a point, the opposite applies and the slower it flies, the shallower the angle of the glide and the further it will fly.
Take that too far and the model will not fly nicely and will 'mush' down quite quickly.

Your task is to find the best speed/angle/distance.

Column 2 (Why?):

I've got the speed of my throw about right, but I just can't get it to fly straight. The wings don't look twisted so what else might be wrong?

Well, that's about it. What do I do next?

I'm surprised that I haven't broken my model yet. It hits things quite fast but just seems to bounce off.

Column 3 (Because):

your model, the speed through the air and the angle of the tailplane. Increasing speed increases lift from the wing and increases down-thrust on the tail. This moves the effective centre of lift ahead of the centre of gravity (C of G) so the model pitches up.

Climbing steeply, the speed drops off, the centre of lift moves back so the model pitches down into a dive.

This can create a never-ending series of stalls until the model hits the ground (usually quite soundly).

You can't force speed into a model that's designed to fly slowly. As you can see, it just skyrockets, loses all the speed you put into it and then struggles to get back to the speed it likes.

Obviously, this is a state we don't want so we begin 'trimming' the model.

Check that the fuselage is straight. Remember, the rudder is part of the fuselage and if that's curved, the rudder will be out of line. You might also check that both wings are about the same weight (when sitting on a table, does the model always fall one way). Sandpaper a heavy wing thinner to balance.

Take this opportunity to just play around with the little glider and get to know what it will or won't do and what it really doesn't like doing.

Go out in a bit of wind and see how it reacts. Try launching it from some high ground so you can see what it does on much longer flights (watch out for head winds coming up the slope or you could see a really long flight!).

This is one good reason for starting out with a very small, simple design. Rather like a bumble bee hitting a window, there's so little weight in the model that it seldom damages itself. Just wait until you start building bigger planes! That's when you'll be glad you have this practical experience behind you.

Chapter 2: Designing your first 'chuckie'

Practice

Now you know some simple rules of flight you can see there's no magic in why models fly. Let's put your knowledge into practice and make a chuckie to your own design.

■ Look through some aircraft books which show 3-views of different types of planes.

Choose something that really appeals to you, but do pick one that's both simple and fairly conventional.

Almost all 3-views found in books will be too small to use without first enlarging them. Let's look at how to do this. There are many different ways.

■ Here are three methods:

- photocopying, using a machine which will enlarge,
- scaling up with dividers or ruler
- making a grid, then drawing by eye using the squares as reference.

Why?

Why do you want me to design my own glider when all I've done so far is build one chuckie?

Right. I can see why I should keep it simple, but wouldn't I learn more from making something unconventional?

What's about the smallest I should make it?

Do I have to follow an actual plane instead of just making up my own design?

Because

As you've seen, a chuckie is easy to build (takes under an hour), uses less than half a sheet of balsa and flies well enough for you to observe *how* it flies. Knowing there's little risk of much going wrong and that you're risking very little anyway, you can give it a go and surprise yourself!

Get to understand the conventional first. Start learning to recognise those normal characteristics which help flight and those which hinder.

The bigger the better, but about 10" is a good compromise at this stage.

Of course not. And, you'd probably make a very good job of it, but this part is as much about enlarging plans as it is about actually designing. You'll learn more doing it this way.

Photo 2:1 *Typical of the 3-views found in many aircraft books.*

AIRCRAFT WORKSHOP: Learn to make models that FLY

A 3-view, particularly suitable for enlarging by using a photocopier

Curtiss P-40 Tomahawk

Wing span: 37' 3¹/₂"
Length: 31' 2"
Height: 12' 4"
Power: Allison V12, 1300 hp
Max speed: 370 mph

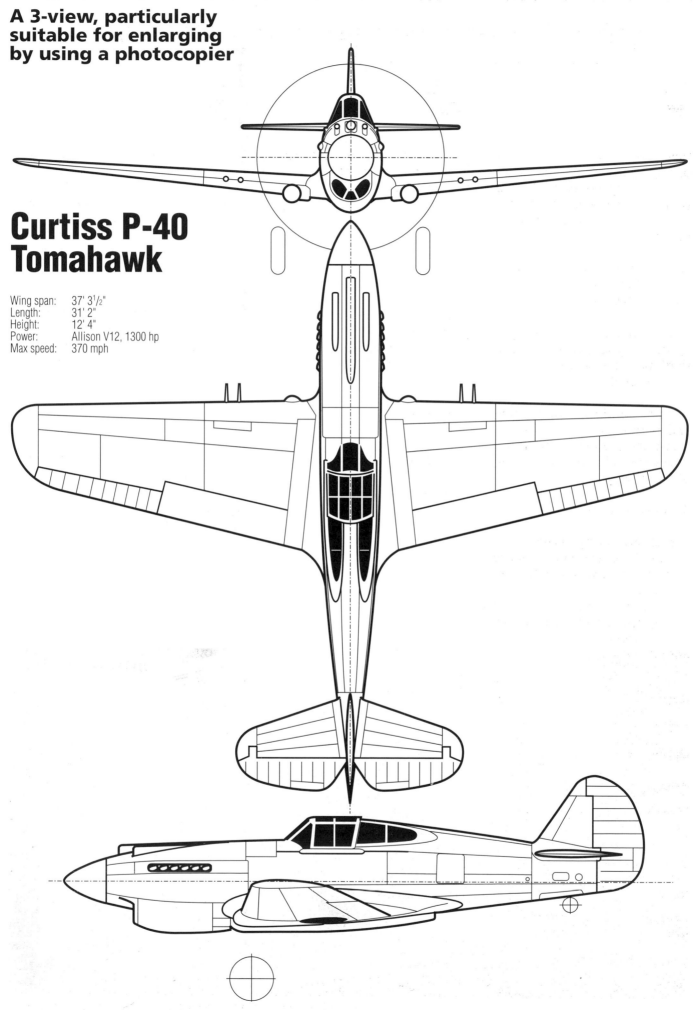

Practice ⬇	*Why?* ⬇	Because ⬇

Let's look at the advantages and limitations of each of these methods.

■ Photocopying

If you have access to a copier which enlarges you have a big advantage.
But remember, the copier is not always as good as you may at first think. It does not enlarge in one huge step. In fact, you will probably want to enlarge to four, six or eight times the size of the original, and this will mean fourth or sixth generation copies. Each time you copy a copy, the quality falls away markedly and the next generation print always looks worse than its previous version.

The quality of the original 3-view; the drawing skill, the reproduction standard, and its size, will all have a great effect on the results you can get when using a photocopier (see below).

This is putting a lot of emphasis on enlarging plans. To be a modeller, do I need to be able to do this or can I not just use full-size plans that are supplied by various publishers?

I have access to a copier, but it won't enlarge. Is this any use to me?

Are photocopiers the only enlarging devices we can use?

If you learn this skill you will be more free to venture into one of the hobby's great rewards, flying your own 'scratch' design models. Many don't experience this adventure and still get a great reward from their modelling. Why not make up your mind after you have designed for yourself a few simple models.

Yes, and you will find there are lots of jobs you'll be able to do more easily because of it, but not as far as helping you with enlarging plans. Your main use will be to make a 'working' copy so as to protect the original.

Great question. No. Some lucky individuals have contacts in the printing industry who can access repro cameras that make precise, one-step enlargements up to quite large sizes. Materials for these machines don't come cheap.

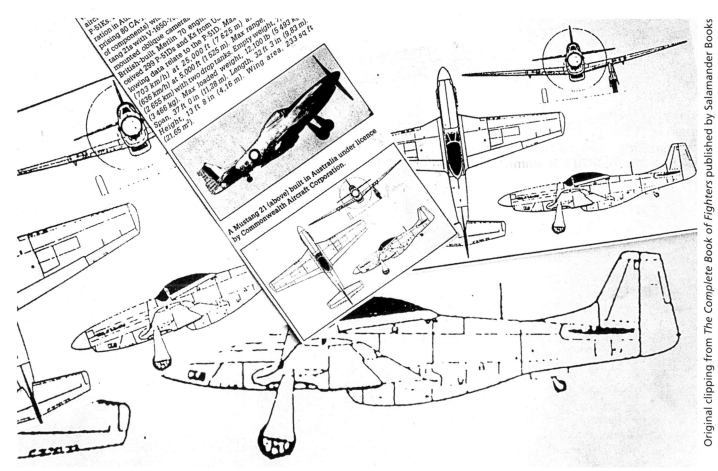

Photo 2:2 *Photocopying from a 1³/₄" span original to a 9⁵/₈" working copy is pushing the system.*

Original clipping from *The Complete Book of Fighters* published by Salamander Books

Practice

Unless you are just going to enlarge at random, you need to calculate what enlargement settings will produce the exact size plan you want.
Assuming this involves several steps, make the first ones at full enlargement and only adjust the final step to produce the exact size.

To calculate, divide say the wing span you want by the wing span on the last print, then multiply by 100 and you will have the % of enlargement required.

Enlarging a plan using a photocopier can be very straight forward, **if you adopt a simple method.** A standard machine which can enlarge will do so by up to 141.42%. At this setting, when you make a copy, then enlarge that copy again, the result will be a plan of exactly twice the size of the original. Using say, international 'A' size paper, the original plan can be a full A4 (210 x 297mm). The first enlargement will then be A3. If this is cut exactly in half and each half is copied again (making sure the cut edge is inside the image area of the machine) you will have two A3 sheets which can then be 'tiled' together with clear tape to form a twice-size working plan of A2 size (420 x 594mm).

Try it, using the 3-view on page 17 as your A4 plan.
With an A3 paper tray fitted, set the machine to maximum enlargement (141%) and, holding the page down flat and square, make the first copy.
Check the exposure to see you do have the best copy the machine can make. When you are satisfied, put the book aside and deal with the copy. Trim it cleanly down the middle and now copy each half using the same settings as before.

Now choose your own 3-view and see how well you can enlarge that one.

Why?

1 Copy the A4 page while enlarging it to A3.

2 On the A3 copy, mark the centre line and, after following the suggestion in '3', cut the A3 page in half to make two A4 pages.

4 Photocopy each A4, enlarging them to A3.

5 On both copies, check that the copier has not cut off part of the image. If so, move the original to give it a bigger border on that edge.

6 On one copy, trim the joining edge exactly on the line you want to meet with the other half. Then, matching the

Most 3-views are in black and white, some have blue backgrounds, while others are in full colour showing paint schemes. Will colour effect the copy quality?

When am I likely to need to make an exact amount of enlargement?

Because

3 As a guide for later on, it is a good idea to draw a cross over each end of the cut line.

two halves of your crosses, lightly tape to hold them in place. Hinge up the top sheet and smear a thin line of balsa cement along the open joint and lower the top sheet back down onto the glue. Run your finger along the join to make it firm.

You now have an A2 sheet exactly twice the size of the original in the book.

Colour can have a big effect. Some colours, even quite light, bright colours will copy as black. Often this will hide detail you want. Experiment with settings for the best available detail.

At this stage you may want to be sure you can fit say, a wing, onto a particular piece of balsa that's left over, or perhaps you just want a model to be the same size as another to make better comparisons with it. Later, this could be quite important

Practice

■ Scaling

Scaling up a plan by using dividers or measurement is often more suitable than photocopying if you want to make big magnifications from the original and if the final size is to be very large.

To protect the original, make a photocopy, then put the original away (if you've ever borrowed a library book and found some vandal has drawn over an illustration, you'll know why we include this step!).

Now decide how much you want to enlarge the plan. If this is say twice, three or four times the original, you will be able to 'step out' the final scale using simple dividers only. If it is to be a fractional size such are 2$\frac{1}{4}$ times or 3$\frac{1}{8}$ you are into a different ball park and it will be necessary to use a measurement system. For our exercise, let's just enlarge the P-80 plan on page 21 to twice size, using simple dividers. Draw centre lines vertically and horizontally through the 3-views on your photocopy. These are to be your 'datum' lines from which all major measurements will be made. Using an A2 piece of drawing paper and measuring from the top of the sheet down, step out twice the space of the A4 and draw the horizontal datum lines. Repeat this for the vertical datum lines by doubling the space from the left edge of the paper. Before going further, check the two sets of lines are at right angles to each other.

Next, with your dividers on the A4, measure how far a wing tip is from the centre datum. Then on the A2, step twice this distance off and make a small vertical mark. Return to the A4 and now measure vertically how far this point is above the horizontal datum. Step this off on the A2 and make a small horizontal mark. Where this mark crosses the previous mark is the position of the enlarged wing tip.

Why?

when for instance, you may want to make a model at a particular scale such as $\frac{1}{4}$ or $\frac{1}{6}$ size. Perhaps you may want to model around an existing part like an engine cowling or propeller spinner available off-the-shelf.

Because

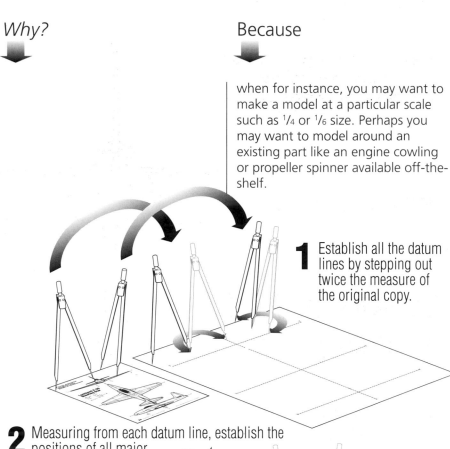

1 Establish all the datum lines by stepping out twice the measure of the original copy.

2 Measuring from each datum line, establish the positions of all major points which can then be joined by straight lines.

3 Step out the minor measurements from established points or from the datum lines.

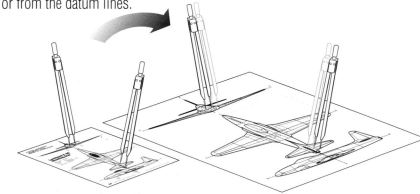

4 By eye, draw in the curves which link the points and lines you have plotted, then add detail (the better your eye, the fewer plots you need to make).

We don't normally use A4 and A2 paper. What sizes are these?

An A1 sheet of paper measures 594mm wide x 840mm deep. When this is halved on its long side it becomes A2, halved again and becomes A3, then A4, A5, etc. An A4 sheet measures 297mm x 210mm (11$\frac{3}{4}$" x 8$\frac{1}{4}$").

20

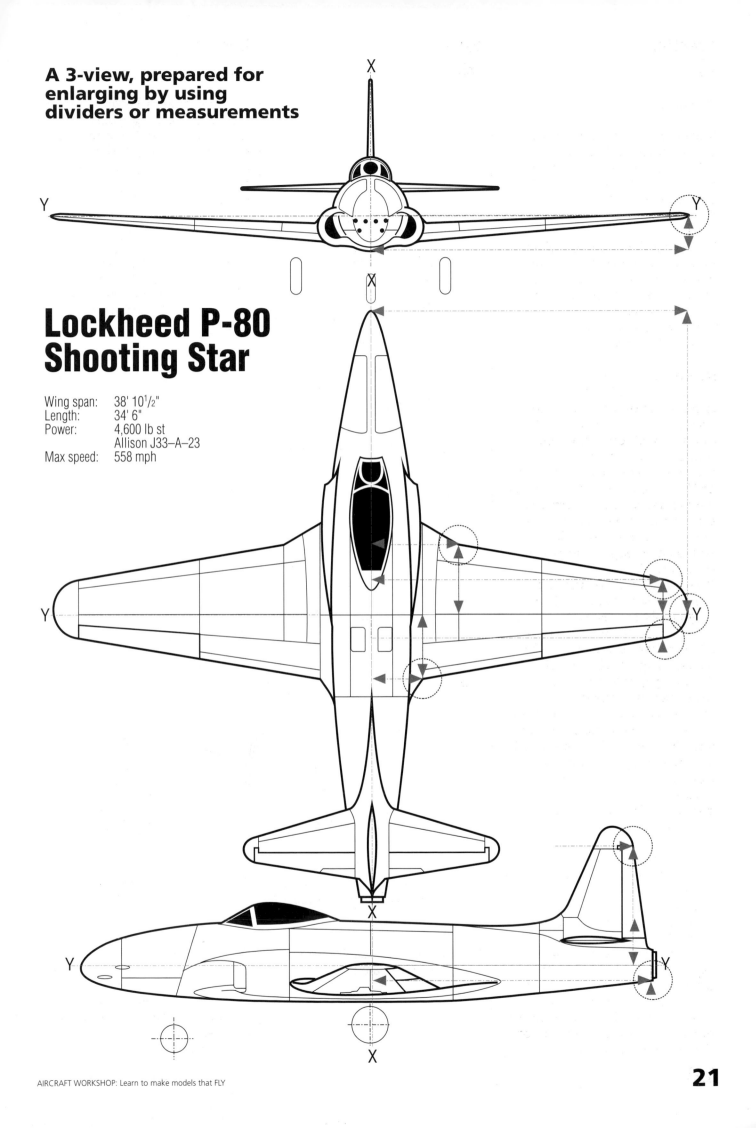

A 3-view, prepared for enlarging by using dividers or measurements

Lockheed P-80 Shooting Star

Wing span: 38' 10¹/₂"
Length: 34' 6"
Power: 4,600 lb st
             Allison J33–A–23
Max speed: 558 mph

Practice

You can alter the scale between the two plans by multiplying each measurement on the first plan by the enlargement factor, then apply the results to the second plan. In this case, by two times (200%).

More complicated enlargement factors like say, 215% can be carried out very easily using 'proportional' dividers. These are double-ended and have an adjustable pivot point. By trial and error the pivot is moved so that when one end measures 100 units, the other end shows 215 units. You then take measurements from the first plan using the 100% end of the dividers and plot on to the second plan using the opposite end.

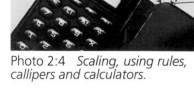

Photo 2:4   *Scaling, using rules, callipers and calculators.*

Why?

This sounds a bit like reading map references where you establish a point by its latitude and longitude.

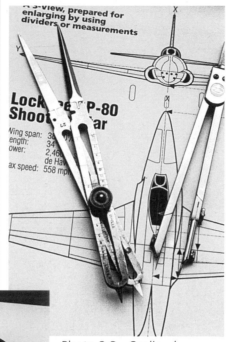

Photo 2:3   *Scaling by simple steps of the dividers.*

Photo 2:5   *The ultimate scaling instruments.*

Because

That's exactly how it works, but instead of latitude and longitude, you work with distances up or down from the horizontal datum line and left or right from the vertical datum line.

Instead of using dividers for these more complicated enlargements, you can use a ruler to measure distances on the first plan, multiply that distance by the enlargement factor, and put down the resulting measurement on the second plan. Rulers are not the ideal instruments for measuring tiny units. Consider buying a calibrated calliper. This is an instrument which can accurately measure between two points, over two points and even the depth of recesses and holes. You will find it invaluable when building a model, but it is also ideal for plan scaling. They come in a range of qualities and for our purposes a cheap plastic model is quite adequate. It will take you little time to become accustomed to using it.

When you are scaling by using a measurement system you will find a little pocket calculator is indispensable for making the scale multiplications. There's no problem if you are working in the decimal system but, if yours is an imperial system using inches, move away from $1/8$, $1/16$ and $1/32$ and start using the language your calculator can compute, that is decimal inches where $1/10$ and $1/100$ of an inch become your fractions (see back page of this book for conversion scales).

Very expensive instruments such as those used by engineers are wonderful luxuries which make scaling plans a lot easier. If you have access to a digital calliper and programmable calculator, the two will work together for a very smooth operation.

Whatever instruments you use, if you become skilled at scaling plans you will be a much more accomplished modeller than a large proportion of your fellow builders.

For grid enlarging. Photocopy onto copier transparency film and use on top of 3-views

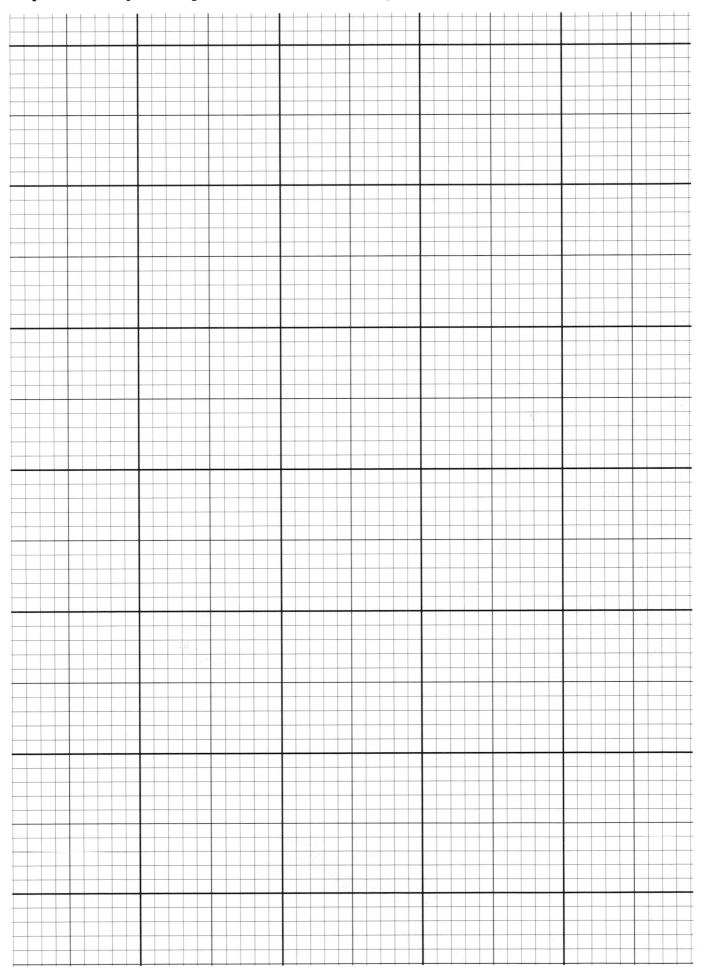

Practice

■ Grid enlarging

Before we had photocopiers, grid enlarging was probably the most common way modellers enlarged plans and today it is still a fairly quick and easy system, especially if you have any drawing skills.

Either use a photocopy of the original 3-view and draw grid lines over it as you can see on the Messerschmitt plan opposite or alternatively make an overhead transparency copy of the grid lines supplied on page 23 and overlay it on top of the original 3-view. Place dominant lines of the grid pattern along each of the centre lines of the 3-view before you square it up. Tape down a couple of opposite corners to stop the overlay from moving while you work.

Decide how much you are going to enlarge the original. For this exercise we will use page 25 and enlarge it by 200%.

Take an A2 sheet of drawing paper (check it is square) and a strip of paper about an inch wide and as long as the long side of the A2. With dividers set to exactly span two squares of the original drawing's grid pattern, step off down one edge of the strip of paper, marking with a pencil, each step as you go, all the way to the bottom of the strip.
Now use this strip to mark out your A2 sheet of paper.

With one end of the strip exactly at the top of the page, transfer its marks to one edge of the sheet. With the same end of the strip to the top, repeat the marks on the opposite side of the sheet.

Turn the sheet at right angles and repeat the process so that all four edges are marked, and the opposite edges exactly match each other.

With a good clean straightedge and using a very sharp pencil, join the marks to form your grid

Why?

I'm no artist. Does this mean this system is not for me?

Will the transparency be right for all enlargements?

I'm still a bit confused. Say it again.

Because

No it doesn't. It just means you will probably have to spend longer comparing your drawing with the original. People with a reasonably good drawing eye find it easier to judge curves and details, relative to the grid pattern. Drawing skill, while it is a big help in seeing whether or not you have captured the correct 'look' of a curved line, it is not an imperative.

A smaller grid than the one provided would be useful when enlarging from a smaller 3-view. Why not make a second transparency with the copier set to reduce it as far as possible? Even if you don't need it now, it will come in handy sometime soon.

See on the Messerschmitt plan how the centre line runs vertically down through the spinner, wings and out through the rudder. Find the corresponding line on your drawing grid and make that the centre line of your enlarged plan. Now do the same for other major lines. To help you remember which is which, lightly number some lines both on the original and on your sheet.
The all-important part of the last few pages was that you decided to have a go.

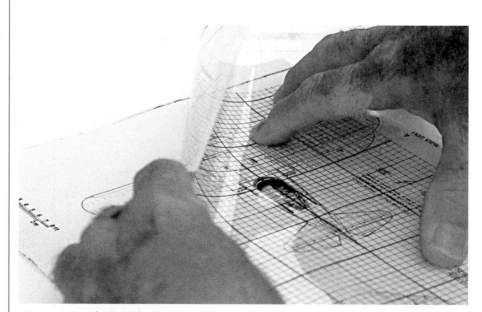

Photo 2:6 *Placing the transparent overlay (photocopied from page 23) over a typical 3-view plan. This is then taped in place and provides reference lines while you draw the full size plan.*

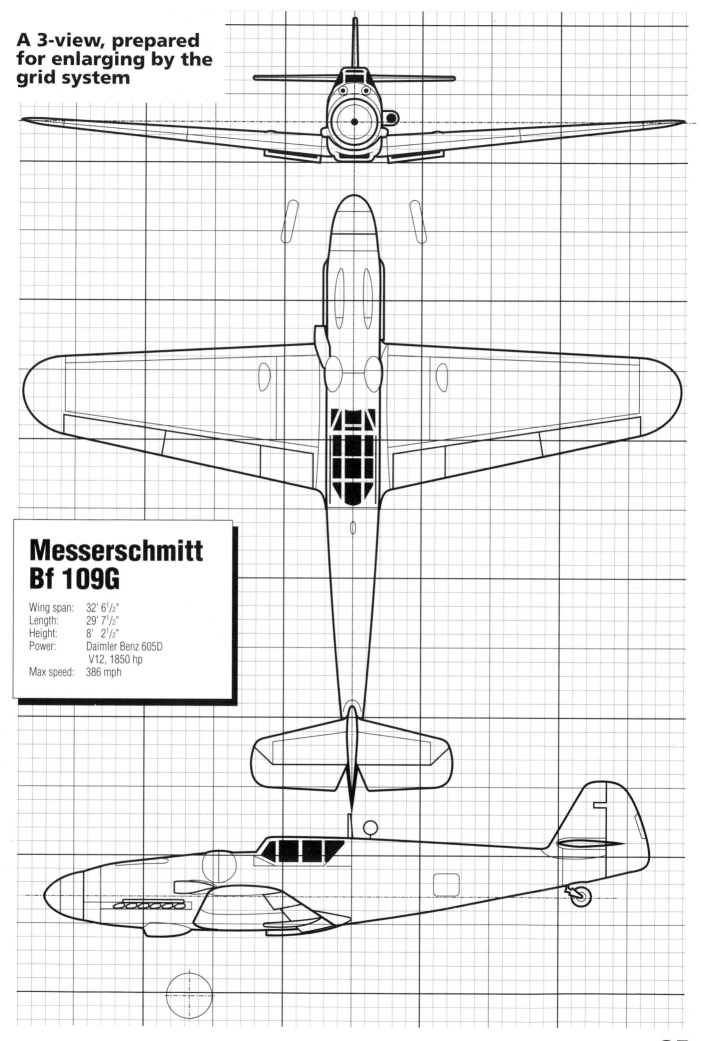

A 3-view, prepared for enlarging by the grid system

Messerschmitt Bf 109G

Wing span: 32' 6$\frac{1}{2}$"
Length: 29' 7$\frac{1}{2}$"
Height: 8' 2$\frac{1}{2}$"
Power: Daimler Benz 605D
               V12, 1850 hp
Max speed: 386 mph

Practice

pattern. To help you find your way, make every fifth line bold, and every second bold line even bolder.

When the grid is finished it is quite a good idea to seal it with a plastic spray to stop it from smudging (don't bother this time but remember to get some from an art materials supplier for future use).

Begin transferring the 3-view from the original onto your drawing by firstly matching the boldest lines on your sheet to those on the original, then you can quickly decide which lines on your sheet will be the centre lines of the views. This establishes the relationship between the two plans.

Match some critical points on the original drawing with locations on your drawing until you can see a general impression of where the main pieces will fall.

Location of wingtips, spinner, back of the rudder, wheel centres and so on are most helpful.

Rule in a few of the important straight lines like the leading edges of the wing, then join them up to other key points.

Now check that you have counted correctly before you go too far.

Just work away at it quietly and you'll be surprised how soon you will see the aircraft appear.

1

On a long strip of paper, step out the grid line spacing at twice the original.

Mark every 5th line bold, then make every second bold line even bolder.

2

With the end of the strip of paper exactly on the top edge of your drawing paper, mark the ends of the horizontal grid lines. Do both sides.
Caution: Don't reverse the paper for the second side.

Your A2 size drawing paper which, before you start, you check to be sure its corners are all square (or your model could end up out of square!).

3

Do the same for the vertical grid lines at the top and bottom edges of your paper.

4

With a very sharp pencil (and keep sharpening it as you go) join the marks to form your grid pattern, using bolder lines for each fifth line and even bolder ones for every second bold line.

5

You now have an A2 page with a grid pattern which represents the grid on your original plan, but which is 200% larger.

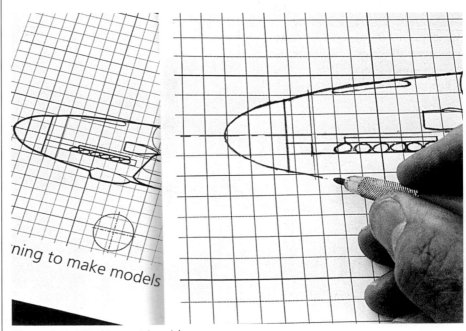

Photo 2:7 *Working with grids.*

■ Summary of enlarging

You have now had a chance to practise three methods of enlarging a plan.

If you have access to the equipment, you probably found the photocopying process by far the easiest.

The scaling system showed that big enlargement factors can be handled well, provided you have some accurate measuring gear.

The grid system is probably easier than scaling but calls for more drawing skill.

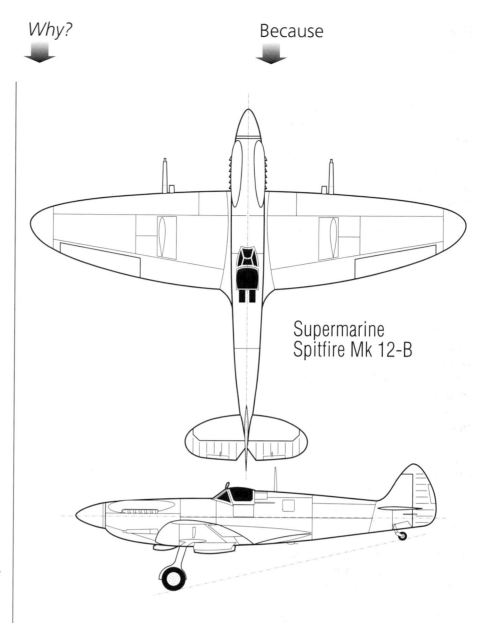

Supermarine
Spitfire Mk 12-B

■ From 3-view to construction drawing

You have three enlarged drawings, each showing the front, side and plan (top) views of an aircraft.

Choose one, and now turn it into construction drawings to build a balsa chuckie.

The Spitfire you built in chapter 1 was drawn from the 2-view opposite. Now study the plans you used on page 9 and see what changes were made, especially to accommodate the wing and tailplane.

Have another look at the diagram on page 15 and see why the changes were made, then go to it.

It may be useful to reread the building instructions given on pages 8–12.

Place tracing paper over your plan and draw in the construction changes, part by part.

Well, that presented me with a fairly steep learning curve. The photocopying was OK but I really started to wonder if I'd manage the scaling exercise. However, I have succeeded and I've a nice little P-80 plan to prove it!

Further on there will be other challenges. If you are prepared to grapple with them the same way, and see them through to a better understanding you will, in fact, be building your skills while you're building your models.

Above all, we hope you enjoyed being challenged because, after all, we are all in this for the fun we can get from it.
See how the airflow over the

Practice

■ Building

When you're happy with the drawing, transfer the tracing to your wood. This time, instead of using carbon paper, prick a whole line of pin points along each outline of a part, just deep enough to leave an easily recognised mark on the wood. Cut out the part by joining the pin dots.
Come back in an hour or so and tell us how you got on.

■ Test flying

Once the glue is properly hard, begin the balancing and test flying sequence.

The one new factor introduced since you test flew our first chuckie is the tailplane/wing angle.

If you got it right you are experiencing no problems.
If not, have another study of the diagram on page 15 and make any changes indicated.

■ Trimming

Incorrect setting of the incidence between the tailplane and wing shows up some of the effects of 'drag'.

Air does not like being disturbed. When your model speeds through it, the air resists being moved out of the way and gets all stirred up. It also resists being rubbed by the surface of the model. All this activity requires energy. That energy is taken from the speed of the model, so it slows down. And that, in a nutshell is DRAG.

Why?

You have made particular mention of the diagram on page 15. What should I be looking for?

Why not use carbon paper as we did on our first model?

Because

tailplane needs to be deflected upward so as to draw the tailplane down. This is to counterbalance the weight in the model's nose and can only happen if the tailplane is set at a different angle to the line of the wing (wing leading edge raised or tailplane leading edge lowered). For this model you are working to a 3° difference.

Throughout the book, where we can, we will introduce you to different methods of doing the same things. This way you can experience a whole range of techniques, then decide for yourself which is the best approach for you. Carbon paper is quick, and easy, but I think it's messy. The pinprick method is clean, but leaves a 'dimpled' edge.

Photo 2:8   *Imagine the drag caused by airflow over the complicated shapes and obstructions of this vintage Stearman Kaydet.*

Photo 2:9 *Compare the smooth lines of this Pulsar with the Stearman above.*

A complicated aircraft such as a WW1 biplane with struts, stay wires, undercarriage and irregular and rough shapes produces a lot of drag. We call this 'parasitic' drag – drag that robs the aircraft of energy while doing nothing to help it to fly.

On the other hand, 'aerodynamic' drag is the resistance which results from producing 'lift'. And of course, lift is what flying is all about (without lift, you don't get flight).

In very simplistic terms, aerodynamic drag results from the work of lifting, while parasitic drag results in useless work.

Back to the model glider:

If the tailplane angle is trimmed too flat (relative to the wing), the plane will have to fly faster to lift the nose. If the speed needed to do this is faster than the parasitic drag will allow the model to fly (terminal speed), the model will continue to dive, right into the ground, regardless of how high it starts from.

In the opposite situation, if the tailplane is trimmed at too great an angle, more weight must be added to the nose to counteract the stronger effect of the tailplane. The wing must then produce more lift to hold up the added weight. This increases aerodynamic drag, so the glider must descend more steeply to gain the speed necessary to produce the extra lift. Consequently, the model does not fly as well.

Good design aims at reducing drag by making better shapes, lighter structures and setting more precise balance/trim adjustments.

The relevance of the angle (incidence) between the tailplane and wing needed to produce lift, and its resulting influence of drag.

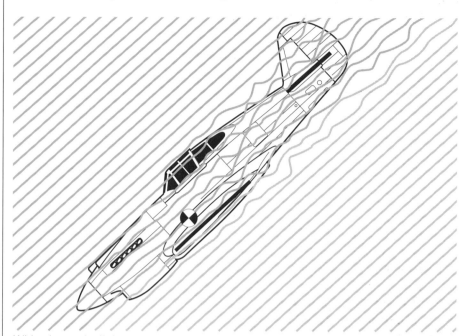

With wing and tailplane set for insufficient lift to sustain flight a dive develops. Parasitic drag limits the speed of the dive to below that needed to produce adequate lift to recover from the dive. A crash is the inevitable result.

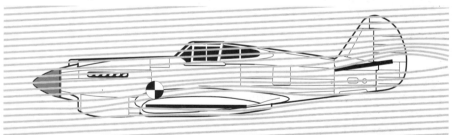

High aerodynamic drag, through too much angle between the tailplane and wing (needed to counter C of G set too far forward), causes the glider to 'sink' rapidly.

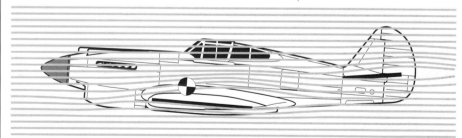

High aerodynamic drag, through excessive lift components needed to counter excessive overall weight, causes the glider to 'sink' rapidly.

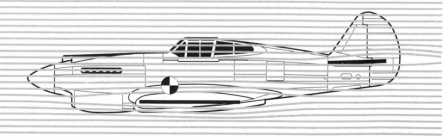

Moderate aerodynamic drag from moderate lift components results in an extended glide.

Chapter 3: Glider with control surfaces

Practice

Why?

Because

■ As our objective is to build radio controlled aircraft, it's time to learn how the controls work and see the effects they produce.

In this chapter you build a larger hand-launch glider which incorporates adjustable 'control surfaces' such as you find on real aircraft.

Each time you fly the model the control surfaces can be adjusted, firstly to trim out a stable glide, then to induce intentional manoeuvres such as port and starboard turns, loops, spins and so on. During the process we encounter terms like 'camber', 'aerofoil', 'angle of attack', 'wing loading' and again, the 'stall'.

The subject model is again our trusty 'Spitfire'. If this bores you, design your own from another 3-view. Enlarge it to about a 2 foot (600mm) wing span and be sure to incorporate the same design features we have added such as the control surfaces and wing 'camber'.

Instructions will be as if you are building from the plans supplied on the opposite page (31). Enlarge the plan to twice size. The fuselage measures 19" (482mm) long if you get the procedure right.

Photo 3:1 *This one looks a lot bigger than twice the size of our first chuckie.*

How long will this model take to build?

Taking your time, you should have this one built during one evening so the glue is hard enough to begin test flying it the following morning.

What is the importance of knowing all these new terms?

This depends upon how far you want to take the sport. The further you go, the more important it becomes in your reading, discussion and practice.

Are there any reasons for continuing to use the Spitfire for the subject model?

The main reason is that it is a design you are familiar with. By building the same design again you will be better able to assess how well it flies in the larger scale and, if you have any problems with its flight, you'll be able to more quickly make the necessary corrections to set it right. However, you could also argue that you learn more by designing your own model. If you want to, use your preferred enlarging method for another plan and follow this building practice.

■ You will need:

Additional tools:	Materials:	
		Cyanoacrylate instant glue (thin)
Small pliers	Balsa Sheet:	Balsa cement
Scissors	1 @ 3" x 36" x ¹⁄₁₆" (75 x 920 x 1.6mm)	Aluminium sheet 0.12" (0.3mm) thick
Sandpaper block	1 @ 6" x 36" x ³⁄₃₂" (150 x 920 x 2.4mm),	– say an old printing plate
	if 6" wide is unavailable, edge-join 2 @ 3"	Pins
	1 @ 3" x 36" x ¹⁄₈" (75 x 920 x 3.2mm)	Fine sandpaper
		Masking tape (used if edge-joining balsa sheets)

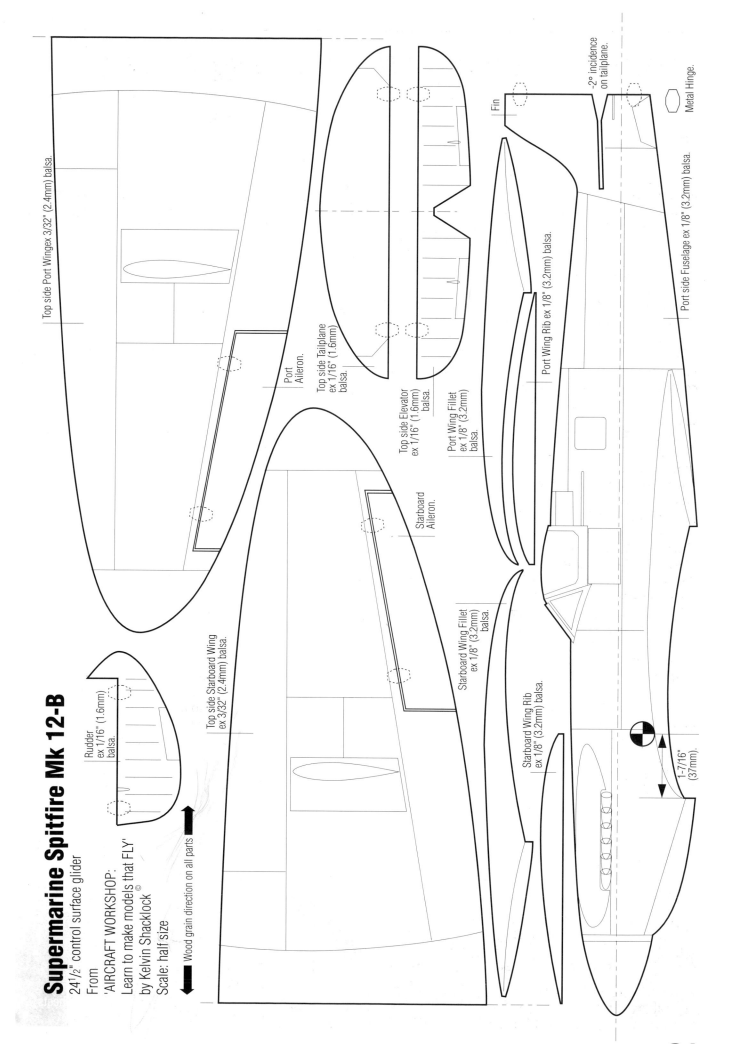

Supermarine Spitfire Mk 12-B

24¹/₂" control surface glider

From

'AIRCRAFT WORKSHOP:
Learn to make models that FLY'
by Kelvin Shacklock ©
Scale: half size

◀ Wood grain direction on all parts

Top side Port Wing ex 3/32" (2.4mm) balsa.

Rudder ex 1/16" (1.6mm) balsa.

Port Aileron.

Top side Starboard Wing ex 3/32" (2.4mm) balsa.

Top side Tailplane ex 1/16" (1.6mm) balsa.

Starboard Aileron.

Top side Elevator ex 1/16" (1.6mm) balsa.

Port Wing Fillet ex 1/8" (3.2mm) balsa.

Starboard Wing Fillet ex 1/8" (3.2mm) balsa.

Fin

Port Wing Rib ex 1/8" (3.2mm) balsa.

Starboard Wing Rib ex 1/8" (3.2mm) balsa.

-2° incidence on tailplane.

Metal Hinge.

Port side Fuselage ex 1/8" (3.2mm) balsa.

1-7/16" (37mm).

Practice	*Why?*	Because

Practice ⬇

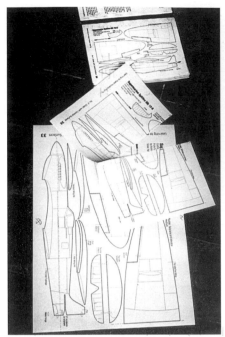

Photo 3:2 *Remember how you scaled up the 3-view using an enlarging photocopier. You can use the same technique here.*

■ Building

Follow the building procedure you used to make our first chuckie.

The initial difference is that you will be using different thicknesses of balsa. Following the plan, mark out and cut each part from the appropriate thickness of sheet balsa. Include the ailerons with the wing panels and only cut them free after general sanding.

Using scissors, cut out 8 metal hinge plates from light aluminium sheet such as used to make regular offset printing plates.

To fit the control panels, at all hinge locations carefully insert your craft knife into the edge of the balsa and make a deep cut. Into the cut, insert a hinge plate on one side only of each hinge joint. Lock in place by piercing from one side of the balsa, then wet with cyano. Slide each control panel with its hinges into their opposite cuts leaving a small gap all round the panel, then repeat the hinge locking process.

Why? ⬇

I can't get balsa sheet that is 6" wide. How do I 'edge-join' two sheets of 3" wide balsa?

I find that marking out the plan onto the wood is a real bind. Have you any other suggestions for doing this?

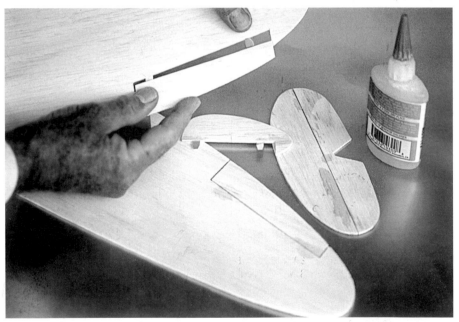

Photo 3:3 *Slide the control panel hinges into the opposite cuts you have made.*

My local printer isn't helpful with supplying an old litho plate. What are the alternatives?

Why use cyanoacrylate to glue the wing panels to their ribs when we use balsa cement for other joints?

Because ⬇

It's easier than it might appear. Firstly, trim the edges of two 3" wide sheets until they snugly fit against each other. Keeping them tightly together, run a strip of masking tape down the join and firmly press it on. Turn over the sheets and lift the joint line so the two sheets hinge apart. Run a little balsa cement along the join edges then hinge the sheets flat so that the join closes against the glue. Weight it down flat and allow to dry. Remove the tape and treat as if it were a single sheet 6" wide.

An adaptation of the 'pin-pricking' method is to run round the outline with a fine craft knife blade. Use the blade to prick through the plan and even make some major cuts right through paper and wood.

By the way, take care not to make two wings for the same side. It's a mistake that's too easy to make!

Look for something about 0.3mm (0.12"). Even better, if you have access to old or damaged 3½" computer disks, cut from the steel slide.

Thin cyanoacrylate is a deep-penetrating glue which can be run into joints after they have been pinned together 'dry'. It's easier to use, but is expensive, so if cost is a factor, use it sparingly.

Practice

Curve each wing panel over its rib. Pin and glue with cyano. When hard, sand each wing 'root' until both wing panels butt together neatly when each wing tip is raised to 1³/₈" (35mm) above the building board. Glue together. Work out your own jigs to hold all major parts in place while gluing, and then assemble.

Clean up with a light sanding then add Plasticine to the nose until balance has been achieved.

■ Design comparisons

This glider has very different design features from our first chuckie. In both models the 'aerofoil' is roughly the same (parallel surfaces top and bottom) but in the new model, the centreline of the aerofoil has been curved or 'cambered'.

You will see from the diagram that a cambered wing panel develops more lift than a flat wing panel. It will also maintain lift at a steeper 'angle of attack' without stalling (and it produces more aerodynamic drag).

Spend a little time over the diagram. It explains a lot about what we will be discussing next and is well worth a thorough understanding.

Why?

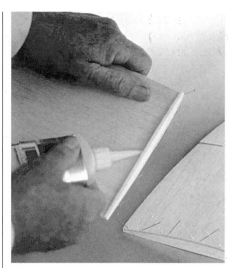

Photo 3:4 *Curve the wing panels over their ribs, pin firmly then wet the join with cyano.*

OK, please explain the difference between 'aerofoil' and 'camber'.

Earlier you referred to the angle of a wing as its 'incidence'. Is this the same as 'angle of attack'?

Because

Take out the pins using your pliers. Before you pull, rotate the pin until you hear a click as it is released from the glue. Now pull. This avoids dragging out a great lump of balsa which is glued to the pin.

It's best to think of an 'aerofoil' as being the cross section shape of a body designed to travel through the air in one general direction with minimum drag. Think of its opposite sides as symmetrical. In this form the aerofoil is a non-lifting shape. The aerofoil is then turned into a lifting shape by curving the centreline in the direction of the required lift (models intended for inverted flight retain a straight centreline).

'Incidence' is the angle that a wing or tail is set at when compared with the aircraft's centreline. 'Angle of attack' is the angle at which a wing or tail is actually travelling through the adjacent air flow (the aircraft could be flying nose high).

Aerodynamic comparisons of lift and drag between a flat wing panel and a cambered wing panel at various angles of attack, illustrating that camber can delay the onset of stall conditions with its resultant collapse of lift.

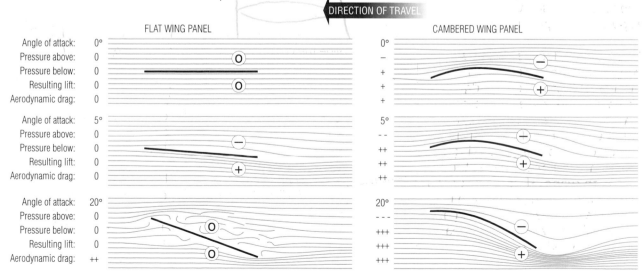

Practice

■ Your model incorporates 'washout' in the wing. Hold up the glider and look from the tip straight into the wing root. See how the near part looks to be sloping downward compared with the inner section. There's less incidence at the tip. This is a built-in safety measure to help avoid a spin.

In simple terms, as the aircraft approaches stalling speed, the outer wing with its reduced incidence, keeps on flying properly even though the inner section is beginning to stall. Since part of the wing is stalled, the whole wing produces less lift, the nose pitches down, the speed increases and the whole wing works again.

If the wingtip stalls first while the inner wing is still lifting, the aircraft will probably overbalance sideways and spin.

■ Some wing plan forms are quite susceptible to stalling from the wingtips inwards (see diagrams on opposite page) and we've seen this is a sure recipe for a short life. While this can be avoided to a large degree by reducing the incidence progressively out toward the tip, another solution is to choose a plan form which automatically 'bleeds' lift from the wingtips, making them less vulnerable to the stall. Wings with parallel leading and trailing edges and squared-off tips are good for this. You will see this plan form used on most model trainers.

The wing to avoid is the highly tapered plan form with broad centre sections and narrow wingtips. The explanation of why narrow wingtips stall early involves some understanding of aerodynamic principles. However, in essence, for a given set of circumstances a small aerofoil stalls before a bigger one. By this definition, a highly tapered wing will stall from the tips inwards.

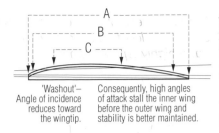

'Washout'– Angle of incidence reduces toward the wingtip.

Consequently, high angles of attack stall the inner wing before the outer wing and stability is better maintained.

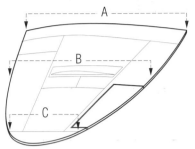

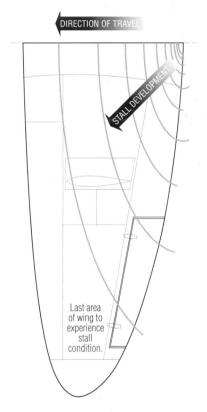

DIRECTION OF TRAVEL

STALL DEVELOPMENT

Last area of wing to experience stall condition.

Because

With an aircraft a classic loss of control situation is where flying speed is insufficient to maintain controlled flight, one wingtip stalls and the aircraft goes into an uncontrolled spin.

A great deal of work has been undertaken to produce wings which stall progressively, beginning at the wing root and only finally influencing the tip. One of the prime solutions is to make sure the outer wing panels don't work as hard as the inner sections. This improves stability but the price is paid in loss of efficiency.

In models we don't need to worry about efficiency the way a commercial operator would so we can build in a generous margin of safety at some cost in efficiency.

Photo 3:5 *Yak-3 displays 'washout'.*

34

Practice	*Why?*	Because

Does this mean that I shouldn't make a scale model of an aircraft which has a highly tapered wing?

Not quite. It really means that you'd be unwise to make one like this until you are an experienced R/C flier and, knowing the aircraft's likely behaviour. You could then avoid situations likely to produce a stall/spin reaction.

The plan form of a wing, that is, its shape when you look down on it, influences the flight characteristics of the plane.

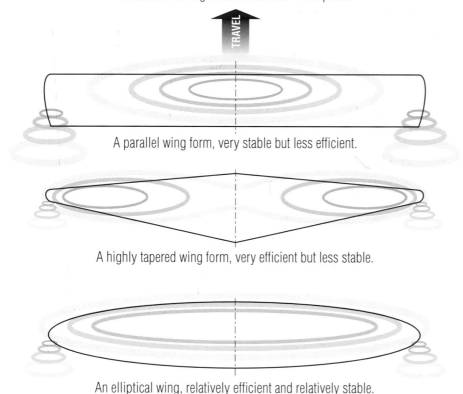

A parallel wing form, very stable but less efficient.

A highly tapered wing form, very efficient but less stable.

An elliptical wing, relatively efficient and relatively stable.

Later we will be taking a second look at the way aileron movement changes the incidence of that part of the wing. When the aileron moves down it increases the angle of attack at the wingtip and heightens the risk of tip stall.

■ The control surfaces, for our purposes anyway, can be looked upon as a way of altering both the camber and incidence on parts of the wing and tail.

Bend one upward and you set reverse camber on the whole panel and it generates negative lift. The panel wants to go down. Bend a control surface down and you increase the camber on the panel so it wants to lift more.

In the same way, setting the rudder alters the camber on the vertical panel. The tail is drawn away from the direction in which you move the rudder.

Go fly your model and observe how it works.

The effective camber of a wing, and its effective incidence, can be altered by bending part of the trailing edge to act against the air flow. Move it upward and it reduces the camber, move it downward and it increases the camber.

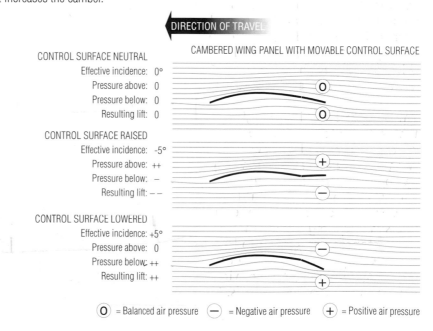

CAMBERED WING PANEL WITH MOVABLE CONTROL SURFACE

DIRECTION OF TRAVEL

CONTROL SURFACE NEUTRAL
Effective incidence: 0°
Pressure above: 0
Pressure below: 0
Resulting lift: 0

CONTROL SURFACE RAISED
Effective incidence: -5°
Pressure above: ++
Pressure below: −
Resulting lift: − −

CONTROL SURFACE LOWERED
Effective incidence: +5°
Pressure above: 0
Pressure below: ++
Resulting lift: ++

(O) = Balanced air pressure   (−) = Negative air pressure   (+) = Positive air pressure

Photo 3:6 *You can now take virtually any 3-view, enlarge it to the size you want, then build the glider YOU want.*

Practice

■ Flight experiments

This is a good model to use to explore flight behaviour under different conditions.

Go to a flat, open field (preferably with about a 6" grass growth) and toss the model around. Adjust the various control surfaces and see the results. Make it fly with a yaw to one side. Load more Plasticine under the balance point and see how it flies with a higher 'wing loading'. Fly it in a light wind, launching it into the wind, down wind and cross wind to compare reactions.

Photo 3:7 *Bungee launching can add lots of fun to your glider flying. It also challenges you to understand what's going wrong and what to do to fix it. Note that this young flier is protecting his eyes just in case the rubber breaks!*

■ Bungee launching

To really see how your model performs you need to see it fly 'at altitude'. The easiest way to achieve this is to add a towing hook (see diagram) to pull it into the air, sailplane fashion. Make up a light 'bungee' which will catapult the model much higher than you can throw it.
Choose a day when there's a light breeze of say 5–12 mph and launch it into the wind, gradually increase the pull each flight.

Be aware, that elastic can break. Protect your eyes.

Drive a stake into the ground. To it tie say 30 feet of ¼" model aeroplane elastic. Add another 100 feet of fishing line and tie a metal ring to the end. Slide the ring over the model's tow hook and walk off down wind. When there's a good pull on the line, point the model to the sky and let go. This is fun!

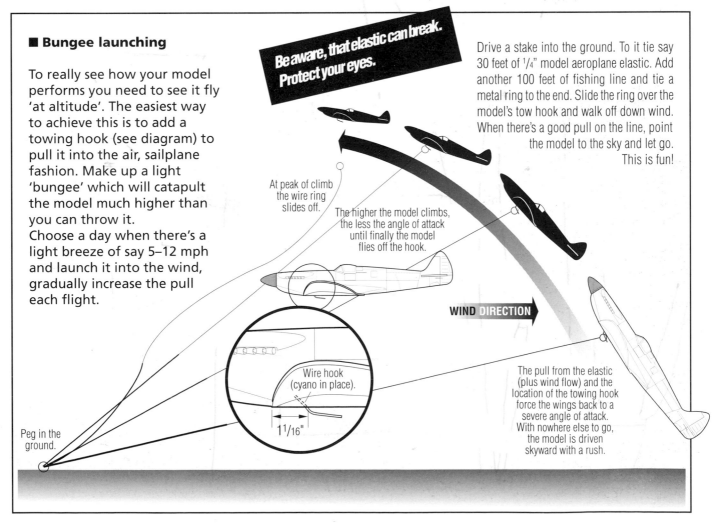

At peak of climb the wire ring slides off.

The higher the model climbs, the less the angle of attack until finally the model flies off the hook.

WIND DIRECTION

Wire hook (cyano in place).

1¹/₁₆"

Peg in the ground.

The pull from the elastic (plus wind flow) and the location of the towing hook force the wings back to a severe angle of attack. With nowhere else to go, the model is driven skyward with a rush.

Chapter 4: Piper J-3 Cub building exercise

While interest in Taylor and Piper Cubs ensure their inclusion in any general study of the evolution of aircraft, the story behind these planes is just as interesting. C.G. Taylor was the surviving brother of the partnership of Taylor Brothers Aircraft Manufacturing Company of the mid-1920s. When the company relocated from Rochester to Bradford, Pennsylvania, William T. Piper became (unwittingly) a shareholder in the company and it was not long before he was appointed to the board.

When the depression of the early 1930s struck, like so many other aircraft manufacturing concerns of the period and despite financial assistance from Piper, the firm went bankrupt. Assets of the company were sold for just $761 to the only bidder, Bill Piper. He then set about organising a new company, Taylor Aircraft Company, made C.G. Taylor the company president and chief engineer and gave him a half share in the business. This operation went on to become the leading manufacturer of light aircraft in this size range, manufacturing the very successful E-2 Cub.

Confrontation between Taylor and Piper over development of the E-2 into its successor, the J-2, led to a split in the partnership, resulting in Piper buying out his partner. Taylor then went on to establish another company, Taylorcraft, while Piper renamed what was now his company, Piper Aircraft Company.

In this way some J-2s, all E-2s and earlier Cubs were 'Taylor' while some J-2s and all later Cubs were 'Piper'.

The Piper J-3 became by far the most famous of all Cubs with manufacture spanning 1937–1942.

Photo 4:1 *For all its popularity and large number manufactured, the Piper J-3 is becoming something of a rare beast to find at today's busy airfields. This immaculate example would turn the head of even the most hardened heavy metal areomodeller.*

Photo 4:2 *'Buttercub' of course painted in the classic Cub Yellow, trade mark of a J-3. This angle gives you an accurate impression of how basic and lightly built the Piper Cubs are. They're simple, efficient and very functional.*

Photos courtesy Graham M. Orphan, Classic Wings Downunder

The different rudder profiles of the two J Cubs give the quickest clue to recognising which is which.

Taylor J-2 Cub   Piper J-3 Cub

Piper J-3 Cub

36" span semi-scale model aircraft
for wind-up rubber power.

Model scale: 11.7: 1 of original aircraft

From
'AIRCRAFT WORKSHOP:
Learn to make models that FLY'
by Kelvin Shacklock ©

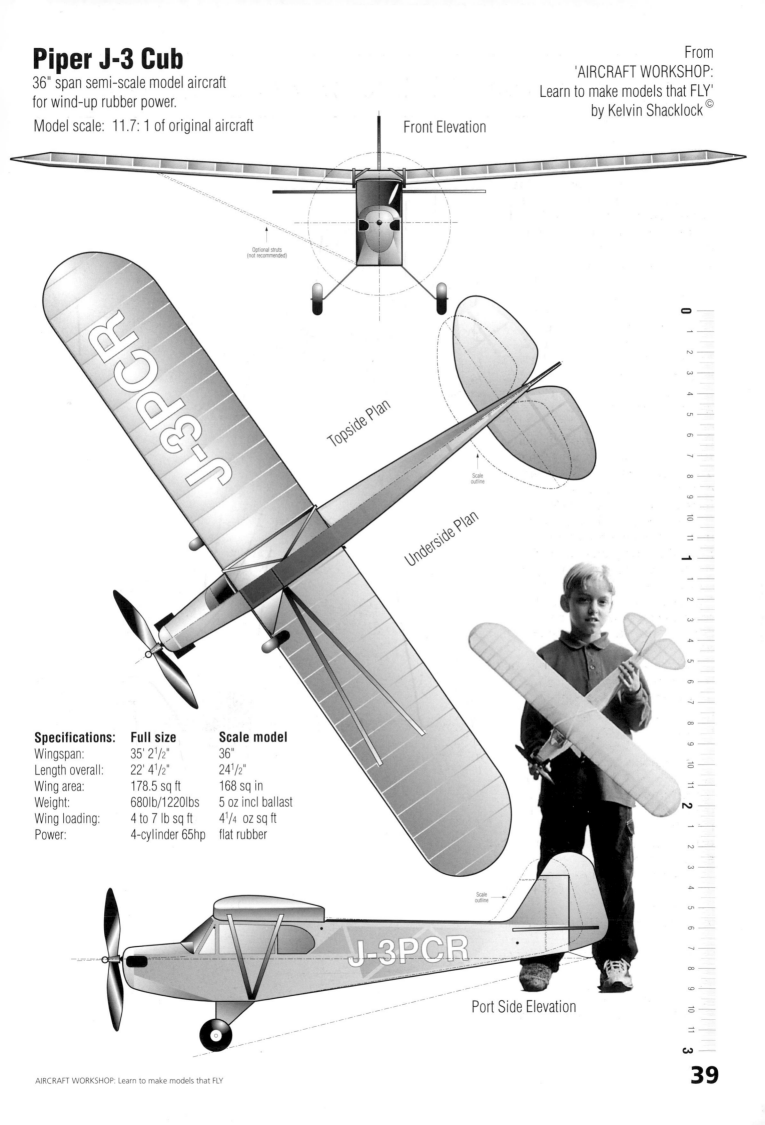

Front Elevation

Optional struts
(not recommended)

Topside Plan

Scale
outline

Underside Plan

Port Side Elevation

Scale
outline

Specifications:

	Full size	Scale model
Wingspan:	35' 2$\frac{1}{2}$"	36"
Length overall:	22' 4$\frac{1}{2}$"	24$\frac{1}{2}$"
Wing area:	178.5 sq ft	168 sq in
Weight:	680lb/1220lbs	5 oz incl ballast
Wing loading:	4 to 7 lb sq ft	4$\frac{1}{4}$ oz sq ft
Power:	4-cylinder 65hp	flat rubber

Photo 4:3 *The little rubber-powered J-3 Cub makes an excellent subject to study the conventional model building methods you will strike again and again as you gain more experience.*

■ This rubber powered semi-scale J-3 isn't a high performance flier. Intentionally it has a heavier construction which is more like a powered model. It introduces you to basic building skills you'll need later. However, its strength will help it survive some hard knocks so that you'll probably have it in flying condition for a lot longer than if it were of conventional weight. The price for weight is performance. In addition it is underpowered. You'd need a huge prop and more rubber power for ROG (rise off the ground) which would destroy any scale appearance. Rather, look on the propeller as increasing the distance your J-3 will glide. Having said all this, the model is easy to build, beautiful to look at and is a treat to see in the air. Building it takes you through a lot of the normal techniques of 'crutch' construction, bracing structures, sheeting, tissue covering, wire work and trimming out. Also, every modeller needs to have made a J-3 at some stage of his modelling life so let's begin.

■ We start out with yet another (but extra easy) way to mark out your wood. All the plans from here on in the book are designed to let you use this method. See the photo along side and the plans on page 41.

What was the point of studying the background of old aircraft like the Piper J-3?

OK, a good point. How do I find out more?

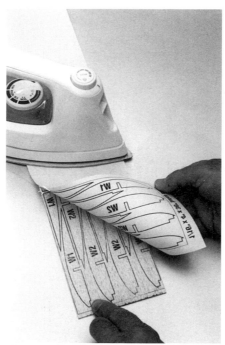

Photo 4:4 *If you have access to a photocopier, here's a magical way to transfer the plan onto your balsa.*

This 'iron on' method of marking up wood looks great. Does it have disadvantages?

You will find that the more you meet with and talk to other modellers the more you'll want to discuss wider issues than just the plane you are building and how it flies. In this case there's quite a good chance someone may refer to your model as a Taylor Cub. Isn't it nice that you now know a little of the background and can comment authoritatively?

For the J-3 and other 'Cubs' Peter M. Bowers has written an excellent book *Piper Cubs*, one of the *Flying Classics Series* (TAB Books, a division of McGraw-Hill, Inc.). The whole series may be well worth looking at.

Recommended Additional Tools:
 Fine files
 Fine wire drill set
 Access to electric soldering iron
 Access to electric iron
 Access to electric drill & bits

Additional Materials:
 Fine wire washers
 Tissue (yellow)
 Model aeroplane dope
 Paint (yellow & black)
 Brushes (for above)

The method works best when the plans are specially prepared with all the parts laid out as they are to be spaced on the wood. Its disadvantage is that the heat bends the wood. However, it soon straightens out again.
Glad you like it.

40

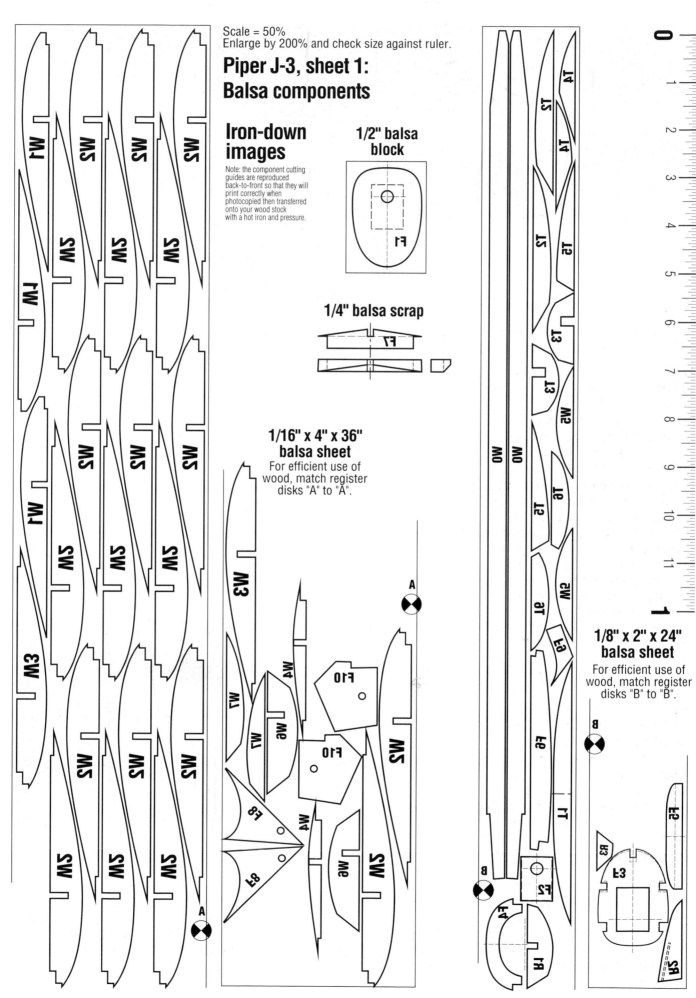

Scale = 50%
Enlarge by 200% and check size against ruler.

Piper J-3, sheet 1:
Balsa components

Iron-down images

Note: the component cutting
guides are reproduced
back-to-front so that they will
print correctly when
photocopied then transferred
onto your wood stock
with a hot iron and pressure.

1/2" balsa block

1/4" balsa scrap

1/16" x 4" x 36" balsa sheet

For efficient use of
wood, match register
disks "A" to "A".

1/8" x 2" x 24" balsa sheet

For efficient use of
wood, match register
disks "B" to "B".

Practice

Here's what to do:

Enlarge sheet 1 to full size. Cut the strips for each sheet of balsa parts and make up the full length strips, interlocking the paper joints so as to conserve balsa (photo 4:5).
Now tape them face down on the appropriate thickness of balsa sheeting.
Use a very hot iron and press down hard on the paper to iron the image onto the wood. Work your way slowly along the sheet until you have transferred the whole (experiment on scrap balsa until you learn how much pressure and time are needed). Strip off the paper and presto, you have the job marked up!

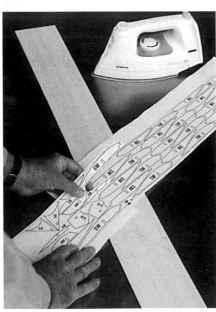

Photo 4:5 *Mark up and cut out all components shown on sheet 1, checking that you are using balsa of the right thickness.*

Now proceed and cut out all the components shown on sheet 1.

■ Take all the W2 wing ribs and sandwich them together as shown in photo 4:6 (now you'll see how accurately you are cutting out the parts).
Sandpaper them until they are all nicely matched and file out all half-checks. Repeat for the three W1 ribs. Hand finish the remaining ribs.

42

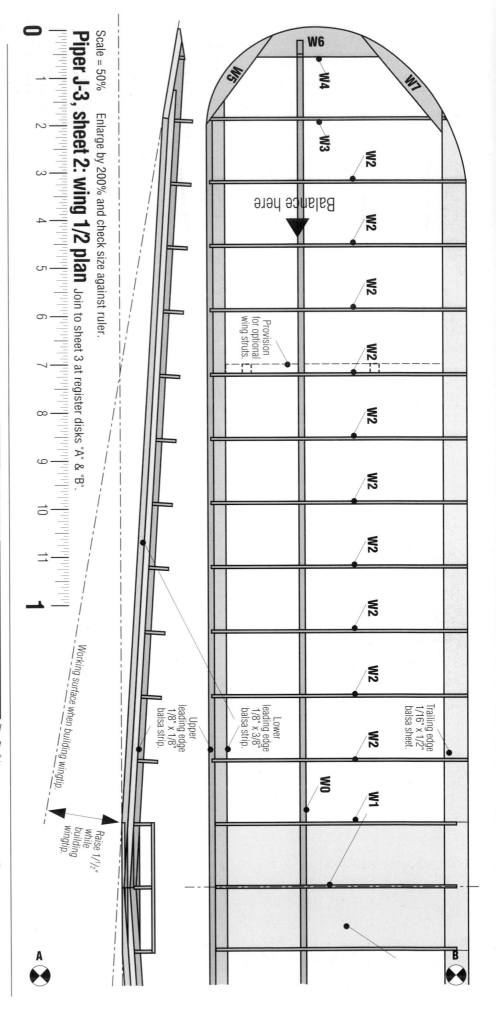

Scale = 50%   Enlarge by 200% and check size against ruler.

Piper J-3, sheet 2: wing 1/2 plan Join to sheet 3 at register disks "A" & "B".

Working surface when building wingtip.

Raise 1½" while building wingtip.

Upper leading edge 1/8" x 1/8" balsa strip.

Lower leading edge 1/8" x 3/8" balsa strip.

Trailing edge 1/16" x 1/2" balsa sheet.

Provision for optional wing struts.

Balance here

Practice

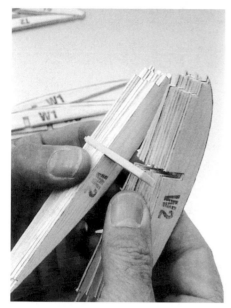

Photo 4:6 *When building a parallel wing like the J-3's, here's a quick trick to help you get all the ribs exactly the same. Align them on a scrap piece of wing spar and pin them together into a solid sandwich.*

Photo 4:7 *Sandpaper the profiles smooth and file out all half-checks to fit the leading and trailing edges. Just in case you get a slight difference between the ends, stow them in their stacked order and place them in the wing in the same sequence as they were stacked.*

This is the technique we will use for all the other models which have parallel leading and trailing edges.

■ Now get a piece of flat softboard at least 3 feet long and 18 inches or more wide to use as your working surface.

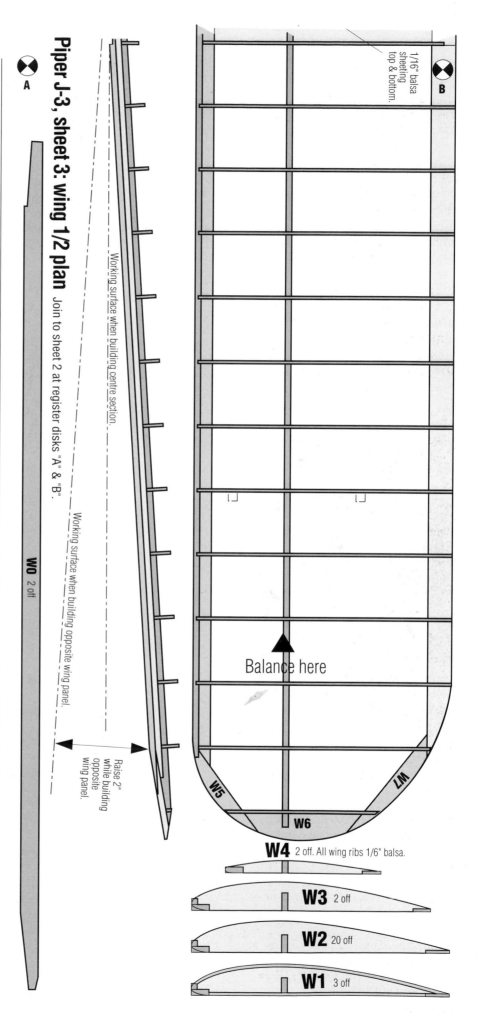

Piper J-3, sheet 3: wing 1/2 plan Join to sheet 2 at register disks "A" & "B".

Working surface when building centre section.

Working surface when building opposite wing panel.

Raise 2" while building opposite wing panel.

W0 2 off

1/16" balsa sheeting top & bottom.

Balance here

W5

W7

W6

W4 2 off. All wing ribs 1/6" balsa.

W3 2 off

W2 20 off

W1 3 off

Practice

Enlarge the wing plans from sheets 2 and 3, tape them down then protect with cling film.

■ Splice together the two main spars W0 and also the leading edge which is made up from $\frac{1}{8}$" x $\frac{3}{8}$" with a $\frac{1}{8}$" square on top (see photo 4:8). These long sloping joints are almost as strong as one piece of wood.

Make up the parts for the trailing edge from $\frac{1}{2}$" x $\frac{1}{16}$" and allow for a splice joint by extending the centre section and chamfering the underside of the overhang by the angle of dihedral. The outer panel trailing edge is also chamfered by the same amount and will be glued on later.

There are three basic steps in building the wing:

■ Begin assembling the centre section of the wing flat on the enlarged plan. Firstly apply the underside $\frac{1}{16}$" sheeting, then the assembled centre spar. Position the spar, leading and trailing edges by temporarily placing a couple of W2 ribs just outboard of the centre section. Complete the centre section with its three ribs and upper $\frac{1}{16}$" sheeting.

■ When the glue is firmly set, remove it from the board, and reposition the spar and leading edge of one side flat down on its wing panel plan and pin in place.

Assemble and glue that side panel as far as rib W3 and leave it to set.

■ Remove the wing from the building surface and reposition it with the outer end flat on the board and the centre lifted to $1\frac{1}{2}$" above the board's surface (see the plan and photo 4:11).

Make up the wingtip and add rib W4. This rib will probably need to be cut in two with the centre removed to accommodate the spar.

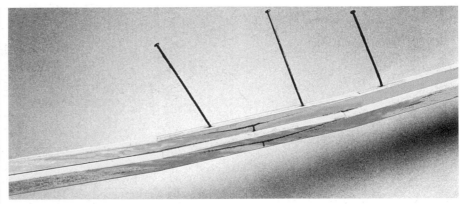

Photo 4:8   *The centre joints of the leading edge members and the central spars are joined with long splice fillets. There are no unsupported structural butt joints in this design (4:9 below shows how even the trailing edge joints are spliced).*

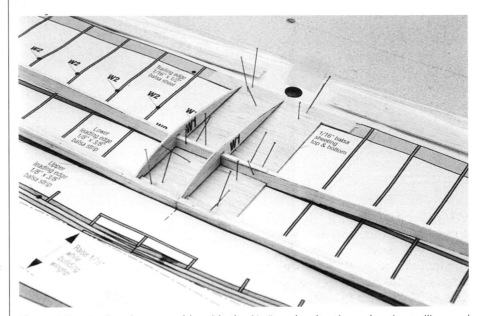

Photo 4:9   *Begin wing assembly with the $\frac{1}{16}$" under-sheeting, plus the trailing and leading edges. Add the centre spar, letting the ribs W1 give it its position.*

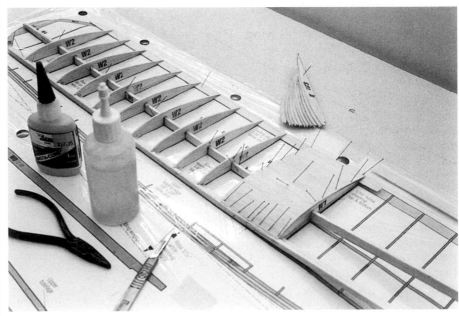

Photo 4:10   *Complete the centre section upper-sheeting then release it from the work surface and tilt it over to assemble the starboard panel with all the W2 ribs.*

44

Repeat the last two steps on the other wing panel and the whole wing is ready for sanding.

Use a medium grit sandpaper with a block and gradually shape the leading edge until it conforms to the cross section shown on the plans.

Take your time when sanding. It is an important job and does take time. Rush it and you're just as likely to damage your work so you could end up spending more time repairing it than the time you tried to saved.

Change to a fine grit sandpaper and smooth the whole wing assembly so that it is ready for doping and covering.

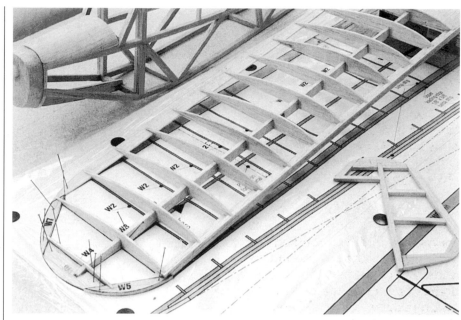

Photo 4:11 *Release the starboard panel from the work surface and tilt it over to assemble the wingtip, adding ribs W3 and W4. Now repeat the process for the port wing.*

■ Handle the wing while it's at this stage. Notice how easily it twists and bends. It's stronger at the leading edge than the trailing edge and it is only at the centre section that you could say it is truly strong. Obviously it's going to have to be much stronger than this before it can be used to support the plane in flight.

Think about the stresses this wing will experience as your model flies. Is it stiff in the best place? If it flexes how will it bend and what effect will that bending have on the flight pattern? If it needs more strength where is that strength going to come from and what is the lightest possible way of doing it?

These are the sorts of questions our aerial pioneers had to address at every point of their building progress. Usually they got it right but of course, sometimes they didn't.

Photo 4:12 *The sanded wing, ready for covering, is an extremely fragile structure, especially when subjected to twisting moments. Later you can compare this with wings you will make which feature 'D' section torque tube construction.*

In 1928 Willy Messerschmitt of Bf109 fame registered his first patent. It covers a single spar wing where the spar and the external skin of the leading $\frac{1}{3}$ section of the wing are combined to form a 'torsionally stiff box'. All his subsequent aircraft designs incorporate this structure. The next wing we build will have this construction and you will be able to compare its twist resistance with this somewhat flimsy design.

The implications from the alternative structures are important. When the 'D' section torsion box is part of the wing, it must be built true and free of any unwanted twists. The wing without this rigidity can be less true in construction but must be held true while the covering is being shrunk to its final tightness. In this case the wing relies on the covering to provide most of the twist resistance.* You need to cut it from sheet balsa.

*Read Frank Vann's biography *"Willy Messerschmitt"* (1993, Patrick Stephens Limited). It makes fascinating reading.

Piper J-3, sheet 4: fuselage 1/2 plan

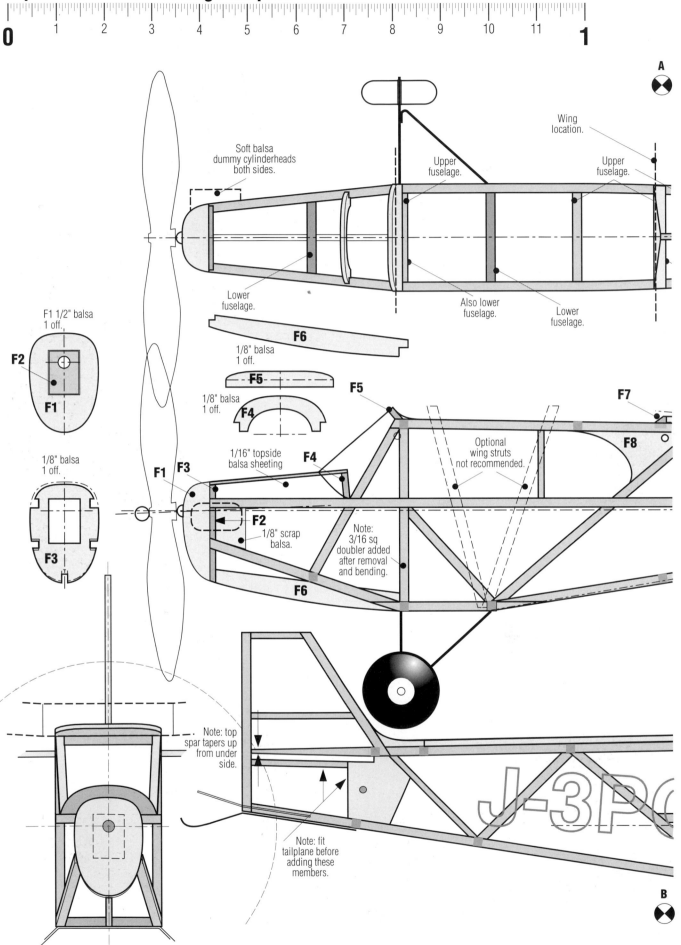

Soft balsa
dummy cylinderheads
both sides.

Upper
fuselage.

Wing
location.

Upper
fuselage.

Lower
fuselage.

Also lower
fuselage.

Lower
fuselage.

F6

1/8" balsa
1 off.

F5

1/8" balsa
1 off.

F4

F5

F7

F8

F1 1/2" balsa
1 off.

F2

F1

1/16" topside
balsa sheeting

F4

Optional
wing struts
not recommended.

1/8" balsa
1 off.

F1 F3

F3

F2

1/8" scrap
balsa.

Note:
3/16 sq
doubler added
after removal
and bending.

F6

Note: top
spar tapers up
from under
side.

Note: fit
tailplane before
adding these
members.

J-3P

46

Piper J-3, sheet 5: fuselage 1/2 plan

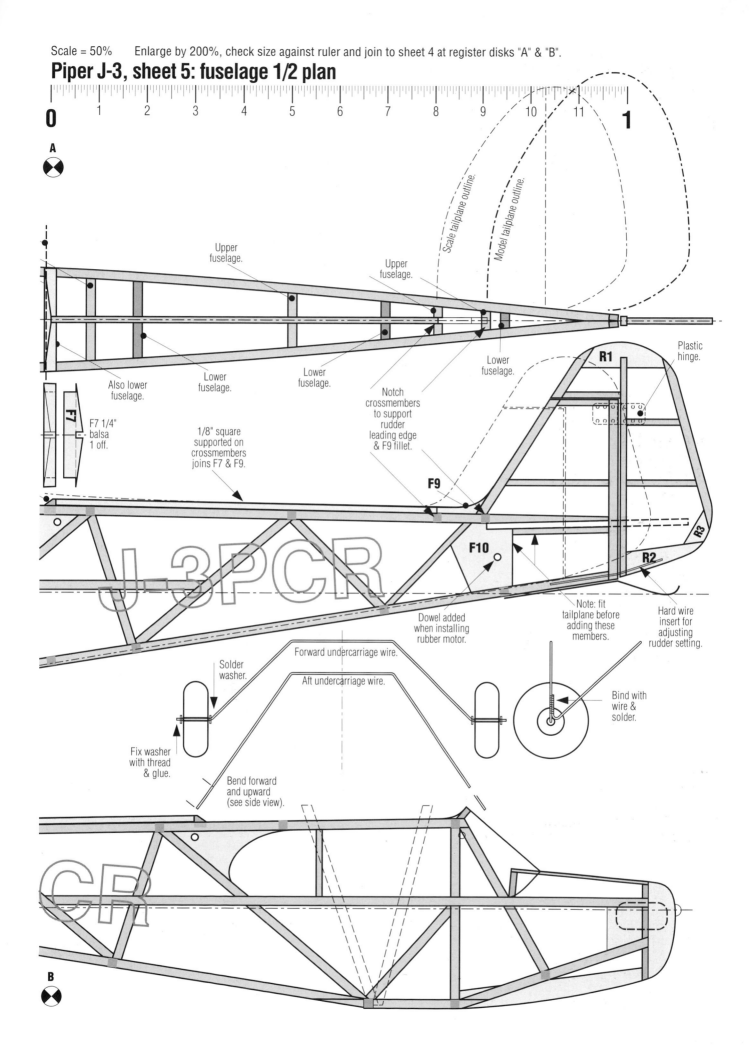

0 1 2 3 4 5 6 7 8 9 10 11 1

A

Scale tailplane outline.

Model tailplane outline.

Upper fuselage.

Upper fuselage.

Upper fuselage.

Lower fuselage.

Lower fuselage.

Lower fuselage.

Also lower fuselage.

Notch crossmembers to support rudder leading edge & F9 fillet.

Plastic hinge.

R1

F7

F7 1/4" balsa 1 off.

1/8" square supported on crossmembers joins F7 & F9.

F9

F10

R3

R2

Dowel added when installing rubber motor.

Note: fit tailplane before adding these members.

Hard wire insert for adjusting rudder setting.

Forward undercarriage wire.

Aft undercarriage wire.

Solder washer.

Bind with wire & solder.

Fix washer with thread & glue.

Bend forward and upward (see side view).

B

■ Fuselage construction

Enlarge the fuselage plan and pin down to the building board the two fuselage side views, covering them with cling film.

■ Build up the fuselage crutches as shown in photo 4:13 from $^3/_{16}$" square section medium grade balsa strip, cutting all the lengths and angles for the top, centre and bottom longerons, then the vertical and diagonals struts. As you go, pin them in place on the plan, but don't glue them yet. Notice that the top longeron is tapered upward to half its width for the tailplane slot (forget this and you're in trouble).
Use $^1/_8$" x $^3/_{16}$" on its flat for the rudder posts. At this stage don't add F10 or the adjoining strut to the rudder post. Also, leave off the under nose spar and its diagonal. When you are satisfied with all the joint angles and fit, glue both crutches.

When hard, remove the crutches from the plan and hold them together at the rudder posts like in photo 4:15 to work out the angle of chamfer for the struts to come together nicely. Notice that the surface of each crutch which was against the plan becomes the outer surface of the fuselage structure. Cut the chamfers and also half check the hinge slot into the rudder posts.

Now set a curve in each crutch by using a hot iron against the inside faces until they bend gently inwards.

Glue $^3/_{16}$" square doublers on the inside of the main cabin posts.

■ On the vertical plan set up the crutches, and while keeping their sides and rudder posts vertical, glue them together at the rudder posts. This is the most critical assembly stage because any alignment error now will be permanently built into the fuselage. Take your time and get it right.

Where do I get the $^3/_{16}$" square balsa strip? It's not a size that's carried by my local hobby shop.

This can be done using a scalpel and straightedge but it's almost impossible to keep the cut square. You really need a balsa stripper. There are various designs but I like the one made by Master Airscrew.

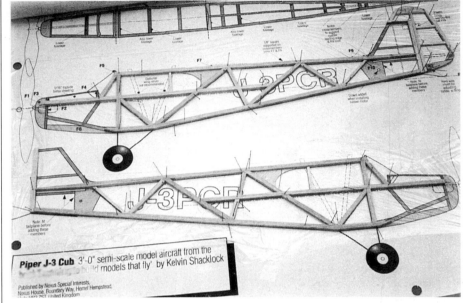

Photo 4:13   *The most traditional of all model aircraft fuselage building techniques – crutch construction. Here the two crutches are ready for removal from the work surface.*

Sorry, I'm getting a bit lost here. Please go over it again.

Where the top and bottom longerons of each crutch come together at the rudder post they need to have a wedge of wood removed from their inside face so that they lie snugly together and allow the two rudder posts to meet face-to-face. The amount of wood you remove affects the angle that the crutches form at the tail. This should match the plan.

This is a new one on me. How do I go about that again?

Place each crutch face down on a suitable hard ironing surface then just gently iron it! You'll see the frame gradually bend up towards you, no problem. Just make sure you bend them the right way.

What's this 'doubler'?

The vertical post running from the front top of the cabin down to the front leg of the undercarriage is made in two halves. During construction of the prototype it was found that this was a weakness so the strut was 'doubled' by gluing a matching strut on the inside running full height from top to bottom. It cured the problem.

48

Proceed to insert the spacers between the frames, beginning at third from the tail and working forward in turn as each spacer dries.

Proceed until it looks as in photo 4:14 then, unless you are using an instant glue, set it aside overnight to harden. Proceed to build the fin, gluing the fillet F9 to its ⅛" x ³/₁₆" leading edge. Then add the ⅛" square struts, gluing them to the aft side of the leading edge. Leave this to harden.

■ Assembling the nose section calls for a little more skill, or really, a little more patience.

Take your fuselage assembly, F3 and F6 and bring them all together to form the nose of your model. Here's how:

Fit one centre longeron of the fuselage into the upper side slot of F3 then gently squeeze the other centre longeron into the opposite slot. Fiddle until you have all this held in one hand. Now wrap sticky tape round the longerons to hold them in the squeeze. Take F6 and fit it into the bottom slot of F3. Then sit the other end comfortably on the centre of the front spacer of the fuselage. Check that F3 is sitting straight up and down and is square left and right. When you're satisfied, run a little cyano into the four joints and allow it to harden.

Cut two ³/₁₆" square struts to fit accurately from the lower fuselage struts to the lower side slots in F3 and glue.

■ Complete the fin assembly by shaping the slot in the centre of the last spacer of the fuselage (photo 4:15). Pin the fin structure and the rudder post to it, add the second last spacer and square it all up. When it looks like photo 4:16 glue with cyano. Now add the top centre strut between F7 and F9 and you're ready to finish off the nose section.

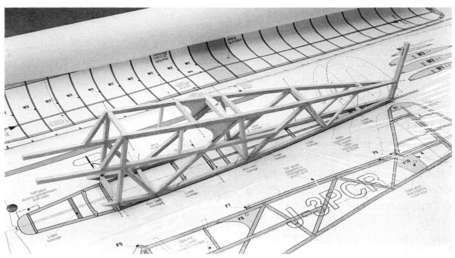

Photo 4:14 *Each crutch has been curved inward to reduce tension. Then they have been glued together at the rudder posts and a few spacers fitted (note: the prototype did not have doublers added at this stage — experience showed that it should have).*

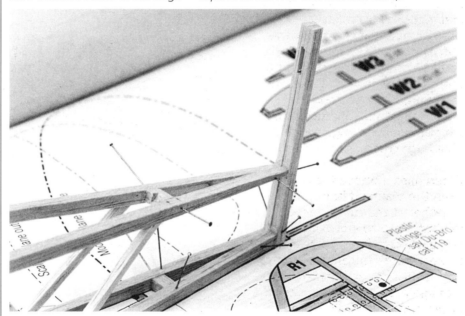

Photo 4:15 *The rudder post and the outer crutch surfaces should sit vertical to the work surface. Note the half check in the last spacer to locate the rudder leading edge.*

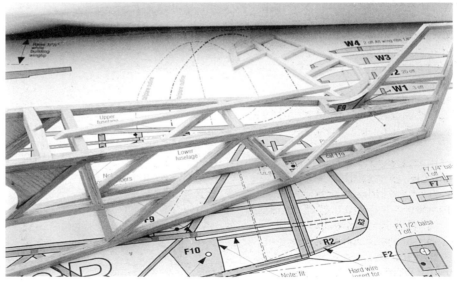

Photo 4:16 *The second last spacer is added to support the rudder fillet F9. Note the shape of F7 which is ready to accept the centre strut.*

Practice

⬇

■ Other than the centre section of the wing, the top of the nose is the only sheeted area of this model. However, this nose piece is quite interesting because the curve is so severe it could prove difficult.

Let's make it easy.
Find a bottle or glass tumbler with straight or tapered lines of similar diameter to the front formers of your model.

Cut a piece of 3/16" balsa to a little longer than the nose section and a little wider than the circumference of former F4.

Pour boiling water over the balsa sheeting. While the wood is hot, bend the balsa round your glass and hold it gently in place with a couple of wide rubber bands. Leave it to dry thoroughly.

Now trim it and glue and pin in place as shown in photo 4:17.

■ Add the scrap filler pieces as mounting surfaces for the dummy engine cylinder heads.

Now you can glue the alignment plate F2 to the back of the nose block F1. The technique is to pin the nose block in its final position and, from the back, insert the alignment plate through F3 and pin it to the block. Now unpin the block from F3 and remove it with the alignment plate still pinned in place. Run a little cyano between them and leave to harden.

Make up the solid cylinder head blocks and angle their mounting surfaces so their outer faces are square and parallel with each other. Don't glue them in place until after you have sanded and sealed the nose block to final shape.

Fit whatever bearing type you can access (large glass bead or soap-wood plug) bend the wire prop shaft and fit the propeller.

Why?

⬇

Photo 4:17 *After the 1/16" sheeting has dried into its curve, cut and shape it to fit the nose struts. Glue before trimming to length.*

I found it quite difficult to judge the final size and angles of cut needed to get the sheeting to fit nicely. Any tips?

Photo 4:18 *Glue the alignment plate to the back of the nose block and drill out the cavity for the bearing plug (or large glass bead). Shape the block to the contours shown on the plan then seal the outer surface with dope to complete the propeller assembly as shown.*

Can't find a wooden plug or a big glass bead. What now?

Because

⬇

Too often we seem to resort to 'planking' an area with strips of 1/8" soft balsa when we could reduce both the work and weight by steam bending lighter sheeting. This works provided we don't have 'compound' shapes (that is, shapes which curve in both directions). The test is to try bending a piece of stiff paper to the final shape. If it won't go, you probably wouldn't be able to get balsa sheeting to adopt the shape either.

Scale logo
(appears on each side of tail fin)

Next time try cutting a template from stiff paper. But remember the paper will be the right size for the inside surface of the wood. Allow extra for the 3/16" thickness where the outer surface will lie.

Modelling often calls for inventive solutions. Look for something made of solid nylon or metal which you can adapt and use. Even the right button might be the answer.

Practice

- The tailplane and elevator are made as one piece on this model. To trim the flight we shall alter the incidence of the wing by lifting the leading or trailing edge.

Building the tailplane is about as conventional a modelling practice as you can get. Enlarge sheet 6, tape it to the board and cover with cling film.

Place all the precut parts down on the plan and cut the main spar from ¹/₈" x ³/₁₆" medium hard balsa. Cut the struts from ¹/₈" square. Pin all parts in place and when you are happy that everything fits accurately, glue with balsa cement.

- While that is hardening make the rudder in the same way. In its case the only difficulty may be cutting the recess in the main spar to accept the hinge. Cut this before you glue the spar into the rudder. This way you can always have several attempts without wasting more than a little balsa. On the down side, you must be careful not to fill the slot with glue when you put it together.

Carefully sand both sides of these tail components and round all outer edges. You might also do a better job than I did in removing the photocopy outlines and coding from the printed parts. If you can still see them on the wood expect them to show through the tissue covering.

- Test fit the finished tailplane into the fuselage. When it is pressed neatly into its resting place under the fuselage top spars, is it square to the fuselage framing? Sight it from both front and back, then file or sandpaper the spars until it's just right.

Pin it in place, sight it square from above as well as from the end elevation, check that you really did taper those spars as per the plan and if all looks well, cyano it in place.

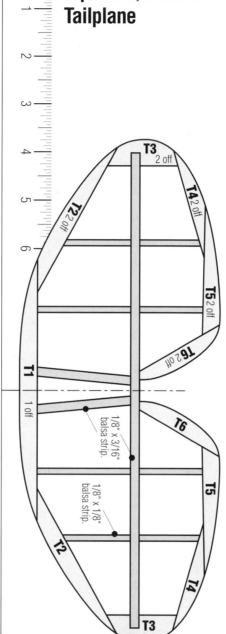

Scale = 50%. Enlarge by 200% and check size against ruler.

Piper J-3, sheet 6: Tailplane

Because

When you are using this building technique and especially when making light structures like these, it is very easy to break the part when you are pulling out the pins. The pin can stick firmly to the wood and the part comes away with the pin instead of staying on the work surface with all the other parts. To avoid this always use a pair of small pliers and rotate the pin before you pull it out. Not only could this save you work but for some reason things never seem to glue together as well the second time round.

There are critical times during assembly of a model when 'getting it right' is absolutely vital to the quality of the final job. The first time with this model was, as we said, when joining the crutches at the rudder posts. This determined whether the fuselage would be square or not. Now we are adding the tailplane. If this isn't square to the rudder it will bother you every time you look along the thrust line. And you'll have a real problem deciding what to align the wings with if you have several alternatives.

While you are waiting for the tailplane and rudder to harden, pick up the fuselage and get familiar with handling these sorts of structures. Try twisting it gently the way we did the wing. This is a very different proposition. Here the fuselage is braced like a torsion tube so it won't twist. It's also braced so it can't be compressed, nor can it rhombus or bend. Yet it is still very light.

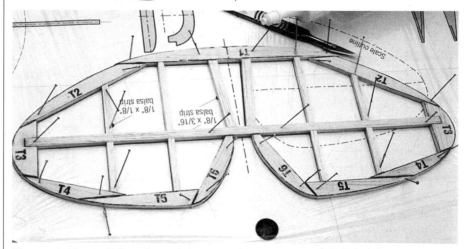

Photos 4.19 *Building the tailplane — about as conventional as it gets.*

■ After drilling the dowel holes, insert under the tailplane the F10 panels and the struts that run back to the rudder posts (photo 4:20). Cut the wing-mounting dowels from ⅛″ dia. wood (I cut up satay sticks) and round off their ends. This is important if you don't want them to puncture the wings when you are carrying or packing the model. Drill their holes and glue in the dowels. Now glue in the rubber-retaining dowel through the F10 panels and trim the ends flat with the sides.

■ Using 0.05″ piano wire bend up the rudder control rod, tail skid and two undercarriage legs.

Drill the rudder control rod cavity through the rudder posts and into one lower fuselage spar. Roughen the wire with sandpaper and cyano it in place (photo 4:20). With your craft knife carve a groove in the underside of the fuselage structure to accept the tail skid (photo 4:20), bind the skid in place with cotton thread and wet with cyano.

Using a razor saw cut grooves across the under fuselage to accept the undercarriage members (photo 4:21), bind with thread and cyano. Leave to set.

With fine florist's wire bind the undercarriage legs per the plan and solder (soft electrical solder is OK on a model of this size – not larger models though). At the same time solder a wire washer to each axle stub to stop the wheels from jamming on the first bend of the undercarriage legs.

Fit the rudder onto its hinge and, holding it against the side of the control rod, mark its position on the rudder. Drill its retaining hole. When everything fits take out the hinge and, keeping the hinge plates clean, wipe a tiny amount of lubricant grease into the hinge joint (this will help prevent glue from locking it up). Refit the rudder and carefully cyano the hinge and control rod in position.

Photo 4:20 *The tail-end is completed when the F10 panels are in place, their struts run back to the rudder post, the rudder control rod is inserted and the tail skid is recessed, bound with cotton and glued with cyano.*

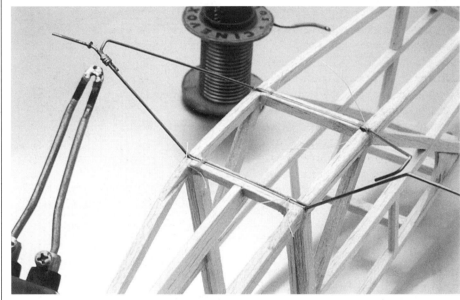

Photo 4:21 *Fitting the undercarriage legs into grooves in the fuselage makes sure the covering will lie flat and smooth. Little details like this make a difference.*

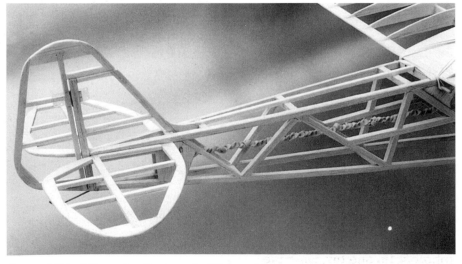

Photo 4:22 *Although adjustment of the rudder means bending the control rod, having a hinge at the top end ensures there will be no stress on fragile parts.*

52

■ If your local model shop caters for rubber power you can probably buy a pair of suitable wheels off the shelf. If not and if you have access to a power drill there's no problem:

Cut two ½" balsa blanks with accurately drilled centre holes (these holes should be just large enough for you to press short lengths of control snake inner rod into them).

Use a long screw which also fits the holes and, with washers both sides of the wheel blank, run a nut up to the wheel and make it moderately tight. Hold the remaining end of the bolt in the drill chuck and you are almost ready to make wheels (photo 4:23). But first, put on a pair of safety glasses.

With medium grit paper in your sanding block and with the drill at full revs, very gently start shaping the wheel, getting it truly round first, then gradually rounding the profile. Smooth with very fine paper, dope it to seal the grain and, if you can run the drill very slowly, even paint the tyre while it revolves (photo 4:24). Cyano a length of plastic tube (ballpoint refill?) into the finished wheel, pop it on the axle, add a wire washer, wrap with thread, check there's a little wheel clearance and then very carefully cyano.

■ Take about 40" of ¼" flat rubber and feed it through the nose, round the tail dowel and back out the nose. Pre-twist each half with about 50 turns, each in the same direction. Then clip the ends together and allow the clip to rotate until the two strands wind up on themselves along their whole length. This allows the model to contain a longer length of rubber without flopping round in the fuselage when the tension comes off. Tie the ends through the propeller shaft loop (photo 4:18) and test wind the propeller. It should run freely and true.

Photo 4:23 *The balsa blank is revolved in the drill while you gently sand it into wheel-shape.*

When I tried this there was a lot of vibration and it seemed to get more out-of-round instead of getting better. Why?

Photo 4:24 *If your drill is variable-speed, you can even revolve it while you paint the tyre.*

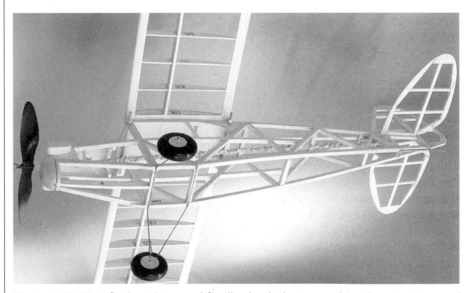

Photo 4:25 *Test fit the wings and finally check that everything lines up true and square. Make any adjustments with a file or sanding block then carefully sand the whole plane until there are no rough spots which will spoil the covering.*

When I look from the front I have got one wingtip higher than the other, especially when I align it with the tailplane. How can I fix it?

This worked really well on the prototype. I did notice though that it was important to keep the drill rigidly held down and the sanding block had to be held firmly but only just touching the wheel. It sounds as if you are trying to take too much off too quickly. Try to just skim the high spots until it settles down.

There's no such thing as 'absolutely' correct. We are all just trying to get things as true as possible. Try filing or sanding down the top of the fuselage strut that is supporting the high side of the wing. There's room for some adjustment here.

Practice

■ Covering your model with tissue paper can be a bit of a challenge. Take your time – it will all turn out right in the end! The prototype is covered with yellow tissue.

Start with a straightforward piece like the tailplane. Using clear model aeroplane dope, paint several coats round all the edges where you want the tissue to stick (photo 4:26).

We are using the dry tissue method, so cut enough covering to amply overlap the area to be done. Position it on the frame then paint dope on top of where you want to start sticking. Stick one end and let it set. Then move to the opposite end and, gently pulling, stick it (photo 4:27). Work the dope through the tissue by rubbing it with your fingertip (be prepared to get plenty of dope on your fingers!). Meantime, start a second panel on the other side. When it's firm work your way right round the frame. Now trim off most of the excess tissue leaving about ⅛" overhang. With scissors slit the edge of the tissue in to the wood wherever there's a curve or corner (photo 4:28). Make lots of cuts while you're learning. Proceed to roll the tissue down over all the edges, doping it as you go. Gradually you'll get the hang of it, and you're away.

Think ahead and remember that the tissue will be coming in from the opposite side too, so allow for some overlap at the joins.

■ Cover the whole model except for the two panels under the nose section. Later you need access here to insert ballast.

■ The model probably looks a bit ragged at this stage so start shrinking the tissue. Make a fine spray and wet the fuselage and tail surfaces. Leave it to dry slowly and see how the tissue tightens. It's really quite a relief isn't it! Now shrink the wings. You do

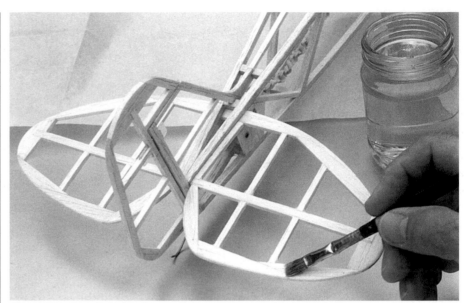

Photo 4:26 *Paint the framework with several coats of dope on all the places where you will want the covering to stick.*

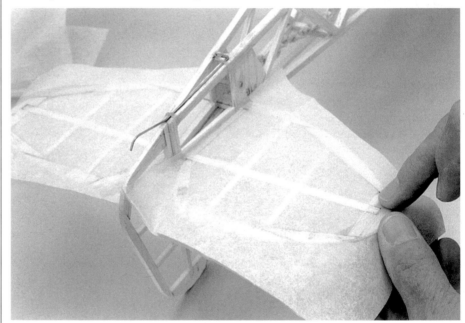

Photo 4:27 *Tack down the covering at the ends and corners, letting it harden before trying to go too far at a time.*

Photo 4:28 *Wherever you are planning joins, trim out the general shape leaving about ⅛" overhang all round. Then, especially on the curves, make lots of little inward cuts so as to ease the tissue down over the edges.*

54

these last because you need some experience to make sure it goes well. The wings will bend slightly and they will twist a little. As long as they both twist the same amount and in the right direction there's no problem (the prototype performed exactly as required). To check, sight from the wingtip to the centre section. The trailing edge should have come up a little so that the centre of the wing has more lift than the wingtip (washout – ref. page 34). If they have not behaved this way you will need to control the twist during the next shrinking process.

■ Starting again with the tail surfaces paint a coating of thin dope over all the tissue and let it dry. The tissue will shrink a little more and the surfaces should now be smooth.

Proceed with the rest of the model. If the wing needs special treatment dope both sides of one wing from the centre section to the second last rib and support each end while it dries. Repeat the process for the other wing. This should control the twist.

Paint the remaining parts with dope. If you are dissatisfied with any of the covering you can always soften the dope and replace the unsatisfactory panels. Set aside for hardening.

■ When you assemble the model as if you were about to fly it, the balancing point will be way back.

Turn the model over and mould some Plasticine behind the joint of F3 and F6. You'll need a lot, and the prototype even has a few pieces of metal tucked in with the Plasticine. Avoid getting this too high where it could interfere with the prop shaft. When correct balance is achieved smooth out the Plasticine and cover the lower panels as the other areas. Shrink and dope.

Tell me more. How do I control the wing while it is shrinking?

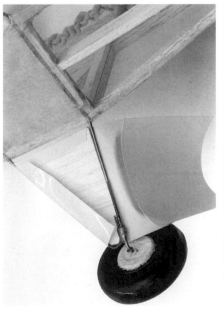

Photo 4:29 *Fill in the undercarriage panels with $1/16$" balsa then wrap with yellow self-adhesive tape.*

Photo 4:30 *After the model is virtually complete, add ballast then cover the underside of the nose section to finish the model.*

Each time you wet the wing, either with water or dope, the tension comes off and the framework can be moved.

If you take a drawer out of a cabinet the top of the two sides can be used to support the wing, while the space between is free to suspend the wet part of the wing without it touching anything that it could get stuck to. Dope both sides of the part of the wing which is suspended and hold the outer ends down on the drawer edges. When the dope dries the wings should be set with both ends parallel. To build in washout, pack up the trailing edge of the outer end of the wing while it is shrinking.

Photo 4:31 *The elegant little J-3 ready for testing, displays all its excellent flight characteristics. Little wonder the real thing was such a popular aircraft.*

■ Remember all the trimming experience you gained with chuckies? Now that experience will help you adjust your J-3 to fly cleanly and well. Choose a calm day and find a nice, open space, preferably with a fair amount of light grass growth to take care of any abrupt landings.

Set the rudder to achieve straight flight or a moderate turn. To adjust the amount of lift pack the leading or trailing edge of the wing. If there's a natural turn that can't be easily corrected with rudder, soften the dope on one wing and correct the amount of twist as described on page 55.

■ This model features both light wing loading and a full aerofoil wing. The aerofoil is more or less a Clark 'Y' (where distinction is made between aerofoil and camber, since the centreline is strongly curved it is described as a cambered aerofoil).

■ If this J-3 is your first made-up model we hope you have a real sense of achievement in completing it. Congratulations.

Well, that was quite a challenge but I'm quite pleased with the results. The part I think I should have done better is in the covering, especially on the top of the wings near the tips.

Show me what you mean by a cambered aerofoil.

Don't be disheartened. The prototype has a wrinkle or two, and just where you describe. There are two contributing factors. Firstly, this part of the wing has a fairly severe compound surface and it is expecting quite a lot from tissue to have it adopt the shape without a pucker or two. The other factor is that we used a dry tissue technique. This is a bit easier for the beginner than using wet tissue and it is less likely to distort the framework because there's less shrinkage.

If you're game, work some dope through the tissue onto the top edge of rib W3 and when it has hardened cut out the last wing panel and cover it separately (wet or dry technique). This gets away from a single piece of tissue having to adopt a compound shape.

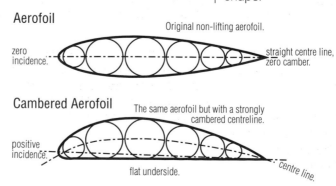

Aerofoil

Original non-lifting aerofoil.

zero incidence.

straight centre line, zero camber.

Cambered Aerofoil

The same aerofoil but with a strongly cambered centreline.

positive incidence.

flat underside.

Centre line.

Chapter 5: Joining a club

Practice

Why?

Because

■ Consider the advantages of belonging to a model fliers' club.

In your day-to-day fun of building and flying models, it makes a lot of sense to belong to a group of people who think the way you think, talk about the things you want to talk about and spend their spare time doing the things you like doing.

Why join a club? I don't know anyone in a club. I know little about making models, or setting them up, and as for flying them, I haven't a clue.

In a club environment you will certainly learn sooner, and at less cost both in terms of damage to your models and your ego.

First, I would rather work away on my own until I know enough to be able to go to a club as an experienced flier on equal terms with everyone else.

Sure, that's an understandable view, but clubs are usually keen to help new members feel comfortable. And, it's in everyone's interest to get you into the air safely and to keep you out of trouble.

Telephone a friend from the club and you have an immediate second opinion. Stuck for a part – and now there's a whole team to direct you to its source.

If I fly on my own I can fly wherever I like, when I like and for as long as I like. In a structured club would I have this freedom?

You are actually not as free to fly your way as you might think. In most countries there are restrictions on the use of air space and you could be breaking the law by flying a model at a location you consider to be available.

See what others are building and compare your own progress with their achievements.

Photo 5:1 *When you first join a club you quickly discover there really are lots of other people who think the way you do!*

■ Although less fun, risk factors are even more important reasons for joining a club.

Let's face it, even in experienced hands, a model that is great fun one second can become an unguided missile the next.

I don't fly where the public come to watch. I go off to a field on my own, minding my own business and bothering no one. Why should I worry about liabilities?

Generally, the more experienced the fliers, the more precautions they will take in the selection of safe flying sites, the way they build, the checks they make before and after flying and the way they fly their routines. With a formal club structure and the combined experience of many, these responsibilities are shared.

Practice

As a member of a club you don't have to re-invent the causes of accidents. Others have been there, done that. Listen and learn so you can reduce the risk of this happening to your model.

You should be flying at an authorised flying site, and operating under approved rules and where the consequences of such an event will be reduced.

If something does go wrong when you are using your model, and a member of the public is injured or suffers damage as a result of your actions, if you are a member of a properly approved and affiliated club you should be indemnified against liability.

Photo 5:3 *'Did anyone happen to see where my P-39 went?'*

■ Even if accessibility to a club flying field is limited, the benefits of belonging to a club should far outweigh the costs or any other restrictions.

Think very seriously before you decide to go it alone.

Why?

Photo 5:2 *Even the most experienced and cautious builder/fliers have accidents. Where an uncontrollable model crashes, by definition, it is out of your hands. And yet, if it's your plane, it is your responsibility.*

I have visited a model flying club and no one seemed very interested in whether I was there or not. Perhaps they are not a very friendly lot out my way. What do you think?

Because

The more planes you watch flying the more you see dangerous situations you never even thought about. If you are flying on your own how broad is your understanding of the need for the various safety procedures? And, how well do you practise them? How confident are you that you are not developing a dangerous habit or two with no one to alert you to what's happening?

We have probably all experienced the feeling you have. And not just with model clubs. Remember that when you first meet with a group of people who are all good friends, they are enjoying each other's company and probably are just not thinking what it was like when they first came out as a stranger.

Photo 5:4 *Clubs often hold special events like this Schneider Trophy and float day. This is an off-site event which, although a great spectacle, gives little indication of what a normal flying day is like. For an overall impression of a club, try to attend both types of event.*

⬇

■ Finding a club

Track down the local radio control fliers' clubs in your area by enquiring from your model supply shop. Then a phone call to the secretary is usually enough to find out where they meet. Expect to be invited to meet them at their next flying day. Take note of any names you are given and when you arrive take the initiative by finding these people and introducing yourself.

Choose your day with a little care. Clubs will like you to attend when they are holding a spectacular

Photo 5:5 *Expect a club flying day to be anything from a group of half a dozen enthusiasts with a few models in a field to a highly organised 'fly-in' with people everywhere, tents, pits, flight lines, competitions and marshals. And remember the weather will always influence the attendance level.*

Some points worth considering when deciding which Model Club you want to join

- How far is the field from your base and can you realistically get to it regularly?
- What restrictions are there on times people can fly and how do these times fit your schedule?
- How is the field affected by weather and does it take advantage of the prevailing local conditions?
- How well placed is the field relative to wind obstructions, flying hazards, forced landing surfaces, etc?
- How safe is the field relative to runway layout, pit location, car parking, public areas, etc?
- Are the members the sort of people you can relate to?
- Is the club looking for new members and do they make you feel welcome?

- What sort of models do the members fly and are these the sort of planes which interest you?
- Does the club become involved in interchange with other clubs in the area, etc?
- Is it involved in national events?
- Do most members fly on one particular mode (Mode 1 or Mode 2 – see chapter 8)? Is this the mode you want to fly on? If not, will this place you at a disadvantage during training?
- What assistance is provided for the novice pilot (eg: training committee, building guidance, flight training, etc)?
- How many models are allowed to fly at any one time and is there congestion waiting for frequency pegs?

- How well-organised is field safety?:–
  - ◆ Novice pilot supervision
  - ◆ Transmitter pound and frequency peg control
  - ◆ Aircraft inspection
  - ◆ Pits access and control
  - ◆ Radio range check
  - ◆ Flight line management
  - ◆ Flight rules control

  Are these controls too rigid or too relaxed for your comfort?
- What does membership cost, what insurance is obligatory and are you comfortable with the financial commitment?
- What other commitments does membership involve (eg: monthly meeting, field and facility maintenance, committee service, etc)?

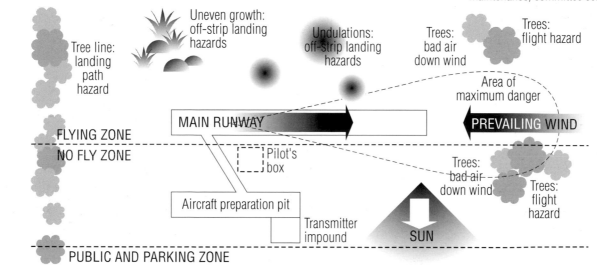

'fly-in' or event of special interest. Go, but don't expect this to be a good time to become known. Rather, pick a normal day that's fine with little wind. Expect most people to be engrossed in activity so that you will probably be the last thing on their minds. Go with the idea of listening, looking and learning. And be patient.

■ Choosing your club

Don't be in too much of a hurry to commit yourself to join the first club you visit. Check out all the clubs in your area and see which will be best for you. When you feel you are ready to join a particular club, begin attending their flying days.

Watch the way different fliers perform over several weeks. See who gets into trouble and who stays clear. Decide who are the fliers on whom you want to model your own flying future.

Photo 5:6 *Perhaps more typical of your average Sunday club meeting with a pleasant day, a few friends, regular flying and a good chat.*

Some people seem to be very unlucky with lots of crashes. Is this a sport where there is a high degree of chance?

You will gradually learn to distinguish between 'bad luck' and 'bad decisions'. Only a very small proportion of crashes can be attributed to lack of luck.

Some good and bad habits you will learn to recognise

✔ Some fliers will first unpack their transmitter/s and take it/them to the impound. They then assemble their models make a few checks and are ready to fly in minutes.

✔ When their radio frequency is available they will collect the transmitter and peg, fuel up, start the engine (perhaps tweak the carb setting) and range-check the radio link.

✔ They then look over the flying field, check wind direction, the circuit being flown, who and how many are flying.

✔ If the flying rules call for a buddy they will indicate to him that they are ready to fly before they taxi toward the strip.

✔ Before moving onto the strip they again check wind direction then where all flying aircraft are positioned.

✔ If none are preparing to land they will confirm with those flying that they are clear for takeoff.

✔ During a final run-up they check that their radio aerial is fully extended, that all controls are responding in their correct direction and amount and that the engine is properly tuned.

✔ As soon as their aircraft is in a stable climb, they move clear of the strip and into the fliers' box (if they were not already standing there during takeoff).

✔ During their flight they will be checking the position of the other aircraft (only using peripheral vision).

✔ If they plan to move out of the flight pattern and there's any chance of overlap they call the manoeuvre.

✔ Preparing to land, they call 'landing' and wait to be cleared by the others.

✔ After landing they clear the strip promptly and move back to the pits.

✔ After shutting down, their first action is to return the transmitter to the impound and replace the frequency peg for the next flyer.

✘ Other fliers unpack their plane in parts all around their tool box and begin the service repairs they saw were needed when they stopped flying last week.

✘ Some will collect the frequency peg and start shuffling batteries until they assemble a set which will perform up to (their) standard.

✘ Then it is time to see if they can cure the engine problems that caused them all that trouble last time.

✘ Many of these running repairs will require the transmitter, so the frequency peg is monopolised during the process.

✘ Once the engine is running it's time to get their plane into the air to see if it will keep running (no time for a range-check, the batteries looked OK anyway).

✘ Just after takeoff the engine cuts. A panic turn back toward the runway (otherwise it might hit the fence), the speed drops, a wing tip stalls and instead of the fence, their model hits the ground, vertically. Oh dear, bad luck!

Although there are times when no amount of prior preparation can eliminate field adjustments and repairs, we owe it to those we fly with to be as well prepared as possible before we arrive at the field.

Chapter 6: Micro T, a 'progressive' trainer

Photo 6:1 *Your Micro T set up as the Mark IV, a 4-channel, radio controlled, powered microlight model aircraft.*

■ The Micro T is a different concept in trainer aircraft.

It is designed to introduce you to one problem at a time, progressively teaching you both building and flying skills step-by-step.

It begins life as a freeflight glider. Then, through a number of minor 'refits' you add components which gradually turn it into a 4-channel powered model microlight aircraft.

Finally, when you are ready to progress on to more complex models, you can make the last changes which convert it into the 'Micro T–Mk V', a very useful camera plane.

■ The Micro T series has a number of design features worth talking about:

● Remember we are learning to make *scale* aircraft. The Micro T looks like a microlight aircraft. It also flies like one. It can safely fly slowly. As a trainer it gives you more time to see what's happening and think out the right correction.

● It is reasonably large and reasonably light. This adds to the impression of slow flight. The engine it uses is a usefully small size suitable for later models you will progress to.

■ In flight the model features 'forgiving' characteristics:

● A rectangular wing plan form:– as discussed, wings with parallel leading and trailing edges and squared off wingtips tend to spill lift from the tips. Like washout, this ensures that at low speed there is less risk of that unexpected disaster from 'tip stall'.

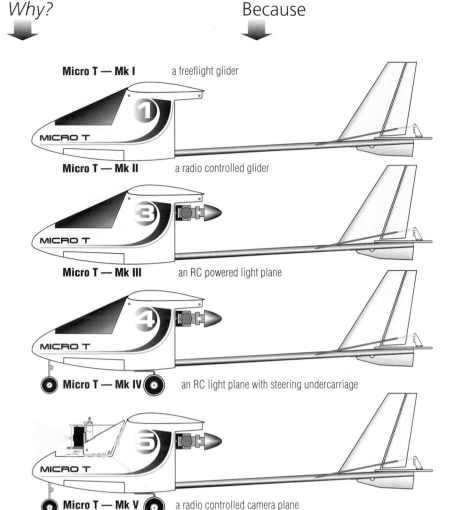

Micro T — Mk I — a freeflight glider

Micro T — Mk II — a radio controlled glider

Micro T — Mk III — an RC powered light plane

Micro T — Mk IV — an RC light plane with steering undercarriage

Micro T — Mk V — a radio controlled camera plane

This model certainly looks different from most trainers I've seen. Has the design been proven with people learning to fly on it?

At the time of writing the prototype has been flown through an extensive set of trials. So far the flight has been proven exactly to spec. Now it is intended to make it a club trainer.

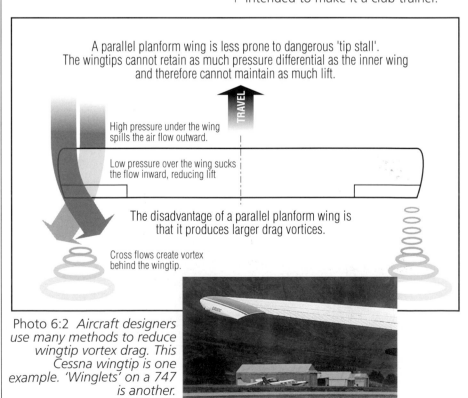

A parallel planform wing is less prone to dangerous 'tip stall'. The wingtips cannot retain as much pressure differential as the inner wing and therefore cannot maintain as much lift.

TRAVEL

High pressure under the wing spills the air flow outward.

Low pressure over the wing sucks the flow inward, reducing lift

The disadvantage of a parallel planform wing is that it produces larger drag vortices.

Cross flows create vortex behind the wingtip.

Photo 6:2 *Aircraft designers use many methods to reduce wingtip vortex drag. This Cessna wingtip is one example. 'Winglets' on a 747 is another.*

Micro T, a lightweight progressive trainer

60" span scale model aircraft for 4-channel radio control
and 0.25 to 0.35 cu in 2-stroke engines (propeller size restriction)
From 'AIRCRAFT WORKSHOP: Learn to make models that FLY'
by Kelvin Shacklock©

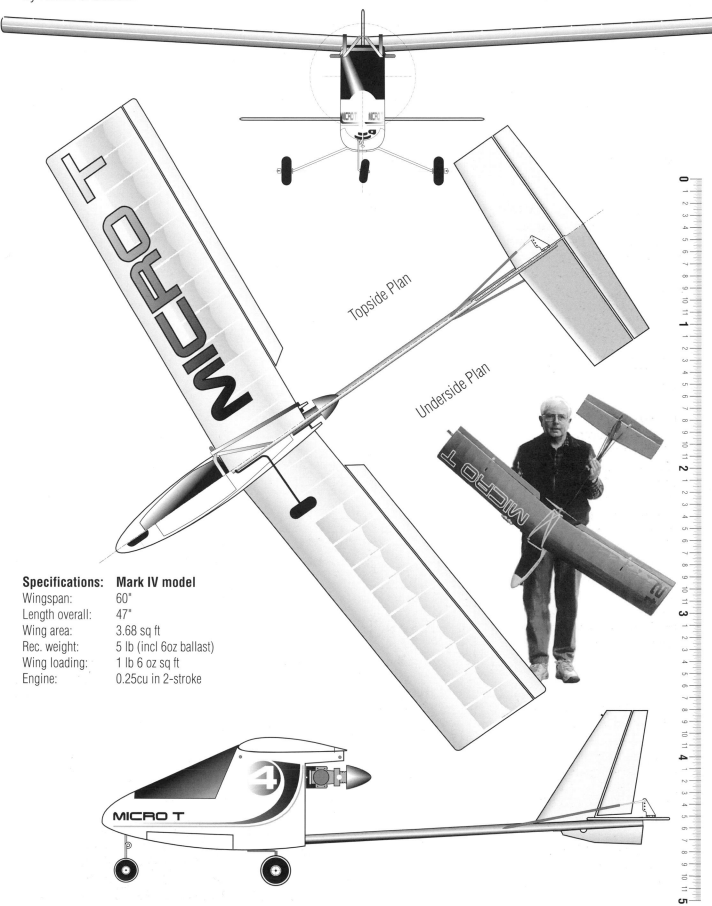

Topside Plan

Underside Plan

Specifications: **Mark IV model**
Wingspan: 60"
Length overall: 47"
Wing area: 3.68 sq ft
Rec. weight: 5 lb (incl 6oz ballast)
Wing loading: 1 lb 6 oz sq ft
Engine: 0.25cu in 2-stroke

Practice

- **Sweepback on the wings:–**
  as your aircraft yaws or flies slightly sideways, like when rudder only is applied, a sweepback ensures that the wing that has been pushed forward produces more lift than the wing that is trailing (see diagram). Lift from the forward wing rolls the aircraft toward the direction of the yaw producing a stable turn.

- **Large tail surfaces:–**
  stability of a model aircraft is generally improved by increasing the area of the tail surfaces. The results vary in combination with the distance between the wing and tail surfaces (pitching moment).

- **A staggered rudder and tailplane:–**
  when the rudder is stationed ahead of the tailplane, spin recovery is much more positive. Without stagger, in a spin the tailplane can shade airflow from the rudder making it ineffective as a corrective control surface.

Photos 6:3 & 4 *Compare the tailplane/rudder relationship on the Pitts (which is intended to be able to spin) with that of the Cessna below which must be spin-resistant.*

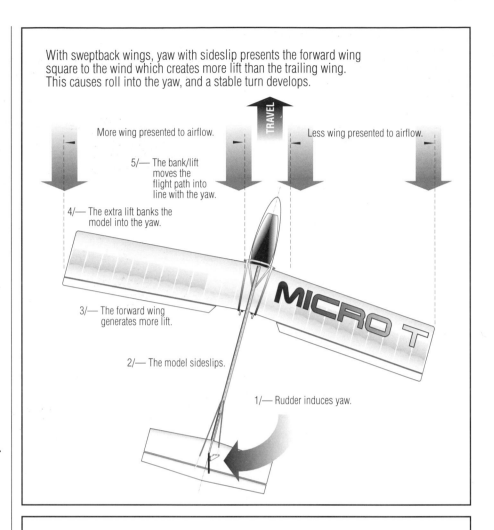

With sweptback wings, yaw with sideslip presents the forward wing square to the wind which creates more lift than the trailing wing. This causes roll into the yaw, and a stable turn develops.

More wing presented to airflow.   TRAVEL   Less wing presented to airflow.

5/— The bank/lift moves the flight path into line with the yaw.

4/— The extra lift banks the model into the yaw.

3/— The forward wing generates more lift.

2/— The model sideslips.

1/— Rudder induces yaw.

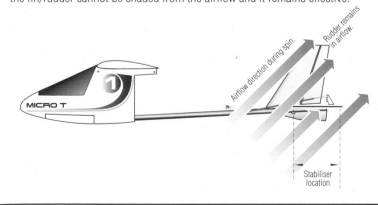

Where the stabiliser/elevator is in line with the fin/rudder, in spin conditions the fin/rudder can be shaded from the airflow and be rendered ineffective.

Airflow direction during spin.   Rudder shaded by stabiliser.

Stabiliser location

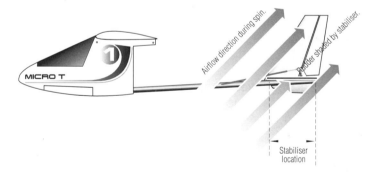

Where the stabiliser/elevator is staggered behind the fin/rudder, in spin conditions the fin/rudder cannot be shaded from the airflow and it remains effective.

Airflow direction during spin.   Rudder remains in airflow.

Stabiliser location

64

Practice

- A long pitching moment:– the more the space between the wing and tailplane of an aircraft, the more smoothly it will respond to elevator control inputs.
  Short moments tend to produce twitchy aeroplanes (see diagram).

- Only moderate dihedral:– plenty of dihedral helps the trainee pilot keep his model on an even keel. However, this also makes the model less inclined to turn when commanded by the pilot. It also makes the model more difficult to control in cross winds. The Micro T combines a low centre of gravity, a high centre of lift, sweepback and only moderate dihedral; a combination designed to produce stability without severely suppressing control.

- Built-in aileron differential:– ailerons interrupt airflow so they cause drag. And, the more they deflect the more drag they cause. Aileron differential is used to alter the amount that an aileron goes down when the other goes up. Now, if the down-going aileron hardly moves at all it will cause little drag while if the up-going aileron moves a lot it will drag a lot. With more drag on the low side of the roll (with its raised aileron) it will yaw the plane into the roll, inducing turn in the same direction as the plane is banking – just what we want!

- Balanced tricycle undercarriage:– the tricycle undercarriage is arranged to make takeoffs easier. The front wheel lifts at low speed and the centre of drag from the wheels moves back to behind the centre of gravity, helping the model to track straight with little need for control from the pilot.

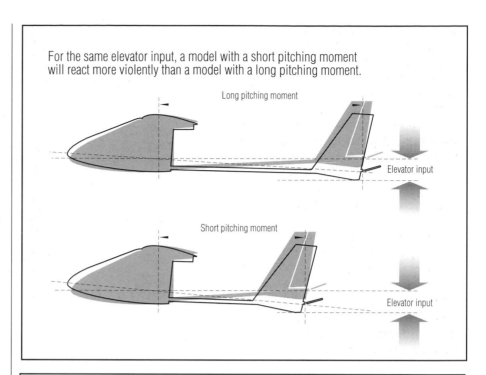

For the same elevator input, a model with a short pitching moment will react more violently than a model with a long pitching moment.

Long pitching moment

Elevator input

Short pitching moment

Elevator input

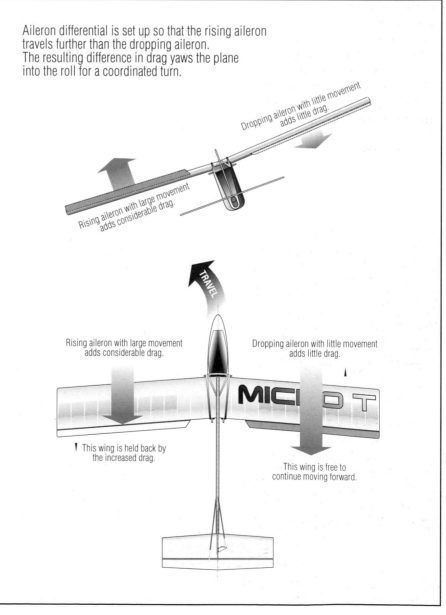

Aileron differential is set up so that the rising aileron travels further than the dropping aileron.
The resulting difference in drag yaws the plane into the roll for a coordinated turn.

Dropping aileron with little movement adds little drag.

Rising aileron with large movement adds considerable drag.

TRAVEL

Rising aileron with large movement adds considerable drag.

Dropping aileron with little movement adds little drag.

This wing is held back by the increased drag.

This wing is free to continue moving forward.

Practice

■ The Micro T also incorporates safety features especially suited to an initial trainer:

● Pusher propeller:– inevitably, while learning there is an increased risk of the trainee pilot losing control of his model. The consequences can be reduced if the model itself presents less danger to others. A pusher propeller makes a dramatic difference to the consequence of a runaway aircraft.

● Exposed control linkages:– clevises, control horns and servos are readily visible/ accessible for preflight checking and maintenance.

■ Simple to build

● Wing:– conventional construction with single aerofoil section; long span ailerons (with built-in differential); and rubber band mounting.

● Fuselage:– pod and boom construction is quick, adjustable for accurate alignment of all sub-assemblies with provision for easy access to all components.

■ Impact resistance and easy repair design:–

● all major parts separate without disturbing glue joints so that components can be easily repaired or replaced individually.

● Fuselage boom is intended to greatly reduce construction time and introduce you to some metalwork.

● Wing/fuselage connection is rubber band mounted to absorb impacts.

● Wing design incorporates closed 'D' section torsion beam with 'bandaged' centre section joint for the strongest job.

Why?

Is tricycle gear an advantage over two wheels and a tailwheel? I thought that as long as the two wheels were far enough forward the model wouldn't tip over on its nose and all would be well.

Because

Tailwheel undercarriage (taildragger) gives a false impression of stability. In fact, as soon as the tail lifts off, all ground resistance is in front of the C of G, rather like an arrow going backwards. If during takeoff the plane yaws sideways the centre of ground drag wants to get behind the centre of mass and the plane tries to flip round into a 'ground loop'. The further you move the wheels forward the worse this gets.

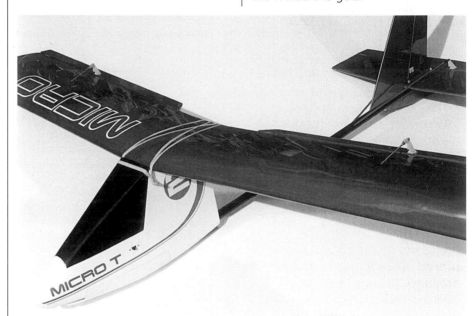

Photo 6:5 *Exposed control linkages are quick to check and adjust while the rubber band mounted wing dramatically reduces 'prang' damage.*

Photo 6:6 *Easily disassembled into its components, the design allows for easy packing and storage, to say nothing of far more straightforward repair.*

If all these features are so good to have in a model, why are they not incorporated in all designs?

It really is a case of designing with a purpose. This model is intended to teach the inexperienced pilot safe building, flying, maintaining and repairing skills.

Chapter 7: Begin building a Micro T

Practice

Photo 7:1 *In this chapter we will progress the building to the Mk I stage: a freeflight glider.*

You decide whether you want to build and fly stage-by-stage, or go straight through to the Mk III or IV model. Either way start here.

■ Building board

Spend a little time and effort preparing so the actual building process is easier, faster and more accurate. Making a building board is well worth it and it will

Building Board Materials:

High density fibreboard, 1/2"–5/8" sheet 6' x 2' (min. 5'8" x 18")

Low density fibreboard, 1/2"–5/8" sheet 6' x 2' (min. 5'8" x 18")

Dressed pine planks, (ex 1" x 4"), 2 @ 6', 1 @ 3', 2 @ 2'

Wood screws

be used on later models. Assemble the wooden frame as shown in diagram 1, ensuring each stick is straight and they are all of equal depth. Work on a really flat surface. Screw down onto the frame the sheet of high density fibre board as shown in diagram 2. Now you have a rigid, flat surface which you can move round, lean against a wall or whatever. Let's set it up for wing building.

From the 1" x 4" x 3' pine, saw two wedges angled accurately so they measure 2" deep at 2'6" from their tapered end tips. Screw

The custom building board is an ideal platform on which to build really accurate airframes, the essence of well aligned aircraft.

Building board frame

END

1"

4"

4"

1"

END

1-6"

2"

Say 5'-8"

1

Building board

Say 6'-0"

1/2" to 5/8"

High Density Fibreboard

2'

END

END

2

Wing building

Say 6'-0"

C/L

1/2"

Low Density Fibreboard

2'

at 2-6"

2"

C/L

High Density Fibreboard

END

3

Wing building

screw down

C/Ls guides for plan alignment

END

4

General building

Remove wedges and replace low density fibreboard

END

5

them in place with their tips a fraction outside the centreline (C/L) of your board (diagram 3).

Mark the exact centre across the low density fibreboard and, on the back surface, knife about half way through and crease. Reverse and position it right-side-up with the crease exactly over the centreline of the board below. Screw it down (diagram 4).

Draw in the centrelines along and across the board. It is now ready for you to start on the wing.

■ Plan preparation

Put into practice the method you learned on page 19 about enlarging plans from the book.

Photocopy/enlarge to 400% sheet 1 showing the cutting patterns for the parts you need for the wing. Tile into strips and iron the image onto your balsa.

Enlarge to 400% sheets 2 and 3 of the wing plans, tiling them together then joining at the registration marks 'A' and 'B'. Check the rule to see you got the scale right. Tape the plan onto the building board, ensuring it is aligned exactly over the centreline of the board. Cover with clear cling film or waxed tracing paper.

■ Wing construction

Cut out all of the components shown on sheet 1.
W15 is a little more complicated than you've made so far. It is a key to some of the strength of the wing union, so spend a little extra time getting it just right. Cut it to the shape shown in the elevation. Notice it is not symmetrical–the starboard side is longer than the port side.
When you look down on it as if it's in the wing, see how the front faces need to be bevelled back to the same angle as that of the wing's sweepback. File, rasp or sand these bevels.

My friends say you don't have to go to all this trouble. They just build their wings straight on any flat surface like a door. Why don't we?

Sure it's conventional practice to build each wing panel on a flat surface, separately, then join them through the centre section. However, there are several reasons we will make a custom building board.

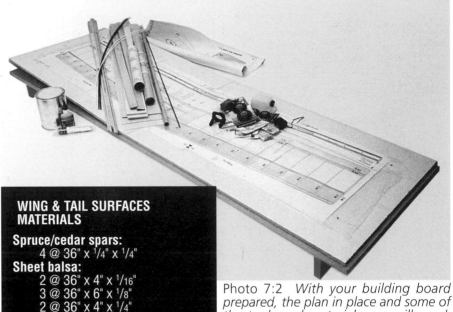

WING & TAIL SURFACES MATERIALS

Spruce/cedar spars:
   4 @ 36" x ¼" x ¼"
Sheet balsa:
   2 @ 36" x 4" x ¹/₁₆"
   3 @ 36" x 6" x ⅛"
   2 @ 36" x 4" x ¼"

Trailing Edge (ailerons):
   2 @ 30" x 1¼" x ⅜"
Glue:
Balsa cement, thin cyanoacrylate, epoxy 2 pot

Materials (for details check plan):
Control snakes (2), threaded pushrods (2), threaded clevises (8), large control horns (4), bellcranks (2), large scale hinges (12), servo tray–horizontal (1), shrink film.

Photo 7:2 *With your building board prepared, the plan in place and some of the tools and materials you will need, you're ready to start.*

It produces an extremely accurate wing (too many new pilots struggle to fly badly aligned models that no experienced person would want to fly). Let's get it right. Also, we will progress to more complex wings where custom building boards are vital, so now's a good time to get into a good habit.

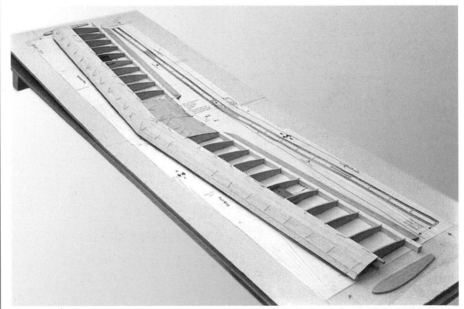

Photo 7:3 *Following the next few pages, your Micro T wing will begin to look like this. And, when you come to remove it from the board you'll be surprised at how strong it feels, especially when you realise just how light it is.*

Practice

When the ribs have all been cut out sandwich them together and true them much the way we did with the J-3 wing. In this case there's a lot more wood so make a pack for each wing and if you

Photo 7:4 *Many of the ribs are the same profile. Clamp them together and sand them to exactly the same shape.*

can hold them square, drill through each pack and bolt them together (see photo 7:4).

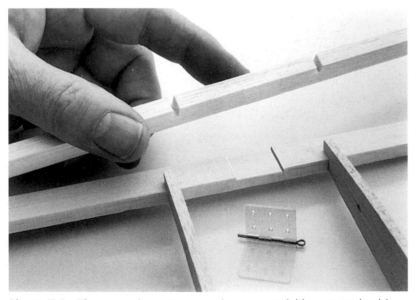

Photo 7:5 *The two-piece rear spar lets you quickly recess the hinge slots into one side before joining them together. You'll find this is much easier than cutting a blind slot. Also, the top member is notched to receive the tail end of each wing rib, ensuring they are correctly spaced.*

Note that all ribs have ¹/₁₆″ sheeting on the forward plane and W7 and W8 plus W0, W1 and W2 have sheeting on the after plane so their profiles are different from the rest of the pack.

Iron-down images

Note: the component cutting guides are reproduced back-to-front so that they will print correctly when photocopied then transferred onto your wood stock with a hot iron and pressure.

Micro T, sheet 1: wing components 0

Scale = 25%   Enlarge to 400% and check size against ruler

1/8" x 4" x 24" balsa   1/8" x 4" x 24" balsa

Spruce or pine etc.
Detail of
1/4" softwood wing spar brace

Elevation
W15
Starboard side   Plan

1/8" x 12" x 17" ply
W14   W14

Detail of W16
(1/8" balsa as shown above)
W16
Elevation
Plan

Practice

■ To start laying up the wing, put down a 1" wide strip of the underside ¹/₁₆" sheeting with its inner end angled to fit the centreline and its back edge on the back line of the main spar. Overhang the outer end beyond the span. Do both wings and glue where the sheets butt join at the centreline.

Angle the ends of two spruce ¹/₄" sq. spars to butt join at the centreline and glue them down on the sheeting so their back edges are flush over the full span.

Put down the two sheeting panels of the centre section so they fit up against the back of the spars and their sheeting. Butt together on the centreline. Make the servo cutouts as shown on the plan.

Strip the ¹/₄" x ¹/₂" rear spars and test fit a few ribs to check the sheeting will place the trailing edge in its correct position. Pin the sheeting in position and glue its leading edge and along the join at the centreline.

■ Make up the two-piece rear spars by rebating slots for the three hinges (per wing) in the lower spars and notching the upper spars to accept each rib (photo 7:5). Test fit with a few ribs and when satisfied remove and glue the two pairs of spars together along their length and pin them in place on the plan.

■ Glue face-to-face ribs W0. Cut a short spruce spar to fit from the outer faces of the two W1 ribs. Pack its underside with a double tapered ¹/₄" x ¹/₁₆" balsa strip so the spruce touches the sheeting at both ends and the centre is supported by the strip over the centreline. Check the position by fitting the W1 ribs. Add the W0 ribs, square up and glue. Starting with ribs W2, progressively place and glue all the ribs except W13.

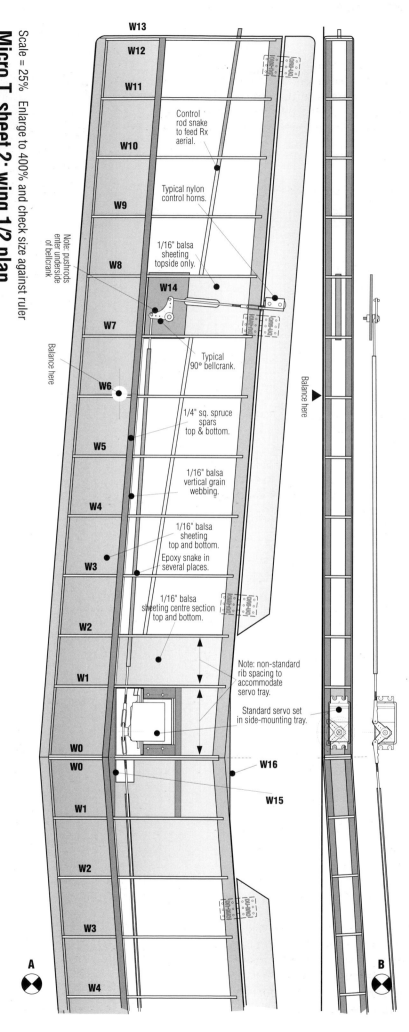

Scale = 25%   Enlarge to 400% and check size against ruler

Micro T, sheet 2: wing 1/2 plan

Note: pushrods enter underside of bellcrank

Balance here

Control rod snake to feed Rx aerial.

Typical nylon control horns.

1/16" balsa sheeting topside only.

Typical 90° bellcrank.

1/4" sq. spruce spars top & bottom.

1/16" balsa vertical grain webbing.

1/16" balsa sheeting top and bottom.

Epoxy snake in several places.

1/16" balsa sheeting centre section top and bottom.

Note: non-standard rib spacing to accommodate servo tray.

Standard servo set in side-mounting tray.

Balance here

■ Lower the upper spruce spars into their rib slots and check for straightness and fit. Angle their inner ends so they butt together cleanly then glue. Meantime let all spars overhanging at the wingtips.

Strip the two ¼" x ½" lower leading edge spars and again adjust where they join. Glue and hold in place with pins. Strip the ¼" sq. upper leading edge spars and pin them before running cyano along the join.

■ With ¹/₁₆" balsa, 'web' the two spruce spars together with vertical grain sheeting to form the back surface of the 'D' section torsion tube (see cross section drawings on sheet three). Web all bays except those outboard of ribs W8 and the two bays inboard of W1.

Slide the ply bellcrank platforms W14 into place, checking the plan to see you have them the right way round (holes inboard and aft). Glue.

Sheet the upper leading edge of each wing panel with ¹/₁₆" balsa running full span, neatly butt join at the centreline and undercut the front edge to lie flat on the leading edge spar. Between ribs W2 and inboard and over the W7/ W8 rib bay, notch the back edge of the sheeting forward ¹/₈" to leave a seating for the trailing edge sheeting.

Glue the gusset W16 to bridge the centreline join of the rear spars.

With your craft knife now remove the wood joining the paired ribs W0 at the back of the main spars and test fit W15. Cut the servo-mounting blocks and test fit against their ribs. Epoxy them and W15 in place and leave to harden.

Clean up any glue overhangs then sheet the centre section on each side paying particular attention to the centreline joint. Remove all the pinning and lift the wing from the building board.

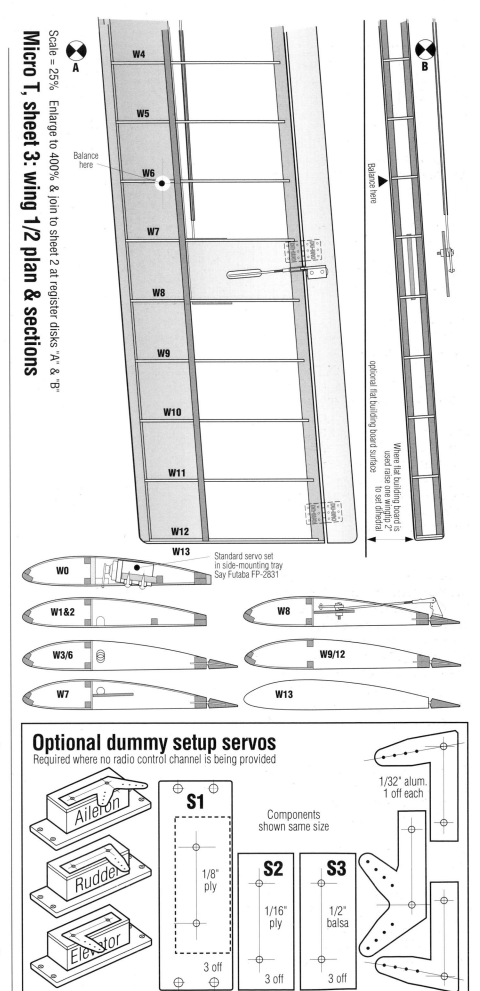

Micro T, sheet 3: wing 1/2 plan & sections

Scale = 25%   Enlarge to 400% & join to sheet 2 at register disks "A" & "B"

Optional dummy setup servos
Required where no radio control channel is being provided

Sheet the rest of the underside leading edge. Cut and fit, but don't glue the ¹/₁₆" sheeting for ribs bays W7/W8. At the wingtips trim all overhangs flush with W12 and glue outer ribs W13 in place.

■ Shape the ailerons from 1¹/₄" x ³/₈" trailing edge, align them with the wing and carve the hinge recesses according to the plan (also refer to the cross sections on sheet 3). Test fit and, provided you are using hinges with removable pins, glue them in place (always add a retaining pin).

■ Decision time. If you are skipping the Mk I stage and going straight into radio control you don't have to make the dummy setup servos (even though they would simplify the job). Over to you, so either make dummies or read 'servo' when you see 'dummy'.

In conjunction with the plan, study the diagram opposite so you understand which parts are what, where they go and how they work.

Build the dummy setup servos shown on sheet 3 then follow the description opposite. To ease and support the work of the main pushrods, epoxy the snake tubes through the ribs per the plan. It is good practice to keep rods straight and to provide support just in case they show a tendency to bend under compression.

When the control system is installed and you're happy that everything is right, lock the bellcrank nuts with glue and prepare to sheet over the two rib bays. With the sheeting you have already test fitted mark up the slot needed to clear the pushrod as it goes to the aileron horn, allowing for it to move down and sideways when it moves the aileron. Cut the slot to size and round the ends. Disconnect the pushrod from the aileron horn, fit and glue. Sand everything to shape as shown.

Photo 7:6 *This horizontal servo tray makes it a lot easier to fit the servo into the wing and you can get it out again with lots less hassle.*

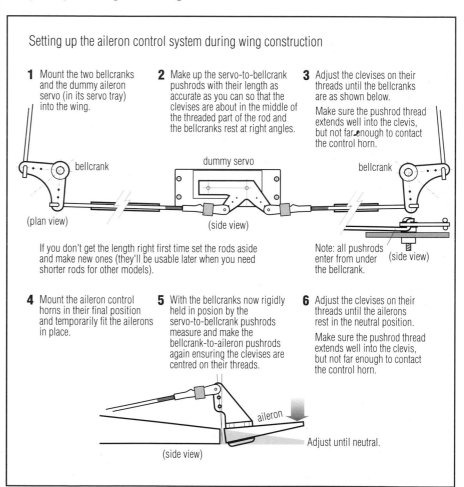

Setting up the aileron control system during wing construction

1 Mount the two bellcranks and the dummy aileron servo (in its servo tray) into the wing.

2 Make up the servo-to-bellcrank pushrods with their length as accurate as you can so that the clevises are about in the middle of the threaded part of the rod and the bellcranks rest at right angles.

3 Adjust the clevises on their threads until the bellcranks are as shown below.

Make sure the pushrod thread extends well into the clevis, but not far enough to contact the control horn.

bellcrank   dummy servo   bellcrank

(plan view)   (side view)   (side view)

If you don't get the length right first time set the rods aside and make new ones (they'll be usable later when you need shorter rods for other models).

Note: all pushrods enter from under the bellcrank.

4 Mount the aileron control horns in their final position and temporarily fit the ailerons in place.

5 With the bellcranks now rigidly held in posion by the servo-to-bellcrank pushrods measure and make the bellcrank-to-aileron pushrods again ensuring the clevises are centred on their threads.

6 Adjust the clevises on their threads until the ailerons rest in the neutral position.

Make sure the pushrod thread extends well into the clevis, but not far enough to contact the control horn.

aileron

Adjust until neutral.

(side view)

It's really quite important. Take a fairly long piece of pushrod and hold it right at each end. Now push your hands together and see how little pressure it takes to have the rod flex. Put a bend it the rod and push again and you'll find the rod has almost no strength at all. If it were, say, the elevator control on your plane and suddenly you needed all the up control you can get . . . whoops.

Practice

- Just before you can say the wing is finished ready for covering, bandage the centre section.

You can use epoxy and very light woven glass rovings, a silkspan or similar lightweight fabric and dope or something similar such as surgical bandage, and dope.

■ Boom construction

The boom of the prototype is made from aluminium tubing $^3/_4$" diameter with a wall thickness of about $^1/_{16}$". Try to get the same but don't worry if it's not exactly to the same specification. However, if it's much heavier you'll have to add considerably more nose ballast.

Cut the tube to exactly 34" long and mark off all the holes and filing angles from the measurements on sheet 4.

It's important you drill the main and tail-fixing bolt holes accurately on the same plane. If you don't have access to a drill press, fit a rod or dowel through the first hole you drill (one of the larger main mounting positions) and use this as a sight while you drill and while file the others.

File the tapered flat for the tailplane, checking that it is at right angles to the fin fixing screws. Angle the flat so that when you hold it hard down on a flat surface it lifts up the other end of the tube by 1$^1/_2$". Epoxy a piece of scrap $^1/_2$" balsa into the tail end and sand flat. Re-drill through from the metal side.

Mark the positions for the control snake exits and drill a $^3/_{16}$" hole at the centre of each. Very gently angle the drill to begin elongating the holes until you've done as much as you can with the drill. Then change over to the rat-tail file and work them into long, smooth exits (photos 7:8 and 7:9).

Photo 7:7 *Safe practice is to bandage the centre section of a wing using some sort of covering fabric and glue combination, preferably lightweight glass woven rovings with epoxy resin bonding.*

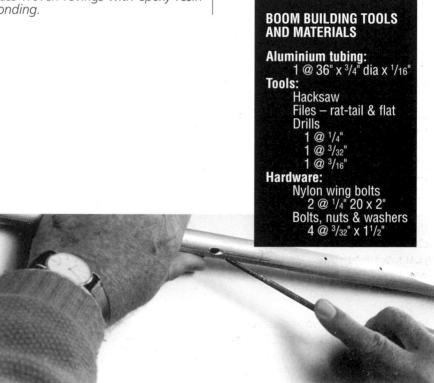

BOOM BUILDING TOOLS AND MATERIALS

Aluminium tubing:
    1 @ 36" x $^3/_4$" dia x $^1/_{16}$"
Tools:
    Hacksaw
    Files – rat-tail & flat
    Drills
    1 @ $^1/_4$"
    1 @ $^3/_{32}$"
    1 @ $^3/_{16}$"
Hardware:
    Nylon wing bolts
    2 @ $^1/_4$" 20 x 2"
    Bolts, nuts & washers
    4 @ $^3/_{32}$" x 1$^1/_2$"

Photo 7:8 *Metalwork is very much a part of aeromodelling. The Micro T fuselage boom is an ideal start. Take your time and you'll soon get it right.*

Photo 7:9 *This shows you why it is important to get nice smooth exits for your control rod snakes.*

Because

Although the wing structure is fairly strong across the centre section join, this added reinforcement has the advantage that it makes sure bending forces are applied to the surface skin instead of simply relying upon the internal framework.

We may use other materials but, wherever practical we will use this technique to increase the strength of the airframes we build.

If before now you've not done any metalwork, do talk over your problems with someone who has. For instance, they can show you how to scribe a parallel line along the length of the tube and 'centre-pop' the places for each hole. Then aligning the drill accurately involves holding the tube firmly without crushing it and controlling the drill angle.

The really important thing is to have a go. There's no better way to learn.

■ Fins & Rudder

Take the boom and position the four fin mounting bolts with their nuts as shown in the plan. Adjust the length of each bolt by moving the first nut along the thread and tighten the second nut to secure it. Make quite sure you have allowed enough thread for the lower fin bolts to hold the tailplane assembly, and for the upper fin forward bolt to also hold the lower fin bracket.

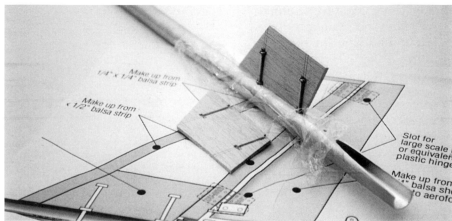

Photo 7:10 *When you epoxy the two upper fin parts together over the mounting bolts you may be surprised how strongly they grip.*

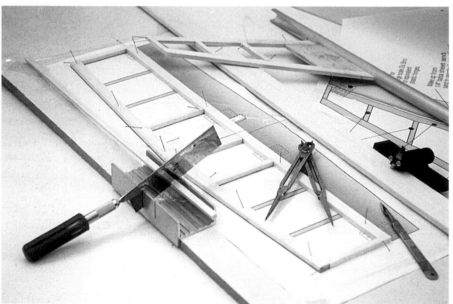

Photo 7:11 *The tail surfaces are built up in a very conventional way working directly onto the plan.*

As we progress to more complex models the text does avoid repeating all the steps we have learned before hand. You will find opposite that we say 'and make up in the usual way'. This is because we covered this technique when we built the J-3 tailplane. Where there could be a difficulty in remembering or it may be a bit tricky we try to give you the page reference so you can go back quickly if you have to.

■ From ⅛" hard grade balsa cut two upper R2 & lower R3 fin parts. Mark them off with the exact outline of the fin screws which will be used to hold them. Then, with your craft knife, make half checks in each part so they can sandwich both screws (see photo 7:10 – Note: only the upper fin is set up in the photo). Clamp the paired sides together to check for accurate alignment along the boom, adjusting the checks until they are dead straight. Take apart, protect the boom with cling film then epoxy the upper fin plates in place using a bulldog clip to squeeze the sides together. Hang until cured so no epoxy can dribble down into the boom holes.

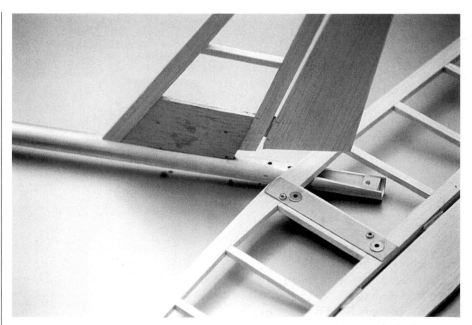

Photo 7:12 *It's less conventional, but it's a lot more convenient to bolt all the tail surfaces together, especially helpful when you start covering!*

Practice

Remove the upper fin assembly from the boom so you can complete the upper fin and work on the lower fin assembly.

Make from say ¹/₃₂" aluminium sheet the lower fin bracket per the plan. Recess the front end of the lower fin plates to enclose the vertical part of this bracket then repeat the epoxy sandwich technique for the lower fin. When hard, notch out a recess to accommodate the protruding end and nut of the second upper fin bolt.

■ Pin the R2 assembly to the plan and make up the fin in the usual way. Consider using two strips of ¹/₈" x ¹/₂" instead of a single ¹/₄" x ¹/₂" for the rudder post. It would be easier to half check the hinges into each side rather than slotting a single piece (the same would apply to the tailplane).

Cut the rudder from ¹/₄" sheet or again, consider using two x ¹/₈" pieces and half checking the hinge slots. If you do the latter, protect the slots to prevent them filling with glue then epoxy the two halves and squeeze them together while curing.

■ Build the tailplane (stabiliser/ elevator) on the plan in the same manner as the fin/rudder.

■ Sand the three assemblies to the cross sections shown then epoxy plates T2 to the top and bottom of the stabiliser.

When hard, accurately mark the position for the front mounting bolt hole and drill this in the stabiliser. Using a spare ³/₃₂" bolt, fit the stabiliser onto the boom and make firm. Swing the stabiliser until it is accurately aligned square to the boom and drill through the second mounting hole into the stabiliser. Remove the bolt and test fit the lower fin, boom and stabiliser. Remove, sand off then test fit the upper fin/rudder and lower fin stabiliser/elevator to the boom

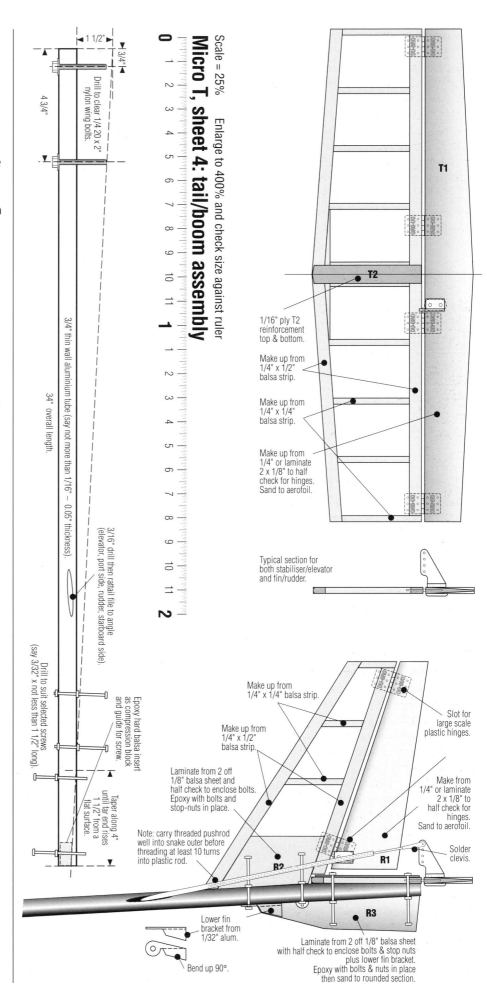

Micro T, sheet 5: fuselage pod

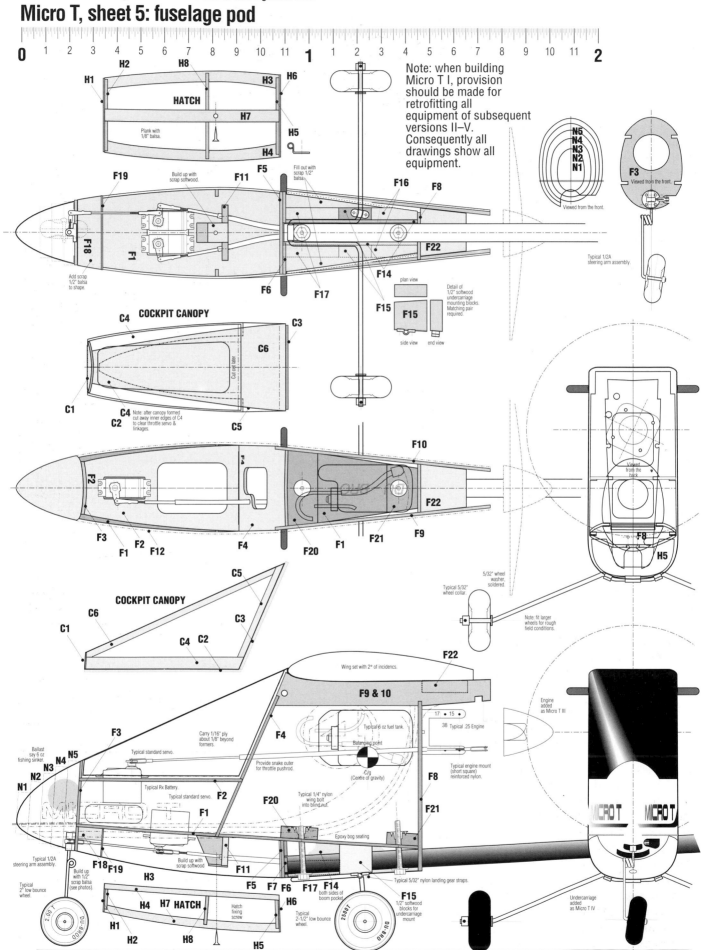

Note: when building Micro T I, provision should be made for retrofitting all equipment of subsequent versions II–V. Consequently all drawings show all equipment.

HATCH

Plank with 1/8" balsa.

COCKPIT CANOPY

COCKPIT CANOPY

Practice

■ Fuselage pod

Enlarge sheets 5 and 6 and apply the plan parts from sheet 6 to the specified wood.

Instead of ironing down the image you could stick down a photocopy of the plan directly onto your wood. Just remember, since the drawings have been reversed, the paper is stuck to the underside of the parts. If you try this method use it first on plywood like the ⅛" sheet of parts shown opposite (photo 7:13). Rubber solution is a quite good adhesive for the job because it doesn't wrinkle or shrink the paper plan the way a water-based paste does. Once the parts are cut out and you remove the paper, get rid of any residue solution at the same time.

Use a fret or scroll saw to cut out all the ⅛" ply parts shown.

■ Test assemble them so your job looks like the prototype in photo 7:14. You will need to use a small flat file to angle the joints which meet at other than right angles.

It's easier to hold everything if you cut a cardboard jig and stand it up inside the main assembly to align F8 exactly square to F1 and F4 at its angle. Cover a corner of a flat bench or table with cling film and weight down F1 ready for gluing. Use epoxy on these joins. Again, when your assembly looks like photo 7:14 and you are sure everything is aligned per the plan, leave it to cure overnight.

■ While you wait, go on sawing out the rest of the parts paying particular attention to keeping the saw cuts vertical, especially on the thicker material. Sandpaper the inside cuts only (most of the outside edges will be worked on later so don't get too carried away with finishing them). Angle any bevel cuts as shown on the plan.

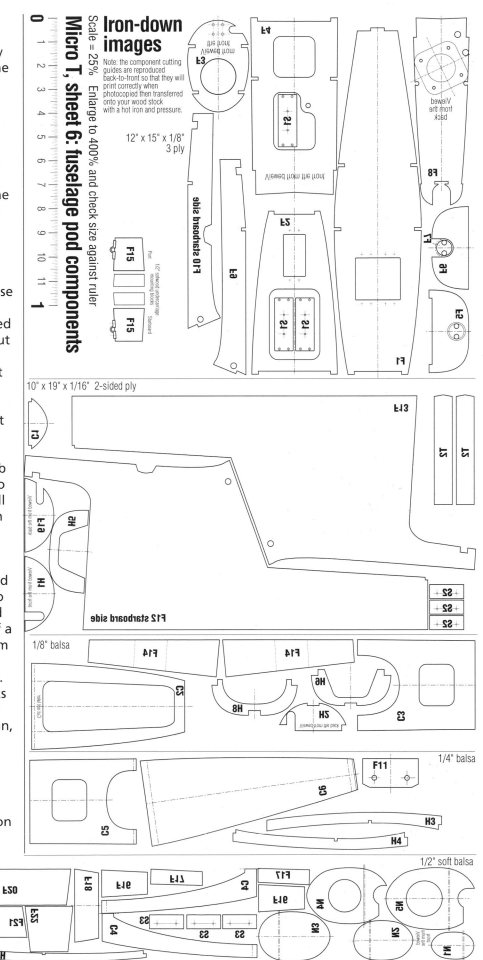

Practice

■ Test fit the ¹/₁₆" ply sides to the main assembly. When the lower and back edges are flush with the frame, there should be about ¹/₁₆"–¹/₈" overhang at the canopy edges (photo 7:15).

Epoxy both sides in place using bulldog clips to position and clamp the sheeting to F9 on one side and F10 on the other. Proceed to pull the sheeting into its curves by binding hard with packing tape. Good contact should be achieved on all the edges including the corners fitting against the front former F3. Again, leave to cure properly before being tempted to remove the tape.

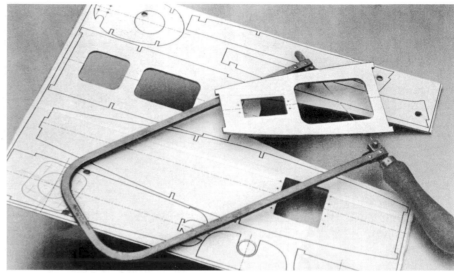

Photo 7:13 *If you can stick a photocopy of the components to the plywood you will find it speeds up the preparation process. Watch out though, water based glues will shrink the image so do use something like artists' rubber cement, etc.*

Photo 7:14 *A card template will help you get the angles right and holds the job steady while the glue hardens. Remember to use cling film protection so the model doesn't become part of the family dining table!*

FUSELAGE POD REQUIREMENTS
Wood:
- 1 @ 12" x 15" x ¹/₈" plywood
- 1 @ 10" x 19" x ¹/₁₆" plywood
- 1 @ 36" x 4" x ¹/₈" balsa sheet
- 1 @ 36" x 4" x ¹/₄" balsa sheet
- 1 @ 36" x 4" x ¹/₂" balsa sheet
- ¹/₂" pine or softwood scraps
- ¹/₄" dowelling

Hardware:
Control snakes (3), steering arm assembly (see plan), wing bolts & blind nuts (2), wood screw, lead sinker, tissue, filler, paint & tape.

Suggested additional tools:
Bulldog clips, fret or scroll saw, sanding disk.

Feel how strong yet lightweight this structure is. We will always try to achieve these qualities.

■ Follow the plan and photos 7:16 and 7:17 as your guide and build up the boom housing. Begin with former F5 and glue F6 and F7 to its face. Set up this assembly under the pod with the boom taped in place. Support it inside F6 and over F7 at the front and hold it in the cutout of F8 at the back. Packing tape will keep everything in place. Glue F5/6/7 into the slots in F1 then glue the sides F14 in place, allowing clearance for the boom.

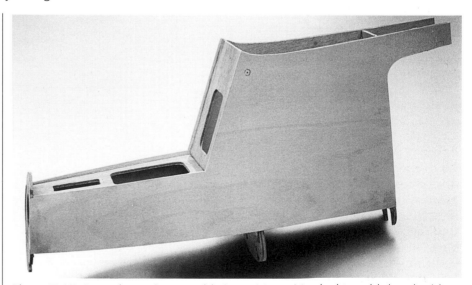

Photo 7:15 *Once the main assembly is set it's no big deal to add the ply sides.*

78

Remove the boom, wrap it in cling film and mix some low-density filler (balloons in epoxy – 'bog'). Put two generous bulks in the boom housing, seat the wrapped boom back in position and let it cure.

■ Fit, position and glue blocks F20 and F21 in place.

Temporarily bolt the tailplane to the boom and locate the boom correctly in the boom housing. Using the tailplane to check you have everything aligned square, carefully drill through the boom's front mounting hole into the pod through F20. Now from the inside and using a larger drill, open out the hole deep enough to accommodate the blind nut. Insert a wing bolt through the boom up into the pod, fit the blind nut and tighten it down into F20. Repeat for the second wing bolt. Undo the bolts and remove the boom, then carefully leak a little cyano round the outside edges of the blind nuts to secure them in place.

■ Build up the outside of the boom housing, firstly with softwood blocks F15 then the balsa parts and scrap as shown in the plan (photo 7:17). Proceed to assemble snake guide F11 and its softwood block plus the balsa block F18 with its former F19.

At this stage it's a good idea to temporarily mount the front undercarriage leg to ensure you retain mounting and function access.

■ The nose block components have been supplied with alignment references. When they are correctly aligned you can sight straight down their datum lines and see everything is right. Pin them in place until you're satisfied, then run some cyano into their joints.

Photo 7:16 *Epoxy 'bog' will set hard and make a good seating for the boom to be tightened against.*

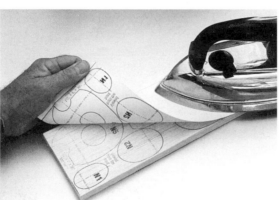

Photo 7:18 *The iron-on photocopy image is probably the best technique for the nose block components.*

I find the iron-on process the easiest and quickest way we have used yet, and can't be bothered with the other methods.

Low-density epoxy/balloon filler is a material we will use repeatedly. Mix a small quantity of 2-pot epoxy on an open dish then add glass balloon extender. Gently mix so the epoxy absorbs as much extender as you can get it to take without it going crumbly. Then apply. In the motor body repair industry this mix is generally referred to as 'bog'.

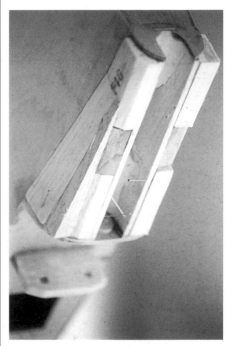

Photo 7:17 *Before you carve and sand the block to shape it can look pretty rough. Don't worry.*

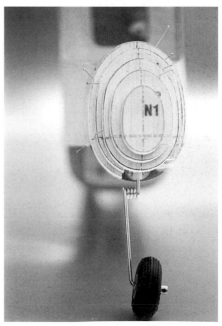

Photo 7:19 *Use the cross lines to help align each laminate of the nose block.*

Practice

■ Before you start shaping the nose block build up the canopy module. Protect the pod with cling film then pin the C2 and C3 parts into the recess in the pod and begin building upon them with C1, C4s, C5 and then C6 (photo 7:20). Now start the shaping process by rasping, filing and sanding.

Fill in the sides with scrap ¼" balsa into the general form and continue shaping (photo 7:21). Expect later to have to use some filler to get the exact shape.

■ Once more temporarily install the nose wheel assembly but this time assemble and couple up the steering linkage to the dummy setup servo per the plan (photo 7:22) and check clearances.

Protect the pod with cling film and build the hatch frame per the plan and photo. See that it clears all the mechanism inside and that the centre 'keel' H7 seats neatly onto the fixing block.

Drill and test fit the fixing wood screw. Apply locator blocks to F1 so the hatch can't swing sideways.

Plank with ⅛" x say ⅜" balsa strips which are bevelled and curved to make up the compound shape. Use lots of pins to hold their bends while the glue dries. Again, if this is your first attempt at planking expect to later use some filler.

Fit the hatch to the pod using the wood screw and gently sand the hatch to a smooth contour with the pod. Sand all three components, adding as little 'bog' as necessary to correct any faults, then sanding off again when cured.

■ Separate the hatch, pod and canopy and apply a generous coat or two of model aeroplane dope. Apply another coat but put down a layer of tissue as you go (cut smaller pieces to cover compound curves). Sand and dope again.

Why?

Photo 7:21 Fill in the canopy sides with scrap ¼" balsa and work it to shape.

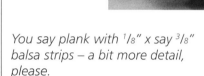

You say plank with ⅛" x say ⅜" balsa strips – a bit more detail, please.

Because

Photo 7:20 *Rasp, file and sand the shapes down to the pattern. Take care and avoid going too deep.*

Sure. Think about the way planks are fitted round a barrel. The sides of the barrel form a compound curve (they bend both ways at once). The same goes for our Micro T hatch. In the same way as planks fit round the barrel, our planks must fit round the hatch. They will be narrowest where the diameter is least and broadest where the diameter is greatest. And along their joins they will need to be bevelled.

Photo 7:22 *Build the hatch frame in place after you have covered the pod with cling film.*

80

■ Undercoat all the outer surfaces of the pod, hatch and canopy with a car painter's high-build sanding paint. Wet and dry it down with a very fine grit paper and paint again, this time sanding most of the paint back to the first coat. Repeat this until the finish is as good as you demand then give another light coat and light sanding. Clean up the edges and test fit all the parts.

■ Run a short piece of control snake outer through F4 and F8, trim it a little longer and epoxy in place. Temporarily fit the wing-retaining dowels.

You're ready to test assemble your Micro T Mk I. Go to it!

■ **Assembly**

This is the time to make any fine adjustments to shape, fit and alignment.

Double check that the fin/rudder lies straight along the boom and that it stands square from the tailplane. See that the tail section is properly aligned to the pod (adjust the boom's rotation in the pod to correct slight errors) then ensure the wings align with the tail. Check that the wing sits comfortably onto the pod and the profiles match (alter the pod to correct angles and any high spots or gaps).

If you are using hinges with removable pins, glue in the last of these at the tail. Mount the elevator and rudder control horns. Set up the snakes through the boom to the dummy setup servos, following the rules about ensuring enough thread is holding all the clevises (see page 72). Also, pay attention to which snakes comes from the rudder and make sure you have led it to the steering servo or you could have some very interesting control problems!

Now take off a little time, stand back and admire your handiwork.

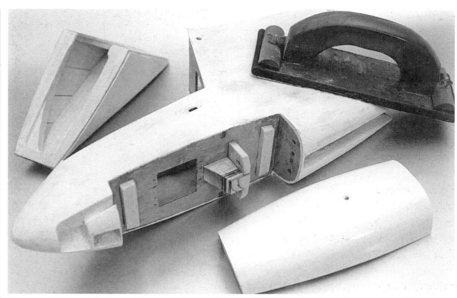

Photo 7:23 *After adding a tissue/dope skin, begin building up a filler and undercoat combination in preparation for painting.*

My rudder is not quite square upright compared with the tailplane. How to I adjust this?

If the rudder is correctly aligned with the pod, adjust the filed flat on the boom or even file the ply packer under the tailplane to bring it into line.

If the tailplane is right and the rudder is wrong loosen the main boom bolts and see if you can revolve the boom enough to correct the rudder then adjust the tail as above.

It's my wings that won't align with the boom or tail.

Take the file to the top of your pod and lower the high side until they come right.

Photo 7:24 *At last you can see the final form, soon to be painted, covered and trimmed with graphics.*

Practice	Why?	Because

■ Covering

The prototype is covered with Metallic Blue heat shrink film. Follow the instructions supplied with the actual brand you use.

Unlike other jobs we have tackled together, with the covering we will begin with the hard bits. In fact, it is really a case of avoiding having any hard bits by starting at the right place.

Covering nicely at the hinge lines usually presents the biggest challenge. With the building technique we have been using there are two possible situations – removable pin hinges and fixed pin hinges. The covering method alters slightly with each type. With the fixed type, glue the hinge flap into only the moving panel. Glue both flaps with the removable type then remove the pin (on each hinge flap always add a retaining pin which passes through the spar and hinge flap. Cut off flush with the other side).

Cover the moving panel first having tucked the hinges through slits cut in the film. Cover the matching edge of the fixed panel with a narrow strip, treating the hinge butts as above. For fixed

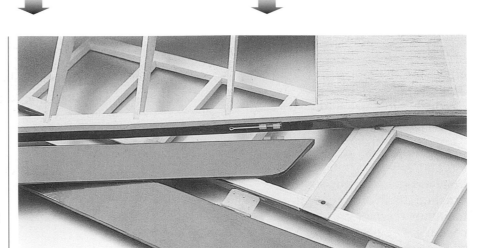

RECOMMENDED FINISHING MATERIALS

Heat shrink film:
    2 x 6' rolls Metallic Blue
Signwriters' computer tape:
    Offcuts in red, dark blue, white and fluorescent red
    Low-tack positioning tape
Paint:
    1 spray can white enamel
    1 spray can black enamel

ADDITIONAL RECOMMENDED FINISHING TOOLS

Specialist modelling iron and heat gun although a satisfactory finish can be achieved using a domestic heat-controlled iron.

I'm getting confused about hinge pins and retaining pins. Please explain.

Photos 7:25 When covering, hinge edges need careful planning if you are to get good clean lines. Removable hinge pins let you avoid the need for gluing after covering.

Although we cyano the hinge flaps into their slots, they can work loose and the consequences are usually total. To avoid this all hinge flaps should be pinned at least once as well as glued. Do this by driving a pin down through the spar, through the hinge flap and out the other side of the spar. Bury the pin head below the spar surface, cut off the other end and push it back slightly for an invisible finish. Then cover.

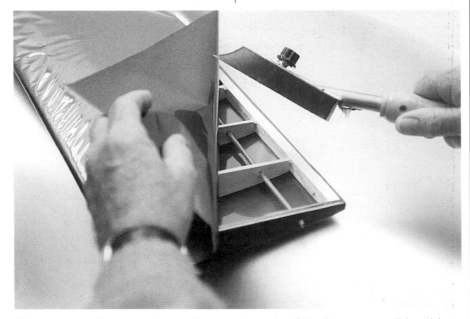

Photos 7:26 There are times when you wonder if the heat gun will be able to remove all the wrinkles. While you're feeling your way, don't try to cover too much with a single piece of film.

Photos 7:27 Slowly work away at the wrinkles, gradually tightening the whole area.

82

Practice

hinges, slit the strip after applying it then install the hinged panel and cyano the hinge flaps from inside the spar. Pin before you cover the fixed panel (photo 7:25).

■ Proceed to cover all panels, working from end to end, side to side, corner to corner, then spotting on opposite sides to maintain a distortion-free covering. Pay particular attention to edges and joins.

Apply the heat gun (or brush the surface very gently with an ordinary electric iron) and work up a glass-smooth surface. Take your time and increase heat very gradually or you could blow a hole in all your good work.

■ Painting

Clean up all hard-surface parts until they have the finish you expect from the final coat of paint. Remember, the remaining paint won't hide any faults you know about and it will probably find a lot you haven't yet seen. As separate parts spray paint the pod and hatch white. Spray the boom and canopy with black. Leave to harden.

■ Detailing

Enlarge sheet 7 and cut the graphics for the wing and pod from signwriters' computer tape (beg or buy offcuts from your local computer graphic signwriter).

Follow the sequence of the photos opposite, 7:28 through 7:32. They show the frequency peg number being cut from fluorescent red for fixing to the port wing of the prototype. The same method applies to all graphic details. Positioning is shown on the plan.

Assemble and align all components so you can now call your model finished and ready for trimming out!

Photo 7:28

Lay up a photocopy over the signwriters' tape so neither can move as you cut round the image with a sharp scalpel.

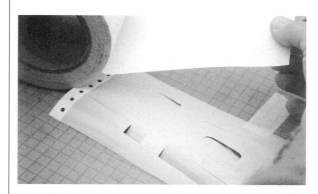

Photo 7:29

Remove the photocopy and cover with low-tack positioning tape.

Photo 7:30

Turn it over, remove the backing to leave the parts you do want and weed out the areas you don't want.

Photo 7:31

Align the tape to the model and touch down. Work from the centre outwards and expel any air bubbles. Burnish down with the back of your fingernail.

Photo 7:32

Gently lift off the low-tack positioning tape and admire your work. If you're very handy with a fine paintbrush you could seal the edges with fuel proofer.

Photo 7:33 *After checking that all control surfaces are firmly set to neutral and the balancing point is as shown on the plan, your Micro T Mk I is now ready for freeflight trials.*

■ Assuming your model weighs out about the same as the prototype add from 4–6oz of ballast into the nose cavity to bring the centre of gravity to the point shown on the plan.
Trim out all control surfaces to flat and test glide, beginning from flat ground and work your way up a slope.

How do I correct any tendencies to turn, stall or otherwise misbehave?

You practised this when you trimmed out the chuckies, glider with control surfaces and then the J-3. The only difference here is that you can make definitive adjustments to the control surfaces by moving the control clevises in or out on their threaded pushrods.
You can refresh your memory by reading pages 14 and 15 again.

Scale = 25%   Enlarge to 400% and check size against ruler.

Micro T, sheet 7: Graphics

0 1 2 3 4 5 6 7 8 9 10 11 **1** 1 2 3 4 5 6 7 8 9 10 11 **2**

MICRO T

1 234

Starboard side

MICRO T

5

Port side

MICRO T

Chapter 8: Choosing a radio

■ The radio for an RC model aircraft is a specialist transmitter which broadcasts within a specific frequency band, legally set aside for the sport. The RC model aircraft frequency band is divided into narrow segments which are numbered for quick ref. (eg: 35.850 mhz = say 42). Radios are supplied with crystals which are tuned to one of these numbered frequencies. **Note: legal bands and numbering systems do differ from country to country.**

At any one time and within a radio range of about 4 miles minimum, only one transmitter may be allowed to send out its signal. Note that if a transmitter is switched on it is considered to be transmitting, regardless of its aerial extension or the position of the sticks (sticks have nothing to do with the transmission of the radio frequency carrier wave). Consequently **there are strict controls over the use of an RC transmitter**.

■ Most modern RC aircraft radios transmit 'FM' (frequency modulation) signals. Older sets send less reliable 'AM' (amplitude modulation) signals. High-end radios can transmit their information as 'PCM'* digitally-encoded computer signals. They can also send the information as 'PPM'**, compatible with lower cost equipment.

■ **Transmitter Channels**

Your basic powered model aircraft transmitter has two 'sticks'. Both work two channels, four in all. Each channel operates a separate function in your plane. You control roll, pitch, yaw and engine speed by moving the sticks to activate one or more of these four channels.

Photo 8:1 *Typical of the range of transmitters you are likely to find at your club: left, a simple 4-channel FM set with adjustable dual rates on the elevator and aileron channels; right, a 7-channel PCM computer-programmable set with channel mixing, snap roll, 4 model memory and in front, a 9-channel PCM computer set with all the bells and whistles.*

I'm serious about taking up the sport so I suppose I should buy the best radio I can afford, then I won't 'grow out of it'. What's your advice?

Good to know you want to make a real commitment, but slow down. Remember that every switch and button that can be set to do something special can also be switched the wrong way so the model does what you don't intend.

Keep it simple, learn to use the basics and consider upgrading later.

What about buying a cheap, second-hand set?

Take advice from someone who can give you good guidance (and not the owner of the set!). In any case, do try to get a brand that will remain compatible with equipment you may want to upgrade to. Some types are interchangeable, others are not.

*   Pulse Code Modulation.
** Pulse Position Modulation

Practice

 Why?   Because

■ Transmitter Modes

The standard setup for a powered, fixed-wing model aircraft transmitter is to have four channels operated by two sticks. Regardless of the total number of channels provided on any particular transmitter set, these four are the primary functions which control pitch, yaw, roll and thrust (engine). These primary channels can be linked to the sticks in either one of two 'modes', Mode I or Mode II.

Mode I has the engine throttle on the right and elevator on the left, while Mode II has them reversed. Both have left hand rudder and right hand ailerons.

■ Arguments over which mode is the better are endless. The important point for you is that once you have learned on one, you would find it difficult to change over at a later date, so consider it carefully.

Enthusiasts of Mode I generally argue they can more precisely control the elevator without affecting roll, and roll without affecting the elevator.

Mode II exponents suggest it is easier to learn to fly on Mode II because it is more natural to 'stir-the-pot' with the right hand, as in a full size 'stick' controlled aircraft.

■ Talk to the members of your club. See which mode most members fly, and find out on which the club would rather you train on. Remember, you don't want to be the only one in the club who flies on that mode or you'll never be able to fly another's aircraft (some people do develop the skill of flying both modes but it's fairly uncommon).

A transmitter can be quite simply altered internally to change it from one mode to the other.

The two standard control modes for radio controlled powered model aircraft

Mode I evolved from early transmitters where first the right hand was used to direct the model. The left hand was added and used for pitch control. As more functions were added sticks became two-function, and the original movements were retained.

Mode I

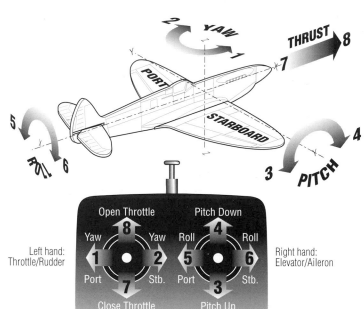

Mode II

Mode II is based upon aircraft practice with the right hand emulating the full size aircraft control column functions for pitch and roll while the left hand works the throttle forward and back and the rudder from side to side.

Why have we two modes anyway? | I suppose Mode II was introduced more recently as a 'natural' method thought to be ergonomically easier to learn.

Practice

■ Basic features

The transmitter radio initiates movement in the plane by activating 'servos'. Normally, the amount of movement made by a transmitter stick is duplicated by an equal amount of movement by the arm of the linked servo. This is referred to as **proportional rates**.

Transmitters can incorporate features which allow you to alter the way a servo arm reacts to stick movement.

■ Unless you are prepared to set up every model with all its servos located to work in the right direction, **servo reversing** is a required feature.

Once the aircraft is set up the transmitter and receiver are switched on, you check that the throttle opens as you raise the stick. If it closes instead you flick the servo reversing switch and suddenly all is well. The same process is used to correct the elevator, rudder and aileron directions of movement.

■ **Trim adjustment** lets you offset the neutral centre of a servo arm's movement. Use these to trim your model for 'hands-off' straight and level flight. When you land note where each control surface rests. Then, one at a time, move each transmitter trim to neutral and adjust its appropriate clevis to reposition that control surface to its noted deflection. The plane should now fly true with each transmitter trim set on neutral. Note the throttle trim adjusts the 'idle' and 'off' positions.

■ Models can prove to be sensitive to 'over control'. A **dual rates** switch lets you reduce the movement of a servo arm to make control less sensitive. The sensitivity can be varied by turning a knob or set screw. Although reduced sensitivity can also be achieved mechanically, you cannot switch from one degree to another during flight.

Why?

This all feels a bit heavy for me. Do I need to go into these complications at this stage?

How important is it that I buy a transmitter with dual rates?

Because

Don't worry if you don't fully understand all this yet. However, it's best if you take a quick overview of what is available, what you need right now and what you may want in the future. Just don't let it bog you down.

Provided you are starting out with a relatively mildly behaved training model you should have no problem. Over-sensitivity can be reduced mechanically by altering the length of servo arms and control horns.

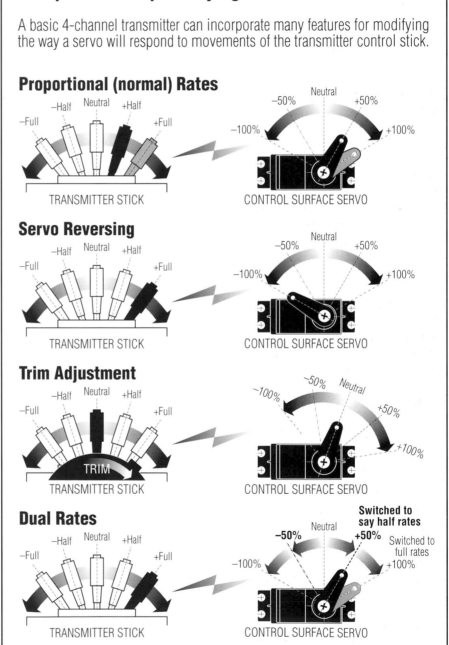

Servo response-modifying features found on many mid-priced FM sports flying 4-channel transmitters

A basic 4-channel transmitter can incorporate many features for modifying the way a servo will respond to movements of the transmitter control stick.

Proportional (normal) Rates

TRANSMITTER STICK — CONTROL SURFACE SERVO

Servo Reversing

TRANSMITTER STICK — CONTROL SURFACE SERVO

Trim Adjustment

TRANSMITTER STICK — CONTROL SURFACE SERVO

Dual Rates

TRANSMITTER STICK — CONTROL SURFACE SERVO

Practice

■ Advanced features

A computer radio can do much more to modify a servo arm's response to stick movement.

■ With **adjustable travel** you can alter the amount a servo moves to each side of neutral. This can however be achieved mechanically.

■ **Exponential rates** allow you to make a servo react differently to movements of the stick near to neutral compared with its reaction to outer movements of the stick. The result is something like having dual rates without the need to switch between them.

■ Most aircraft can be trimmed to fly manoeuvres better when there is input into more than one function (say rudder plus aileron). This can be done electronically with **channel mixing** in the computer transmitter.

The mixing function is ideal for 'V' tails and 'flaperons'.

Another example (shown opposite) is flap/elevator mixing where input on the flap channel will automatically adjust the elevator setting to compensate for any tendency for a model to pitch up or down when flaps are applied.

■ General features

Even simple transmitters can have **additional channels** for other functions such as retracting the undercarriage, lowering flaps, etc. Seven channels would be about all you're likely to use.

■ Two compatible transmitters can often be linked through a **buddy system** of plugs, cable and switch. It works like dual control in an aircraft with an instructor and pupil. It would be a good idea to check out your club to see if a buddy plug is something you could benefit from while you're learning to fly.

Why?

How many channels should I try to get on my first transmitter?

While I'm learning would a buddy facility be a valuable feature?

To use a buddy lead, must I be flying on the same mode as my instructor?

Because

You should have four and these may be enough. If the transmitter is still a simple one you can go for two more channels, but remember, it could be quite a while until you use either of them.

Yes. Fortunately you can get this facility on many, even low-end, transmitters. It does however rely upon someone else having compatible gear, a buddy lead and the knowledge needed to set up the two transmitters properly.

No, as long as the gear is compatible you each fly your own mode and there's no conflict.

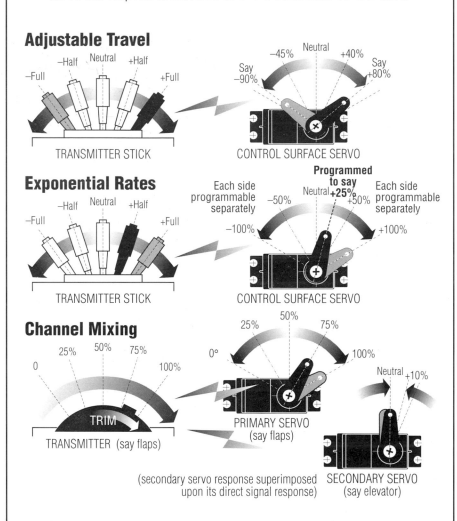

Servo response-modifying features found on high-end, multi-channel computer transmitters

Additional features high-end transmitters have for modifying the way a servo will respond to movements of the transmitter control stick.

Adjustable Travel

TRANSMITTER STICK — CONTROL SURFACE SERVO

Exponential Rates

TRANSMITTER STICK — CONTROL SURFACE SERVO

Channel Mixing

TRANSMITTER (say flaps) — PRIMARY SERVO (say flaps) — SECONDARY SERVO (say elevator)

(secondary servo response superimposed upon its direct signal response)

Practice

■ Each aircraft you build will probably require a slightly different radio setup – servo reversing, control balancing and so on. Transmitters with **model memory** allow you to switch electronically from one plane to another. It automatically selects the setup you developed for each model in the system. This is an advanced feature and is one you won't need to worry about for some time yet.

■ Some computer radios can be set up so that if there is interference on the signal to your plane, it will adopt a **fail-safe** mode. This can be programmed to shut down the engine and set the control surfaces to a predetermined attitude until the signal is restored. This is a nice feature but remember, just because the controls return to say neutral, it does not mean that the plane will necessarily adopt straight and level flight (it may have been in say, a vertical dive when contact was lost).

■ Battery Packs

Most radios are fitted with rechargeable NiCad batteries. The ability to recharge is essential and you need to develop a sound programme of battery recharging management. However, even in some transmitters fitted with NiCads, the batteries can be contained as individual cells which are clipped in and out of a battery holder instead of being 'hard-wired' as a pack, which is treated as a single unit. One of the cardinal rules for the correct management of NiCads is that all the cells in a pack are treated in exactly the same way. There is no benefit from being able to pop in a single replacement cell. The disadvantage is that there is far greater potential for a total power failure with all those loose contact points between cells. At best, a power failure means a crash.

Why?

If I don't have the model memory feature, how difficult will it be when I change from one model to another?

Because

If you are operating a simple radio, the setup will be relatively simple too. Most likely you will change a few servo reversing switches. Stick a label on the back of your transmitter to remind you of the settings for each plane and it's no big deal.

Photo 8:2 *When you have your hands full learning to coordinate four-function control of a trainer, you really can do without the terrifying array of switches and knobs you find on a high-end computer radio.*

Photo 8:3 *Even after you have progressed to a high-end radio, you can happily also use this simple 4-channel set. On a busy club day you can beat the congestion for a frequency peg by using a second transmitter flying a different plane on an alternative frequency.*

Chapter 9: Radio control in the Micro T– MkII

Practice

Why?

Because

You have learned a lot about building, trimming and flying freeflight gliders. You know what good flight looks like.

Now you have bought your radio and have a reasonable grasp of how it works.

It is time to install some of that gear into your plane and start controlling from the ground what the model does in the air.

■ Installing the gear

When you purchased your radio the box probably included all the gear you need:

- radio transmitter (Tx)
- matched radio receiver (Rx)
- flight battery pack
- battery charger
- 3–4 servos with mounting accessories
- Switch harness

Check you have everything and read the instruction booklet.

Photo 9:1 *Wherever possible all your radio gear should be padded against vibration damage. This battery pack can now be stuffed into the nose cavity where it will be both secured and protected by a good layer of foam.*

I bought my radio second hand and all I got was the transmitter, a receiver on the same frequency and a battery charger. What else do I need?

I hope you also received the instruction booklet. If not, ask for it. It's nice to be able to check out the functions and how to use them.

You will need a number of other accessories. The important thing to watch for is that their connecting plugs are compatible with your gear (there are several different systems).

Purchase a switch harness. This fits in your plane and connects the flight battery, on/off switch and radio receiver. It also incorporates a charging socket.

Each plane needs a flight battery. Get one as a hard-wired pack of 4 NiCad cells, nominally rated at 4.8V DC.

You'll need some servos. The number depends on how far you are going right now. To the Mk II stage you'll need 3. You'll need 4 for the Mk IV model. If you have a 5-channel radio and plan to make the Mk V version you'll need one more.

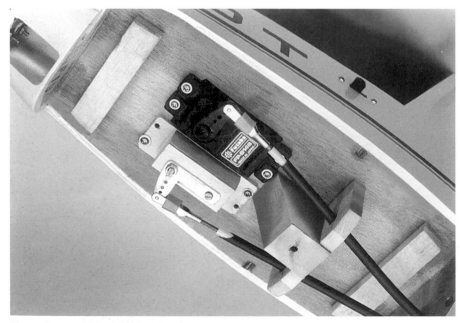

Photo 9:2 *Installing the first servo to provide rudder control in the Micro T — MkII.*

Practice

The rest of the gear is already installed in your Mk I model. It is now just a case of fitting the radio equipment in position and replacing the dummy setup servos with the real thing.

Why?

How skilled do I have to be to set up my plane so it works properly and is safe?

Because

The schematic below shows the function of each of the parts in the system. If you understand this clearly you should have little problem (but before you fly, have someone with experience check it out for you).

A schematic of the link between your radio transmitter (Tx) and your aircraft. In this case, the particular radio channel shown is channel 4, the rudder. Sideways movement of the left transmitter stick initiates a radio signal to the receiver (Rx) which activates servo 4 in the model.

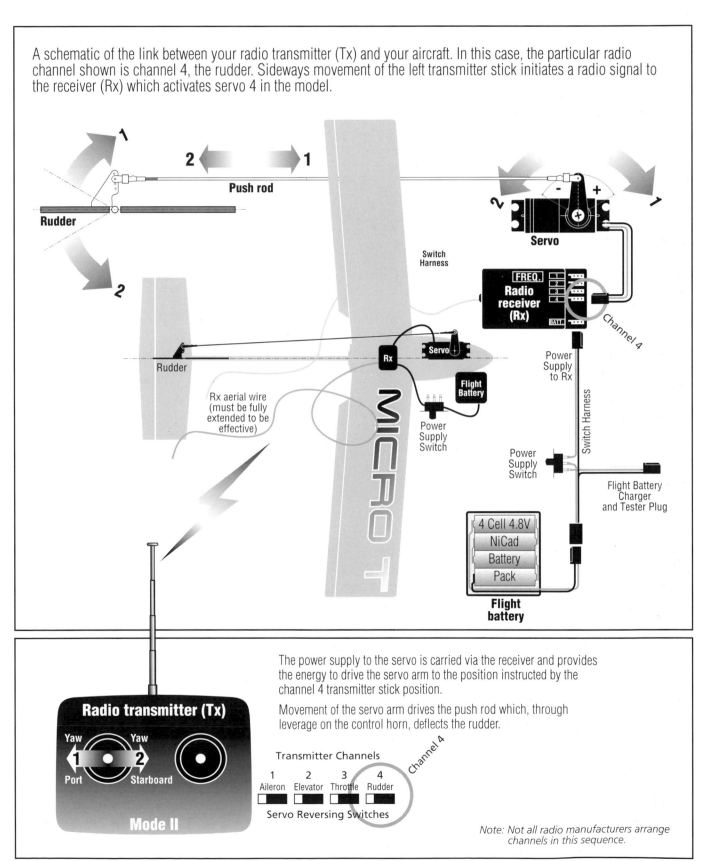

The power supply to the servo is carried via the receiver and provides the energy to drive the servo arm to the position instructed by the channel 4 transmitter stick position.

Movement of the servo arm drives the push rod which, through leverage on the control horn, deflects the rudder.

Note: Not all radio manufacturers arrange channels in this sequence.

Practice

■ In the side of the fuselage pod mark the position for the receiver switch, cut the mounting hole, and install the switch harness.

Proceed to wrap the flight battery pack in foam (see photo 9:1) to protect it against vibration. Later when you add an engine the plane will vibrate. Plug it into the servo harness, then stuff it into the cavity between the canopy and hatch, pushing it as far forward as it will go.

Now replace the rudder dummy setup servo with the real thing (photo 9:2). Take off the servo arm, connect it to the rudder clevis and meantime just rest it back on the servo shaft.

Add foam to the cavity behind the battery and cut a recess for the receiver. Pull the servo wire up past the foam. Unwrap the aerial wire and tuck the receiver into place. Thread the aerial wire inside F2 and F4, then up to the wing mounting area.

Plug both the power supply from the harness and the rudder servo lead into their receiver sockets (photo 9:3). See it is switched off.

Assuming you are nowhere near model flying activity, raise the transmitter aerial up one stage and switch on both the receiver and transmitter (also assuming they are both charged).

Move the left stick (if Mode II) from side to side and watch the servo respond. Ensure the transmitter trim is set to neutral, hold the rudder central and press the servo arm down onto the shaft. Insert the retaining screw and tighten.

Move the left stick again and watch the rudder move. Check that when you apply left rudder on the stick that the rudder panel moves to port (left when viewed from the tail). If not, flick the servo-reversing switch for that channel and test again.

92

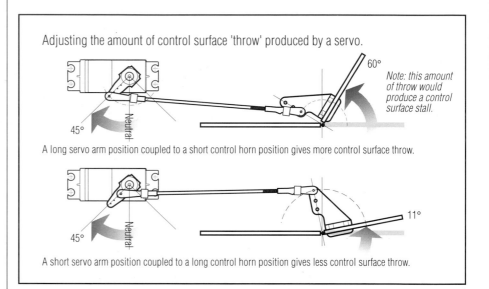

Making and adjusting the pushrod for neutral trim.

1 Connect the servo into the Rx. Turn 'ON' the Rx and the Tx. Set that channel trim to neutral.

Position the servo arm at neutral and tighten.

2 With the screw clevis halfway along the thread of the rod and the control surface held at the neutral position, measure and make the pushrod assembly to the correct length.

3 Connect the pushrod assembly from the servo arm to the control horn.

Make fine adjustments to the pushrod length by screwing in or out the threaded clevis.

Make sure the pushrod thread extends well into the clevis, but not far enough to contact the control horn.

Adjusting the amount of control surface 'throw' produced by a servo.

60°

Note: this amount of throw would produce a control surface stall.

45° Neutral

A long servo arm position coupled to a short control horn position gives more control surface throw.

45° Neutral 11°

A short servo arm position coupled to a long control horn position gives less control surface throw.

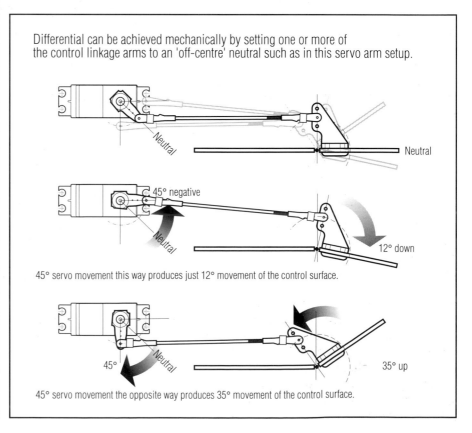

Differential can be achieved mechanically by setting one or more of the control linkage arms to an 'off-centre' neutral such as in this servo arm setup.

Neutral — Neutral

45° negative — 12° down

Neutral

45° servo movement this way produces just 12° movement of the control surface.

45° — Neutral — 35° up

45° servo movement the opposite way produces 35° movement of the control surface.

Practice

Observe how much movement you get from the rudder when you move the stick hard over. The prototype handles well with about 1" each way. Change the throw by moving the clevis further out on the rudder horn to reduce movement or further out on the servo to increase it (see the centre diagram opposite). If you need greater adjustment move the appropriate clevis inboard (try to keep both clevises as far out as you can). Fine tune the exact position of the rudder when the transmitter trim is neutral by adjusting a clevis on its tread as before. Switch off the Tx and Rx.

■ You must decide how many channels you will activate before you test fly. Some will want all three, others one at a time. This description covers all three.

■ Install the elevator servo in exactly the same way as you did for the rudder and adjust for a neutral setting.

The aileron servo requires some modification to its control horn. See photo 9:4 and turn back to sheet 2, page 70. Look at the centre of the wing elevation showing the servo and pushrod assembly. Cut two of the arms off a large 4 arm servo horn so it looks like the plan. Disconnect the clevises from the dummy aileron setup servo and remove the servo tray. Replace the dummy with a servo. Plug in this servo to the Rx, and with the Tx aileron trim set to neutral, activate it and the Rx. The servo will flick to neutral. Press the arm onto the shaft so the arms are exactly even both sides and tighten. Turn off and reinstall the servo tray, fitting back the clevises as you do it.

Feed the aerial through the snake tube in the wing (photo 9:6), plug in the servo and fit the wing. Now fire up the Tx and Rx again and check out the aileron movement, adjusting as before. Even out any small difference between them by adjusting clevises at the ailerons.

Why?

I notice you say to raise the transmitter aerial one stage before switching on. Is this just so the signal will be stronger?

Because

No, that's not the real reason. You should not operate the transmitter without an aerial or you can damage the circuitry. Get into the habit of always having 5" or 6" of aerial showing before you switch on.

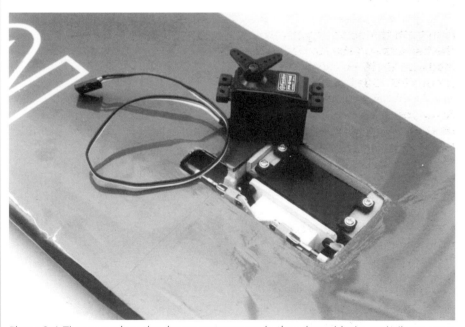

Photo 9:3 *Pack the radio receiver so you can access the plug panel. Later on the aileron servo will plug in when you assemble for the day and unplug again when you pack up.*

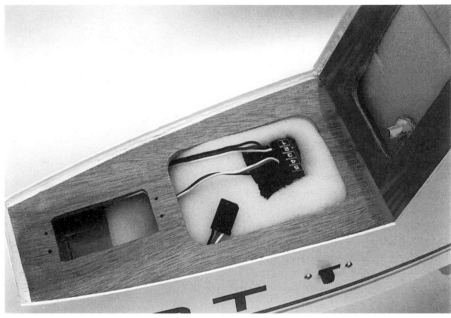

Photo 9:4 *Time to replace the dummy setup servo in the wing with the real aileron servo (notice the twin-arm servo horn used to produce aileron differential).*

Why keep control rod clevises as far out as possible on control horns?

Any slop in the pushrod assembly is a smaller component of the total movement when the rod moves a long way instead of a short way. So, always aim for long movements in the pushrod assemblies.

Practice

■ Your plane is about ready for flight tests so it's time to get yourself ready. And please, preparing yourself is just as necessary as preparing your plane.

Presuming you have never controlled a model before, put some time aside to think it through before you go to the field . . . well before.

Go back to your little chuckie and with your radio transmitter in your lap, move the model through some manoeuvres while you work the sticks. Input some roll to port and bank the model. Have the model turn through a 180° then move the stick to the opposite side and level it out. Input some rudder control . . . now think . . . the model is coming towards you . . . which way will the model respond? Now pitch up the nose and lower it again. Practise.

To help you sort things out start with the rudder and follow through the sequence shown in the top diagram, page 95. In your mind, fly the model round the circuit and work the rudder stick to increase or reduce the turn. Notice there is a point in the circuit where suddenly you must switch your mind from being behind the plane to being in front of it. Then as it begins to pass across in front of you suddenly you are behind it again. These are the points where control reversal comes into and out of play. Soon you will learn to recognise these points quite unconsciously.

Notice also that the diagrams always show the model out in front of you. Remember, you don't fly round yourself. There should be a line, real or imaginary, which you are standing behind and you never let the model cross that line.

Practising this way is a whole lot less heartbreaking (and less model breaking) than learning in real life.

Why?

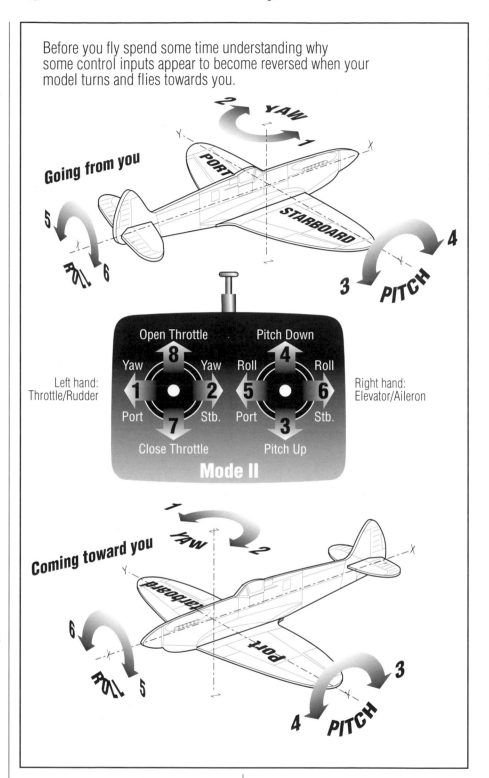

Before you fly spend some time understanding why some control inputs appear to become reversed when your model turns and flies towards you.

Surely to begin with it would be easier to fly round yourself so you can always follow the action? I don't see the problem.

Because

Remember you are not the only person needing to be considered. In fact, when you are flying your first duty is to consider everyone else ahead of yourself. There must be a recognised area where people can stand, park their cars, and prepare their models without the risk of being hit by a model. Hence the 'no fly zones'. There should always be a recognised flying circuit, landing area and so on.

94

Concentrate on learning to cope with rudder reversal first.
Learn this on the ground. It's a whole lot cheaper than trying to learn it in the air.

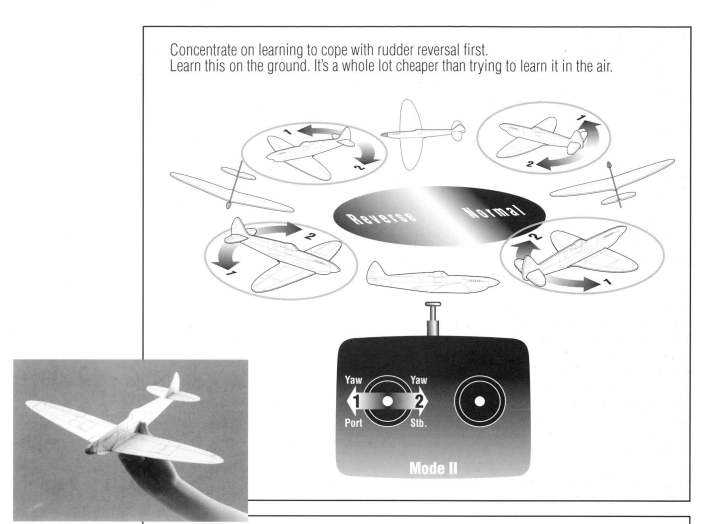

Photo 9:5 *Pick up your little chuckie and take it through the motions of flying a circuit. See how confusing it can get when it comes towards you and the input controls appear to be reversed, compared with when it is going away from you.*

Aileron reversal is similar to rudder reversal. Again, learn about it on the ground by thinking it through and becoming familiar with it before you fly.

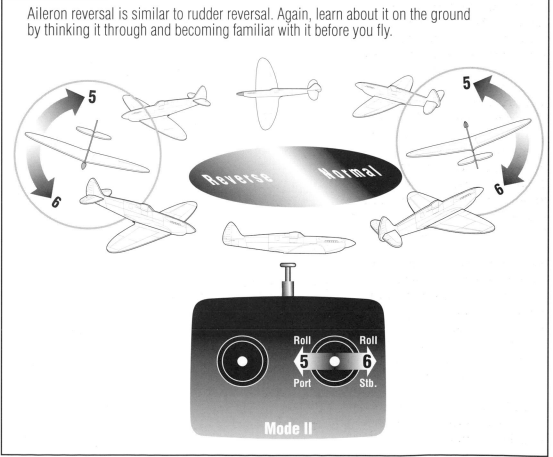

Practice

■ When you feel ready or at least know there's not much more you can do to prepare yourself, it's time to go flying. At home test-assemble the model just as if you were at the field:

● Place the wing close to the pod and feed plenty of aerial wire down the hole in the inner pushrod that you are using as a draw rod for placing the aerial (photo 9:6).

● With the canopy removed, feed the aileron plug and wire down behind the former F4 towards the receiver.

● Put the wing in place and plug in the aileron servo to the Rx.

● Replace the canopy and place a few rubber bands over the top end of the canopy, back around the dowels, forward and over the wing and back to hook onto the overhang of one side of the pod. With each band alternate which side you hook to (photos on the first pages of chapters 11 and 13).

● Turn the model upside down and gently feed in the aerial wire as you slowly withdraw the pull rod. All the wire should enter the snake with about 1/4" of wire showing when the rod is removed. Never try to fly unless the aerial is properly in place.

● Right the model and apply a few more bands to retain the wing. Check it has a good grip, the wing is in the right place and you can't lift the wing.

Try to arrange with a buddy who flies to meet at the flying site. Better still see if he can also come and check over your plane sometime beforehand or you risk discovering a problem which can't be fixed at the field. The night before put both your transmitter and receiver on to charge and leave them charging overnight.

Why?

I'm on my own and feel quite apprehensive about heading off to make my test flight. Am I just 'chicken'?

Why all the fuss of feeding the aerial out through the wing. Can't we just feed it down the fuselage boom where it can stay as long as the model lasts?

Well why not roll it up inside the fuselage pod?

Because

No way. You've put a lot of work and effort into building your Micro T and now we expect you to go and put it all at risk with a new pilot and no instructor! Nevertheless, the time has come. We will try to make it a very gradual and painless exercise.

Photo 9:6 *The inner pushrod of a control snake makes an ideal draw rod for pulling the aerial out through the wing. As a warning that you have overlooked installing the aerial, fit a piece of vivid marker tape over the outside end of the draw rod. Once you've got an engine, if you ever forget to pull the aerial through into the wing, the propeller could turn it into a lot of short wires!*

Afraid not. Firstly, we have the problem of the boom being made of metal. If we put the aerial lead down there, or even strap it on the outside of it, we would be shielding the wire from receiving its signal. Secondly, we are going to add an engine with a pusher propeller. This is in an ideal place to chop up the aerial wire if we don't have it safely tucked away. The wing has been chosen as the best compromise position even though it has to be inserted into its tube each time you assemble the plane.

The length of your aerial is designed to fit the radio signal. It should always be installed so it is extended to its maximum possible length. Good question though.

While I remember, when you switch on your transmitter, always have at least one segment of the aerial extended, or you may cause damage to the set.

Practice   *Why?*   Because

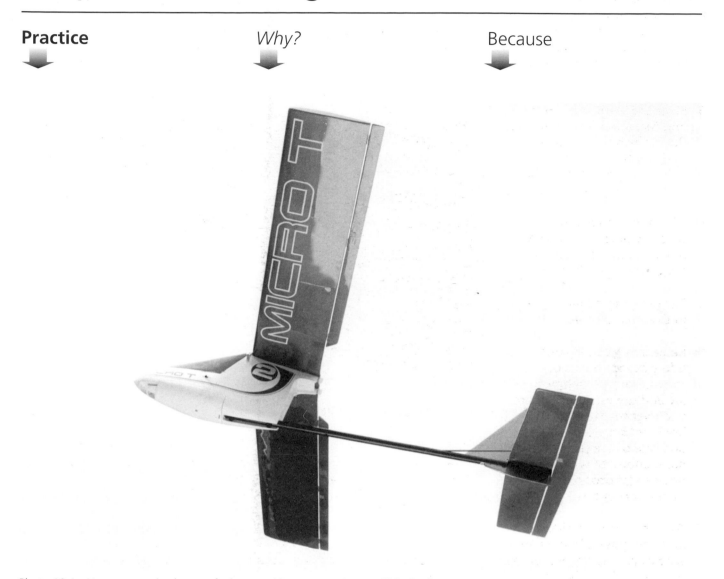

Photo 10:1   *Now you are in charge of where and how your Micro T will fly (well up to a point!).*

■ Over the past few weeks you have been checking out the various flying sites which might be available and suitable for your RC glider. You have settled for a field that's not too steep and rounds out with a broad, flat base before the hedges. It faces the prevailing wind and today's forecast is for light winds.

■ You have arrived at the field. If it is a controlled site or anyone else is flying within radio range, find out what transmitter rules apply. Until then, leave your transmitter in the car, switched off. Assemble your model and check it over thoroughly as you go. When everything looks right seek clearance to use your radio.

The club I have joined isn't into gliders. Should I go off on my own?

There are a few people flying here but there doesn't seem to be any control over transmitter frequencies. What should I do?

It's always more fun if you are with someone else. Talk at your club and see if there isn't someone who will come and give you a hand. It is not like aeromodellers to be disinterested in almost anything that flies, especially if it's an area they don't usually become involved with. Try again but if you don't succeed find somewhere quiet and go on your own. At least you will be able to choose your own pace.

Make yourself known to them and check on the local rules about flying. Explain what gear you have and see if there is a frequency clash. If it is as informal as you describe, you will probably find they each know what frequencies the others fly on.

■ Frequency Clearance

Obey the local rules which prevent radio accidents (eg: check that the frequency peg for your transmitter is free, take it, claim your radio and put the peg on your set). Switch on both the aircraft and transmitter. With the aerial up one extension only, test the controls . . . left rudder moves port . . . elevator up when you pull back . . . aileron rises to meet the stick (when you're astride the model facing forwards) . . . all movements are full and free.

■ Range check

With the aerial still only at the first stage extension walk away about sixty paces and see that all surfaces respond correctly (a buddy can hand signal their movements).

■ Pre-flight brief

Up until now you have used the control surfaces to adjust trim – to correct a tendency to drop one wing, to straighten the flight path or to adjust the pitch attitude. All of these involved setting a control surface into a new, but fixed position.

Now you are being introduced to the second use of control surfaces – to manoeuvre the plane.

Making the plane say turn, involves interfering with its trimmed flight attitude. Now the control surfaces are moved to a new position until the desired response is achieved. In many cases, especially in banking manoeuvres, the controls are immediately returned to their neutral trimmed position. In other words, for many aircraft, once a turning attitude has been established, the trimmed plane will go on turning. If you continue to input turning controls the plane will turn tighter and tighter until it enters a spiral dive (all the way to the ground).

Photo 10:2 *If you are flying anywhere within about 4 miles of other modellers you must respect radio frequency conventions. A model club usually uses a frequency peg board to ensure only one transmitter at a time can be operated on any particular dedicated frequency. This is a typical board at a local RC club.*

What actually happens if I turn on my transmitter when some one else is using the same frequency?

The most obvious effect will be a certain irritation from that person who was happily flying his ¼ scale 40cc competition-winning scale SE-5 which is now buried amongst some granite boulders over there. You see, your radio blankets and confuses the signal from the other user's transmitter as soon as both are switched on. The aircraft immediately goes into spectacular contortions. Sometimes the other user's model will be on the ground, but it could just as easily be in the air heading towards some people. Either way it is a very serious offence.

Would you please run over than turning procedure once again.

When you want to turn a motorcar you turn the wheel towards one side and hold it there until you want the car to stop turning. With an aircraft when you want to turn, you put the stick over, and as soon as the plane is banking enough you return the stick more-or-less to neutral while the plane continues to turn (perhaps with small additional inputs depending upon the aircraft). When the plane has turned enough you put the stick over the other way to return it to straight and level.

The usual remedy for overdoing control is to let go of the stick, see what attitude the plane adopts and then input a correction. This shows that even though you have control, it is important that your model is trimmed out to fly straight and level (or in this case, on it's set glide path), hands off.

■ Trimming out

Very quickly you will know if your model is out of trim because you will have to hold a stick off centre or forward-or-back to get it to fly true.

Start out with short glides and see what corrections you have to hold. Move the appropriate trim tabs in the same directions as you held the sticks, and try again. When you don't have to alter a trim, that channel is 'trimmed'. With a model which is nicely trimmed you now have a chance to learn how to properly fly it. If it takes your buddy to trim it, don't worry – it can be tricky.

■ Flight manoeuvres

The first 'manoeuvre' is a turn. From straight and controlled glide, just ease in a little rudder and ease off again. The prototype drops the wing slightly and the nose gently dips. Correct with slight up elevator, but not too much (if the nose pitches up let go the stick). You must maintain a good flying speed and remember, in a turn it is more likely to stall than in straight and level flight.

Add a dab of rudder if that wing has returned to level before the model is coming back to you. And again, feed in just a touch of up. Now the plane is heading back towards you and will soon run out of airspace if you don't turn it away from the slope, so initiate the turn again by adding a little rudder and a touch of up elevator. The ground is coming up fast so watch it, watch it, keep it coming. Now a little up. Kiss the ground. Doesn't it sound easy?

What do I do if the model suddenly starts the dreaded spin?

Photo 10:3 *When trimming out, see if you need to hold a transmitter stick out of line to get the model to fly straight. If you do, before the next glide, move the transmitter trim over in the same direction as you were holding the stick and now see if it flies straight. When it does, you can consider the model to be trimmed correctly on that channel. Do the same for each channel.*

Firstly, it's extremely unlikely that you will accidentally spin this model. Having said that, there are a few classic situations where the novice can set himself up for just such sudden uncontrolled manoeuvres. They all really involve a stall (which can develop into a spin).

The most common is on takeoff (or just after hand launching). Too much up elevator is fed in with too little flying speed – one wing drops and there's a violent turn toward the dropped wing. Full aileron against this sort of turn usually increases the problem and it should be corrected with rudder only. If this happens close to the ground the solution becomes academic because it's all over in what seems a split second.

The same effect occurs when a turn is too tight, flying speed is too slow and the model is asked to climb, all at the same time. Instead of curving into the turn, the model suddenly drops the outer wing and the opposite turn results, usually violently. Recovery can only come from increasing flying speed, usually meaning a dive. Again, lack of sufficient altitude to complete the full recovery is unfortunate (engine cut on takeoff provides two of the same three components. Try to turn back and you add the critical third component and that's usually it! Always pitch the nose down and hold straight until you have a safe flying speed).

Photo 10:4 *Later, when you are satisfied that you have the model correctly trimmed, set the clevises (see page 92). Take one function at a time, note the exact position of the control surface, move the trim to neutral and adjust the clevis to duplicate the offset.*

Practice	*Why?*	Because

■ Debrief

Too often the experience of that important first RC flight is lost by putting it behind you and moving on too quickly. Think about it. Go over each phase with your buddy and have him describe to you what he thinks happened. Compare his view with yours. This way you learn.

Now, if everything went well, wasn't it great? But, if it all got screwed up don't be too disheartened. Just try to establish what went wrong and how it can be avoided next time.

■ Vicarious flying

This might sound a bit far-fetched but you can learn by visualising your model going through its paces while you mentally work the controls.

Think each manoeuvre through. Imagine the nose dropping in a turn and what you do to correct it . . . imagine you have over corrected and the nose pitches up into a stall . . . snap the imaginary stick forward and save it . . . imagine the hedge looming up and how you just avoid it by pulling a tight turn and landing.

Even at risk of the rest of the family believing you have really lost it this time, sit down with the transmitter in your hands and imagine the model flying through a routine as you work the sticks. The technique works and as we've said, it's cheaper to crash a dream than the real thing.

When you are learning to fly, fear of causing a crash can actually cause just that! Freezing on the sticks, not knowing what to do next, and forgetting which control produces the actions you want, are all common problems for the beginner. The sooner you can become familiar with your equipment and develop reflex reactions the sooner you will relax.. Then it becomes great fun!

Photo 10:5 *When you are ready to launch your model off the hillside, first, think about the path you want the plane to fly. Note the obvious hazards like those two trees. Where are the best landing sites? Remember, if you are to avoid hitting a rising slope, you must make your turns away from the hillside. And, stop the model from drifting too far away so keep turning it back toward you then roll it away. To help you judge your landing height, pick a sunny day so you can watch the shadow come up to meet your plane.*

That deals with the more common problems but, if a spin does develop is there a technique I can use to recover from it?

Photo 10:6 *You will attract comments from the family when you sit in your favourite armchair with your eyes shut, clasping a transmitter while you do some vicarious flying! But it's great preparation.*

Yes there is. We've seen how the Micro T is designed to minimise the possibility of a spin. However, if one does develop this model will automatically recover quickly, hands-off. If you 'freeze' and hold up elevator it may well become 'locked in' and spin all the way to the ground.

You can generally presume that when an aircraft is spinning, the wing panels and the horizontal tailplane are stalled so their control surfaces are ineffective. Provided the design makes sure the rudder is not blanketed by the tailplane, rotation is stopped by giving opposite rudder. Some down elevator assists the aircraft to develop a dive, air begins to flow over the wings and tailplane as speed increases, so you can start to apply up elevator to get back to level flight.

All this is something you can practise when you feel ready. Just remember that altitude is you greatest friend so start out from a good height.

Chapter 11: Adding the engine for a MkIII

Practice

■ The engines we will be using for the models in this book range from a smallish 0.25 cubic inch (4cc) to a sizeable 2 cu in (33cc). Most models are basic 2-stroke, relatively inexpensive types and popular brands.

For the Micro T prototype model we use an OS 0.25 FS engine. It's ideal as a first motor being small, uncomplicated and conventional in its features. Its power is at the lower limit recommended for the model. If you pay a little more for say a OS 'FX' version you will have a more lively plane. On the down side, if you want to use the same engine when you build the 'Spirit of St Louis', you'll need to slightly alter the drawings for the dummy engine because the Surpass is longer in the shaft.

Whatever you choose, when the engine is angled far enough to give clear access to the glow plug, check that the regular muffler stands off far enough to clear the bodywork (Photo 11:1). Alternatively, replace the standard muffler with a 'Pitts' style one. You could mount the engine nearer to horizontal for better access (but check that the carb needle adjustment is free of the wing mounts).

■ Mount the engine on a standard 0.25 size reinforced nylon engine mount, and drill it accurately to take the engine mounting bolts. Fit the engine and trim the bolts to the right length, allowing for spring washers and double nuts. Add a 9" diameter x 6" pitch pusher propeller to the engine. With the wing in place, hold this engine assembly against the back of the pod and find its best position so the muffler clears the bodywork, the prop clears the boom and there's access to the

Photo 11:1 *Here's what we will be doing as we add the engine to our Micro T. The challenge of this layout is to mount the engine high enough to swing a 9" prop, have the muffler clear of the pod and still be able to access the glow plug and needle valve.*

Photo 11:2 *The range of engines we'll be using begins at 4cc for the Micro T up to 33cc for the Spitfire.*

Model	Engine size	
	cubic inches	cubic cm
. . . .	0.10	1.5
. . . .	0.15	2.5
Micro T and 'NYP' . . .	0.25	4
56" span Schneider . .	0.45	7.5
60" span Sea Fury . . .	0.60	10
1/4 scale D.H.71.	0.70	11.5
. . . .	0.90	15
. . . .	1.20	20
. . . .	1.80	30
1/5 scale Spitfire	2.00	33
. . . .	3.00	50
. . . .	4.00	65

Photo 11:3 *The two common types of reciprocating model engines: the 2-stroke (left) and 4-stroke (right – we'll deal with 4-stroke engines later in chapter 18).*

Photo 11:4 *Amongst the 2-strokes there are a multitude of different configurations, each for a special purpose. Meantime, stay with the basic sports type.*

Note: When this model was prepared, the tendency toward mounting the needle valve behind the cylinder was not common practice. Now you could provide an alternative mount and place the needle valve for convenience, on the starboard side.

If your choice of engine retains the forward position, make the fuel tubing extension to the needle valve as shown in photo 11:7. Check that it grips properly and allows you to revolve the needle from fully closed to right out (to let you clean it).

Notice there are three tubes coming from the fuel tank. There's your filler,

Photo 11:5   *Our choice of engine is nothing spectacular but just a good and reliable, totally conventional OS 0.25 FS.*

glow plug, and the carb needle adjustment clears the wing mounts. Centre it on the centreline of the pod and mark its location (the plan shows the accurate position and angle). Take the engine off the mount and replace the mount against the pod. Mark the mounting holes. Drill then refit the engine assembly and bolt it to the pod.

■ Now set up the throttle linkage. Feed a control snake outer through formers F4 and F8 and epoxy in place. When cured mount the throttle servo on its tray with the shaft aft, and its plug in channel 3 of the Rx then switch on both the Rx and Tx.

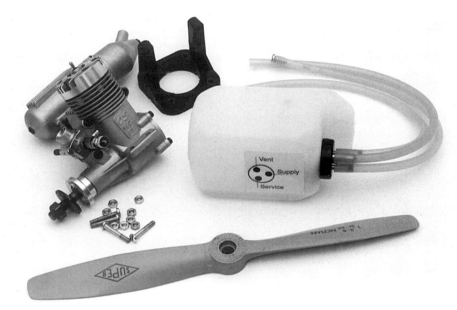

Photo 11:6 *Engine accessories you'll need: the engine mount and mounting screws with washers and two sets of nuts; the fuel tank and fittings; plus a pusher propeller. To operate the throttle you also need an additional servo with push rod and clevises.*

Photo 11:7   *The engine module ready to bolt to the firewall. Note the fuel tubing extension to the needle valve. Lock nuts make sure the main mounting bolts don't come loose. Another precaution worth taking is to fit a spinner which will retain the propeller nut and washer if the engine backfires and throws the prop – quite likely to happen, especially with a new motor.*

the supply to the engine, and the pressure tube which will couple to the engine muffler. When the engine is running there is positive pressure inside the muffler. We take a line from this high pressure zone and feed it into the fuel tank. This pressurises the tank and improves the delivery of fuel to the carburettor.

The broad principles of the 2-stroke engine are relatively simple to explain and understand.
Take the time to get to know how your engine works so you'll have a better idea of what's wrong when it doesn't!

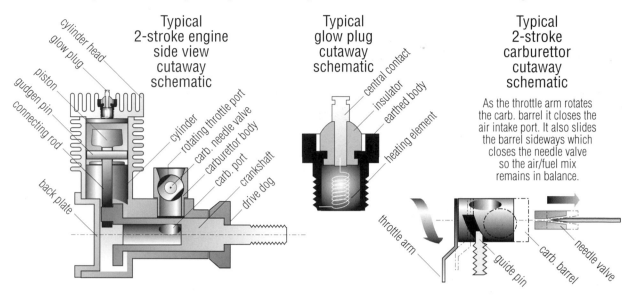

Typical 2-stroke engine side view cutaway schematic

cylinder head
glow plug
piston
gudgen pin
connecting rod
back plate

cylinder
rotating throttle port
carb. needle valve
carburettor body
carb. port
crankshaft
drive dog

Typical glow plug cutaway schematic

central contact
insulator
earthed body
heating element

Typical 2-stroke carburettor cutaway schematic

As the throttle arm rotates the carb. barrel it closes the air intake port. It also slides the barrel sideways which closes the needle valve so the air/fuel mix remains in balance.

throttle arm
guide pin
carb. barrel
needle valve

1 As the piston rises it rotates the shaft which opens the port to the carburettor.

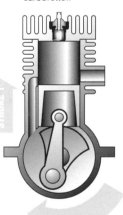

2 The rising piston sucks fuel/air into the crankcase through the hollow crankshaft passage.

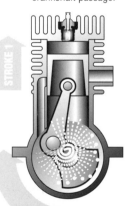

3 The crankshaft port closes and the piston comes down compressing the crankcase gasses.

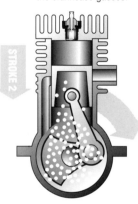

4 Eventually the piston exposes the bypass port letting the gasses rush up into the cylinder.

5 As fuel/air rushes into the upper cylinder it blows existing gasses out the exhaust port.

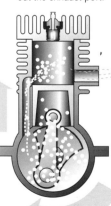

6 The rising piston now compresses the fuel/air in the cylinder and the glow plug starts an explosion.

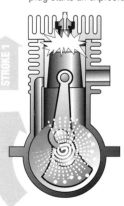

7 The exploding gas drives the piston down and it again compresses the crankcase gasses . . .

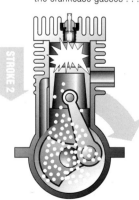

8 . . .the piston lets the gasses rush into the cylinder and . . . your engine is running!

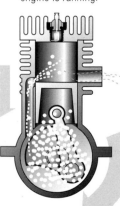

The 2-stroke engine: one combustion event for every two strokes (one up, one down)

Practice

Set the Tx throttle stick and its trim to shut (both fully down) and fit the control arm to the servo at about 45° back and out to the port side. Move the throttle stick up and down to check the servo is working in the right direction (forward to open, back to close). Zero the throttle again and switch off the Rx first then the Tx. Move the engine's throttle arm right back to shut, then make up and fit the control rod with its clevises to connect the throttle arm of the motor to the servo arm, checking that its adjustable length is about centred.

Fit the control rod and adjust its length so that the carb moves from just closed to just fully open when the throttle trim is right down. Listen to hear if the servo hums. If it does, lengthen the control rod a turn and try again. Now move the throttle trim and stick right up. See if the carb is fully open and check that the servo does not hum. If all's well, you're finished. If not, you must adjust the linkage, possibly by moving one of the clevises further in or out on its arm until it's right.

■ Lastly, we fit the fuel tank. Its position can be quite critical. The centreline of the tank should be no higher than the needle valve nor more than ½" below it.

Our model fuel tanks are designed for 'tractor' aircraft (engine in front, tank behind). As this is a 'pusher' aircraft, the tank is in front of the engine. To maintain the proper supply during acceleration or climbing, the pick-up needs to be at the back of the tank. This means we still mount the tank as if the engine was ahead of it, but must carry the fuel and pressure lines round the side of it, back to the engine and muffler.

Now, watching that you don't kink any of the tubing, wrap the tank in soft foam and tuck it down into the pod. It's done!

Why?

Why all the foam padding round the fuel tank. I can't believe vibration is going to damage the fuel!

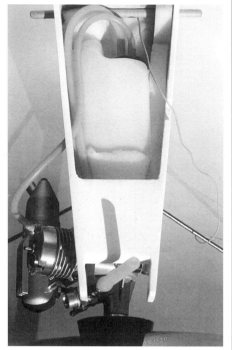

Photo 11:8   *Looking down from behind the pod, you see the general arrangement of engine, needle valve extension and fuel tank system.*

Because

Well, in effect, that's just what it can do. When your fuel is all whipped up like a milk shake it gets full of air. And, air is just what your engine doesn't want in the fuel line. It's called 'foaming' and is quite a common cause of inconsistent engine performance.

Another cause of air in the fuel can be a pinhole in the supply line which can be quite hard to track down. Treat the tubes with respect to reduce the risk.

Even an air leak in the needle valve thread can do it.

Photo 11:9   *The throttle servo is mounted near the nose to help keep the C-of-G as far forward as possible. This necessitates a fairly long linkage which is fine, provided the rod can be kept virtually straight along its length. Here it is also guided inside a snake.*

Photo 11:10   *With the pod lying on its side, the throttle linkage at the engine end is clearly visible (note the small bend in the pushrod to clear the engine mounting bolts – the only bend in the rod overall).*

104

Chapter 12: Managing the engine

Get yourself properly organised before you attempt to run your new engine. It should be correctly installed in the plane with all linkages connected, the radio charged and functioning. Check that the propeller nut is really tight. For safety, it is preferable to have the washer, nut and propeller hub enclosed within a bolt-on spinner.

■ The fuel should be thoroughly mixed and made-up to the manufacturer's specification. At this stage a castor oil mix has some real advantages over synthetic oil mixtures. It should be absolutely clean, and stored in an airtight metal container. Filter it before it goes into your plane.

■ You should have read, thoroughly understood and have followed all the instructions supplied with the engine. In particular you should have taken notice of the safety instructions and realise these engines are not toys – they can bite . . . and badly.

■ Don't just think of what you'll need to get the engine started. Be ready to clean up the castor-laden exhaust mess when you've finished. Here's a good, and cheap cleaner you can mix up in an old spray bottle:

Methylated spirits	¼ cup
Household ammonia	1 tsp
Dish detergent	1 tsp
Water .... top up to	500ml

Shake to mix.

■ To start the engine, firstly you must heat the spiral element in the glow plug to a bright golden orange. You can do this with either a continuous current of 1.2 volt DC or with a 'pulsed' supply at a higher voltage. We'll assume

Photo 12:1 *About the minimum field kit you can start out with. For the safety of your fingers, add a 'chicken stick'.*

Why should I only use a metal storage container for my fuel?

Methanol, the base ingredient of a glow plug motor's fuel, is hydroscopic – that is, it can absorb moisture from the atmosphere. Plastic storage containers can allow

Photo 12:2 *Glow driver with it's own built-in rechargeable battery is simple.*

Photo 12:3 *A chicken stick saves your fingers from bad bruising or much worse.*

Photo 12:4 *Glow driver panel needs a 12V DC power source and delivers an adjustable 'pulsed' 12V power to the plug.*

Photo 12:5 *Electric starters can run from the same power supply you use for the glow driver panel.*

you are going to begin by using a single cell rechargeable glow driver which clips directly onto the top of the plug and supplies about 1.2V continuous supply.

Remove the plug and test the element by clipping it into the driver. If it glows brightly, replace it in the engine (use a cloth or you'll burn yourself). This test shows that both the driver is adequately charged and the element is in good condition.

Alternatively it can be heated by a pulsed 12 volt DC powerboard (photo 12:4). Never directly connect your glow plug to a battery of more than a single cell (1.2 volts) or it will burn out.

Generally speaking, to avoid overheating your glow plug, the battery power supply to it should be connected only while starting the engine and during initial warm-up (15–20 seconds). When the engine is running, heat of combustion from one revolution maintains the element temperature sufficiently to ignite the next combustion and so on.

■ First run – to set the mixture, close the needle valve. Test that it is properly closed by fitting a piece of fuel tubing to the fuel inlet nipple and blow. No air should escape. Now, open the needle jet to the manufacturer's recommendation (usually between 2 and 3 turns).

Connect the transparent fuel tube between the tank and carburettor, fuel up, turn on the Tx and Rx, open the throttle fully and choke the engine by flipping the prop while blocking the carburettor air intake with your finger. Watch to see when fuel fills the tube, then flip it two of three more turns. Remove your finger and flip the prop a few more times to distribute the mixture through the system. This ensures you have not drawn so much fuel into the cylinder that

moisture through the walls even when they appear to be sealed airtight. Not so with metal.

Photo 12:6 *Later on you might want to make up a full field outfit with glow driver, electric starter, fuel pump, battery Volt meter and on-field battery charger.*

Will it cause any damage if I leave the power on the glow plug?

Leaving the power on too long will lessen plug life and can burn it out. Power supply from better pulsed powerboards self-regulate to the plug temperature and generally may be left on longer with less risk of burn out.

Why wouldn't the needle valve close properly in the first place?

Manufacturer's swarf or dirt can sometimes stop the needle from seating properly. Don't force it. Take out the needle and clean the thread, and see that it's seating correctly without any air escaping.

Photo 12:7 *By the time we complete chapter 22 we'll be looking for some fairly heavy field equipment to backup a plane the size of Warwick Blackman's 1/5 scale P-51.*

106

Practice

you have 'hydrauliced' the piston against the cylinder head.

Close the throttle to about ¼ open and connect the battery to the glow plug. To test that the plug is heating and that the engine is ready to start, take a good grip of one blade of the propeller and pull the prop round over the compression stroke. Feel for a distinct kick as it goes over top-dead-centre. If you don't feel this kick turn off the power and choke another couple of turns. Repeat the test. If you still don't feel the kick, remove the glow plug and see if the element lights up when you connect it to the battery. If it doesn't, test your battery against another glow plug to see if you need to replace the original plug or recharge your glow driver battery.

Secure your model, either with a buddy holding it or with it tethered to the ground. With the throttle still at ¼ open, power the glow plug and, using a 'chicken stick' or electric starter, flip the motor (anticlockwise). It should start immediately.

If the engine bursts into life, revs up then dies suddenly, the mixture is set too lean. Open the needle valve about ¼ turn and try again, repeating it until it runs continuously. Alternatively, if it just putters, blows smoke and gradually dies, the mixture is too, rich. Close the needle slightly.

Once the engine is able to run continuously, open to full throttle and adjust the needle until you hear distinct tone changes between 2- and 4-stroking (abrupt changes in pitch). Close the needle two clicks and it should 2-stroke continuously, but with enough fuel in the system to ensure that your new engine is getting enough lubrication.

Run a few tankfuls at this rich setting before closing the needle, click at a time, to achieve full performance.

Why?

'Hydrauliced" ? Please explain.

Because

Liquid fuel will not compress. If, under these conditions, the motor is forced to turn, something will break. Any liquid fuel in the cylinder will increase the compression. This can cause 'pre-ignition'. The mixture explodes before the piston reaches top-dead-centre, the engine backfires, and throws off the propeller.

Some extra safety precautions

✔ Mount your propeller with a spinner which screws against a backplate and encloses the retaining nut. Tighten.

✔ Keep yourself, and anyone watching, out of the line of the propeller arc. Remember, the end of that propeller can be going almost as fast as a bullet.

✔ Use a chicken stick or electric starter. Your finger is an inappropriate tool.

✗ Don't just hold your plane with one hand and start it with the other. Have a buddy help you or use a tether.

✗ Don't operate an engine that you can't bring to a stop by shutting the throttle and lowering its idle trim control.

✗ Don't operate an engine where there is inadequate spectator control or you are being uncomfortably crowded.

Starting procedure checklist

✔ Check engine mounts are secure, linkages correctly adjusted, propeller tight and free from damage of any sort.

✔ Tx with its frequency peg, collected from the transmitter pound.

✔ Rx and Tx switched on.

✔ Rx and Tx batteries fully charged. All aircraft functions working and all throws are correctly set for this model.

✔ Fuel tank filled with fuel of the correct specification, filtered to remove any solids and stored free of moisture.

✔ Glow driver charged and producing adequate heat to the plug.

✔ The model secure, with either a buddy helping or the plane tethered.

✔ The engine choked to remove air from the fuel tube and a small charge in the engine.

✔ A few flicks to distribute the fuel/air mixture through the engine.

✔ Check spectators are at a safe distance and out of the propeller arc.

✔ Set throttle to about 1/4 open.

✔ Connect power to the glow plug.

✔ Proceed to flick start.

Basic troubleshooting

The engine just will not fire –
  ☞ Choke to ensure it is receiving fuel.
  ☞ Remove the glow plug and check it is heating properly. If not, test your power supply on another plug. If OK replace the plug with another of the correct specification.

The engine is not receiving fuel –
  ☞ Check that the tank is full.
  ☞ Check the fuel tube for air leaks.
  ☞ Remove the needle. Blow air into the tank through the pressure tube until fuel squirts out the needle hole and reset the needle.
  ☞ Check that the fuel 'clunk' is sitting properly.

The engine dies as soon as the throttle is opened –
  ☞ It is probably set too lean. Open the needle valve a few clicks.
  ☞ Check there are no bubbles moving along the fuel tube. Look for leaks.

The engine won't come up to full revs –
  ☞ It is probably running too rich. Close the needle a few clicks.

The engine dies on takeoff –
  ☞ As a preflight precaution, open the throttle and hold the model straight up and also straight down to see if it cuts out. If so, it is probably too lean. Open the needle valve a click or two and try again.

Chapter 13: Now the Micro T– MkIV gets wheels

Practice

Photo 13:1 *With wheels attached and a steerable nose wheel you can begin taxiing practice, especially bringing the plane towards you and keeping it running straight.*

■ Take the front undercarriage leg assembly and its steering linkage which you test fitted in Chapter 7, and now permanently install it in the nose of your model (photo 13:2).

Pay particular attention to aligning the steering control arm to the wheel position and tightening the arm screw against the leg. I file a flat on the shaft to help keep it rigidly in position.

Couple the linkage to the rudder servo arm as shown, then fire up the radio and adjust it until the wheel and rudder are exactly aligned to neutral centre.

Photo 13:2 *The steering linkage setup is important – notice the wheel steering pushrod is set as far inboard as possible on the servo arm, and as far out as possible on the wheel assembly arm (the rudder linkage is set out as far as possible on the same servo arm).*

A. Rivers

108

Tips to help you set up a friendly tricycle undercarriage.

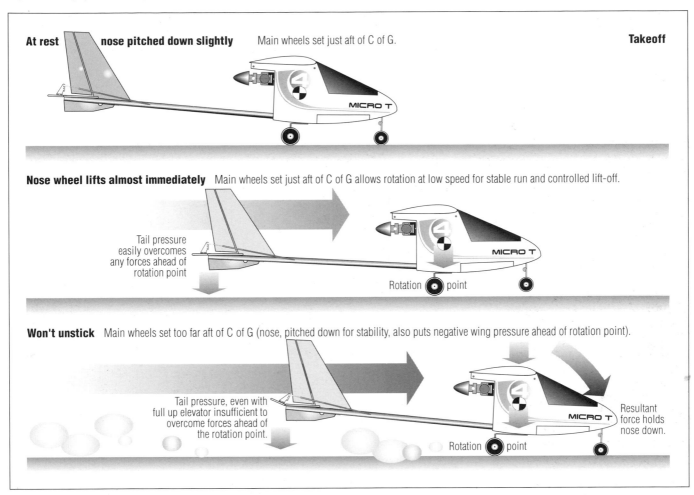

At rest   **nose pitched down slightly**   Main wheels set just aft of C of G.   **Takeoff**

Nose wheel lifts almost immediately   Main wheels set just aft of C of G allows rotation at low speed for stable run and controlled lift-off.

Tail pressure easily overcomes any forces ahead of rotation point

Rotation point

Won't unstick   Main wheels set too far aft of C of G (nose, pitched down for stability, also puts negative wing pressure ahead of rotation point).

Tail pressure, even with full up elevator insufficient to overcome forces ahead of the rotation point.

Rotation point

Resultant force holds nose down.

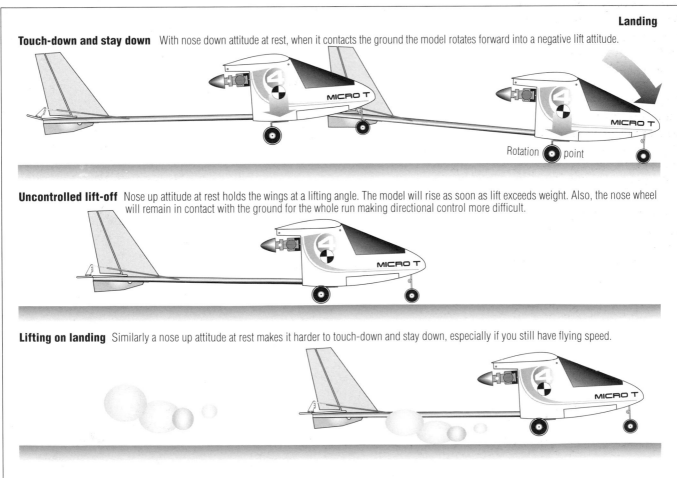

Landing

Touch-down and stay down   With nose down attitude at rest, when it contacts the ground the model rotates forward into a negative lift attitude.

Rotation point

Uncontrolled lift-off   Nose up attitude at rest holds the wings at a lifting angle. The model will rise as soon as lift exceeds weight. Also, the nose wheel will remain in contact with the ground for the whole run making directional control more difficult.

Lifting on landing   Similarly a nose up attitude at rest makes it harder to touch-down and stay down, especially if you still have flying speed.

Practice ⬇

Because ⬇

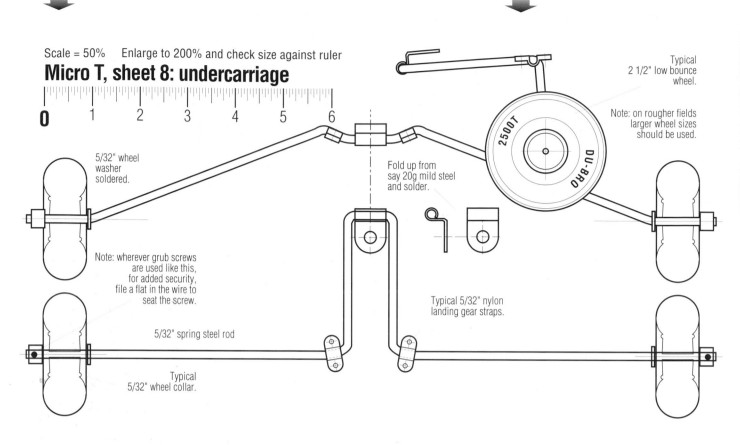

Scale = 50%   Enlarge to 200% and check size against ruler

Micro T, sheet 8: undercarriage

0 1 2 3 4 5 6

Typical 2 1/2" low bounce wheel.

Note: on rougher fields larger wheel sizes should be used.

5/32" wheel washer soldered.

Fold up from say 20g mild steel and solder.

2500T DU-BRO

Note: wherever grub screws are used like this, for added security, file a flat in the wire to seat the screw.

Typical 5/32" nylon landing gear straps.

5/32" spring steel rod

Typical 5/32" wheel collar.

Bend up the main undercarriage legs from ⁵/₃₂" rod and the fixing bracket from say 20g mild steel or brass. Test fit the forward boom bolt through this bracket and adjust it until the rod sits nicely against the under face of the pod. Securely solder the bracket to the rod (ordinary soft solder has proven adequate on the prototype model).

Solder a retaining washer on the inside of each axle. Fit the wheels and mark the place for flats to be filed to help retain the wheel collars. Assemble on the plane, then locate and screw on the landing gear straps.

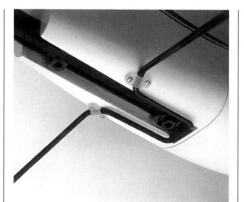

Photo 13:3 *The main anchorage of the wheel assembly is at the wing bolt while the two trailing edge brackets keep it aligned and control any side movement.*

The retaining washers which you solder to the axles are intended to stop the wheels from riding onto the bent part of the axles where they would jam. This is a standard practice which we will use on other models. Take care to remove any solder that may get onto the bearing part of the axles. This too would cause the wheels to jam.

Always make sure the wheels are free to revolve smoothly, they are lubricated to stop 'chatter' and they are set on the true line of travel. A takeoff can give quite enough trouble without adding the unnecessary difficulty of a poorly setup undercarriage.

A. Rivers

110

Chapter 14: the Micro T–MkV photo plane

Photo 14:2 *This neat little package straps on to your Micro T whenever you want to take photos from the air.*

Photo 14:1 *When your primary training days are over your Micro T can be promoted into the role of Club Photoplane by simply replacing the canopy module with the camera module and upgrading the receiver to 5 channels. The module is held in place with elastic bands so you can take it off and on any time. Now see the world as your models see it! And by using disposable camera packs, you don't even put an expensive camera at risk.*

'What can the model see from up there?' This question has intrigued modellers right from the earliest days of model flying.

What's so special about the Micro T camera module? Can't I turn any plane into a camera plane?

It is not sufficient to just strap a camera onto a plane, set up a servo to fire off the shutter and trust to luck that all will be well. It probably won't be.

Photo 14:3 *The MicroT configuration with the engine, propeller and exhaust spray all behind the wing, makes it an ideal photo plane. To convert your Micro T-MkIV to a photo MkV you need to be operating at least a 5-channel radio system, then make this strap-on camera module and enjoy the fun of aerial photography!*

Once you are comfortable that you can handle your Micro T in most situations, consider building the photo module. It is very little extra work and you will get loads of fun.

■ Gear and materials

You must have a transmitter with at least 5 channels. If you have a choice, the most convenient to assign to the camera is the undercarriage channel. This lets you hit the switch to take the shot, then switch back before you wind-on to the next frame.

Naturally, you'll have to match up the aircraft's receiver with the Tx, so it needs to be 5 or more channel.

A standard servo is used to trigger the shutter. This can be the cheapest you can get. Even an old suspect one which you have recovered from a crash will do since little hangs upon a servo failure.

The rest of the material can probably come from your scrap balsa and ply stock pile, a length of ¼" dowel, a wire off-cut, and a couple of undercarriage straps and you're in business.

Photo 14:4 *A test fitting of the partially completed prototype shows clearly how the servo holds the shutter release arm up off the camera's shutter button. When you activate say the retract switch on your transmitter the servo revolves, allowing the spring to pull the release arm down onto the shutter button and 'click', you have your first aerial photograph.*

Remember the first time you handled a camera? You were told to hold it steady and don't 'push' the shutter button down, just squeeze it. Photography from the air has just the same rules.

If the camera is not sufficiently insulated from the aircraft, engine vibration will shake it during the time the camera shutter is open. This will blur the image exposed onto the film.

Another problem is exhaust. If the camera is behind the propeller, the chances are the lens will get all covered in oil. Again, not a help when you want a good shot.

A third advantage of the Micro T layout is that the camera can be pointed straight ahead. This helps you aim at the subject you want to photograph.

If you want to get really sophisticated, use a self-winding camera and you can take a number of photographs without landing to rewind between shots. Whatever, it's lot of fun.

Micro T, sheet 9: camera module

0 1 2 3 4 5 6 7 8 9 10 11 1

CM6 CM13 CM9 CM2 CM5 CM1 CM10 CM12 CM10 CM8 CM4 CM12 CM15 CM6 CM13 CM14 CM9

Plan

CM5 CM4 CM2 1/8" sq. balsa strips

1/8" sq. balsa strips

CM4 CM3

End Elevation

Note: the camera is held from moving upward by CM2, downward by CM3 and sideways by the two 1/8" sq. strips. Adjust to fit the camera of your choice.

1/16" scrap CM10 CM4 CM5 CM2

Typical 1/8" nylon landing gear straps.

CM11

CM1

CM6
1/8" balsa

CM8 CM4

CM12 CM13 CM9 CM14 CM3 CM15

Side Elevation

Say Fuji 'QuickSnap' disposable camera

End Elevation

Practice

■ The camera

The drawings have been prepared for you to use a Fuji 'QuickSnap' disposable camera. However, it won't take much to adapt these so your module will hold any other compact 35mm, as long as it's small, lightweight and you're prepared to put it at risk. I wouldn't consider anything like a single lens reflex camera on either weight or risk grounds at this stage. If the camera is a self-winding one, it offers the big advantage that you can take several shots without coming down to rewind. Just remember to check that you have not dramatically altered the balancing point of your model when you add a different camera – the disposable ones are very light.

■ Setting up and using

Pad the module so that there are no hard contact points between it and the plane. Then, don't have the bands so tight that the padding becomes rigid (nor loose enough to let the camera come adrift).

Just take a little extra care when you fly for a photograph – it would be too easy to get carried away with the picture and forget about the flying hazards!

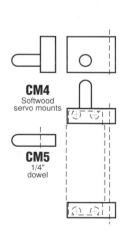

Photo 14:5 *While the measurements supplied are for a standard disposable camera, if you want to use another type such as an auto-wind, modify the housing measurements and the shape of the shutter release arm so it will fit the camera of your choice. Remember, aero modelling isn't just following a plan, it's also inventing, developing and modifying!*

Scale = 50%   Enlarge to 200% and check size against ruler

Micro T, sheet 10: camera module components

0 1 2 3 4 5 6 7 8 9

1/8" 3-ply, 5-1/2" x 4"   1/8" x 4" x 9" balsa sheet

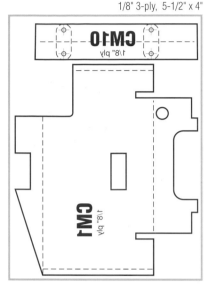

CM10
1/8" ply

CM1
1/8" ply

CM8
1/8" balsa

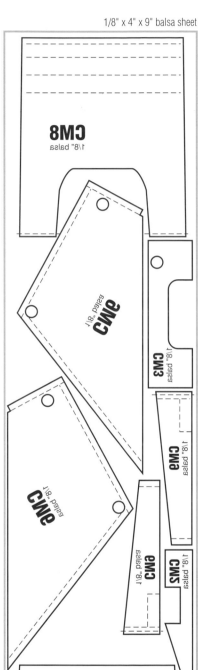

CM6
1/8" balsa

CM3
1/8" ply

CM7
1/8" balsa

CM9
1/8" ply

CM2
1/8" ply

CM1
1/8" ply

Iron-down images

Note: the component cutting guides are reproduced back-to-front so that they will print correctly when photocopied then transferred onto your wood stock with a hot iron and pressure.

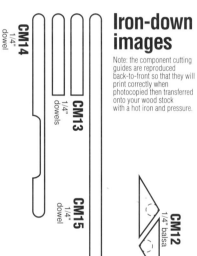

CM14
1/4" dowel

CM13
1/4" dowels

CM15
1/4" dowel

CM12
1/4" balsa

CM4
Softwood servo mounts

CM5
1/4" dowel

Practice

■ As a modeller you will learn to recognise certain design features in full-size aircraft. Some features are a strength in some fields and a weakness in others. Remember, aircraft are designed for specific purposes.

When you decide to model an aircraft make sure you know beforehand what its purpose is. Use this as a guide to what the model should do well and what it may not even want to do at all!

■ The relationship between power, weight, wing loading, flying speed, lift and drag should be the subject of your primary assessments.

Why?

Where do I start?

Photo 15:1   *Considered by some as the pinnacle of aircraft development from WWI, the Sopwith Triplane by designer Herbert Smith.*

Because

Read all you can. There's a wealth of enthralling material written about flying in the World Wars, the 'golden era' of aerial exploration, pushing the boundaries, and classic air racing*. The early aviators experienced many of the problems you will be able to relate to as you make and fly models.

Browse the magazine racks and bone up on what's going on in aviation circles.

Photo 15:2   *It is a brave modeller who tackles a machine which flies as near the stall as this 1910 Bristol Boxkite replica stationed at Old Warden.*

The historical period of your plane will be a major clue.

Early flying machines suffered from low-powered engines which were heavy. Designers needed to compensate by building very light structures with large lifting panels. The strength of these constructions relied on high-drag struts, stay wires and obstructions. When the planes did fly, their speed was little above the stall, a situation leading to difficult flight control.

Later, in America during the racing era it almost became 'power at all cost'. Some of these racers appear to use engines to replace wings. They often make good models nevertheless!

Photo 15:3   *Perhaps typical of the type of aircraft which might capture your attention: the very potent Sukhoi 31 aerobatic marvel from Russia. The power-to-weight ratio of this demon makes it a little wild for the novice pilot but great fun to look forward to.*

* Do read: Richard Bach's (Jonathan Livingston Seagull) *"Stranger to the Ground"*, *"Nothing by Chance"*, *"A Gift of Wings"*, *"Biplane"*, etc. (Granada Publishing).
A classic World War One novel featuring the Sopwith Camel is the late V.M. Yeates' *"Winged Victory"*, (Granada Publishing) while for World War Two, Derek Robinson's *"Piece of Cake"* (1984, Pan Books) is hard to beat.

Practice

■ It will be seen by the 'Progress of Flight Speed Records' (shown below) that it was really only after WWI that aircraft were endowed with the power to allow designers to build aerodynamically clean airframes which in turn allowed high air speeds.

The inter-relationship between power, speed, lift and weight soon becomes obvious.

Photo 15:4 *Lots of visual clues here: the Chance Vought F4U Corsair, built for speed and altitude, became the first US fighter to exceed 400mph in level flight. The wings were 'cranked' to allow that massive 13 foot prop to clear the deck. With over 2,000hp hauling about 10,000lbs to over 37,000ft altitude, we are talking brute force and heavy metal. Check out those flaps which allow carrier deck operation. Gliding ability does not figure highly amongst the characteristics of these breeds.*

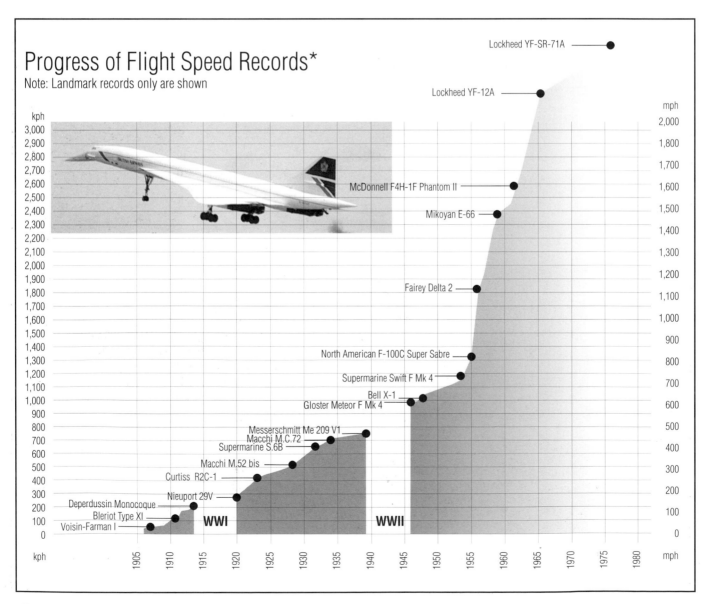

Progress of Flight Speed Records*
Note: Landmark records only are shown

Practice

Instead of using high power for outright speed, many aircraft use extra power to overcome the drag of a high-lift wing and so force it through the air to create high lift.

This high lift can be used for STOL (short takeoff/landing), extra payload, increased altitude or a combination of these benefits.

See the 'Progress of Flight Altitude Records' (shown below).

Photo 15:5 *The Polish PZL-104 Wilga 4-seat light utility aircraft breathes 'lift' from every line. You don't often see such speciality high-lift wings on a light plane without thinking about the design purpose behind the feature: ultra-short takeoff and landing, stable slow-speed flight (37 knots), glider towing, aerial photography or spotting exercises.*

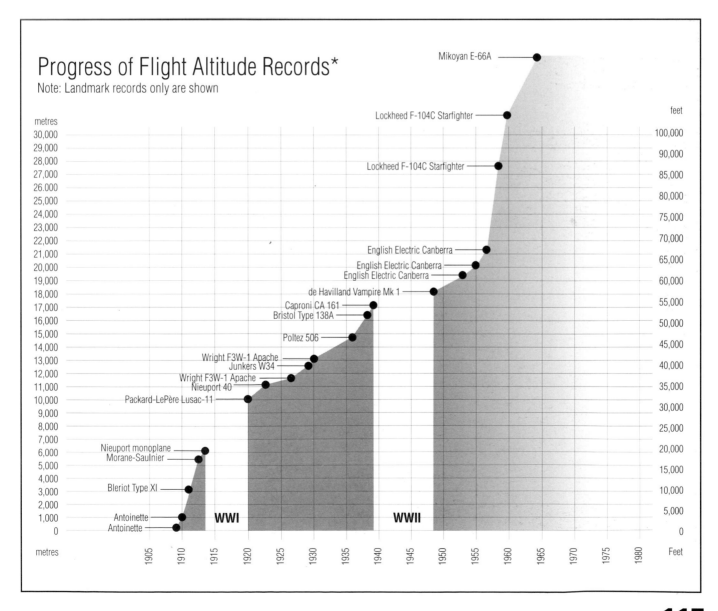

Progress of Flight Altitude Records*
Note: Landmark records only are shown

■ Lift which can be converted into payload is, in many aircraft, used for fuel. Over the past 40 years the evolution of more powerful, lighter engines, improved streamlining and more reliable components, flight distances have extended dramatically.

See the 'Progress of Flight Distance Records' (shown below).

■ Look at the sample aircraft presented in this chapter and seek the clues that tell you more about their flying characteristics.

Photo 15:6 *The clean lines of the de Havilland D.H.89 Dominie Rapide are one of the designer's counters for the low power (suggested by the small size of its propellers). Another is the aircraft's light construction which is evident from the fabric-over-stringer fuselage treatment. As an early passenger transport the design objectives must have included speed and payload (passengers, baggage and fuel capacity). A modeller's dream, but not to be undertaken by the faint-hearted!*

I didn't think that building model planes was so involved. Does everyone take it this seriously?

No. And everyone must find their own level of interest. However, the more seriously you do take it, the more pleasure you'll get.

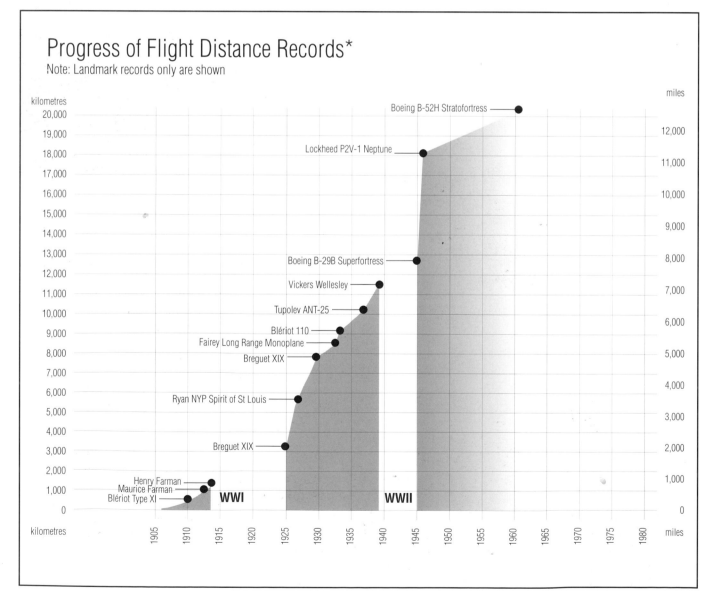

Progress of Flight Distance Records*
Note: Landmark records only are shown

Boeing B-52H Stratofortress

Lockheed P2V-1 Neptune

Boeing B-29B Superfortress

Vickers Wellesley

Tupolev ANT-25

Blériot 110

Fairey Long Range Monoplane

Breguet XIX

Ryan NYP Spirit of St Louis

Breguet XIX

Henry Farman
Maurice Farman
Blériot Type XI

WWI   **WWII**

118

Accepting that this is a sport, not an obsession, take the opportunities to visit local airfields, talk to fliers, maintenance people and private owners.

Many smaller fields have interesting aircraft and you could be surprised to see what does drop in. Get to know what is flying in your area and research the details of anything that you find particularly interesting. You could well decide to one day make a scale replica of one of these planes.

Attend flying meets and displays when you can. Watch the real thing perform both standard manoeuvres and aerobatic routines. This will help you develop your flying techniques.

Photo 15:7 *A different concept of power is demonstrated in the Pitts Special S1 –power combined with light wing loading. Result is astounding aerobatics.*

Photo 15:8 *A somewhat less obvious clue identifies this as a Sea Hurricane. Early WWII aircraft must be seen as much less powerful than later versions.*

Photo 15:11 *Aircraft restoration gives us the chance to study construction details that are normally a mystery beneath the skin. This Hurricane is being rebuilt at Christchurch, New Zealand.*

Aircraft rebuilding and restoration is very relevant to the model scene, both for the subject aircraft involved and for the opportunity to study full size construction methods. See if there's some restoration work going on in your area.

Another is the home-built field. Modelling is often a realistic outlet for the would-be amateur builder/ flier so there's no problem with going to look or even drool a little.

Frequently it is the aircraft museums which inspire the modeller most. There is little to compare with spending time with an actual aircraft you have read of, or with studying a particular make and model that you want to build.

Photo 15:9 *Shuttleworth's replica 1910 Avro Mark IV built by the Hampshire Aeroplane Club must be seen flying to be fully appreciated – sheer magnificence!*

Photo 15:10 *A very rare WWII restoration: the Polikarpov I-153 of Sir Tim Wallace's Alpine Fighter Collection, a high performance (286mph) 1939 bipe.*

Photo 15:12 *The ubiquitous Tiger Moth, 2-seat primary trainer of the WWII period and post war aero club stand-by.*

Photo 15:13 *Alex Henshaw's famous Mew Gull G-AEXF which still holds the world solo speed record for Gravesend to Cape Town—30 hrs 28min flying time!*

Photo 15:14 *This one is a trap for the uninitiated — Grumman Ag-Cat, all metal and built in 1970, specifically for agricultural aviation purposes.*

Photo 15:15 *Every line of the Sky Arrow 480 T suggests aerodynamic efficiency coupled with structural weight reduction such as a strut-supported wing.*

Because

■ Museums

Belgium:
Royal Army Museum, Brussels; some 100 aircraft, some dating from 1911.
Canada:
National Aviation Museum, Ottawa; over 100 examples.
Czechoslovakia:
Military Museum – Air and Space Section, Prague; 136 or so aircraft.
France:
Air and Space Museum, just north of Paris; over 300 examples.
Germany:
German Museum of Achievement in Science and Technology, Munich; about 80 aircraft.
Italy:
Museum of the History of Italian Military Aviation, Vigna di Valle; almost 100 aircraft, with interesting Schneider Trophy examples.
Poland:
Museum of Aviation and Space, Rakowice; over 100 examples.
Sweden:
Malmen Air Force Museum, Linköping; about 75 examples.
United Kingdom:
Imperial War Museum, Duxford; almost 100 military aircraft.
Science Museum, London; over 50 aircraft dating from 1910.
Shuttleworth Collection, Old Warden; especially important for its flying examples of more than 50 aircraft dating from 1910.
United States of America:
United States Army Aviation Museum, Alabama; about 115 aircraft.
Pima Air Museum, Arizona; over 160 examples.
The Air Museum 'Planes of Fame', California; 70 aircraft.
San Diego Aerospace Museum, San Diego; over 70 aircraft.
New England Air Museum, Connecticut; 115 examples.
National Air and Space Museum, Washington, DC; with well over 300 aircraft.
Naval Aviation Museum, Florida; over 100 aircraft.
Old Rhinebeck Aerodrome, New York; over 60 examples.
United States Air Force Museum, Ohio; almost 200 aircraft.
Confederate Air Force Flying Museum, Texas; notable for its collection of over 90 flyable WWII aircraft.
Experimental Aircraft Association Museum, Oshkosh; world renown for display of over 200 recreational aircraft.

The list is almost endless.
Check out your local area. You could be very surprised at the examples of fine aircraft you can study near home and at your leisure.

120

Chapter 16: Modelling a full-size aircraft

Practice

■ The ultimate modelling achievement is to 'discover' an individual aircraft that is everything you believe in, to recreate it as a model, then control it through realistic flight manoeuvres.

Almost everyone who starts out wants to build either a Spitfire or a Mustang. But before getting too excited, it's important to assess where you're at with your building and flying skills. If you build beyond your comfort level you can upset your progress in both disciplines.

Meantime, choose a design you can build without getting overwhelmed and one which flies within your capability. When you feel you can handle a bigger challenge then aim a little higher.

Let's look at some possibilities.

■ Start by looking at the flying surfaces because these will tell you most about how the model will fly. Some of the following will suggest good characteristics:

● Is the wing fairly lightly loaded for a good glide angle?
● Is the wing plan parallel or if not, is it only gently tapered?
● Is the wing span reasonably generous without being excessive?
● Does the plane have good spacing between the wing and tailplane?
● Does the tailplane 'shade' the rudder?
● Does the original have a reasonably good power-to-weight ratio?

When you're satisfied look at building aspects.

Why?

Do you mean a certain model of aircraft such as a 'Spitfire' or 'Mustang' or do you mean for example, the actual F4U-1A Corsair number "29" as flown by Lieutenant Ike Kepford, US Navy ace of Sqdn VF-17?*

An attractive photo in a magazine can be the start of your research. A picture of Jungmeister G-AYSJ started the model below.

Photo 16:1 *The author's 1/4 scale model of restored Bücker Jungmeister G-AYSJ in the colours of the 1930s German sport-flying association, owned by British aviation writer, James Gilbert. The model is a modified Dave Platt design, 15cc Supertige.*

Do you think I'm ready to build a scale model?

Because

While each one of us is looking for different rewards from our modelling, once you have built a scale model or two, try researching and reproducing the *actual* aircraft that did something special. It's fun!

You must not let yourself be pushed into something you are not yet comfortable with. If you really feel you are not ready, use another plan, or relax and assemble a kit.

Photo 16:2 *Getting bigger – 1/3 scale, 70cc Christen Eagle this time, set up to represent N41ET as flown by the Eagles Aerobatic Team Leader, Charlie Hillard at Reno 1987.*

* For this aircraft's details see *"Famous Fighters of the Second World War – Second Series"* by Williams Green (1962, Macdonald & Co Ltd).

Practice

■ The construction method for the model is often suggested by the shapes found in the actual aircraft. Look for easy solutions:

● Is the fuselage suited to a standard 'crutch' approach? Slab sides are easiest to build and cover. Compound curves are the most difficult.
● Does the fuselage taper straight to the tail so you can bend a simple turtleback over the topside?
Are the wings positioned so you can arrange for them to be removable without destroying the fuselage's basic strength?
Can the wing ribs be shaped together in a 'sandwich'?
Will you have to mould a special cockpit canopy?
Does the undercarriage retract and if so, will you use retracts in the model or settle for the non-retract solution?
Are most of the shapes fairly straight forward to build?

■ You will need access to shapes and dimensions of the full-size aircraft. Do you have 3-view plans and if not, can you track down a set? There are a number of excellent plan services round the world. Write for catalogues.

When you have the drawings, what size will you build?
There are several restrictions which will influence the size of your models:

The overall costs of materials, equipment and operating.
● The 'at risk' values that you are prepared to put in the air.
● Your timetable and available construction hours.
● The size of your work area.
● Your storage facilities.
● Your transport capacity.
● Existing engine/s, equipment on hand.

Generally, build as large as you comfortably can.

Photos 16:3 *The Starlet homebuilt.*

Photo 16:4 *The Lancair IV.*

Photos 16:5 *The Polikarpov I-16*

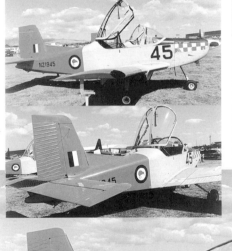

Because

In choosing the various aircraft to model in this book I looked over many full-size aircraft. The examples here demonstrate some of the features considered before settling on the Ryan for chapter 17.

The Starlet has real eye appeal which I thought you'd like but too many of the shapes are compound, the wing tapers and it would take longer to build. Takeoffs and landings look like a challenge. Rejected meantime.

The Lancair offers good ground handling from the tricycle undercarriage but all those flowing lines would make this as hard to build as any warbird. Rejected.

The Polikarpov looks cute on the ground and marvellous in the air. But again, difficult ground handling, a very short pitch moment so probably a handful in flight and compound shapes all over the place. Never really a serious contender.

The Airtrainer has a whole lot going for it. Look over the construction lines and you'll see it could be built fairly easily with slab sides, a straight taper on the turtleback, but a slight taper on the wings so individual wing ribs would be needed. However, not bad. The tail surfaces are pure text book for spin recovery and the tricycle gear would make ground handling a piece of cake. Only real problem would be that cockpit canopy. Just a bit too difficult yet.

Photos 16:6 *The NZAI CT4B Airtrainer, a very serious contender.*

122

For our next project I eventually settled on building the 'Spirit of St Louis', a high wing monoplane with parallel wings, strutted, but unfortunately a 'taildragger' undercarriage, though good for training. Fully fabric covered. It suits conventional crutch construction, the wings ribs can be shaped in a 'sandwich' and no special building skills are needed beyond what we've done to date.

We build it at a size that's suitable for the engine we used in the Micro T, an OS Max FS 0.25. On a relatively light, high wing monoplane this would suggest about 4'6" span and an all up weight of something like 4 lbs.

■ We are learning to build scale and this calls for added detail. Unfortunately, detail usually also means weight. So the compromise will lie between a highly detailed

Photos 16:7　*The Bulkow Junior*

It seems that most planes have individual features that will be hard to model. For the stage I'm at is it too optimistic to make a scale plane?

Another promising plane was the Swedish 'shoulder wing' Bulkow Junior. Having a strut-supported wing this model could be built very lightly. The wing is parallel (although swept forward slightly) and the fuselage has straight lines and square corners. It has tricycle undercarriage and nicely placed tail surfaces. But once again, that cockpit canopy! What we needed was a really straight forward aircraft which, if it involved complications, the builder could decide to leave off the model without feeling cheated.

No, Lindberg's 'Spirit of St Louis' fills the bill nicely. The plan offers plenty of interesting detail but, if you want to get flying scale without too much building, leave off the detailed scale undercarriage and dummy engine and you're in business.

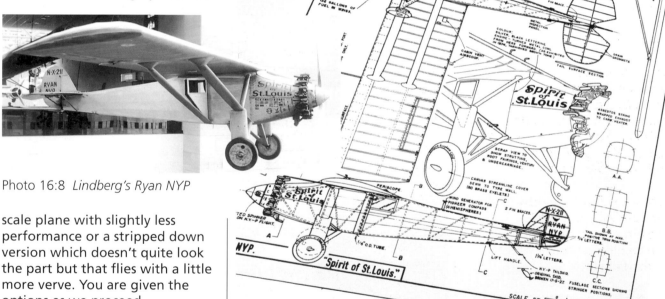

Photo 16:8　*Lindberg's Ryan NYP*

scale plane with slightly less performance or a stripped down version which doesn't quite look the part but that flies with a little more verve. You are given the options as we proceed.

■ Ther are many aspect to model-making: crafting with our tools; problem solving as we encounter new challenges; patience to get things right; and a sense of judgement as to what to include on a model and what to leave off.

In the next chapter you will see how one person solved some design problems. There will be many other ways of solving them. You can start to think laterally.

Photo 16:9　*Once the Ryan had been chosen, I sent for the plans. 3-views and sections were supplied by Nexus Special Interests Ltd, Plan Service, Nexus House, Azalea Drive, Swanley, Kent BR8 8HU, England. Surface mail to the opposite side of the world took just under one month, no problem.*

Can I really expect that the model will fly nicely?

Yes, many characteristics of full-size planes carry over to the model, particularly if you build big.
You also need to build comparable characteristics such as relative wing loading, power-to-weight and of course, a matched centre of gravity. Keep the weight down. Light weight means easier flying.

Chapter 17: Let's build a sports-scale plane

The Ryan M-2 which was modified for Charles Lindberg's Atlantic crossing makes an interesting modelling project.

A standard M2 was re-specified to give the plane the extra lift needed to raise 2,500lbs of fuel carried at takeoff, and to be burned during the following 33 hours that it would take to fly from New York to Paris, nonstop.

The wingspan was increased to 46 feet. The tail surfaces were left intentionally small to avoid increasing drag, even though the plane would be skittery and need continual attention. There was no forward vision. Lindberg wanted the safety of sitting behind the fuel tank; and this had to be located about the centre of gravity so that consumption did not seriously affect trim stability. He also felt there would be little need for forward vision during the crossing (a small forward-looking periscope was provided but seldom used). The undercarriage was increased in size and beefed up to handle the extra weight.

■ The visual changes are retained in the model. However, particularly for the relatively new pilot, the instability produced by under size tail surfaces is un-acceptable, so design concessions have overridden scale reality and the tail surfaces are larger. Also the fuselage is longer, behind the wing for stability and in front of the wing for balance (without ballast). Otherwise we follow the outline quite closely. One major problem with the scale outline is the propeller spinner. The original aircraft has a very short, large diameter nose and I have not found a commercial spinner that conforms to the profile.

Photo 17:1 *Today Lindberg's Ryan 'Spirit of St.Louis' has pride of place, hanging from the ceiling of the main gallery at the Smithsonian Institution National Air and Space Museum, Washington D.C.*

Why do you call the model a 'sports-scale' plane rather than a scale model?

We are saving that description for later on when we try much harder to replicate the details of the full size aircraft. At this point we are making compromises in the interests of making the model simple to build and not too excessively expensive to crash.

Photo 17:2 *Now this presents you with a signwriting challenge! The model shows its own engine cylinder head plus a ring of matching dummies. Note the model's incorrect spinner shape is disguised by moving the joint line further aft.*

124

Ryan NYP 'Spirit of St.Louis'

54" span scale model aircraft for 4-channel radio control
and 0.25 cu in 2-stroke engines
From 'AIRCRAFT WORKSHOP: Learn to make models that FLY'
 by Kelvin Shacklock ©
Model scale: 10.2: 1 of original aircraft

Specifications:	Full-size	Scale model
Wingspan:	46' 0"	54"
Length overall:	27' 7"	35⁵/₈"
Wing area:	330 sq ft	3 sq ft
Rec. weight:		3 lb 15 oz
Wing loading:		21 oz sq ft

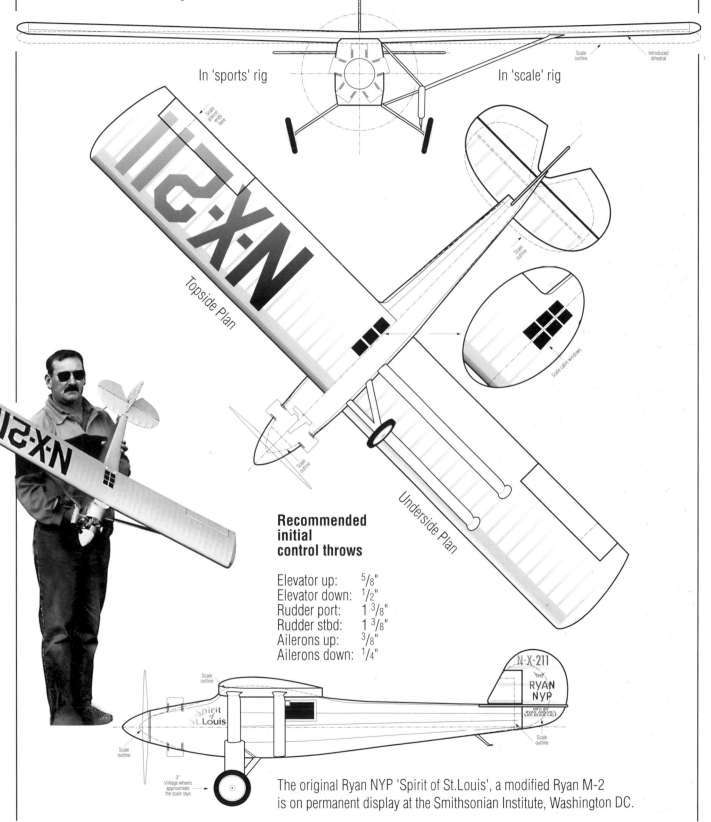

In 'sports' rig

In 'scale' rig

Topside Plan

Underside Plan

Scale cabin windows

**Recommended
initial
control throws**

Elevator up: ⁵/₈"
Elevator down: ¹/₂"
Rudder port: 1 ³/₈"
Rudder stbd: 1 ³/₈"
Ailerons up: ³/₈"
Ailerons down: ¹/₄"

N-X-211

RYAN
NYP

The original Ryan NYP 'Spirit of St.Louis', a modified Ryan M-2
is on permanent display at the Smithsonian Institute, Washington DC.

■ You will find this an interesting modelling project for quite a few reasons. As you go along, you can make decisions on how far you want to take the scale detail. For example, you don't need to decide on a dummy engine until you start building the cowling. And if you make a sports cowling meantime, there's nothing to stop you making a scale one later. The same applies to the wing struts and undercarriage detail (provided you built in the blind nuts in the wing as you made it).

It also introduces a number of design solutions which may not otherwise have occurred to you. The dummy engine doesn't attempt to replicate the original, but still gives an impression of a radial engine. Since the actual engine forms a part of it, you don't end up with a scale engine with one foreign cylinderhead sticking out like a sore thumb. And, after all, who remembers exactly how the original looks? Then there's the complicated-looking undercarriage suspension which on this model actually works in reverse, making it easier to build and still effective in use.

Photo 17:3 *The fully framed model ready for painting then covering. All equipment has been test-installed and checked for fit and function. In 'sports' rig you could ignore the dummy engine, wing struts and undercarriage suspension.*

Photo 17:4 *All the major subassemblies can be removed for covering, access or damage repair.*

This chapter emphasises the need for a modeller to develop skills at finding simple design solutions to apparently complex problems.

Enjoy the challenge and see if you can come up with better solutions than the ones provided here. After all, the plans you are using now and will use in the future have been put together by people just like you and me, so why shouldn't you have some better answers?

Photo 17:5 *In scale rig the model attempts to give the overall impression of the actual plane, rather than follow the specific true-to-life detail. It looks as if it has a fully functional 5-cylinder radial engine. Does it matter that the original has 9 (or is it 7) cylinders? And, who would guess that the undercarriage shock absorbers are in fact under tension instead of compression? Surely, unless you're in an official scale competition, general impression is the important consideration.*

126

■ Starting with the wing, it has been designed as a builder's wing. That is, if you enjoy building you'll thoroughly enjoy making this one. Sure, it has more ribs than you actually need. Halve the number if you really want to, but these are set at scale spacing to look really impressive. On the plan It looks complicated because there are quite a lot of parts but they are simple shapes, easy to make and they fit together well. The end result is a light, strong and attractive wing that's really no great sweat.

The aerofoil we have chosen is very traditional. It is a 'Clark Y' aerofoil which in fact has a fairly high degree of camber built into the formula. So much so that the aft 75% of the underside is flat. It has the reputation for being well mannered and provides good lift at relatively low speeds.

To produce wing ribs which conform to the Clark Y profile (or any other we might have chosen) we refer to published tables which give the measurements for the location of the wing's surface at various stations across the chord (see page 128). In this case we have used tables from the book *Model Aircraft Aerodynamics* by Martin Simons. Once we have the outline and have settled on a suitable structure we develop a template of the actual wing rib.

■ Building the Wing

Use the same building board setup as you used on the Micro T.

■ Now we try yet another technique for getting the shape of your wing rib down onto the wood. Make a metal pattern or template. Here's how.

Enlarge the wing rib template shown on page 128 and using double-sided tape, stick the copy to an aluminium printing plate offcut. With sharp scissors, trim the outline then notch out the four wing spar cutouts. File to

Photo 17:6 *Aircraft of this vintage, and a lot of more modern ones, have quite a rough finish on the surface. Much of it is caused by the structure beneath the fabric. If we build the model in a similar way the final look can be very convincing.*

Building the prototype became a lot of fun so it was decided to go all the way and incorporate 'rib stitching'. If you want to have a go too, before you cover the model skip ahead to Chapter 18 and read all about how it's done.

Photo 17:7 *Taking quite a fancy to this model, the author decided to finish the wings and tail surfaces with authentic looking stitching on all the ribs.*

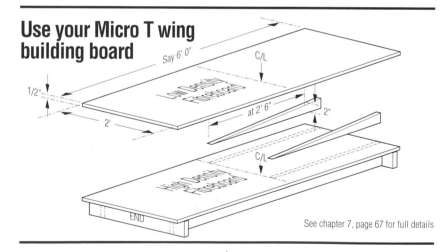

Use your Micro T wing building board

Say 6' 0"

C/L

1/2"

2'

Low Density Fibreboard

at 2' 6"

2"

C/L

High Density Fibreboard

END

See chapter 7, page 67 for full details

Do I have to understand all this technical stuff about aerofoil design before I can design my own scratch models?

If you have a technical bent you will thoroughly enjoy working with the theory. However that's not for everyone, and a good gut feeling for shapes and a little reading can usually get you by without too much difficulty. I think it's true that some accurate shape, halving the thickness of the outline. Drill the aileron torque rod hole to size. Leave the paper and tape fixed to the template as both a guide for further modification and also to keep the aluminium quite stiff. Drill two location pinholes to let you pin it to the wood so it won't move as you cut round it.

Now is the test to see how well you have learned to control your balsa knife. If you are getting good clean cuts that are nice and

modellers make too much of the need for sophisticated shapes when making a power model that is not too dependent upon super efficiency before it will appear to fly very well. That is not to say that it could not be made to fly even better if a great deal more work were invested in its design. It's really a case of what you want to do and how far you want to take it.

Published coordinates for Clark 'Y' aerofoil
(simplified for clarity)

Chord station X	Upper surface YU	Lower surface YL
0.00	3.50	3.50
2.50	6.50	1.47
5.00	7.90	0.93
7.50	8.85	0.63
10.00	9.60	0.42
15.00	10.68	0.15
20.00	11.36	0.03
25.00	11.60	0.00
30.00	11.70	0.00
40.00	11.40	0.00
50.00	10.52	0.00
60.00	9.15	0.00
70.00	7.35	0.00
80.00	5.22	0.00
90.00	2.80	0.00
100.00	0.12	0.00

We choose the traditional Clark 'Y' aerofoil for the NYP

Plotting the Clark 'Y' aerofoil from published figures*

Preparing a chart

Upper surface of aerofoil YU

Lower surface of aerofoil YL

Datum line

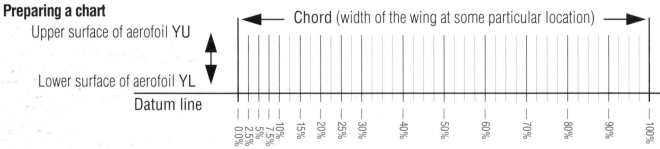

Chord (width of the wing at some particular location)

Chord station X (as a percentage of the cord back from the leading edge)

Plotting the coordinates

Wing thickness to be 12% of the chord

Divisions scaled so 11.70 = 12% of chord

Datum

Wing chord

Chord station X

Drawing the aerofoil

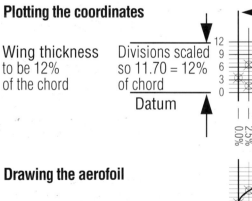

Resultant outline

Construction drawing

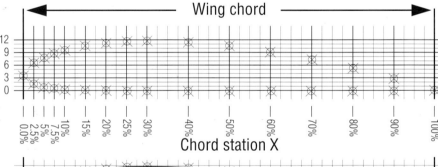

Make the wing rib template
(shown at 50% of full size)

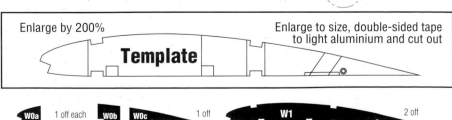

Enlarge by 200%

Enlarge to size, double-sided tape to light aluminium and cut out

Template

Wing rib schedule
(shown at 25% of full size)
Cut all from 1/16" balsa

| W0a | 1 off each | W0b | W0c | 1 off | W1 | 2 off |
| W2 | | | | 30 off | W3a | 14 off / W3b 18 off |

*For further study read *Model Aircraft Aerodynamics* by Martin Simons (1999, Nexus Special Interests)

Practice

vertical, you'll find this technique produces beautifully accurate wing ribs that hardly need a touch of sanding. Each one will be the same as the previous one. All the slots will line up. All the holes will be in just the same place. This is when you bless parallel wing designs.

Use the guide lines on the template to make up all the different ribs you need to complete the wing (Photo 17:10).

■ Iron down the images for the 3-ply parts and wingtips, then cut and sand them to size. At the same time print down the centre section sheeting guide.

■ Put the plan on your building board but locate it so you can drill holes straight down from the aileron linkage points without hitting any structure underneath (photo 17:13). Cover with cling film.

■ This wing is constructed a little differently from the previous ones in that here we are using rib capping strips. These are $1/16$" x $3/16$" flats which glue top and bottom of each wing rib where there's no overall sheeting. It reinforces the lightweight ribs and, provided you don't use too much glue, makes for a lighter and stronger wing.

This is an excellent project for you to try out different glues and learn about their special qualities. We will use three different types – aliphatic resin, epoxy resin and thin cyanoacrylate.

■ Begin by pinning the lower trailing edge to the plan. Then add aft part of the underside leading edge sheeting – only the aft part because this is flat against the building board. Rather than try to pack the front edge up to touch the ribs, we leave it off and add it after we lift the wing. Note that the aft edge of this sheeting stops midway under the front spar to leave a landing for the

Because

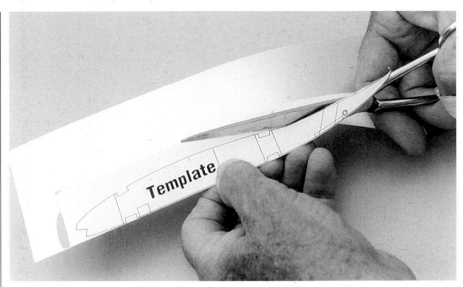

Photo 17:8 *Using double-sided tape to stick the photocopy to an offcut from an aluminium printing plate, make an accurate pattern for rib W2.*

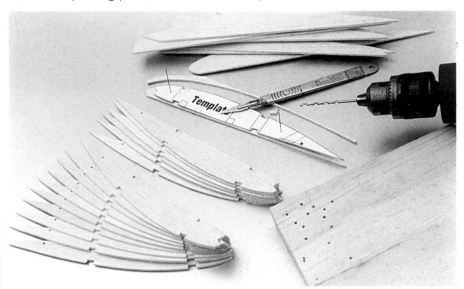

Photo 17:9 *Cut a set of rough blanks from $1/16$" balsa, then use the template to accurately cut and drill the final profiles. With care you'll find this is a really accurate way to make ribs for a parallel wing.*

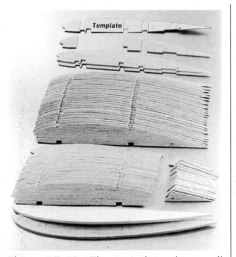

Photo 17:10 *The template shows all the combinations needed to make a full set of wing ribs. Here's what they should look like before sanding.*

Capping strips reinforce the lightweight ribs and, provided you don't use too much glue, make the wing lighter and at the same time stronger. The covering also can get a better grip on the broad capping strip compared with a narrow rib, so again the finished wing is stronger.

On our next model we will add stitching to the capping strips so a very realistic covering can be achieved. On the prototype we have jumped ahead to that chapter and added stitching, simply because the wing looked too good to leave bare. You can do the same without too much problem.

Practice

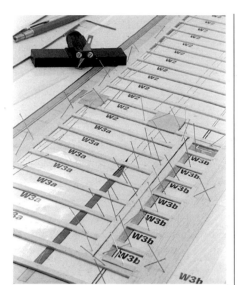

Photo 17:11 *Cut $^1/_{16}$" x $^3/_{16}$" capping strips and lay them up on the plan.*

capping strips to fix to the spar. Make cutouts to let the leading W5 strut plate fit into this strip.

Add the pre-printed centre section sheeting panels and glue.

Cut $^1/_{16}$" sheeting into $^3/_{16}$" strips. Using the aliphatic resin, proceed to fit, glue and pin all the underside rib capping in place (incorporate the aft 3-ply strut plate W5) including the ailerons, their leading edges and the aileron opening trailing edges.

Add the 3-ply W6 aileron hinge plate and the two $^1/_4$" softwood servo mounting spars (chamfer their undersides to the dihedral angle). Check their position accurately by test-fitting the W1 wing rib before the glue goes off. Also add the aileron torque rod plates W12 making sure there's space for the outside aileron rib to seat on its capping strip.

■ Take 4 spruce spars and chamfer the inner end of each to the angle of the dihedral so the centre joints can be spliced. Use the epoxy glue and place the starboard leading spar down to overlap the centreline by the splice length and glue over the full span. Use a rib to test the position and diagonally pin over the spar to hold it down in position. Add the port side spar

Ryan NYP, sheet 1: wing 1/2 plan

Scale = 25%   Enlarge to 400%, check size against ruler and match to Sheet 2 at "A" and "B" registers.

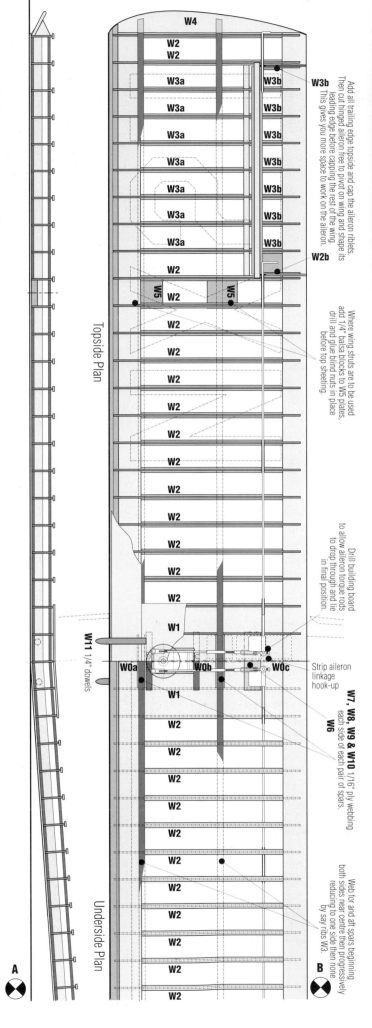

Practice

with the splice beginning at the centreline. Use the same procedure with the aft spars but begin with the port side.

■ Now make up the special aileron control torque rods using the following sequence (this order is essential):

● Cannibalise parts from a suitable aileron linkage hook-up pack by cutting each torque rod and taking the nylon bearing plates. Drill to $1/8"$.

● Make up a longer pair of torque rods from $1/8"$ steel rod. Before you make the second (outboard) bend in each rod, thread on the nylon bearing plate then three pieces of neat-fitting brass tube, each cut to $1\frac{1}{2}"$.

● To test fit on the plan drop the longer arms down through the holes drilled in the building board. Space out the bearing plates and brass tubing as shown and see that the return bends lie nicely into the aileron locations.

■ Begin assembling the wing by threading onto each torque rod all the ribs beginning with one W1, 13 W2s out to the aileron bay and ending with one W3b aileron riblet. Lower each rod into place and check they are all there, right way up and in the right sequence.

Use crossed-over pinning to fit each rib into final position then slide the brass tubes into their locations. When all joints fit and everything's nice and square, dribble thin cyano onto all the joints. Take care you don't get any into the torque rod tubes!

Cut a pair of tubes $2\frac{1}{2}"$ long for the outer aileron hinges and assemble the outer two bays of riblets (2 W2s and 2 W3bs) and cyano.

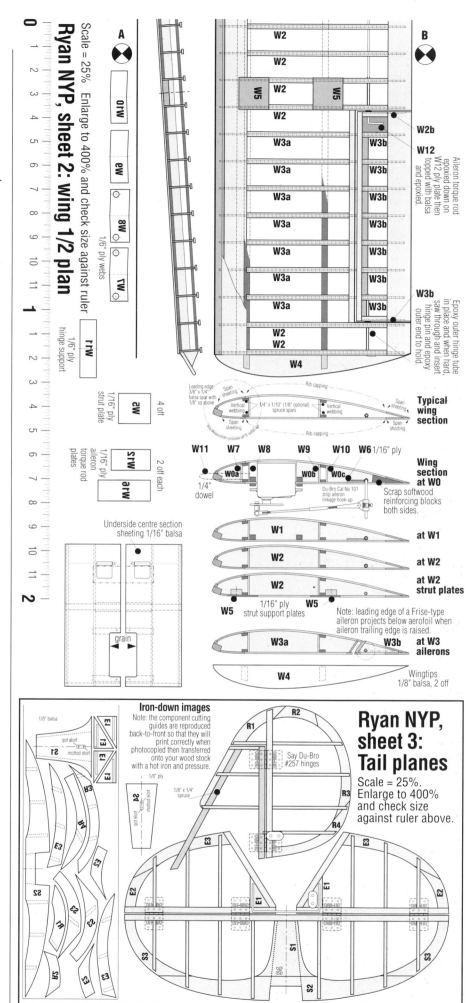

Practice

Use a fine, light saw blade to cut through these outer aileron tubes where the ailerons meet the wing. Insert hinge pins through the tubes and epoxy the outer ends to retain them in position.

From ⅛" sheet make the aileron leading edges with angled cuts to match the slope of the riblets. Glue, then add the intermediate riblets to the ailerons. Insert the remaining wing ribs, gluing with aliphatic resin as you go.

■ Take four more spruce spars and splice them as pairs. Epoxy, clamp and leave to cure.

Test fit the upper spars into the ribs. When a good fit is achieved throughout, lift them out, dab a little epoxy in each rib slot, re-insert the spars, weigh down and leave to cure. To be quicker you might also add the centre section 3-ply webs W7 to W10 and epoxy them at the same time.

Fit the 3 separate parts of the centre rib W0 and glue.

Use vertical grain 1/16" balsa and web both sides of both spars from ribs W1 out about 6 bays then one side only out to the aileron gap, gluing with aliphatic resin as you go.

Insert the leading edge balsa spars. Drill, fit and glue the dowels.

■ If you intend to fit scale wing struts make provision now. Glue ¼" balsa backing blocks to the plates for blind nuts to be fitted. Drill them out and epoxy nuts in place.

■ Remove the wing from the building board to bevel the aft side of the trailing edge down to the line of the wing ribs then back to the board.

The wing is still easily twisted so we will now build in washout.

Photo 17:12 *Add the pre-printed centre section sheeting panels and glue. Add the aileron hinge plate and the two ¼" softwood servo mounting spars.*

Photo 17:13 *Begin assembling the wing by threading onto each torque rod all the ribs beginning with one W1, 13 W2s out to the aileron bay and ending with one aileron riblet W3b.*

Photo 17:14 *Cut a pair of tubes for the outer aileron hinges and assemble the outer bays to hold the tube and cyano.*

Photo 17:15 *Add the aileron leading edge then bring in all the remaining riblets and glue.*

Photo 17:16 *Epoxy the 3-ply webs W7 to W10 over the centre joints for the spars. While you have the epoxy mixed, add a scrap of ply to the top of the torque rod bearing plates to hold them down (and the aileron rods where they are enclosed within the ailerons).*

132

Practice

Pack the centre-front of the wing up about ¼" from the building board. Weigh down the outer panels so they are flat on the board and the whole trailing edge sits down flat.

Add softwood reinforcing wedges to the innermost bay's trailing edges (to withstand the pressure of the wing mounting bolts) and then glue the upper trailing edge of ¹⁄₁₆" balsa.

While the wing is still twisted, sheath the upper forward and centre section in the usual way.

Cut some ¹⁄₁₆" balsa into ³⁄₁₆" strips. Bend them over the rib tops and fit flush between the aft edge of the leading edge sheeting and the front of the upper trailing edge. Fit and glue these 'capping' strips to the top of all the ribs from the centre section sheeting out to one bay before the aileron.

Cap the leading edge of the ailerons then run caps over each riblet to fit flush with the trailing edge (photo 17:20). Leave to set.

Remove the wing from the board and sight the washout which is now set into the wing structure. The wing will feel much stiffer and the outer panels should be permanently twisted slightly downward.

■ Cut the ailerons free so they pivot in the wing. Shape their leading edges per the plan.

Add the aft enclosures to the aileron bays then cap the remaining parts of the wing.

■ Add the wingtip formers and sheath the remaining underside leading edge to complete the torsion box.

Sand the leading edges to shape and lightly sand the whole wing. Epoxy/bandage the centre section in the usual way (keep epoxy off those dowels!).

Why?

I notice that you are giving less and less chance for me to ask questions. Is this intentional?

Because

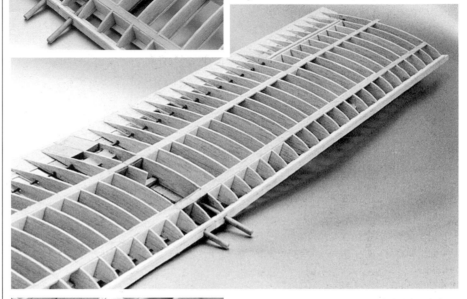

Photo 17:17 *The 3 parts of wing rib W0 butt against the centre section webs and complete the framework.*

Photo 17:18 *Note that the webbing is extensive near the centre section and gradually reduces in strength until there is no webbing on the final half dozen bays.*

Photo 17:19 *¼" balsa backing blocks are added to hold the blind nuts that you'll need if you are going to add scale wing struts.*
Also notice the aileron torque rod has a covering plate epoxied over it to reinforce its connection to the aileron.

Photo 17:20 *The wingtip formers angle up quite steeply which is in character with the real thing. This shot also shows the rib capping on the wing ribs, aileron bays and aileron riblets.*

Only up to a degree. As we've said, model making is very often a case of problem solving. While there are always dozens of different solutions, the question you must keep asking yourself is 'have I found the best solution to this particular problem?'. Better answers mean better models. So yes, I am keen that you should develop the ability to find solutions for yourself. On the other hand, I certainly don't want to leave you with a problem you can't solve.

Scale = 25%   Enlarge to 400% and check size against ruler.

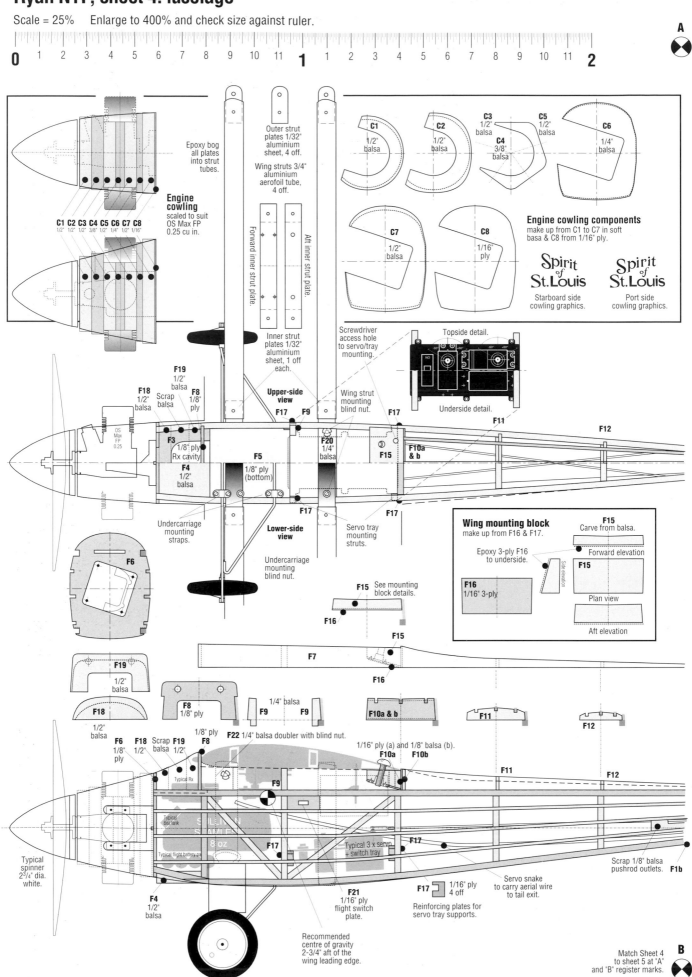

Epoxy bog all plates into strut tubes.

Outer strut plates 1/32" aluminium sheet, 4 off.

Wing struts 3/4" aluminium aerofoil tube, 4 off.

Engine cowling scaled to suit OS Max FP 0.25 cu in.

C1 C2 C3 C4 C5 C6 C7 C8
1/2" 1/2" 1/2" 3/8" 1/2" 1/4" 1/2" 1/16"

Forward inner strut plate.

Aft inner strut plate.

Inner strut plates 1/32" aluminium sheet, 1 off each.

C1
1/2" balsa

C2
1/2" balsa

C3
1/2" balsa

C4
3/8" balsa

C5
1/2" balsa

C6
1/4" balsa

C7
1/2" balsa

C8
1/16" ply

Engine cowling components
make up from C1 to C7 in soft basa & C8 from 1/16" ply.

Spirit of St.Louis
Starboard side cowling graphics.

Spirit of St.Louis
Port side cowling graphics.

Screwdriver access hole to servo/tray mounting.

Topside detail.

Underside detail.

F19
1/2" balsa

F18
1/2" balsa

Scrap balsa

F8
1/8" ply

Upper-side view

F17   F9

Wing strut mounting blind nut.

F17

F11

F12

OS Max FP 0.25

F3
1/8" ply Rx cavity

F4
1/2" balsa

F5
1/8" ply (bottom)

F20
1/4" balsa

F15

F10a & b

Undercarriage mounting straps.

F17

Lower-side view

F17

F17

Servo tray mounting struts.

Undercarriage mounting blind nut.

Wing mounting block
make up from F16 & F17.

F15
Carve from balsa.

Epoxy 3-ply F16 to underside.

Side elevation

F15
Forward elevation

F16
1/16" 3-ply

F15
Plan view

Aft elevation

F6

F15
See mounting block details.

F16

F15

F7

F16

F19
1/2" balsa

F18
1/2" balsa

F8
1/8" ply

1/4" balsa

F9   F9

F10a & b

F11

F12

F6
1/8" ply

F18
1/2"

Scrap balsa

F19
1/2"

F8
1/8" ply

F22 1/4" balsa doubler with blind nut.

1/16" ply (a) and 1/8" balsa (b).

F10a   F10b

F11

F12

Typical Rx

F9

Typical 8oz tank

Typical flight battery pa...

Typical 3 x servo + switch tray

F17

F17

Scrap 1/8" balsa pushrod outlets.

F1b

Typical spinner 2 3/4" dia. white.

F4
1/2" balsa

F21
1/16" ply flight switch plate.

F17

1/16" ply 4 off

Reinforcing plates for servo tray supports.

Servo snake to carry aerial wire to tail exit.

Recommended centre of gravity 2-3/4" aft of the wing leading edge.

Match Sheet 4 to sheet 5 at "A" and "B" register marks.

Ryan NYP: sheet 5: fuselage

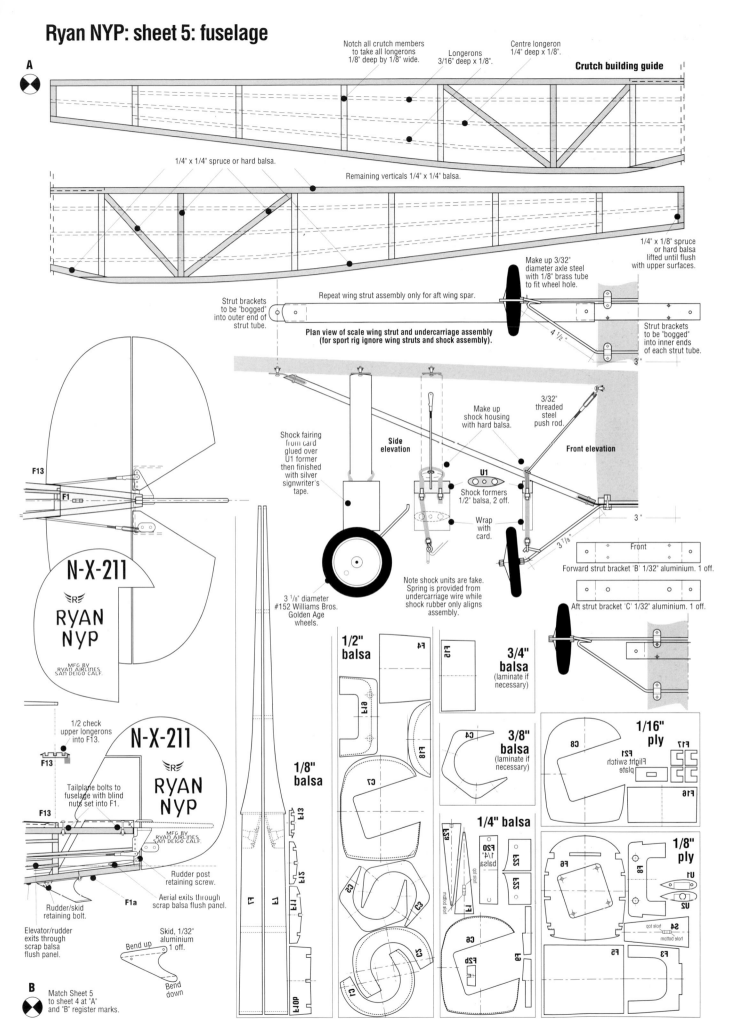

A

Notch all crutch members to take all longerons 1/8" deep by 1/8" wide.

Longerons 3/16" deep x 1/8".

Centre longeron 1/4" deep x 1/8".

Crutch building guide

1/4" x 1/4" spruce or hard balsa.

Remaining verticals 1/4" x 1/4" balsa.

1/4" x 1/8" spruce or hard balsa lifted until flush with upper surfaces.

Make up 3/32" diameter axle steel with 1/8" brass tube to fit wheel hole.

Strut brackets to be "bogged" into outer end of strut tube.

Repeat wing strut assembly only for aft wing spar.

Plan view of scale wing strut and undercarriage assembly (for sport rig ignore wing struts and shock assembly).

Strut brackets to be "bogged" into inner ends of each strut tube.

4 1/2"

3"

F13

F1

N-X-211

RYAN NYP

MFG BY RYAN AIRLINES SAN DEIGO CALF.

Shock fairing from card glued over U1 former then finished with silver signwriter's tape.

Side elevation

Make up shock housing with hard balsa.

3/32" threaded steel push rod.

Front elevation

U1

Shock formers 1/2" balsa, 2 off.

Wrap with card.

3/32"

3"

3 7/8"

3 1/8" diameter #152 Williams Bros. Golden Age wheels.

Note shock units are fake. Spring is provided from undercarriage wire while shock rubber only aligns assembly.

Front

Forward strut bracket 'B' 1/32" aluminium. 1 off.

Aft strut bracket 'C' 1/32" aluminium. 1 off.

1/2 check upper longerons into F13.

F13

Tailplane bolts to fuselage with blind nuts set into F1.

F13

F13

F1a

Rudder post retaining screw.

Aerial exits through scrap balsa flush panel.

Rudder/skid retaining bolt.

F1a

Elevator/rudder exits through scrap balsa flush panel.

Skid, 1/32" aluminium 1 off.

Bend up

Bend down

N-X-211

RYAN NYP

MFG BY RYAN AIRLINES SAN DEIGO CALF.

1/2" balsa

F4

F14

3/4" balsa (laminate if necessary)

1/8" balsa

C7

C4

3/8" balsa (laminate if necessary)

1/16" ply

C8

F21 Flight switch plate

F17

F16

1/4" balsa

F20 1/4" balsa

C6

C5

C3

C1

F2b

C2

1/8" ply

F6

F8

U1

U2

F5

F3

B Match Sheet 5 to sheet 4 at "A" and "B" register marks.

Practice

■ Building the Fuselage

Start constructing the fuselage by making up the ¼" square spruce and balsa crutches. As you can't pin through spruce, use the little clamps as shown in the diagram. Wood screws can also act as stops for wedge clamps (Photo 17:21). For the prototype, epoxy glue was used on the basic frame.

Note from the plan that the last vertical member is ⅛" deep and held up flush with the upper face of the crutch.

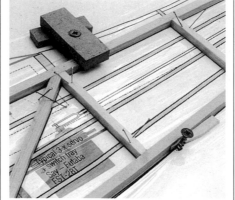

Photo 17:21 *Two clamping methods for holding down and tensioning spruce while you build the fuselage.*

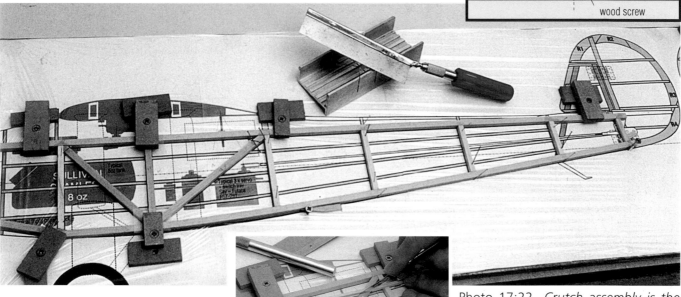

Mark the positions where the central ¼" x ⅛" longeron and ³⁄₁₆" x ⅛" upper and lower longerons will go then notch out their slots to ⅛" deep. Test the fit as you go with a scrap balsa longeron.

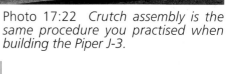

Photo 17:23 *Mark in where the longerons will fit.*

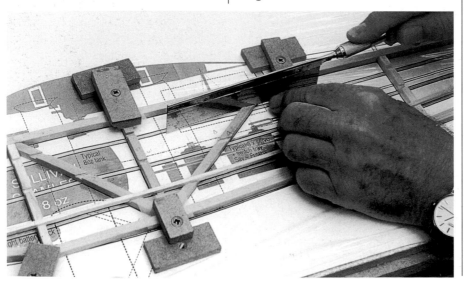

Because

Cut a set of scrap packing blocks and straps. Drill the straps to take wood screws and use them when you want to clamp down components onto your building board. These simple clamps become part of your tool kit. Also, a few finely tapered wedges will always come in handy.

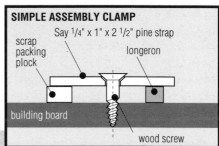

SIMPLE ASSEMBLY CLAMP
Say ¼" x 1" x 2 ½" pine strap
scrap packing plock
longeron
building board
wood screw

Photo 17:22 *Crutch assembly is the same procedure you practised when building the Piper J-3.*

You may wonder why the last vertical member of the fuselage crutch is only ⅛" deep and is held up to the top face of the crutch. This is to provide a recess for the rudder post to slide into, making it possible to have removable tail surfaces. And, that will make covering a whole lot easier later on. It also lets you remove any damaged part of the tail and make a new one without resorting to major surgery.

Photo 17:24 *Use a razor saw or sharp scalpel to notch out the vertical members for longerons to be inserted later.*

136

■ Notch out the spruce longerons at the tail end of each crutch as shown in photo 17:25.

Cut all the topside spacers and hold them down on the plan. Bring the crutches into position (the top edge of each crutch is straight so that for assembly they can be turned upside down and held flat on the building board). Add the underside spacers and hold them in place by squeezing the crutches together with scrap ply 'U' shaped clamps cut to size (photo 17:26).

When everything's snug, square and true, run cyano into all the joints and leave to harden.

■ Fit the longerons into the notched sides of each crutch. When they lie at the right depth, cyano (photo 17:27).

■ Add the servo tray bearers and ply reinforcing plates F17, fixing the tray with its servos in place at the same time to get a good fit.

Fit out the hardware: engine and mount, fuel tank, plumbing and throttle linkage; even firing up the servos to get the right linkage functions at this early stage while you have clear access.

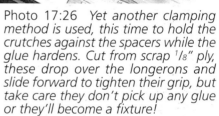

Photo 17:25 *The spruce longerons are notched out to make provision for the rudder post. Clean out any glue before bringing them together for assembly.*

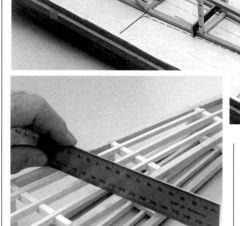

Photo 17:26 *Yet another clamping method is used, this time to hold the crutches against the spacers while the glue hardens. Cut from scrap ⅛" ply, these drop over the longerons and slide forward to tighten their grip, but take care they don't pick up any glue or they'll become a fixture!*

Photo 17:27 *Fit the longerons to the correct depth so there's a straight line from the centre longeron out to the top or bottom corners. Sand if necessary.*

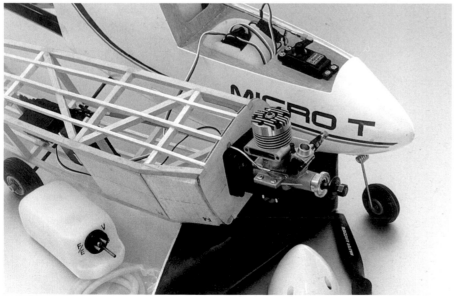

Photo 17:28 *Set up the servo tray and linkages as soon as you can – access will never be easier than right now (to fire up the servos before the radio and battery gear is installed connect them into a 'going' model). Note the fuel tank outlets are labelled to save a lot of confusion later on.*

Photo 17:29 *Test fit the tank, drill out the feed line passages and test-connect the tubes to confirm they have unrestricted routes.*

Practice

Why?

Because

■ Make up the two wing mounting blocks – dowel block F8/F19 and wing bolt block F15/16/10a/10b (photo 17:30). Epoxy and leave to harden.

We are now going to use a technique that you will find useful for all sorts of tricky assembly situations. In this case, the hard bit is getting the mounting blocks in the right place on the fuselage so the wing fits properly.

Firstly, fit each block to the wing, making sure they fit snugly (photo 17:31). Now place the wing on the fuselage. When it's lined up, check that the blocks make good contact with the fuselage longerons. Put epoxy on the contact areas, reposition the wing and bind it in position with masking tape to hold it true until cured. Then you can disconnect the wing from the mounting blocks which remain on the fuselage, in the correct place and properly aligned.

■ Completing the fuselage and engine cowling is straightforward, so proceed by following the plan, the photos and their captions.

Photo 17:30 *Locating the two wing mounting blocks onto the fuselage: the dowel block forward and the wing bolt block aft are ready to be fixed.*

This seems a very clever way of holding individual parts in exactly the right place while they are being glued. What other situations would be suitable for using this technique?

Photo 17:31 *Fit both blocks to the wing. Position the wing in its final place on the fuselage. Epoxy. Leave to cure.*

Photo 17:32 *When the glue is hard unbolt the wing and withdraw it from the dowel block. Both blocks are now fixed to the fuselage in their correct position.*

Photo 17:33 *Laminate the cowling in its three sections. Shape the centre section then laminate it to the aft section.*

Photo 17:34 *Drill out the mounting holes, insert washers then screw the aft part to the firewall. Now align and expoxy the front section to the cowling.*

There are lots of times. When aligning an engine cowling, undercarriage assembly or some other detachable part, it's often easier to attach a mounting block to the part, then put glue on the mounting block and set everything in place. When the glue's hard you can just detach the part and the mounting block stays in its final place on the model.

138

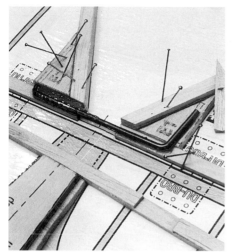

Photo 17:35 *The wire torque rod is set into grooves cut in the upper and lower spars and fillets, then epoxied.*

■ The tailplane is made in the conventional way, with the two elevator halves fixed together with a wire 'U' torque rod epoxied into the spar and fillet sandwich (photo 17:35 and 17:36). Mark the position of the wire so you can avoid it when you later fit the elevator horn.

Fit the tailplane by taping it accurately in position, then drill down through it and the plate F1. Fitting blind nuts to F1's underside (photos 17:37 and 17:38).

■ Test fit the fin by sliding its leading edge down through the tailplane and out through the underside of the fuselage, while easing the rudder post into its slot at the back of the fuselage. From ¼" scrap make up the lower guide to fit the leading edge where it exits the fuselage. Remove the fin and glue. Try the rudder in place using hinges as shown in the plan. The only tricky bit is trimming the lower hinge flap to seat properly into the 2-piece rudder post.

■ Make up the aluminium sheet tail skid and test fit with the fin in place (photo 17:39).

Disassemble all components for painting and covering.

Why do I have to use epoxy glue when I'm making laminated parts?

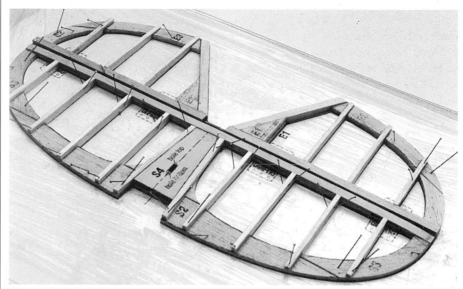

Photo 17:36 *Tailplane and elevator are assembled against each other to ensure the hinges align accurately and there's a minimum air gap. Sand back the top and bottom edges of the elevator spar to allow the elevator movement.*

Photo 17:37 *Test fit the fin's leading edge down through the tailplane and out the fuselage while you ease the rudder post into its slot in the fuselage.*

Photo 17:39 *The tail skid screws to the fuselage and bolts through the leading edge of the fin to retain both.*

Perhaps it's not strictly essential but glues that rely on evaporation take a very long time to harden if they are enclosed within a laminate.

Photo 17:38 *Everything should fit neatly with the fin vertical and aligned with the centre of the fuselage.*

With my model flying from a relatively rough grass runway I found this tail skid was fairly vulnerable and I ended up replacing it with a rounded balsa half teardrop block. If scale is not too important to you, you may consider the same alternative.

Practice

Why?

Because

■ The OS Max. FP 0.25 engine muffler cannot clear the fuselage of this model. You have various options. The two most straightforward are to either select a 'Pitts' type alternative and delete the lower dummy cylinderhead or, if you or a friend have some metalwork skills, make a simple adaptor that relocates the standard muffler further out (the plans allow for the latter).

Either way, assemble your unit then test fit the cowling base until it can freely slide on and off.

■ Make the dummy cylinderheads from disks cut from some suitable plastic sheet. I used a circle cutter and ABS sheet of three thicknesses.

Assemble (with wet solvent between the layers) on a long ¼" bolt, tighten and dip in solvent. Leave to harden.

Photos 17:40 *The standard muffler arrangement of our engine needed modifying to increase the standoff distance from the centre line.*

The adaptor used on the prototype model was made without sophisticated tools. The block was squared off with the disk sander, the holes measured and marked off with a scriber and rule, then I used a drill press to align the holes. To cut out the exhaust passage I drilled lots of small holes and carefully cut away the remainder with a very small and sharp cold chisel. It's amazing how well you can work aluminium if you just keep working away, one piece at a time and in no great rush.

My disks of plastic have lots of little rough edges and I don't seem to be able to get them off.

I had some of that too. Firstly I put the ¼" bolt into my drill chuck and spun each dummy cylinderhead quite fast while I held fine sandpaper against it, finishing it off by painting

Photo 17:41 *A plumber's circle cutter does quite a good job of cutting out components for a dummy radial engine. If you want to cut out several at a time, hold the layers together with clamps or vice-grips.*

In each head, drill out the six screw holes and a large central hole, wide enough to clear a glow plug at the top and reduced to fit the plug's thread. Saw and file grooves across the heads to represent the cooling fins. To lighten, drill out as much of the inside as you can safely remove. Spray paint, then add old plugs and screws. Add a locating disk of balsa to the cowling core to take each cylinder.

Photo 17:42 *The dummy engine construction is real model maker's art!*

solvent over the fins until the edges dissolved away. When they hardened they were quite smooth (well almost). I painted them silver.

140

Practice

■ The scale undercarriage calls for quite accurate wire bending and a good vice will make it easier. Where the distance between bends cannot be directly taken from the drawings, actual measurements are shown. Also, study the photos so you understand the layout before you start.

The front leg should be silver-soldered to the aft leg. To make the job easier and more accurate the prototype model undercarriage was assembled in a jig (photo 17:43).

You'll find the wheels have ⅛″ axle holes. If you're clever with a fine drill follow the system shown in photo 17:44 and add a ⅛″ brass tube sleeve over the ³/₃₂″ wire. The wire should stop short of the full wheel width so you can drill a tiny hole through the brass tube and insert a little split pin. Soft-solder the tube and inside washer to the axle wire.

■ Use medium size fuel tube to set up the undercarriage shock absorbers. You'll find that you can push the tubular retaining plugs into the tube making it too fat to pass through the holes in the former U1. This allows you to adjust the tension on the tube and, once in place, it will stay put.

After it is in place and adjusted satisfactorily, wrap card to form the outer fairing, cover with silver signwriter's tape and glue the inner top edge to former U1 to keep it in place. Keep scraps of these materials because the fairings are replaced rather than repaired (it's easier).

Follow the plan and all will become clear!

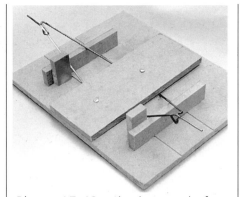

Photo 17:43 *Jigging up before soldering the undercarriage wires.*

Photo 17:45 *Test fitting of the scale undercarriage, wing struts and suspension assembly.*

Because

The undercarriage jig is just a flat piece of particle board with two grooves cut across it which locate the legs at the right spacing. When you screw a flat down on top, it will lock the legs in place. Pack up the outer legs to the right angle and bring them together for silver-soldering.

Photo 17:44 *Looking towards the front (starboard wheel) showing the suspension hook, axle washer, tube and splitpin assembly.*

Fuel tubing can be like a rubber band. But, instead of having to tie knots you can get the same result in a neater way if you poke oversize hollow plugs into the tube. These will cause solid obstructions which will prevent the tube from sliding through holes that it would normally easily slide through. Place the plugs with an insertion rod made from ³/₃₂″ wire soldered inside ⅛″ brass tube (photo 17:45).

Photo 17:46 *The full treatment: the engine dummy complete with fake fuel leads, undercarriage shocks enclosed and the paint job sealed beneath a layer of clear polyurethane to reduce fuel damage. Now, let's go flying!*

Practice	*Why?*	Because
⬇	⬇	⬇

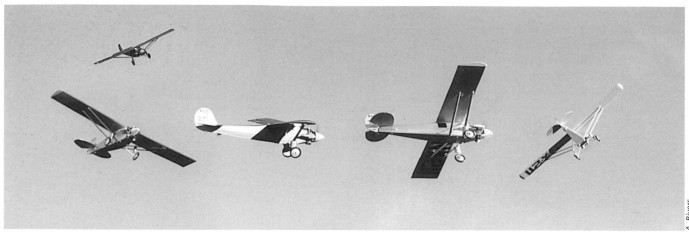

A. Rivers

Photo 17:47 *The Ryan is a pretty little plane combining good manners with good looks — from whatever angle, in the air or on the ground I think you'll find this is a very satisfactory little model.*

■ The prototype model has the wheels, spinner, cowling and forward section of the fuselage painted in metallic silver then signage applied, all under clear. All 'fabric' areas are covered in silver shrink film and the wing registrations are cut from signwriter's tape, as are the windows. These and the door are framed in chrome tape. The results look great.

■ With the wings just resting in place, the aileron servo plugged into the receiver and the power turned on, double check all servo directions are correct. With all transmitter trims set to neutral, adjust any clevises so all control surfaces rest at neutral (page 92). With all transmitter dual rates off compare control surface movements with the recommendations shown on the plan. Alter any throws to match the plans.

■ Fit the wings and test the balancing point of your model against the recommended location shown on the plan and adjust accordingly (note: a slight nose-heavy position is acceptable – a tail-heavy position is NOT).

■ Read the third column on this page and quietly think things through before your first flight. Then, when you start to feel really comfortable practise some of the manoeuvres shown on page 143.

Now that I'm ready to test fly my model, what can I expect in the way of differences in handling behaviour from the Micro T-Mk IV?

The first and biggest difference you will find is in the takeoff. With the main wheels not far in front of the balancing point, the model will tend to tip forward onto its propeller, especially at low speed. To correct you need to apply up elevator for the first part of the run, gradually reducing it to neutral as soon as the speed builds up. Take care you don't lift off too soon or you'll drop a wing and perhaps crash.

Being a 'taildragger' you will also find the model does not automatically 'track' straight so you must steer it all the way. Let it come out of line too far and you could 'ground loop'. Shut the throttle!

Photo 17:48 *You will find the Ryan is a practical weekend flier, robust enough to take some knocks, reliable and still, more or less, a scale model. Happy flying.*

Having now scared you properly, once in the air you'll enjoy a little more power, a quicker response and more manoeuverability.

Cross-wind Takeoff (Mode II)

Remember, if the plane's going *from* you, the rudder stick leans *down* wind. Ailerons oppose the rudder. Bank to windward.

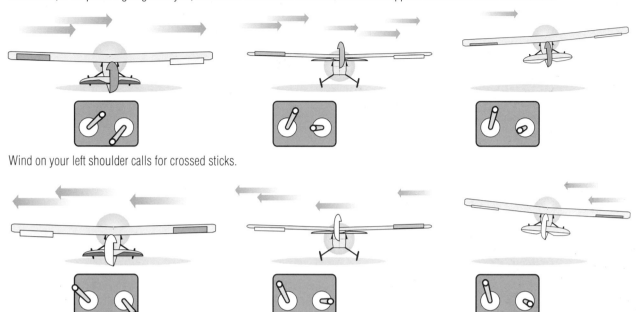

Wind on your left shoulder calls for crossed sticks.

Wind on your right shoulder calls for splayed sticks.

Cross-wind Landing (Mode II)

Remember, if the plane's coming *towards* you, the rudder stick leans *up* wind. Ailerons oppose the rudder. Bank to windward.

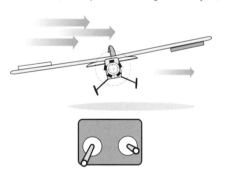

The objective is to have the plane sideslip into the wind just equaling the down wind drift of the plane. The plane then tracks straight along the landing strip through to the roll out.

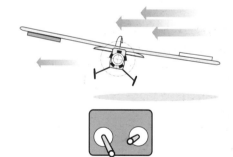

Tail draggers and ground loops

The dynamics of a tail dragger aircraft are more complicated than those of a tricycle geared plane. The aerodynamics (once the craft is airborne) are the same, but, while a tail dragger is running along the ground it is potentially unstable. The drag from the main wheels is ahead of the centre of mass (otherwise the plane would overbalance forward). Just like an arrow flying backwards, once the tail lifts off the ground the tail dragger wants to reverse ends. If it succeeds the resulting manoeuvre is what is called a 'ground loop'. Your task is to immediately respond to any deviation from the line and correct it with rudder. Be prepared so if a ground loop develops, shut the throttle, fast.

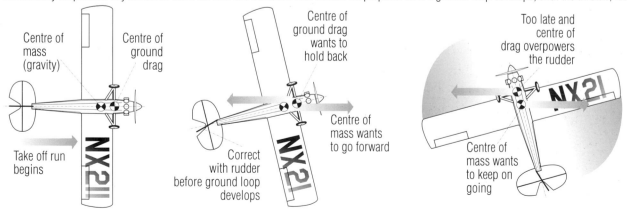

Chapter 18: Building a 1/4 Scale D.H.71

Practice ↓

Why? ↓

Because ↓

■ Start a controversy by saying you are building a Tiger Moth monoplane!
This little-known aircraft has largely been lost from the history books, but in fact it was the first de Havilland design to carry the now famous title, 'Tiger Moth'.

Only two aircraft were built. They were intended to provide parallel test beds for comparing the company's new 5.23 litre Gipsy engine with their standard Cirrus, G-EBQU being the Gipsy-powered plane.

G-EBQU broke the 100km speed record at 186.47 mph on 24 August 1927 and the British altitude record of 19,191 ft while still climbing at 1,000 ft/min! After being shipped to Australia in 1930, on 17 September of that year and re-registered as VH-UNH it crashed, killing its inexperienced pilot.

The other aircraft, G-EBRV raced in the 1927 King's Cup Race but was withdrawn when weather conditions deteriorated to a dangerous level. This aircraft was destroyed by German bombing in October 1940.

■ What I find most interesting about this little plane is its historical lineage. It was conceived at a time when huge amounts of development money were being expended on Schneider Cup supremacy yet this little plane appears to have been developed on a shoestring budget. Later, when aircraft competed in the great air race from UK to Australia, it was the same company's D.H.88 Comet which, produced in record time and numbers, took top honours. Note the many obvious similarities in the two de Havilland aircraft.

Photo 18:1 *De Havilland D.H.71 'Tiger Moth' G-EBQU at Hendon, England, 30 June 1928. Note the original open cockpit which was later replaced with the streamlined semi-enclosed canopy, neither giving the pilot good visibility!*

Photo 18:2 *The prototype model is based upon G-EBQU, the original Gipsy-engined version which was eventually shipped to Australia.*

Why did you choose this particular aircraft to model?

As a subject for your first 1/4 scale, size was the first attraction (the original was just 22'6" wing span). It is also a classically clean design and, like the original, the model would turn in a sparkling performance from relatively low engine power.

Photo 18:3 *Just as this D.H.88 Comet is credited with being the forerunner of the Mosquito, surely the original Tiger Moth deserves more recognition for the part it must have played in the evolution of this famous de Havilland racer.*

De Havilland D.H.71 'Tiger Moth'

67½" span scale model aircraft for 4-channel radio control
and 0.70 cu in 4-stroke or 0.50 cu in 2-stroke engines
From 'AIRCRAFT WORKSHOP:
Learn to make models that FLY'
by Kelvin Shacklock ©

Specifications:	Full-size	1/4 scale
	(normal wing)	
Wingspan:	22' 6"	67½"
Length overall:	18' 7"	57"
Wing area:	76.5 sq ft	4.94 sq ft
Weight:	905 lb	119 oz
Wing loading:	11 lb 11 oz sq ft	24 oz sq ft
Power:	135hp Gipsy	0.70 4-stroke
Max speed:	166 mph	

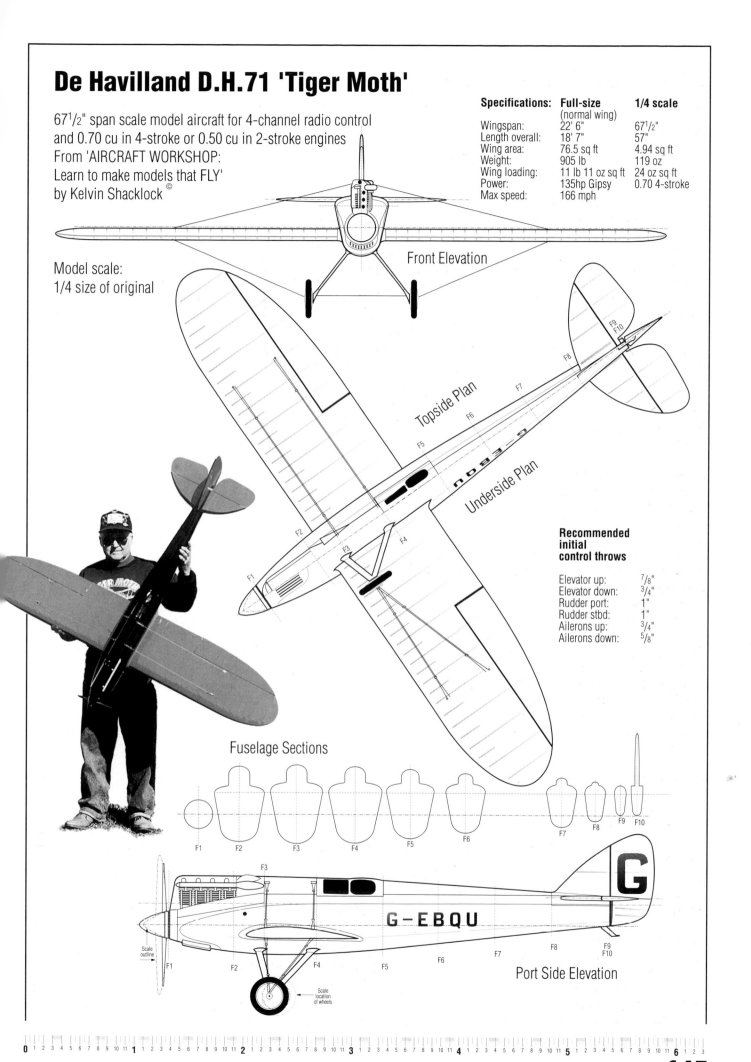

Model scale:
1/4 size of original

Front Elevation

Topside Plan

Underside Plan

G-EBQU

**Recommended
initial
control throws**

Elevator up:	⁷/₈"
Elevator down:	³/₄"
Rudder port:	1"
Rudder stbd:	1"
Ailerons up:	³/₄"
Ailerons down:	⁵/₈"

Fuselage Sections

F1 F2 F3 F4 F5 F6 F7 F8 F9 F10

G
G-EBQU

Scale
outline →
F1 F2 F3 F4 F5 F6 F7 F8 F9 F10

Scale
location
of wheels

Port Side Elevation

■ Again, a sound building board can almost guarantee you an accurate model that flies true.

In researching this model, what sources did you find for information?

There were several good reference pieces: The English magazine *'Aero Modeller'*, May 1974 carried an article and drawings by Mr Harry Robinson (reprints available from Nexus plan service); *'Flight'* magazine of September 22, 1927 was excellent and the book *'De Havilland Aircraft'* was a third.

Now, invest a little time and effort preparing to build, then the actual building process is easier, faster and more accurate.

In this case the building board is a critical part of the aeroplane.

The original plane has a flat wing (no dihedral). Build the model that way and it looks as if the wingtips droop, so we are going to put in a gentle curve upwards to compensate.

The building board is a carefully designed platform which is dished up towards the wingtips and twists in a little washout while you are building the wing.

Make up the board to stage 4 as shown in the drawings and you can't go far wrong, with one exception –

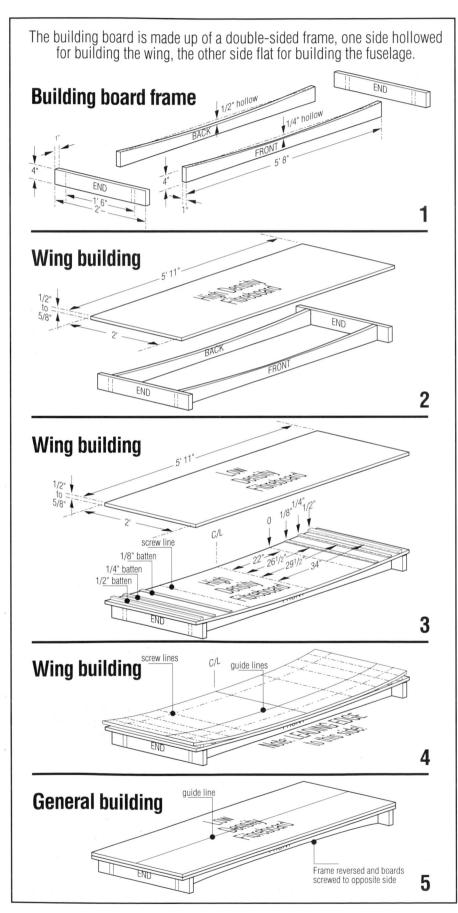

The building board is made up of a double-sided frame, one side hollowed for building the wing, the other side flat for building the fuselage.

Building board frame

1/2" hollow
BACK
1/4" hollow
FRONT
END
1"
4"
END
4"
1' 6"
2"
1"
5' 8"

1

Wing building

5' 11"
High Density Fibreboard
1/2" to 5/8"
2'
BACK
FRONT
END
END

2

Wing building

5' 11"
Low Density Fibreboard
1/2" to 5/8"
2'
0 1/8" 1/4" 1/2"
22" 26½" 29½" 34"
C/L
screw line
1/8" batten
1/4" batten
1/2" batten
High Density Fibreboard
END

3

Wing building

screw lines
C/L
guide lines
Note: LEADING EDGE to this side
END

4

General building

guide line
Low Density Fibreboard
END
Frame reversed and boards screwed to opposite side

5

Building Board Materials:

High density fibreboard, $^1/_2$"–$^5/_8$" sheet 6' x 2' (not less than 5'8" x 18")
Low density fibreboard, $^1/_2$"–$^5/_8$" sheet 6' x 2' (not less than 5'8" x 18")
Dressed pine planks, (ex 1" x 4"), 2 @ 6', 2 @ 2'

Scrap battens, 2 @ 24" x 1" x $^1/_8$" 2 @ 24" x 1" x $^1/_4$" 2 @ 24" x 1" x $^1/_2$"

Nails, screws.

when you build the wing **make certain the front of the wing is to the front of the board.** Get it wrong and you could have a very nasty aircraft! The building board is topped off with the low density fibreboard to let you easily pin, nail and screw into the surface.

Mark the centrelines so you can align the plan accurately.

Practice

■ The plans

When the building board is ready enlarge the wing plans just as we did for the Micro T.

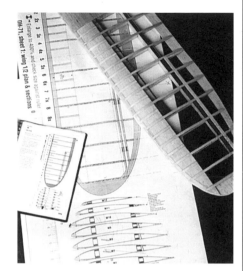

Photo 18:4 *To again confirm the effectiveness of the enlarging technique described on page 21, I photocopy/enlarged an early proof of these pages and obtained excellent full-size plans from which the prototype model was built.*

Mount the joined sheets on the building board, *ensuring the leading edge faces the front of the building board.* Cover with cling wrap or waxed paper.

■ Building the wing

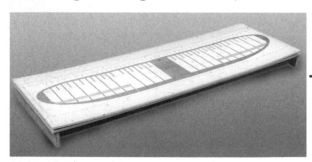

Photo 18:5 *The plans taped out on the building board and covered with a film of cling wrap, ready to be built upon.*

Here we shall use some new techniques like laminated balsa sheet for the aileron trailing edges and wingtips plus split-cut laminated strips for the outer leading edges.

Look over Sheet 3 and identify the parts and where they are used.

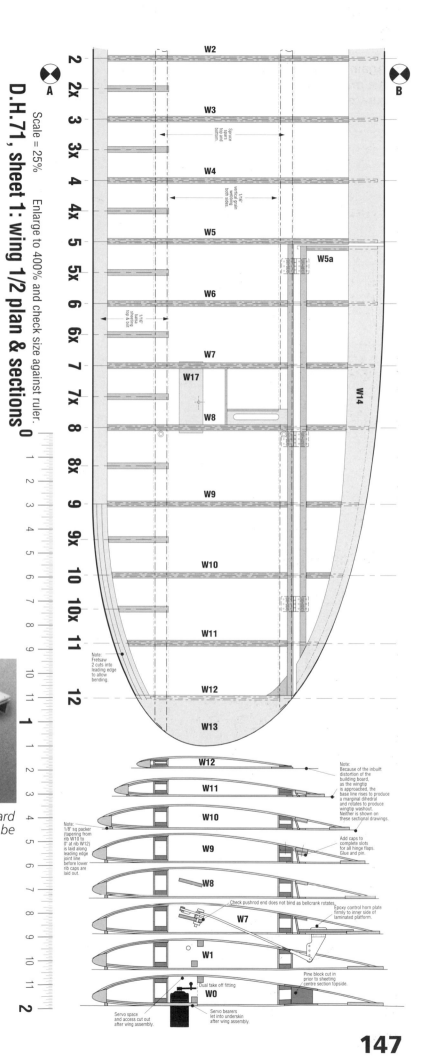

D.H.71, sheet 1: wing 1/2 plan & sections

Scale = 25%   Enlarge to 400% and check size against ruler.

Practice

Like the Ryan, these wing ribs are capped top and bottom so the underside is laid up first.

■ Begin with four W14 trailing edges. Epoxy laminate 2 of each face-to-face and pin down on the plan so they adopt the set curve of the building board surface. Leave them to harden while you cut out the other components.

Make up 4 main spars measuring about 6'7" (spliced and epoxied if necessary to get the length). From the plan mark off on these the centreline and rib stations. Chamfer the outer ends of the spars from $^3/_{16}$" thick at rib W9 down to $^1/_{16}$" thick at the tips.

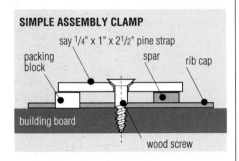

SIMPLE ASSEMBLY CLAMP

say $^1/_4$" x 1" x 2$^1/_2$" pine strap

packing block

spar

rib cap

building board

wood screw

Photo 18:6 *Laying up the wing with the spar and leading edge sheeting assembly lying on the left, ready to be glued down over the rib capping. It will be clamped down in the same way as the aft spar is shown. Note all the holding pins are clear of the position to be taken by the assembly (the half rib capping has been taken beyond the spar line to allow pinning).*

148

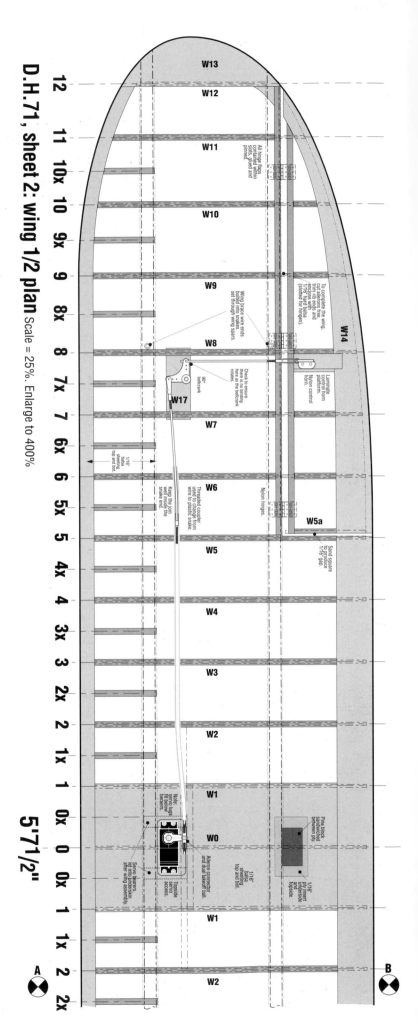

D.H.71, sheet 2: wing 1/2 plan Scale = 25%. Enlarge to 400%

5'71/2"

Practice

On the upper/aft spar notch the underside to recess the aileron hinges (see W9 cross section on Sheet 1 for details).

Cut the underside leading edge sheeting to size (diagonally butt-joint to make up the full span length). Glue one spar to its aft edge and set aside to harden.

■ Take a full span length of ⅛" square balsa scrap, and beginning from rib W10 taper it to zero thickness by rib W12. Lay it on the plan along the aft side of the leading edge. This is used as a packer to raise the rib capping and sheeting up to the curve of the wing ribs (see cross sections).

From ¹⁄₁₆" balsa lay up centre section sheeting (with the ¹⁄₁₆" ply mounting plate let in) and with ¼" wide strips make up the aileron cutouts and all full rib capping. Pin in position on the plan, gluing each to the trailing edge as you go. Add the ½ rib capping but extend each back past the spar line for pinning. Take a second wing spar and glue it at all contact points then clamp it down in the aft spar position (photo 18:6). Add glue, then lower the forward spar with its leading edge sheeting into place and clamp down.

Photo 18:7 *After the 'D' section sheeting is complete, the leading is pulled in toward the tip and, when seated correctly, flooded with cyano.*

D.H.71, sheet 3: wing components

Scale = 25%   Enlarge to 400% and check size against ruler

[ruler: 0 1 2 3 4 5 6 7 8 9 10 11 **1** 1 2 3 4 5 6]

Using a hot iron, transfer down onto dry balsa

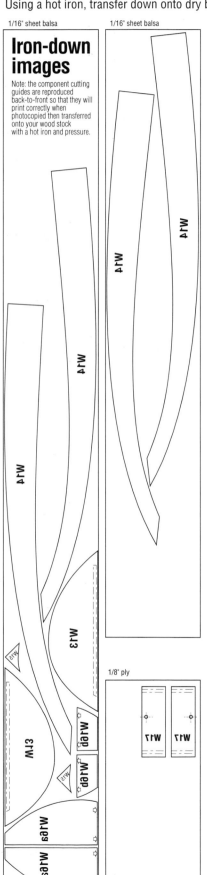
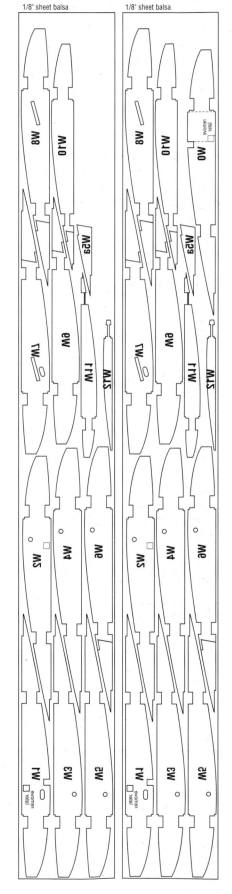

Iron-down images

Note: the component cutting guides are reproduced back-to-front so that they will print correctly when photocopied then transferred onto your wood stock with a hot iron and pressure.

AIRCRAFT WORKSHOP: Learn to make models that FLY

149

Practice

■ Proceed in the conventional way to position the ribs, assembling the centre section with the servo mounting spars inserted before gluing. Lay the upper spars in place and weigh down to hold the ribs in place as the glue hardens. Work out toward the tips. With all ribs in position, add the upper spars and web with ¹/₁₆" balsa.

Apply the ¹/₁₆" balsa sheeting to the upper leading edge but, before sheeting the centre section, insert the wing mounting block, the ¹/₁₆" ply panel and support packing (photo 18.8).

■ With the W17 ¹/₈" ply bellcrank platforms and aileron horn insets in place, temporarily fit the aileron servo, bellcranks, horns and linkages. From scrap balsa make up the pushrod outlets and their supports per the plan (photo 18:9).

Temporarily fit the hinges into their spar recesses and cap with scrap balsa. The aileron hinge flaps fit flat against the capping strip and are then overlaid with recessed scrap to make up their slots.

Remove the aileron horns and their linkages then cut the ailerons free from the wing, sliding them off their hinges. Complete the aileron bays and aileron leading edges as shown on the plan. Refit and check for freedom of travel with minimum air gap. Note: the hinges are not glued and pinned until during the covering stages.

It's quite a good practice to refit the linkages and fire up the servo to confirm sufficient movement is maintained. Check that nothing in the system is catching or binding. After all, it is easier to correct any little faults now before the wing is covered!

■ Sand off to covering quality and set the wing aside.

Why?

You mention 'spliced' together if necessary to get the length. What's this 'spliced'?

You don't really get too helpful when you say to finish off the aileron bays and aileron leading edges.

Because

A join is often needed when you can't get wood that's long enough for the job. A 'splice' is an angle joint which is intended to give maximum gluing surface. So, make long, narrow joins wherever more than one strip of wood must be joined to make a longer strip. Where several joined strips are being used in a structure, position their joints in different places and avoid maximum stress areas.

Photo 18:8 *Pay particular attention to building up the wing mounting block so all squeezing action of the wing bolt is absorbed by solid pine and plywood.*

Photo 18:9 *The aileron linkage is conventional, using a 90° bellcrank. Aileron differential is achieved by moving the aileron horn toward the trailing edge.*

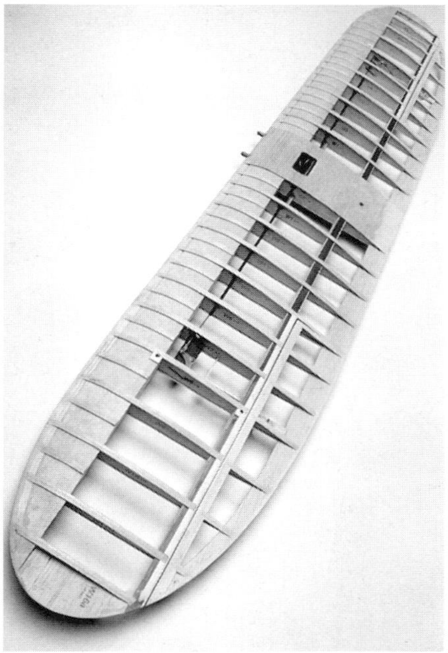

Photo 18:10 *The wing completed with the ailerons trimmed out and hinged. Note the photo shows dowels. These are actually drilled out only after fitting to the fuselage.*

As you've probably noticed, fine description can sound far more complicated and off-putting than the actual process deserves. Just follow the cross section drawings and you'll find it's really no big deal.

150

D.H.71, sheet 4: tail surfaces

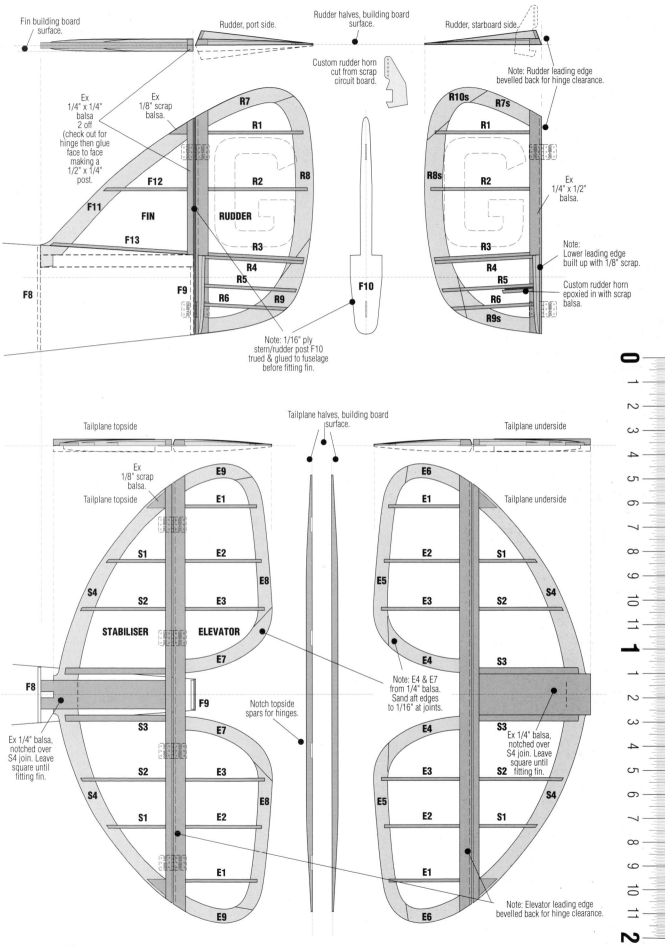

Fin building board surface.

Rudder, port side.

Rudder halves, building board surface.

Rudder, starboard side.

Custom rudder horn cut from scrap circuit board.

Ex 1/4" x 1/4" balsa 2 off (check out for hinge then glue face to face making a 1/2" x 1/4" post.

Ex 1/8" scrap balsa.

R7

R1

R8

F12

F11

FIN

R2

RUDDER

F13

R3

R4

R5

F9

R6

R9

F8

Note: Rudder leading edge bevelled back for hinge clearance.

R10s

R7s

R1

R8s

R2

R3

Ex 1/4" x 1/2" balsa.

Note: Lower leading edge built up with 1/8" scrap.

R4

R5

R6

R9s

Custom rudder horn epoxied in with scrap balsa.

F10

Note: 1/16" ply stern/rudder post F10 trued & glued to fuselage before fitting fin.

Tailplane topside

Tailplane halves, building board surface.

Tailplane underside

Ex 1/8" scrap balsa.

Tailplane topside

E9

E1

S1

E2

S4

S2

E3

STABILISER

ELEVATOR

E7

F8

F9

Notch topside spars for hinges.

Ex 1/4" balsa, notched over S4 join. Leave square until fitting fin.

S3

E7

S2

E3

S4

E8

S1

E2

E1

E9

E6

E1

E2

S1

E5

E3

S2

S4

E4

S3

Note: E4 & E7 from 1/4" balsa. Sand aft edges to 1/16" at joints.

E4

S3

Ex 1/4" balsa, notched over S4 join. Leave square until fitting fin.

E3

S2

E5

S4

E2

S1

E1

E6

Note: Elevator leading edge bevelled back for hinge clearance.

Tailplane underside

Scale = 25%   Enlarge to 400% and check size against ruler.

Practice

■ The tail surfaces:

This is the usual process of working flat on the building board (which you will have reassembled as a flat surface). Because the rudder and tailplanes are quite thick and curved on their outer faces, we make them in two halves, each flat on the centreline. When the halves are finished we glue them face-to-face.

This method makes fitting hinges easy because we recess the spars before we begin gluing them. It forms beautifully accurate slots in the finished panels. Also, it lets us recess a piano wire reinforcement 'U' brace right into the heart of the elevator connection shaft which is a design weakness in many models.

When you are gluing the tail surface halves together hold them firmly by binding with masking tape round the spar areas and with bulldog clips on the edges. Just make sure the hinge slots are cleaned out of any surplus glue.

■ On the prototype model I incorporated a custom rudder control horn which was cut from an off-cut of an electronic circuit board. This is a good, strong material which can be sawn, filed and drilled to form all sorts of linkage arms, bellcranks and the like. It works well. If you follow this approach do ensure the pushrod holes you drill are a good, neat fit on the clevis shaft. Epoxy it in place and surround it with scrap balsa to give the covering a surface to 'land' on.

■ The fin (which isn't made in two halves) is for incorporation into the fuselage and is reinforced with a $^1/_{16}$" ply rudder post that is added only after the tailplane and elevator assembly has been permanently fitted. This means you can't finish off the tail end of the fuselage until quite late in the building process.

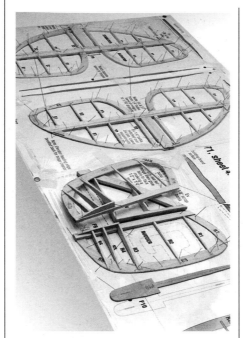

Photo 18:11 *All tail surfaces except the fin are built flat on the plan in the usual way. The difference here is that you make pairs of each which join face-to-face on the centre plane. This way they are built truly flat although in fact they have curved outer faces. Like all laminating jobs, I prefer to use a non air-drying glue so have epoxied mine together.*

Photo 18:12 *Before you join the top and bottom faces of the elevator, bend up a $^3/_{32}$" wire 'U' brace and recess it into both faces then epoxy everything together (mark the wire's position on an outside face so you can avoid it when adding the elevator control horn).*

D.H.71, sheet 5: tail surface components

Scale = 25%.
Enlarge to 400% and check size against ruler

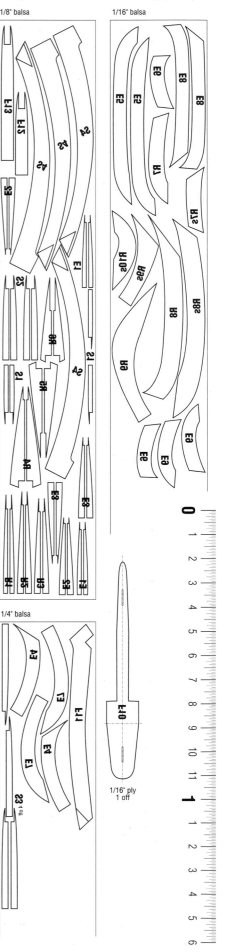

152

Practice ⬇	*Why?* ⬇	Because ⬇

■ **The engine:**

We are now going to talk 4-stroke engines. I couldn't visualise this old timer screaming through the sky sounding like a banshee, so chose to design it for the more tranquil sound of a 4-stroke 'putter'. And have no regrets.

Now I'm getting to know more modellers I find some use 4-strokes all the time. So far we have only discussed using 2-stroke engines. Why?

Well they are relatively cheap, reliable and give great performance. Having said that, many modellers wouldn't install anything but a 4-stroke because of their more realistic sound.

Schematic of 4-stroke engine back view cutaway

exhaust valve
inlet valve
rocker arm
inlet port
push rod
cam & camshaft

Note: camshaft/s geared to crankshaft rotating 1 revolution per 2 revolutions of crankshaft.

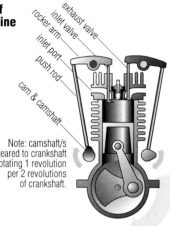

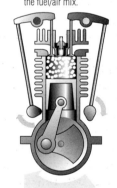

Photo 18:13 *This type of model seemed more suited to the muted sounds of a 4-stroke engine so it has been incorporated in the design drawings – if you'd rather use a 2-stroke, there's no problem, but do modify the plan to fit your engine installation.*

1 From top-dead-centre the piston begins the induction stroke as the cam opens the inlet valve.

2 The piston sucks fuel/air into the cylinder through the inlet port via the open valve.

3 At bottom of the stroke the cam has rotated enough to close the inlet valve.

4 With both valves closed the piston comes up to compress the fuel/air mix.

STROKE 1: INDUCTION

STROKE 2: COMPRESSION

5 Near the top of the compression stroke the pressure & glow ignites the fuel/air.

6 The exploding gases drive the piston to the bottom of the working stroke.

7 As the piston rises the exhaust cam begins to open the exhaust valve port.

8 The piston drives out the burnt gases, the exhaust valve closes as the piston reaches the top-dead-centre.

STROKE 3: IGNITION

STROKE 4: EXHAUST

The 4-stroke engine: induction, compression, ignition and exhaust (1 combustion event for every 4 strokes).

■ **The engine module:**

The fuselage is designed round a very strong ply and bearer box that carries the engine, fuel tank, wing mount, servos and power supply.

The engine is soft-mounted to the box (to reduce vibration) on a relatively light $1/8$" aluminium plate. It is intended to buckle on impact, rather like the 'soft' crumple zone at the front of a modern car (it will be easier and cheaper to fix the plate than either the plane or engine).

■ Make up the box to the stage shown in photo 18:15 with the soft mount, fuel tank (padded), servos and throttle linkage fitted and working.

The scale fuselage is quite short in the nose so as much weight as possible is brought forward as ballast. The prototype model has $1/2$" square mild steel packing under the engine lugs to achieve balance. Remove the soft mount.

■ From $1/8$" ply make firewall F2 to slide neatly over the front of the assembly and seat against the sides where they form the front of the wing mount. Glue it in place absolutely square in both directions.

■ **Building the fuselage:**

Place the top view of the fuselage plan on the building board with the aft line of the firewall F2 exactly on the edge of the board. Protect it as usual. Place the engine module upside down on the plan and check the plan is properly aligned before you clamp it down hard.

Take two $1/4$" sq spruce struts and clamp them down per the plan. Add formers in the conventional way.

From here the photos and their captions are enough guide for your level of building experience.

Photo 18.14 *The engine soft mount calls for some metalwork. This was cut out of $1/8$" aluminium plate using a fine blade in the scroll saw. A light lubricant improves the cutting. Just take your time and let the blade do the work.*

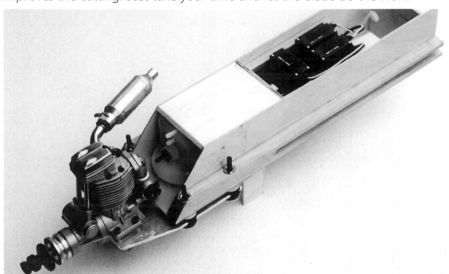

Photo 18:15 *The engine fuel tank and servos are all contained in the power module (note the shape of the engine mounting plate is updated on the plan).*

Photo 18:16 *The engine installation package includes a plug-in power supply to the glow plug, Rx power supply and double circuit switching, charging plug and through-the-cowling choke and mixture control. Nose ballast on the prototype was added by using mild steel for the engine packing blocks.*

154

D.H.71, sheet 6: engine module

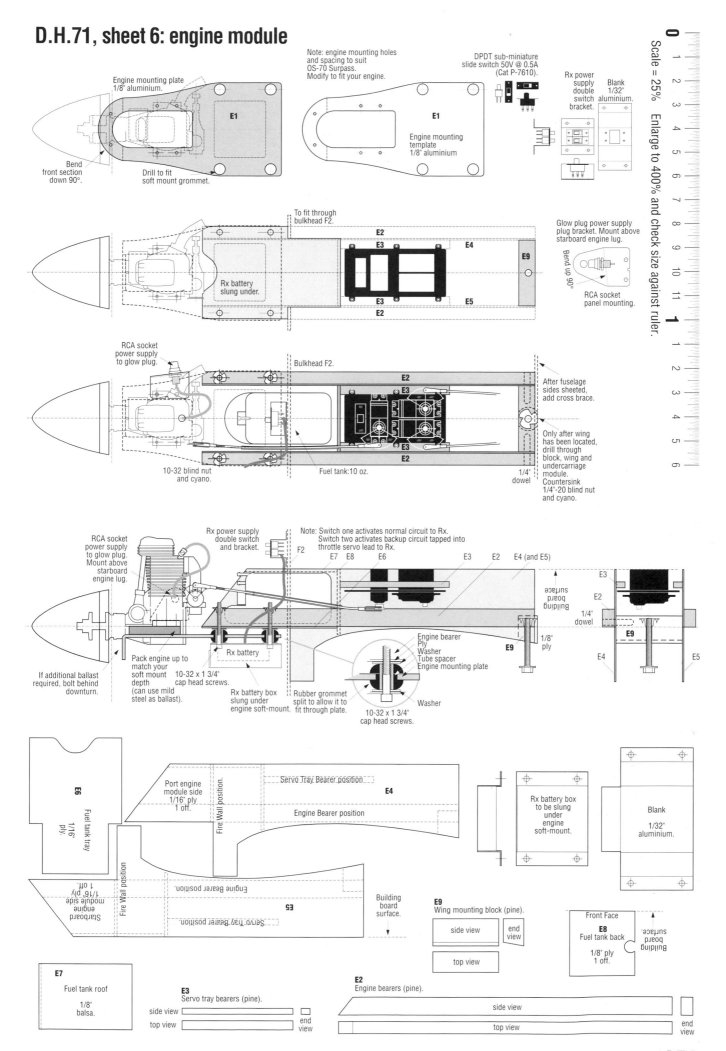

Note: engine mounting holes and spacing to suit OS-70 Surpass. Modify to fit your engine.

Engine mounting plate 1/8" aluminium.

Bend front section down 90°.

Drill to fit soft mount grommet.

E1

Engine mounting template 1/8" aluminium

E1

DPDT sub-miniature slide switch 50V @ 0.5A (Cat P-7610).

Rx power supply double switch bracket.

Blank 1/32" aluminium.

Scale = 25%   Enlarge to 400% and check size against ruler.

To fit through bulkhead F2.

Rx battery slung under.

Glow plug power supply plug bracket. Mount above starboard engine lug.

Bend up 90°.

RCA socket panel mounting.

E2   E4   E9

E3

E3   E5

E2

RCA socket power supply to glow plug.

Bulkhead F2.

After fuselage sides sheeted, add cross brace.

E2   E3

E3   E2

10-32 blind nut and cyano.

Fuel tank: 10 oz.

1/4" dowel

Only after wing has been located, drill through block, wing and undercarriage module. Countersink 1/4"-20 blind nut and cyano.

RCA socket power supply to glow plug. Mount above starboard engine lug.

Rx power supply double switch and bracket.

Note: Switch one activates normal circuit to Rx. Switch two activates backup circuit tapped into throttle servo lead to Rx.

F2

E7 E8   E6   E3   E2   E4 (and E5)

Building board surface.

E3

E2

1/4" dowel

E9

E4   E5

If additional ballast required, bolt behind downturn.

Pack engine up to match your soft mount depth (can use mild steel as ballast).

10-32 x 1 3/4" cap head screws.

Rx battery

Rx battery box slung under engine soft-mount.

Rubber grommet split to allow it to fit through plate.

Engine bearer Ply Washer Tube spacer Engine mounting plate

Washer

10-32 x 1 3/4" cap head screws.

E9

1/8" ply

E6

Fuel tank tray 1/16" ply.

Port engine module side 1/16" ply 1 off.

Fire Wall position.

Servo Tray Bearer position.

E4

Engine Bearer position

Fire Wall position

Starboard engine module side 1/16" ply 1 off.

Engine Bearer position.

E5

Servo Tray Bearer position.

Building board surface.

Rx battery box to be slung under engine soft-mount.

Blank 1/32" aluminium.

E9 Wing mounting block (pine).

side view   end view

top view

Front Face **E8** Fuel tank back 1/8" ply 1 off.

Building board surface.

E7 Fuel tank roof 1/8" balsa.

E3 Servo tray bearers (pine).

side view   end view

top view

E2 Engine bearers (pine).

side view

top view

end view

D.H.71, sheet 7: fuselage

Scale = 25%   Enlarge to 400% and check size against ruler.

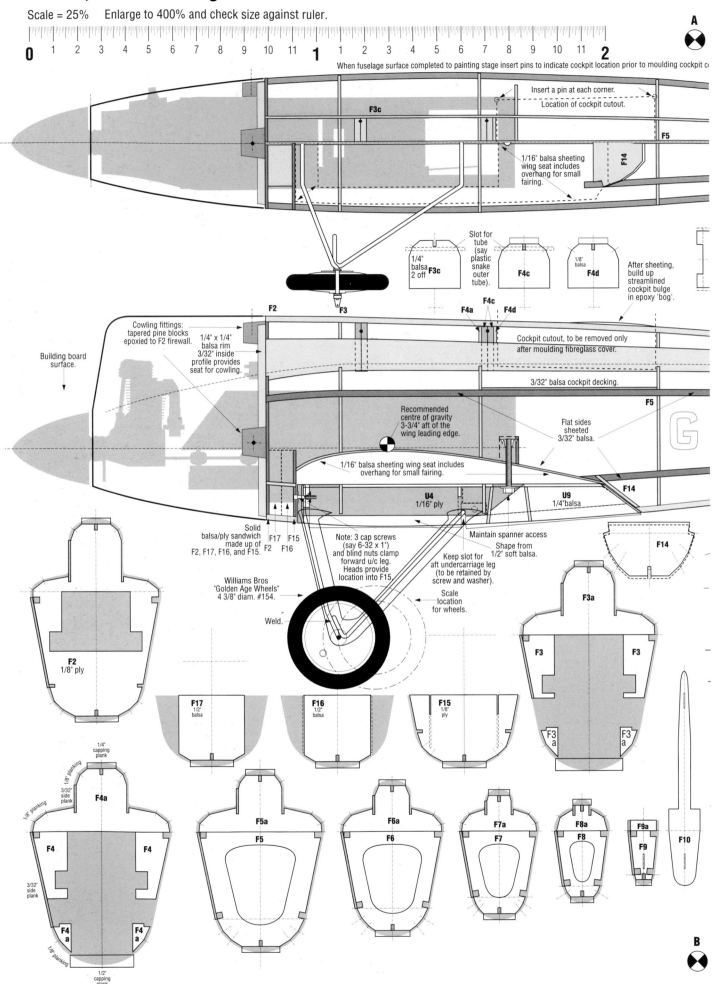

When fuselage surface completed to painting stage insert pins to indicate cockpit location prior to moulding cockpit c...

Insert a pin at each corner.

Location of cockpit cutout.

F3c

F5

F14

1/16" balsa sheeting wing seat includes overhang for small fairing.

Slot for tube (say plastic snake outer tube).

1/4" balsa 2 off **F3c**

F4c

1/8" balsa **F4d**

After sheeting, build up streamlined cockpit bulge in epoxy 'bog'.

F2   F3   F4a   F4c   F4d

Cowling fittings: tapered pine blocks epoxied to F2 firewall.

1/4" x 1/4" balsa rim 3/32" inside profile provides seat for cowling.

Building board surface.

Cockpit cutout, to be removed only after moulding fibreglass cover.

3/32" balsa cockpit decking.

F5

Recommended centre of gravity 3-3/4" aft of the wing leading edge.

Flat sides sheeted 3/32" balsa.

1/16" balsa sheeting wing seat includes overhang for small fairing.

U4 1/16" ply

U9 1/4" balsa

F14

Solid balsa/ply sandwich made up of F2, F17, F16, and F15.

F17 F15
F2   F16

Note: 3 cap screws (say 6-32 x 1") and blind nuts clamp forward u/c leg. Heads provide location into F15.

Williams Bros "Golden Age Wheels" 4 3/8" diam. #154.

Maintain spanner access

Shape from 1/2" soft balsa.

Keep slot for aft undercarriage leg (to be retained by screw and washer).

F14

Weld.

Scale location for wheels.

F3a

F3   F3

F2 1/8" ply

F17 1/2" balsa

F16 1/2" balsa

F15 1/8" ply

F3 a   F3 a

1/4" capping plank

1/8" planking

3/32" side plank

F4a

1/8" planking

F4   F4

3/32" side plank

F4 a   F4 a

1/8" planking

1/2" capping plank

F5a

F5

F6a

F6

F7a

F7

F8a

F8

F9a

F9

F10

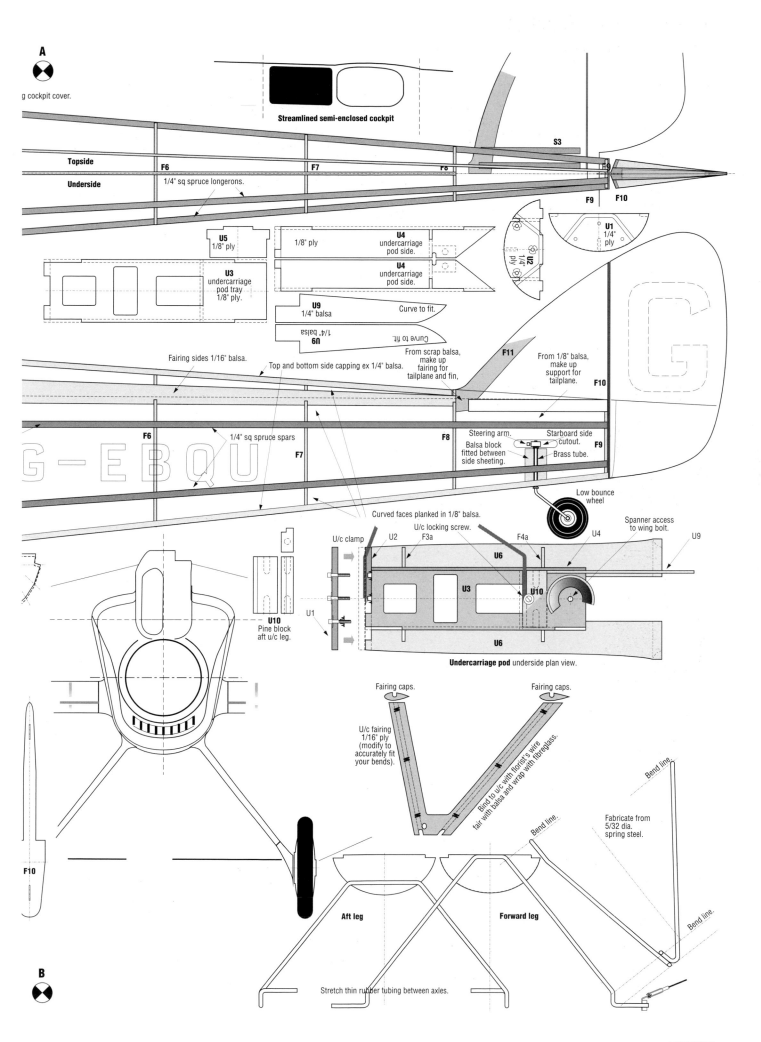

A

g cockpit cover.

Streamlined semi-enclosed cockpit

S3

Topside F6 F7 F8 F9

Underside 1/4" sq spruce longerons. F9 F10

U5
1/8" ply

U4
undercarriage
pod side.
1/8" ply

U3
undercarriage
pod tray
1/8" ply.

U4
undercarriage
pod side.

U9
1/4" balsa Curve to fit.

U9
1/4" balsa Curve to fit.

U1
1/4"
ply

U2
1/4"
ply

Fairing sides 1/16" balsa.

Top and bottom side capping ex 1/4" balsa.

From scrap balsa,
make up
fairing for
tailplane and fin,

F11

From 1/8" balsa,
make up
support for
tailplane.

F10

F6

1/4" sq spruce spars

F7

F8

Steering arm.

Starboard side
cutout.

Balsa block
fitted between
side sheeting.

Brass tube.

F9

Low bounce
wheel

Curved faces planked in 1/8" balsa.

U/c locking screw.

U/c clamp

U2 F3a

U6

U3

U10

U6

F4a

U4

Spanner access
to wing bolt.

U9

U1

Undercarriage pod underside plan view.

U10
Pine block
aft u/c leg.

Fairing caps. Fairing caps.

U/c fairing
1/16" ply
(modify to
accurately fit
your bends).

Bind to u/c with florist's wire
fair with balsa and wrap with fibreglass.

Bend line.

Fabricate from
5/32 dia.
spring steel.

Bend line.

Bend line.

F10

Aft leg **Forward leg**

B

Stretch thin rubber tubing between axles.

Photo 18:17 *F2, F3 and F3 formers are glued to the engine module. Then construction over the plan begins with the fuselage crutch made from spruce longerons.*

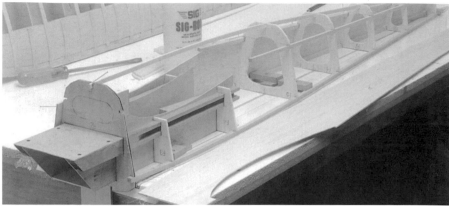

Photo 18:18 *Sheeting the flat sides involves careful fitting. Before you glue, remove any clamps which could become enclosed within the forward sections.*

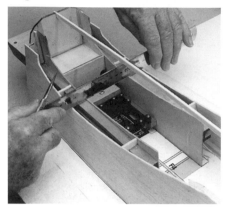

Photo 18:19 *True the line across the wing bay in preparation to sheeting the contact area. Also note that the front of the whole assembly can be firmly held down on the building board with a screw clamp through the switch bay of the servo tray. This can stay put until the underside is completed.*

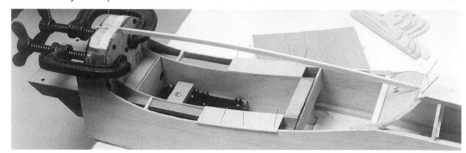

Photo 18:20 *Pre-drill the matching holes in formers F15, U1 and U2, then make up the bulkhead sandwich and epoxy. Proceed with sheeting the wing bay.*

Photo 18:21 *Plank over the underside of the bulkhead and when hard trim the aft face flush and smooth. Cap and plank the underside of the fuselage from F14 aft.*

Photo 18:22 *Carefully locate, seat and align the wing in its final position. Bind it in place with tape. Recheck it for square to the fuselage, and parallel to the surface of the board. With great care to keep the drill horizontal and parallel to the fuselage centreline, drill the two dowel holes through the bulkhead and into the wing. Mark the centreline of the fuselage onto the trailing edge of the wing, then remove the wing, fit the wing dowels and epoxy.*

Photo 18:23 *Make up the basic undercarriage pod assembly. Align the wing and bind at the trailing edge. Add the undercarriage pod and when everything is true, drill the wing mounting bolt hole down through the pod, wing and fuselage block.*

Photo 18:24 *Remove from the board, add the blind nut and bolt together. Replace on the building board.*

158

Photo 18:26 *Remove the under-carriage legs and reassemble with cling film separating all removable parts then continue building the pod.*

Photo 18:27 *The pod is capped with soft ¹/₂" balsa and planked with ¹/₈" balsa.*

Photo 18:25 *The spanner access hole to the wing bolt on the prototype model has a round wall. This was made over a tapered sauce bottle protected with cling film. ¹/₁₆" balsa was softened in boiling water, wrapped round the bottle in two layers and glued with white, water soluble PVA glue. This was held in place with cotton thread and left to dry out. A square hole would be more simple, but not as pleasing – over to you.*

Photo 18:28 *Remove the wing and cling film then smooth the underside to shape.*

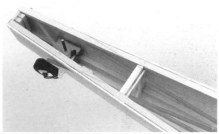

Photo 18:29 *Add the tailwheel assembly incorporating the steering arm, and tighten permanently.*

Photo 18:30 *Align, install and support the control snakes, then formers.*

Photo 18:31 *Snake liners for landing wires should be free to slide through their balsa formers.*

Photo 18:32 *Plank the topsides, completing one side of the cockpit fairing. Drill out the landing wire holes and slide the snake liners through before completing the other side. Again, drill out the landing wire holes and slide the liners through and trim off flush on both sides. Fix the liners with cyano.*

Photo 18:33 *Shape and smooth the fuselage end to end, top to bottom, filling if necessary until satisfied. Cover with heat shrink fabric, shrink and dope.*

Practice

■ Fibreglassing the cowling:

Don't be frightened off making components in fibreglass. In this case we make a foam plastic core, slightly smaller than the final size to allow for the thickness of the glass (about $^3/_{32}$"). The core is

Photo 18:34 *This is the final result of making the expanded polystyrene mould, casting a fibreglass cowling over the EPS and shaping it into the lines of the fuselage.*

shaped, smoothed and painted then coated with resist ready for glassing over.

It's rather like working with paper maché except that the paste is sticky, dribbly resin and the glass cloth is much springier than the wet paper. Otherwise, fibreglassing is really quite straightforward.

■ Epoxy resin is the easiest system for the amateur. Following the manufacturer's safety recommendations, mix a small amount at a time and don't rush. Large quantities in confined spaces generate heat which, at best makes the resin cure too quickly and at worst can cause a fire. Take care and keep an eye on the pot, being ready to move it outside if things go wrong! Have a container of universal thinners at hand to clean up as you go. Wash out the brush between epoxy mixes and clean you hands regularly.

With sharp scissors, cut a variety of small pieces of woven rovings (say 2 oz cloth) and apply them one at a time, working in the resin with a stiff (cheap) paint

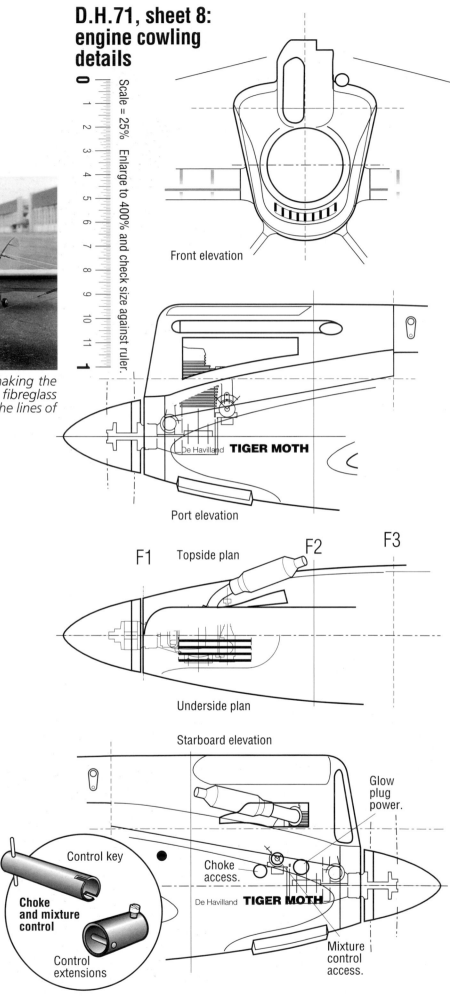

D.H.71, sheet 8: engine cowling details

Scale = 25%   Enlarge to 400% and check size against ruler.

Front elevation

Port elevation

De Havilland **TIGER MOTH**

F1   Topside plan   F2   F3

Underside plan

Starboard elevation

Glow plug power.

Control key

Choke access.

Choke and mixture control

Control extensions

De Havilland **TIGER MOTH**

Mixture control access.

160

brush. Overlap the pieces and keep the cloth wet, but not overloaded. Tight corners need small pieces of cloth to handle the curves. Thin strips and triangles are handy. Since the model will be tail heavy we are not too worried about adding weight. Nor do we need a lot of strength so this is a good object to practise on. When you think it's about thick enough, cover the job with cling film and bind it against the core to remove any air spaces. Work out any bubbles with your fingers.

■ Shape the final casting with a file, using epoxy bog to develop the squared corners and finished shape. Fill and paint.

Photo 18:38 *Protect the fuselage/ cowling joint with cling-film, then glass up to a thickness of about ³/₃₂". Don't worry too much about weight here – this model tends to be tail heavy. Cover with cling film and bind in tightly against the EPS core. Leave to cure.*

Photo 18:40 *The paint layer is a good guide when you come to chipping out the EPS core (I prefer this to dissolving the core with petrol – it's less messy).*

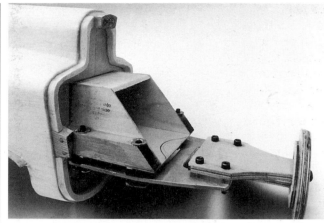

Photo 18:35 *Begin forming the cowling by making a dummy engine plate which matches the unit you are using. Make a circular disk that represents the back of your spinner. Bolt this to the engine plate so that it sits about ¹/₈" nearer the engine than the final spinner position (to allow for cowling clearance).*

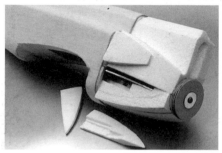

Photo 18:36 *Using blocks of expanded polystyrene (EPS), build up the cowling shape, but about ³/₃₂" smaller to allow for the thickness of the fibreglass.*

Photo 18:37 *Work at it so that when you remove the spinner disk the EPS can be slid off and on the fuselage. Fill, shape, paint and apply resist.*

Photo 18:39 *Here's where you get the benefit of being able to slide the EPS block off and on instead of breaking it off. Just take it off to work on it and replace it to check the fit. Now hollow out the EPS.*

Photo 18:41 *The completed cowling, filled, painted and fitted. Only the silencer and prop/ spinner need to be taken off for cowling removal.*

Practice

To mould the canopy over the bulge in the fuselage we build up a boxing over formers F4 and F5. This should leave about 1/16" clearance for a Plasticine 'gasket' to seal against the fuselage. Mark its position for later reference by pressing a pin into the fuselage at each corner of the canopy. The pin heads will show in the mould and later in the casting. Later when you cut the hole in the fuselage you will know the moulding will fit. When you make

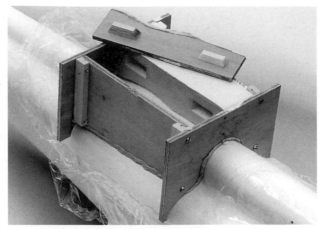

Photo 18:42 *The boxing incorporates a dividing wall so the mould can be made in two halves. This wall has register tongues so the mould halves will align together automatically when the mould is assembled after drying.*

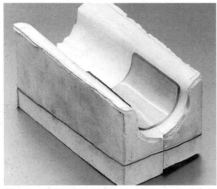

Photo 18:43 *Once the mould is thoroughly dry, warm it in the oven then heat acrylic sheet and press it into place to form the clear glass section.*

Photo 18:44 *Coat the mould and clear glass with PVA resist, wedge the clear glass accurately in place and glass up with cloth and resin.*

Photo 18:45 *Add balsa formers to maintain the fibreglass shape, remove from the mould, remove the clear glass section (I broke mine!) and clean up.*

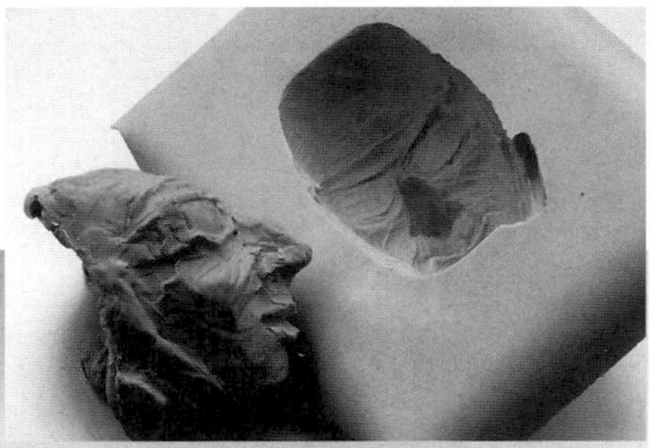

the boxing, make sure it covers a larger area than that marked by the pin heads. The fibreglass moulding will be cut down to fit. Vaseline the fuselage and boxing before pouring builders' grade plaster into the boxing. Cast one

Photo 18:46 *You can sculpt your own pilot from Plasticine. Take a plaster of Paris mould, apply plenty of resist and cast the face in resin and balloon 'bog'.*
Note: unless you are prepared to spend a lot of time eliminating 'undercuts' be prepared to break the plaster away from the resin casting.

Dashboard template, actual size. Cut from 1/16" ply, back with 'instruments' and glass with medical tablet dispenser bubbles.

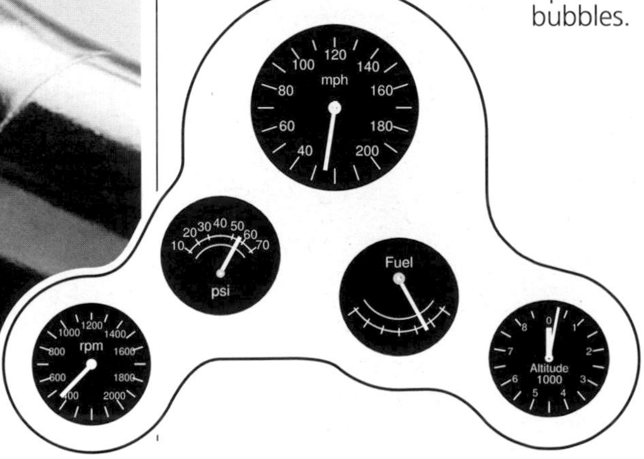

Photo 18:47 *The completed 'streamlined' semi-enclosed canopy with 1/4 scale 'pilot' in place and the clear glass removed to show the instrument panel more clearly.*

162

Practice

Photo 18:48 *The fabric covering of an aircraft is not smooth. Our objective is to make the model look fabric covered.*

half at a time, the second half after removing the divider and applying Vaseline to the adjoining surface. When they are both hard, remove, dry and seal with plenty of parting agent. Follow the photos 18:42 to 18.45.

■ Make up the dashboard as shown on the template then, if you want to make your own pilot, have a go at sculpture!

■ Wing Stitching

Detail adds a great deal to the realism of a model. Rib stitching will make a major contribution. The little device shown here is something I've used on many models and it offers a really easy way to achieve a convincing finish. Follow the photos. It's easy.

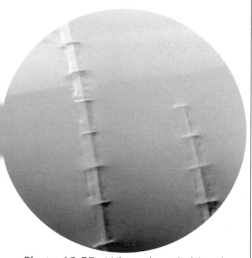

Photo 18:55 *When the stitching has been covered with shrink film the results can be very convincing.*

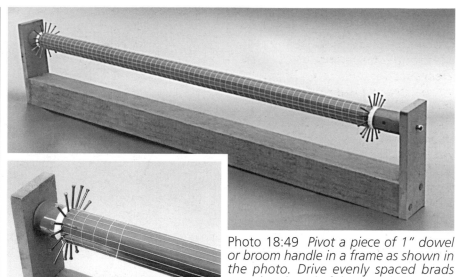

Photo 18:50 *Stretch linen thread or cotton between all the brads and tie. Now wind on a length of cross thread.*

Photo 18:52 *When it hardens off the surface is a smooth transparent skin with the threads making strong ridges.*

Photo 18:49 *Pivot a piece of 1" dowel or broom handle in a frame as shown in the photo. Drive evenly spaced brads round each end of the dowel. Cover the surface from end to end with shiny packing tape to resist PVA glue.*

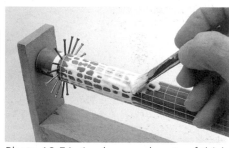

Photo 18:51 *Apply several coats of thick, water soluble PVA glue (allowing each coat to dry) until the surface is covered.*

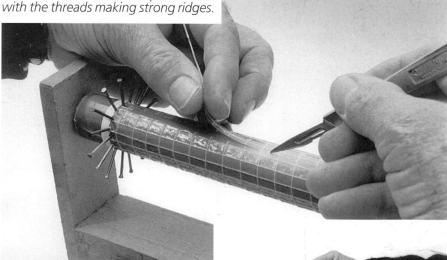

Photo 18:53 *Using a very sharp knife, cut along between the straight threads and remove one row of stitching at a time. Handle gently and you will have clean, even strips ready for applying to the rib capping of your wing and tail surfaces.*

Photo 18:54 *Smear a little PVA glue on the rib capping and lay the stitching strip down in it, pulling it straight. Gently press down into the glue and leave it to set.*

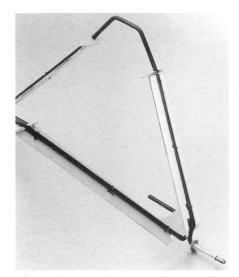

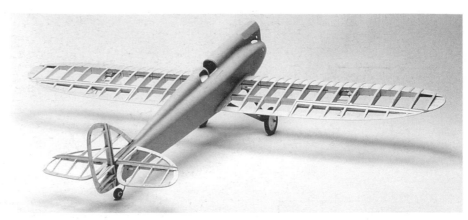

Photo 18:57 *All structure, filling and sanding is complete, equipment has been test-installed and checked for function and it's ready for painting and covering.*

Photo 18:56 *Thin ¹/₁₆" ply is wired to the inside face of the undercarriage legs and their fairing plates are glued in place. Balsa fillets are glued on the ply to make up the aerofoil. Wrap with glass cloth and epoxy. Fill with bog then file and sand to the final shape.*

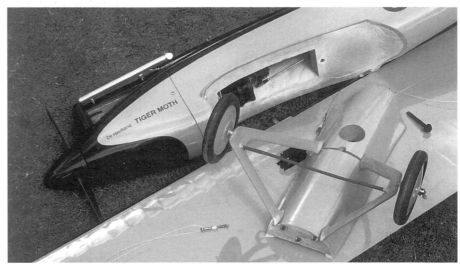

Photo 18:58 *Breakdown for transport and storage is very convenient with a single bolt assembly, then the six clevises are attached to secure the stay wires. Normally I transport the fuselage with just the undercarriage module attached.*

A. Rivers

Photo 18:59 *There are few moments in modelling to equal that feeling when you open the throttle for a model's first flight. Pick a nice sunny day and savour the moment!*

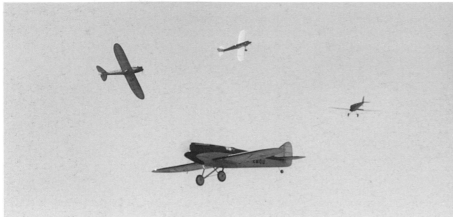

A. Rivers

Photo 18:60 *Although designers seem to always describe their creations as brilliant fliers, this model is an absolute natural, behaving beautifully both on the ground and in the air.*

Photo 18:61 *I'd like to think that some photos say it all.*

Footnote: *This has turned out to be quite an exceptional little aircraft fulfilling the promise of those clean 3-view lines. I run it slightly over-propped to keep the noise down, but it can still show a clean tail to many more powerful models. It handles decisively at both full and reduced power and shows no nasty stall characteristics. For the past 12 months it has been my favoured model and Sunday flier where it quite often attracts a pleasant comment. Certainly, it is no flamboyant show-stopper, but rather a quietly unobtrusive, beautifully-mannered little lady that's a delight to fly. I am a non-competitive flier but at our recent club fly-in where there were in excess of 100 models she apparently caught the judge's eye. Imagine my surprise and pleasure when the de Havilland Tiger Moth monoplane was awarded the 'Judge's choice' trophy for 1999.*

Chapter 19: Sport kit to Schneider racer

British aviation legend has been woven round Supermarine, Reginald Mitchell, Rolls Royce, the Royal Air Force High Speed Squadron, Lady Houston, the Schneider Cup and the evolution of the Spitfire. It is fascinating reading. Just the words 'Schneider Cup' evoke this amazing era.

Of all those beautiful float planes that battled for national honours in the cup contests, one of the most beautiful was the S-5. 'N220' piloted by Flt. Lt. O.E. Webster, who won the 1927 race at an average speed of 281.63 mph. Although the S–5 was powered by a Napier engine, (Mitchell turned to Rolls Royce before the 1929 contest) it is very much part of the Spitfire legend and makes an ideal 'original'. After the challenge of our last building project it comes as light relief to build this fun plane with floats.

This is a quick and relatively inexpensive way to get float plane experience. We start with a good but basic sport kit like Model Tech's 'China Clipper' and, making a series of add-ons, convert it into an S–5 Schneider look-alike. Later you could invest the time and money in building a true scale Schneider cup winner, any one of a range of wonderful aircraft from Supermarine, Macchi, Curtiss or Gloster stables.

We will assume you have purchased the Model Tech kit (if you've had to settle for something similar you must make size changes to the add-ons to see everything fits).

You will also need to buy or make a suitable cowling. The prototype uses a SIG moulding.

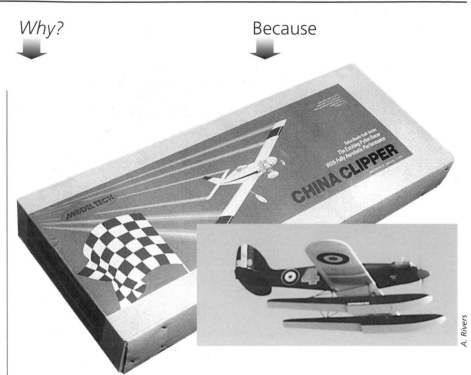

A. Rivers

Photo 19:1 *Model Tech's 'China Clipper' is an extremely basic and thoroughly sound sports aircraft which provides the elementary components on which we build. The method we use will suggest all sorts of kit adaptations you could make for other simple planes.*

My local shop can't supply this particular kit. What alternatives do you suggest?

When you consider how little of the original lines are apparent in the finished model you could modify many basic low-wing sport models of the 0.25 – 0.40 engine, 48" span size. Modify any plan parts to make them fit and it shouldn't be too hard.

Photo 19:2 *Straight out of the 'paint shop' and ready to begin sea trials. Flamboyant by any standards and especially so of the period we represent – however, this is FUN sport so we've gone right over the top . . . and why not!*

Sport kit conversion to Supermarine S-5 fun-scale

57" span fun-scale model float plane
for 0.45 to 0.50, 2-stroke engines
From 'AIRCRAFT WORKSHOP:
Learn to make models that FLY'
by Kelvin Shacklock ©

Model scale: 5.6 : 1 of original aircraft

Front Elevation

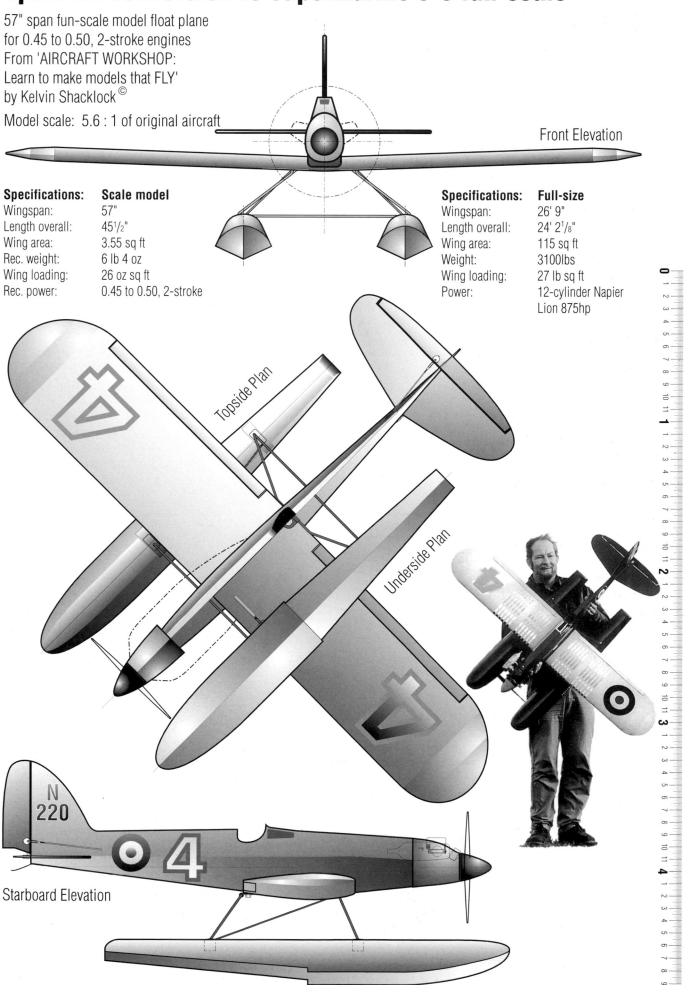

Specifications:	**Scale model**
Wingspan:	57"
Length overall:	45$\frac{1}{2}$"
Wing area:	3.55 sq ft
Rec. weight:	6 lb 4 oz
Wing loading:	26 oz sq ft
Rec. power:	0.45 to 0.50, 2-stroke

Specifications:	**Full-size**
Wingspan:	26' 9"
Length overall:	24' 2$\frac{1}{8}$"
Wing area:	115 sq ft
Weight:	3100lbs
Wing loading:	27 lb sq ft
Power:	12-cylinder Napier Lion 875hp

Topside Plan

Underside Plan

Starboard Elevation

N 220

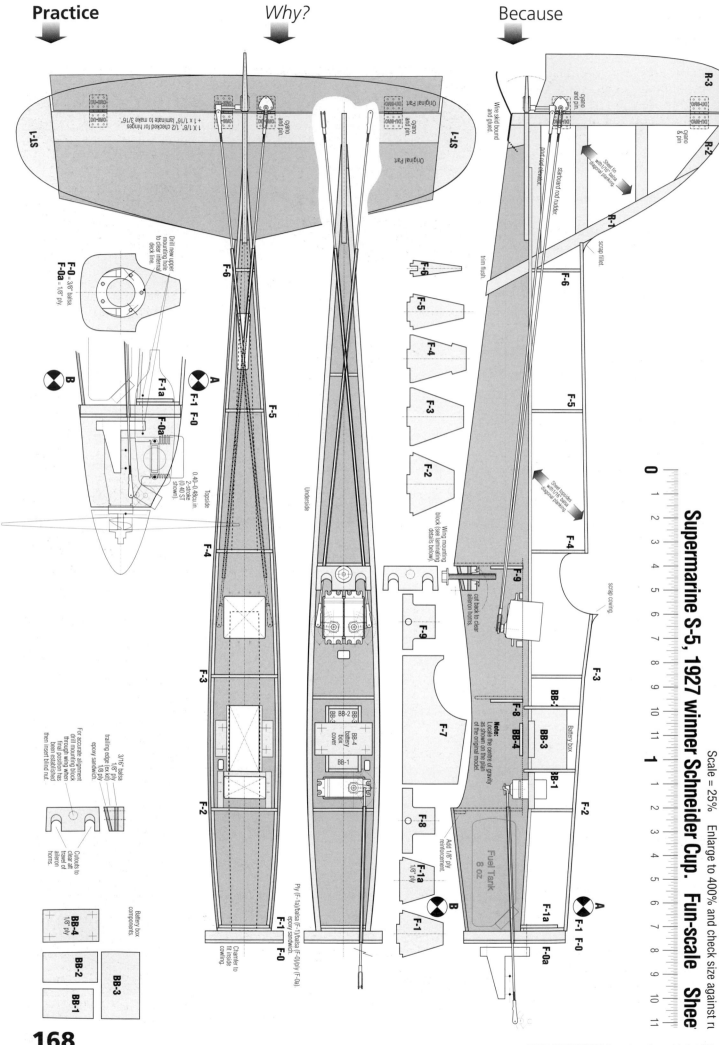

Supermarine S-5, 1927 winner Schneider Cup. Fun-scale Sheet

Scale = 25%   Enlarge to 400% and check size against ru

AIRCRAFT WORKSHOP: Learn to make models that FLY

In the kit you will find an assembled fuselage and sheeted foam-core wing plus all the components to build the sports racer. The book plans cover all the extra parts you'll need and are provided as 'iron on' in sheet 2.

■ Fuselage and tail feathers

On the plan opposite see how to increase the size of a kit tailplane by inserting wood between the original stabiliser and elevator; then the span, by adding tips.

Sand it to shape and fit it to the fuselage. This will provide the sightline for all the rest of the assembly, so take your time to align it accurately.

Make up the fin on the plan. Then carefully plot your cuts on the fuselage so that the leading edge of the fin slips through the top and bottom surfaces, while the stern post sits nicely against the end of the fuselage. Align the fin square to the tailplane and dead straight along the fuselage. Glue.

■ Along the top of the fuselage mark the positions and tongue widths of each of the formers and cut their slots. Cut out the formers F1 to F6 and cockpit doublers F-7, fit and glue. Add the ⅛" fuselage capping fore and aft of the cockpit making a break at F-3.

Epoxy sandwich balsa former F-0 and its 3-ply face F-0a together.

Run ⅛" square junction longerons along the topsides of the kit fuselage from F-1, and taper them out to blend smoothly into the fin/tailplane joint. This longeron should lie inside the face of the kit fuselage sides so that there is space for the ¹⁄₁₆" sheeting to finish flush. Now is the time to get this right (photo 19:6).

Epoxy the F-0 assembly to the front of the fuselage leaving provision for the cowling thickness to align with the fuselage capping.

Photo 19:3 *Identify all the parts in the kit and check them against the plan.*

Photo 19:4 *After modifying the tailplane, begin by mounting it accurately.*

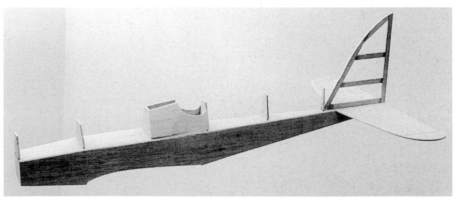

Photo 19:5 *Make cutout slots for the formers and front fin spar, then fit them.*

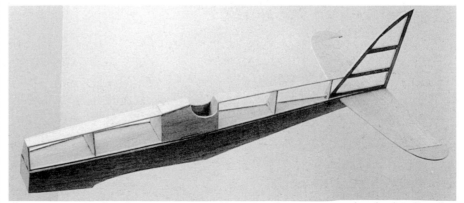

Photo 19:6 *The fuselage capping and junction longerons make the landing for planking, so it's important they're correctly positioned inside the skin line.*

Practice

■ Test the cowling for fit and alignment then temporarily hinge the rudder and elevator in place.

Add control horns to the tail surfaces and then follow the plan to install their servos. These mount against the inside of the kit fuselage topsides and protrude into the cockpit area. Add the softwood mounting blocks to accept their fixing screws.

Now you can accurately plot the straightest possible lines for the control snakes, and cut the necessary paths. Note: On the prototype the kit fuselage former lying under F-5 needs to have its upper member cut away. A nail saw helps here (photo 19:8).

Make up the push rod assemblies so the snake outer tubes extend beyond the projected fuselage surfaces (photo 19:9). Fit to the servos and control horns, and adjust for neutral inputs.

■ To leave more room in the radio compartment we are building a battery box into the upper fuselage (photo 19:10).

We also locate the throttle servo to mount against the inside of the kit fuselage topside. This gives a better line for the throttle linkage to the carb. Cut the appropriate holes and add the softwood backing blocks (photo 19:11).

■ Test fit the engine and mount, making provision for the blind nuts to hold it. Aligning the motor to fit the prototype cowling calls for a new location for the tops screws. This is because the standard holes in the mount clash with the topside of the kit fuselage. The prototype has a round mount, so only one hole can be made at the top. This looks fine (photo 19:12). Glue the blind nuts in place, especially the top one, as there is no access to it after the fuselage has been sheeted.

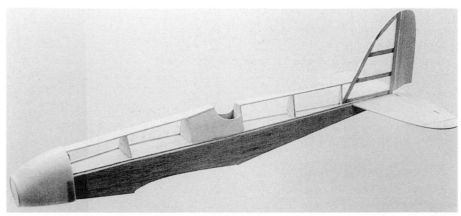

Photo 19:7 *Hinge the rudder and elevator components and see the cowl fits.*

Photo 19:8 *When you've settled on the servo locations, plot the rod cutouts.*

Photo 19:9 *There's a smooth straight line from servo arm to control horn.*

Photo 19:10 *To give plenty of space for the radio gear, make this battery box.*

170

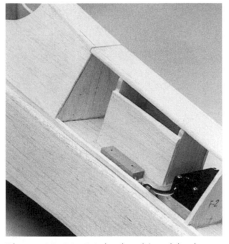

Photo 19:11 *Make backing blocks to take the screws from the throttle servo and battery box lid.*

■ Diagonally sheet the fuselage topsides, carrying the sheeting from the firewall aft to the tip of the fin (photo 19:13). Sand to conform to the lower fuselage and capping. Round a good leading edge on the fin.

■ Although you now begin building the wing, when you come back to fitting it to the fuselage you will be adding the wing fillets, so we describe it now.

With the wing ready for covering, protect it with cling film and mount it to the fuselage. Test fit the fairings and see they contact the wing evenly and are the right shape. Remove them and bevel them to a triangular cross section. Smooth, then glue them to the fuselage while pressing them down against the wing for a good fit (photo 19:14).

■ As supplied, the kit appears to be fairly lightly constructed round the wing dowel plate. In the prototype this is doubled with a second 1/8" ply plate drilled and epoxied to the front of the existing plate.

■ **Wings**

It's easier to modify the wingtips before gluing the wings together. To begin, print the plan parts on your wood, cut them out and sand them to size.

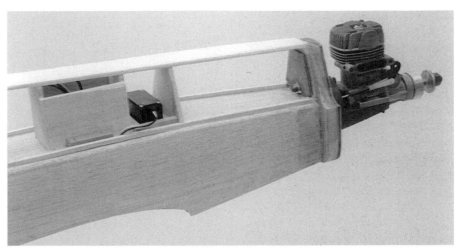

Photo 19:12 *Note there's not much room for that top engine mount screw and its captive nut, even after drilling a higher hole in the engine mount.*

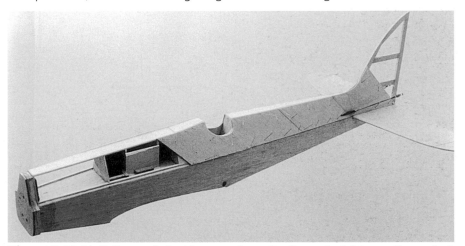

Photo 19:13 *1/16" diagonal planking runs from the firewall, right over the cockpit sides and through to the tip of the fin.*

Photo 19:14 *The wing fairings are pressed down onto the protected wing panel, glued and pinned in place for a really neat fit.*

Do we need to take any special precautions to waterproof the electrical gear?

This depends quite a bit on where you plan to fly. The prototype only goes near fresh water. There's an extra smear of Vaseline round joints and bearings of the servos and the radio is in a plastic bag with a tieoff. The battery switch is well covered with grease. I think I'd be even more cautious if I were flying from salt water.

Practice

Check the kit wing against the enlarged plan (photo 19:15) to ensure sizes are correct.

Make up the new wingtips by gluing the WT-1s to the WT-2s over the plan. Assemble ribs WT-4 over the spar extensions WT-3. Bring both subassemblies together to complete the tips.

Cut recesses into the end ribs of the wing to accept the new wingtip assemblies. When everything aligns, glue (photo 19:16).

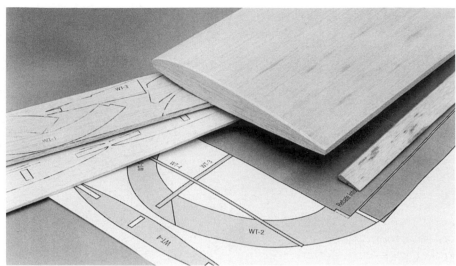

Photo 19:15 *We replace the kit's wingtips with made-up extensions that are fully rounded. Note the ailerons do not go full span (so we can use those supplied with the kit).*

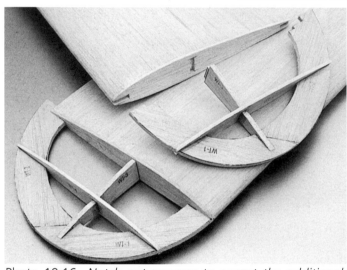

Photo 19:16 *Notch out recesses to accept the additional structure so it's easier to locate them. It's also stronger.*

Photo 19:17 *Use trailing edge blocks from the kit to finish the line of the wingtip through to the aileron.*

Photo 19:18 *Carve out the servo cavity and passage for the servo lead to come out. Make provision for the 3-ply servo tray to tuck in under the $^1/_{16}$" sheeting so it will all glue together for a neat mounting.*

Use a trailing edge block supplied in the kit to complete the outer wing (photo 19:17). Blend the tip lines smoothly into the wing surfaces with a sanding block.

Photo 19:19 *Fit the standard wing joiner supplied in the kit. We will use this to mount both the wheels and floats.*

172

Practice

■ Bring the two wing halves together and, allowing for the correct dihedral, check their fit.

Mark the position of the servo tray and trim the upper sheeting to clear the servo, but leave a lap to cover the sides of the tray. Cut out the servo cavity and make a channel for its electrical lead. Hollow under the sheeting just enough to allow the 3-ply servo tray to slide under (photo 19:18) as the two wing halves are brought together. Turn over the wing and test the fit of the standard wing joiner in its pre-machined slot.

Apply a liberal coating of epoxy, and join the wings, including the joiner and servo tray within the joint. Support rigidly until cured.

■ Install the aileron torsion rod assemblies by slotting the aft edge of the wings to take the bearing plates. Recess grooves in the wing and trailing edge blocks for the rods (see photo 19:20). Carefully lubricate the rod only enough to resist glue, and set the trailing edges in place. Leave to harden but periodically check that the torsion rods revolve freely.

Bandage the centre joint with fibreglass and epoxy. Make up a bevelled block of hard balsa to fit to the centre section upper leading edge. It should be short enough to fit between the fuselage sides and deep enough to accept the wing mounting dowels. Glass bandage this in place and do the same with the wing bolt plate on the underside of the trailing edge. Hold with tape over cling film until cured.

■ Laminate and epoxy the special wing bolt block shown on sheet 1. Epoxy it into the fuselage and let it harden. Place the wing in position and check for clearance from the aileron torsion rods as they move through maximum deflection.

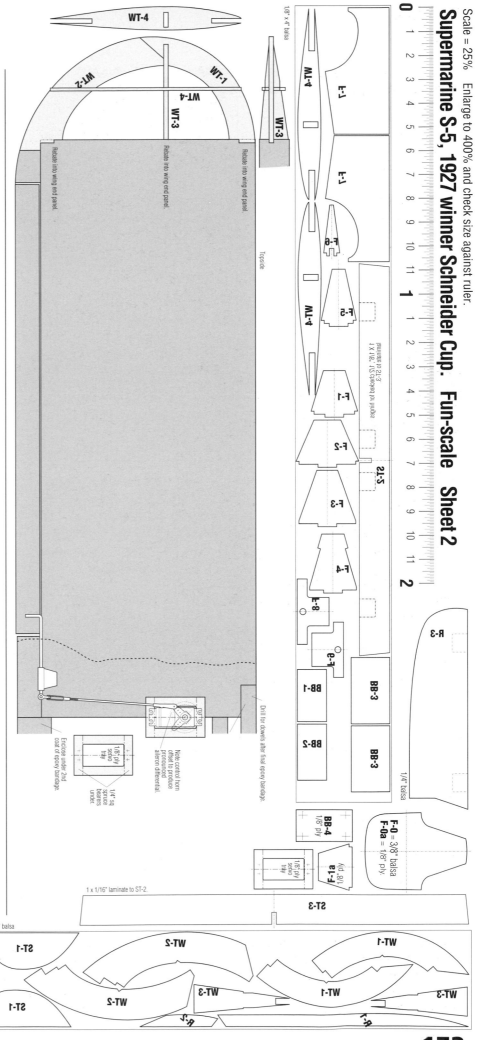

Locate the wing accurately within the fuselage saddle, and drill the dowel holes through from the fuselage former into the leading edge (use a hand-held bit).

Cut the dowels, fit them into the wing, epoxy and leave to cure.

Replace the wing into the fuselage, check fit and alignment. If all is OK, drill the hole for the wing mounting bolt through the wing and on through the block in the fuselage. Remove the wing and enlarge the hole in the block to accept a blind nut. Tighten the wing against the blind nut until it is pulled into the correct position. Remove the wing and glue the nut in place. Now fit the fuselage fairings as described earlier.

■ Floats

The floats are cut from EPS (expanded polystyrene) and covered in glass cloth.

■ From an old printing plate cut the 'light aluminium template'.

■ Use either a hot wire or fine-bladed bandsaw for steps 1, 2 & 3 as shown on the plan (see the results in photo 19:24).

Step one is to produce a 3' strip of EPS which is shaped to the section shown as (1) in the plan.

Step two (2) is to locate the template against the deepest face of the EPS section. Pin it there. With the opposite face of the EPS flat on the work surface, cut vertically down along the stepped edge of the template to form one of the undersides of a float. Make two pairs of matching opposites.

For the third step (3) reverse the EPS and fit the template against the second deepest face. Align the top of the template to the edge of the EPS. Again, cut down vertically against the opposite face to form the upper side of each float half. Epoxy the paired halves together on the centreline,

Photo 19:20 *Aileron torsion rods are recessed into the rear spar and fairings.*

Photo 19:21 *When bandaging the wing with fibreglass, avoid the aileron rods.*

Photo 19:22 *Glass in blocks with the second layer and cover with cling film.*

Photo 19:23 *Check clearance for the aileron rods in the wing mounting block.*

174

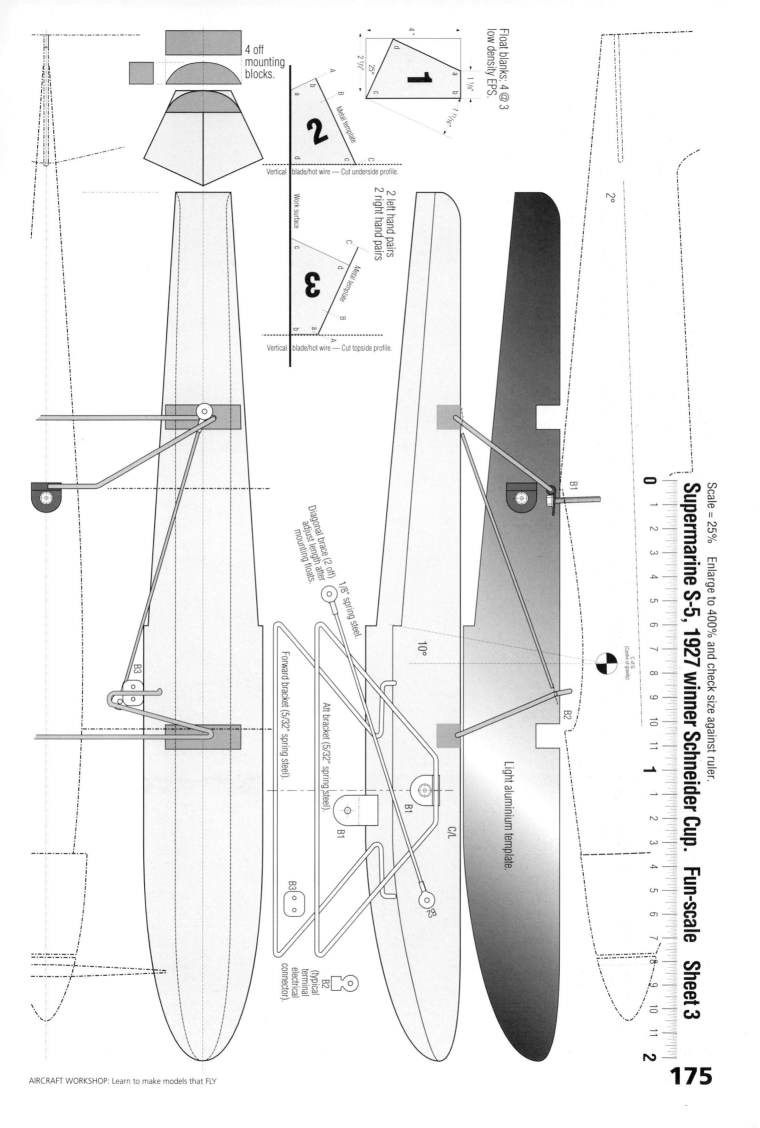

4 off mounting blocks.

Float blanks: 4 @ 3 low density EPS.

4"

25°

2 1/2"

1 1/8"

1 11/16"

1

A — A
a
b
B
a
B
b
c — c
d
d

Metal template

2

Vertical blade/hot wire — Cut underside profile.

Work surface

2 left hand pairs
2 right hand pairs

c — c
d
d
B
B
a
a — A
b
b

Metal template

3

Vertical blade/hot wire — Cut topside profile.

2°

B1

10°

C of G
(Centre of gravity)

B2

Light aluminium template.

Diagonal brace (2 off)
adjust length after
mounting floats.

1/8" spring steel.

Forward bracket (5/32" spring steel).

Aft bracket (5/32" spring steel).

B1

C/L

B3

B2

B3

B2 (typical terminal electrical connector).

B3

B1

inserting the softwood mounting blocks at the same time.

Sand the cured floats to their final shape ready for glassing (4).

The prototype floats have carbon fibre ribbon set into the glass, bridging the somewhat weak step area. Alternatively you could have a full profile of say $^1/_{16}$" ply sandwiched between the halves.

■ Glassing is in two stages: 8 oz cloth on the undersides first. When set, 4 oz cloth is added to the topsides carrying through to overlap onto the undersides by $^1/_2$" or so. All edges are left rounded to about $^1/_4$" radius to help avoid corner bubbles. Wrap with cling film and bind with tape until cured (photo 19:25).

Make up an epoxy/balloon filler to achieve a smooth finish and to put sharp edges on the under faces (photo 19:26).

■ Make up the front and back wire brackets using a flame to get neat and tight bends. Silver solder the plate for the aft bracket which will be gripped by the wing bolt.

■ Groove recesses in the float mounting blocks to accept their brackets. Do this with a power drill with a bit of the same diameter as the bracket wire.

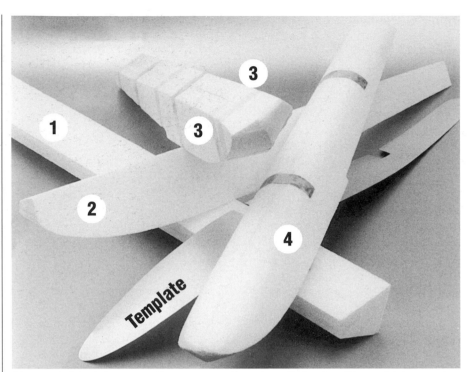

Photo 19:24 *Polystyrene floats are cut from bevelled strips (1) to which you pin a light metal template, once on the centre face (2) to cut the undersides then on the bevelled face (3) to cut the topsides. Naturally, you must make matched pairs. These are epoxied together then sanded to the final shape (4) ready for glassing.*

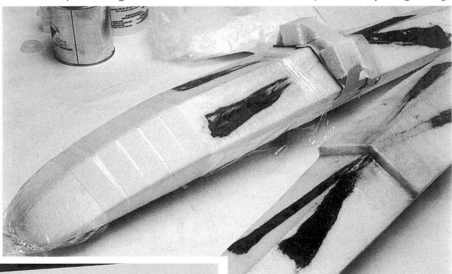

Photo 19:25 *The prototype has carbon fibre reinforcing over the step area. Glassing's a bit of a fiddle and, short of vacuum bagging, settle for wrapping in cling film and strapping with masking tape to hold it tight while curing.*

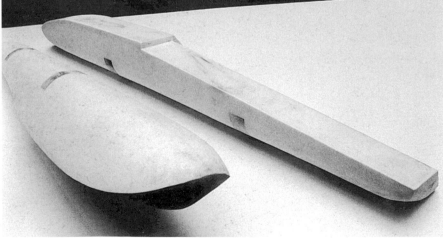

Photo 19:26 *Once the floats are glassed use epoxy/balloon filler to true up the faces and develop clean sharp edges on all the running lines. Sand to a glasslike finish and paint.*

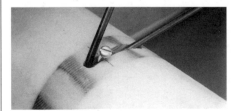

Photo 19:27 *Carve grooves to fit the float brackets into the mounting blocks. Use selftap screws to fix them in place, and epoxy.*

176

When everything fits nicely, drive a selftap screw into each block to retain the brackets within their slots (photo 19:27). Check the alignment and reassemble using epoxy to seat the brackets permanently into the floats. Add the diagonal braces later.

■ Finishing

The prototype is covered in OzCover, a clear shrink film which is designed to be painted. This is used on all except the floats, which are undercoated straight over the glass/filler and painted along with all the other parts.

Considerable license has been taken with decals and signage as this is seen as a fun-scale plane.

Photo 19:28 *Final assembly to check the fit before covering with OzCover, painting and fitting out. Remember also to pre-assemble with wheels in place of the floats.*

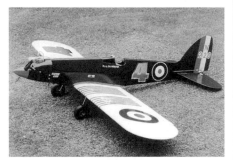

Photo 19:29 *Initial tests were carried out from land. This proved to be a good guide to the plane's behaviour when finally fitted with floats.*

What effect do the floats have on the way the model flies?

It doesn't have as much effect as you might imagine. There's a bit more weight, a bit more drag and a little less stability on the roll axis. Otherwise it's much the same as with wheels. The increased tail surfaces seem to take care of any potential problems.

■ Flying

The author has no previous experience of flying off water but taking off with the prototype presents no great problem. Alignment into the wind is critical otherwise there's a tendency to bury the lee float (especially with a starboard wind).

Its airworthiness is unquestioned. There's plenty of aileron differential so little need for the fourth channel once a good flying speed has been achieved. It has low wing loading but quite a lot of drag (so don't imagine you are going to stretch a glide very far).

Hold a long, gentle flare and let her settle softly when she's ready.

Photo 19:30 *From maiden flight onward, the S-5 is fun to fly, looks the part and handles the circuit with precision and speed.*

Chapter 20: Building a 60" Hawker Sea Fury

Now we are going to have a go at heavy metal warbird modelling. This design has six radio channels: the standard four we've used to date, plus flaps and retracts. We use seven servos and compressed air (for the undercarriage). The model is powered by a 0.60 cu in 2-stroke which can develop over $1^{1}/_{2}$ bhp and it is soft-mounted. All this gear and a substantial airframe structure mean that when the model is fully detailed and balanced, it will too easily weigh in the 9 lb range, and that's in a 60" aircraft. So, let's do all we can to keep the weight down because, no matter how careful we are, the model will have a fairly high wing loading. It is assumed you have developed the building and flying skills over past projects to handle this one. When you start flying, keep up the speed, and be smooth and gentle on those sticks.

Hawker Sea Fury

60" scale model aircraft for 6-channel radio control
and 0.90 cu in 4-stroke or 0.60/0.90 cu in 2-stroke engines
From
'AIRCRAFT WORKSHOP: Learn to make models that FLY'
by Kelvin Shacklock ©

Model scale: 1/7.7 size of original

Specifications:	Full-size aircraft	Scale model
Wingspan:	38' 5"	60"
Length overall:	34' 8"	54"
Wing area:	208 sq ft	4.6 sq ft
Weight:	14,650 lb	9 lb 3 oz
Wing loading:	70 lb 5 oz sq ft	32 oz sq ft
Power:	Bristol Centaurus 18 cylinder 2480 hp radial	0.60 cu in 2-stroke glow
Max speed:	420 knots at 18,000 ft	

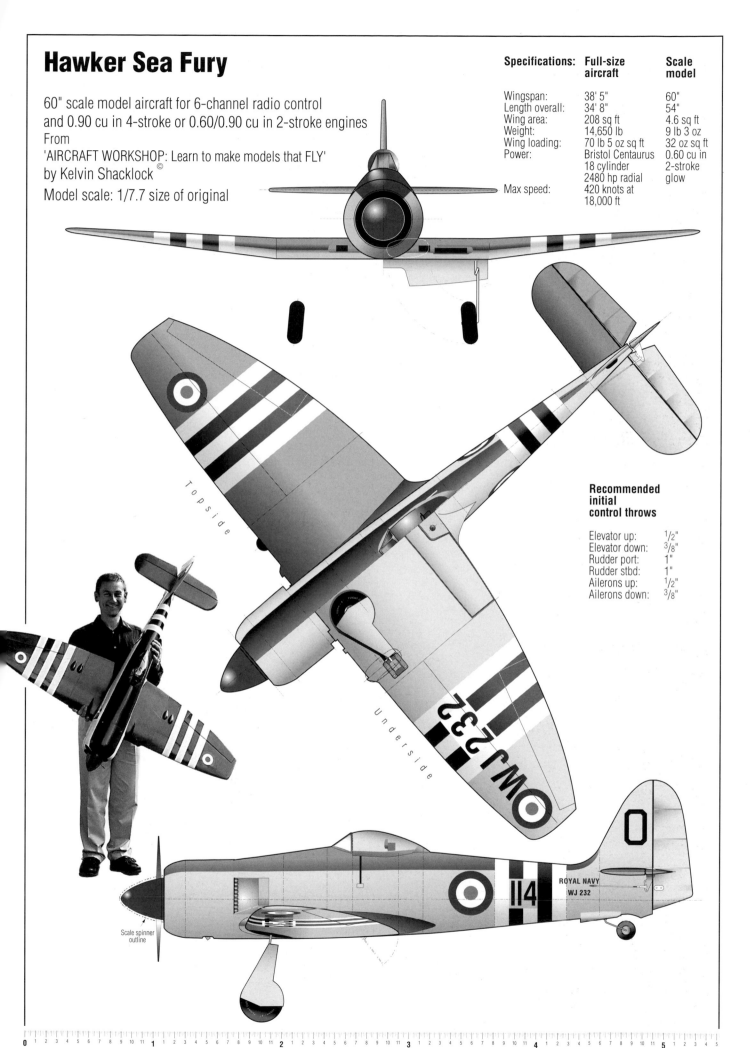

Topside

Underside

Recommended initial control throws

Elevator up:	1/2"
Elevator down:	3/8"
Rudder port:	1"
Rudder stbd:	1"
Ailerons up:	1/2"
Ailerons down:	3/8"

Scale spinner outline

ROYAL NAVY
WJ 232

WJ 232

Practice	*Why?*	**Because**

■ An actual aircraft:
If you can, base your model on a plane you know. In my case I have used WJ232 as my 'target aircraft'.

Why not just follow the plan detail and photos of your model?

No problem, but why not practise a little research on your own?

Photo 20:1 *The target aircraft – Sea Fury Mk FB.11 ZKSFR (WJ232) based at Ardmore, New Zealand. Built as a 'Baghdad' Fury sold to the Iraqi air force, it lacked hydraulics for wing folding and an arrester hook. In 1986 the plane was acquired by a consortium that had it restored to Sea Fury specifications, and finished it in the scheme of WJ232 of the Royal Navy carrier HMS 'Ocean'. In the hands of Lieutenant Peter 'Hoagy' Carmichael RN, WJ232 earned a place in history when it shot down a MIG 15 jet fighter during the Korean War.*

■ The manufacturer:
Hawker Aircraft Company. Sopwith Aviation Company, makers of the famous Sopwith Pup and Camel aircraft of World War I was, after the war, hit by the recession and went into receivership in 1920. What emerged was the HG Hawker Engineering Company. The next year the company suffered a worse blow when their chief pilot, Harry Hawker, was killed in a Nieuport Goshawk. Today his name has been perpetuated through the company's long list of extremely successful aircraft that bear his name.

What's the historical significance of studying the manufacturing company and design background of this particular model of aircraft?

Hawker aircraft, under Sydney Camm and his design team, was responsible for a remarkable line of distinguished aircraft: the Hawker Hart bomber (1928), faster than its contemporary fighters; the Hart Fighter (1930) renamed 'Demon' two years later; the Hawker Fury I (1931), first RAF fighter to exceed 200 mph;

Photo 20:2 *The model makes a very convincing replica of the real thing. Just the tiny propeller is the big giveaway.*

■ The Designer:
Sir Sydney Camm
Born: Windsor, England, 1893
Died: 12 March 1966
Knighted: 1953
Founding member of the Windsor Model Aeroplane Club which, in 1912, designed and flew a man-carrying glider.
Chief designer and head of the Hawker Aircraft design team at Kingston-upon-Thames, Surrey, England from 1925.

Hurricane, mainstay of British against the Luftwaffe bomber onslaught during the Battle of Britain; Tornado/Typhoon and the Tempest/Fury/Sea Fury series of piston-engined aircraft; into the jet age with the Hunter then the P.1127, prototype of the world's first operational vertical takeoff and landing fighter, the Harrier.
His active life spanned the era that took aviation from man-carrying kites to Concorde.

180

■ The aircraft:

A total of 864 aircraft were produced. Developed during World War II, the plane did not enter service until after the war. It eventually saw active service in the Korean war and served with distinction undertaking ground attack missions, air spotting for naval gunnery and photo rec.

■ The model:

As you have progressed to this sort of model featuring retracting undercarriage and flaps, you'll need a six-channel radio and quite a lot of practice with a model like your D.H.71.

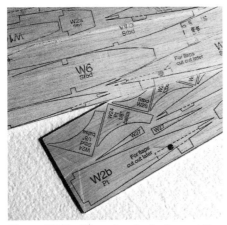

Photo 20:5   *The plan includes cutting patterns for the balsa and ply parts, so begin by marking up your wood.*

■ Building the wing

Again a custom building board is recommended for the wing assembly, but this time notice that the wing ribs incorporate tabs. These hold each rib at the right position to develop washout at the wingtips (later you will cut them off before sheeting the lower surfaces of the wings). Other differences are that this wing is sheeted both sides right back to the trailing edge. It also incorporates two aileron servos, air retracts and servo operated flaps. All this calls for more planning before you start, making sure you keep building in the right sequence.

■ Fit the flaps servo to rib W1 then follow the usual technique of splicing the lower wing spar. Set up the ribs over it and the

When are we going to build a model that only needs a flat bench space?

Recommended building board

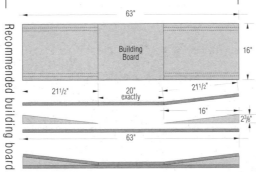

Photo 20:3   *Without this building board you could end up with a tricky alignment job on your hands – with it it's a piece of cake.*

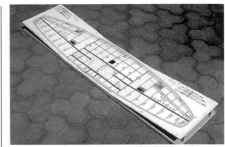

Photo 20:4   *Double check the wing sections of the plan fit accurately.*

Sorry if it's a bit of a bore, but the building board really will save you time in the long run. And it's so much easier when you can screw down clamps for a great grip while glue hardens.

You can use parts of previous boards to make this one because you don't really have to follow all the outer measurements. Just be sure to get the centre section right and follow the plan for the angles of the outer panels.

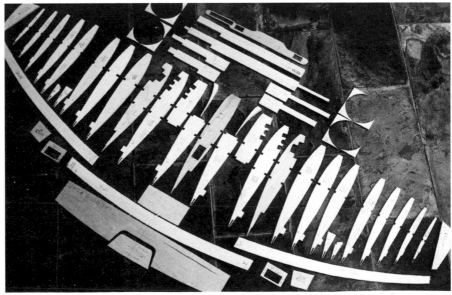

Photo 20:6   *After you've cut out all the parts for a section like the wing, it's not a bad idea to lay them out so you understand just where everything fits. It also helps you become more familiar with the job ahead.*

Sea Fury, sheet 1: wing   Scale = 25%   Enlarge to 400% and check size against ruler.

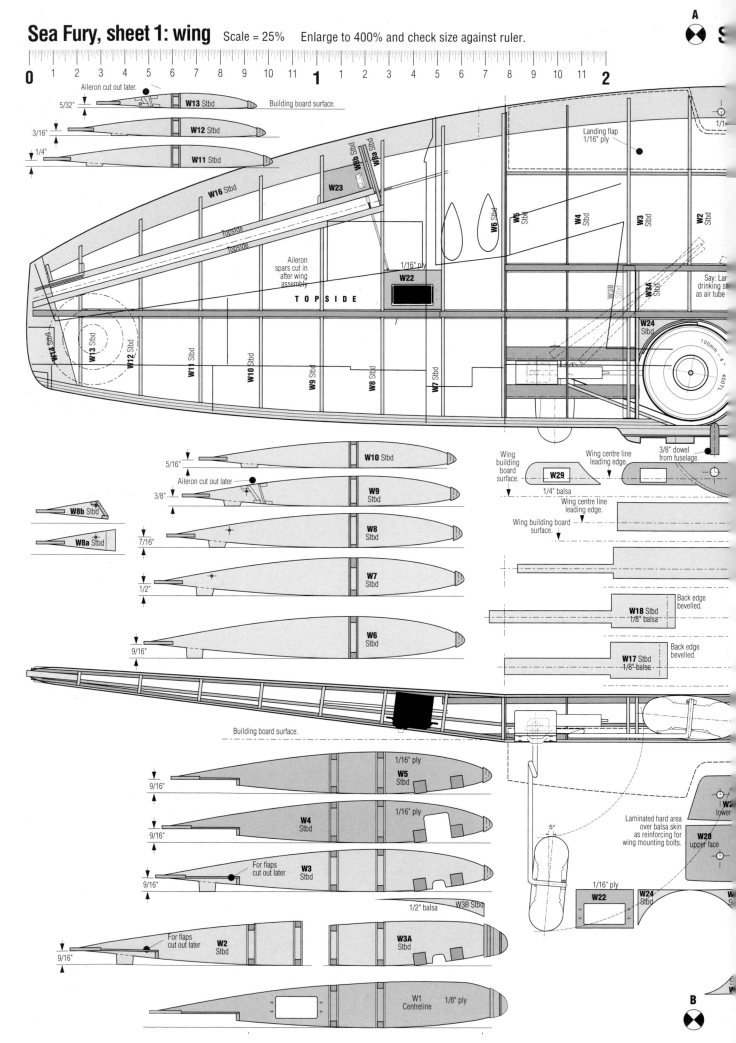

0 1 2 3 4 5 6 7 8 9 10 11 **1** 1 2 3 4 5 6 7 8 9 10 11 **2**

Aileron cut out later.

5/32"   W13 Stbd   Building board surface.

3/16"   W12 Stbd

1/4"   W11 Stbd

W16 Stbd

W23

Topside
Topside

Aileron spars cut in after wing assembly

T O P S I D E

1/16" ply

W22

W14 Stbd
W13 Stbd
W12 Stbd
W11 Stbd
W10 Stbd
W9 Stbd
W8 Stbd
W7 Stbd

W6 Stbd
W5 Stbd
W4 Stbd
W3 Stbd
W2 Stbd

Landing flap 1/16" ply

W3B Stbd

W3A Stbd

Say: Lar drinking s as air tube

W24 Stbd

100mm – 4" 400TL

3/8" dowel from fuselage.

5/16"   W10 Stbd

Aileron cut out later

3/8"   W9 Stbd

W8b Stbd

W8a Stbd

7/16"   W8 Stbd

1/2"   W7 Stbd

9/16"   W6 Stbd

Wing building board surface.

Wing centre line leading edge.

W29

1/4" balsa

Wing centre line leading edge.

Wing building board surface.

Back edge bevelled.

W18 Stbd
1/8" balsa

Back edge bevelled.

W17 Stbd
1/8" balsa

Building board surface.

1/16" ply
W5 Stbd

9/16"   W4 Stbd   1/16" ply

9/16"   For flaps cut out later   W3 Stbd   1/16" ply

1/2" balsa   W3B Stbd

9/16"   For flaps cut out later   W2 Stbd

W3A Stbd

5°

Laminated hard area over balsa skin as reinforcing for wing mounting bolts.

W28 upper face

1/16" ply

W22

W24 Stbd

W1 Centreline   1/8" ply

Sea Fury, sheet 2: wing

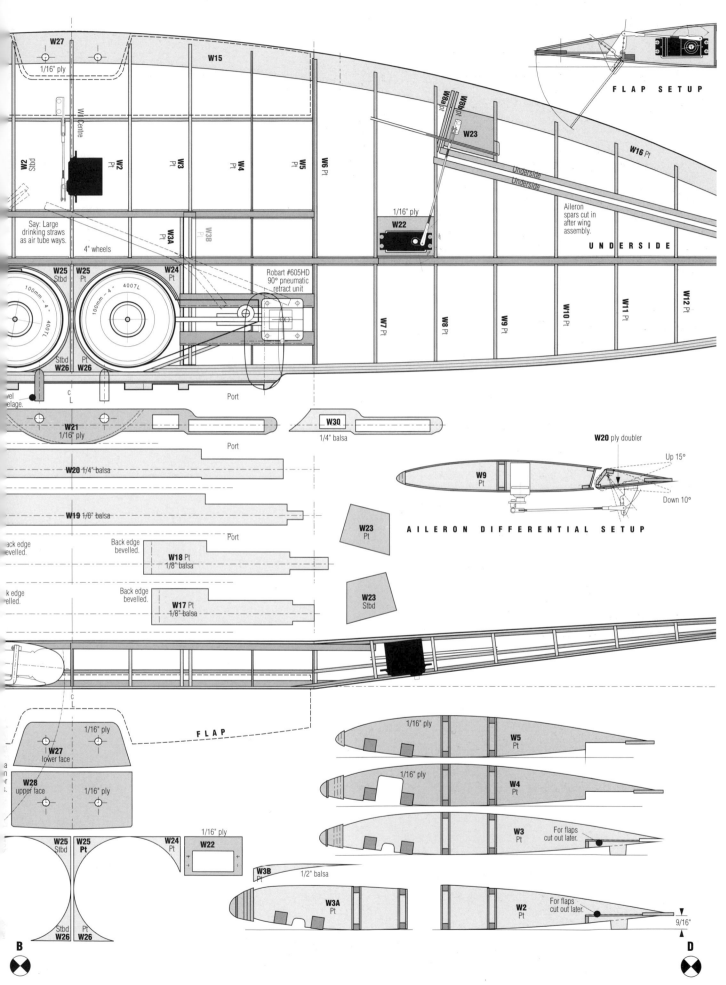

W27
1/16" ply

W15

W1 Centre

FLAP SETUP

W8a pt W8b pt

W23

W2 Stbd

W2 Pt

W3 Pt

W4 Pt

W5 Pt

W6 Pt

W16 Pt

1/16" ply

W22

Underside
Underside

Aileron
spars cut in
after wing
assembly.

UNDERSIDE

Say: Large
drinking straws
as air tube ways.

4" wheels

W3A Pt

W3B Pt

Robart #605HD
90° pneumatic
retract unit

W25 Stbd

W25 Pt

W24 Pt

100mm ~ 4" 400TL

100mm ~ 4" 400TL

400TL

W7 Pt

W8 Pt

W9 Pt

W10 Pt

W11 Pt

W12 Pt

Stbd Pt
W26 W26

C
L

Port

W21
1/16" ply

W30

Port

1/4" balsa

W20 ply doubler

Up 15°

W20 1/4" balsa

Port

W9
Pt

Down 10°

W19 1/8" balsa

Back edge
bevelled.

Back edge
bevelled.

Port

W23
Pt

W18 Pt
1/8" balsa

AILERON DIFFERENTIAL SETUP

ack edge
elled.

Back edge
bevelled.

W17 Pt
1/8" balsa

W23
Stbd

C
L

FLAP

1/16" ply

W5
Pt

W27
lower face

1/16" ply

1/16" ply

W4
Pt

W28
upper face

1/16" ply

1/16" ply

W3
Pt

For flaps
cut out later.

W25
Stbd

W25
Pt

W24
Pt

1/16" ply

W3B
Pt

1/2" balsa

W22

Stbd Pt
W26 W26

W3A
Pt

W2
Pt

For flaps
cut out later.

9/16"

D

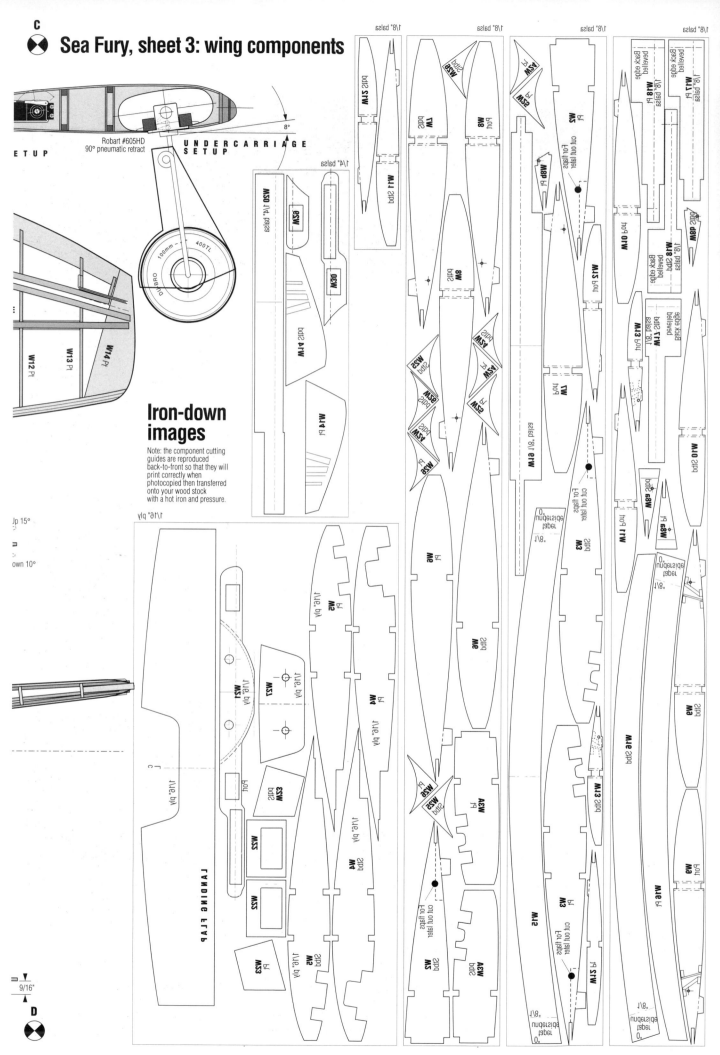

Sea Fury, sheet 3: wing components

Iron-down images

Note: the component cutting guides are reproduced back-to-front so that they will print correctly when photocopied then transferred onto your wood stock with a hot iron and pressure.

Robart #605HD
90° pneumatic retract

UNDERCARRIAGE SETUP

184

other spars and undercarriage bearers. Insert the brass hinge tubes through ribs W7/8/9 and W13/14 as you go and add the top spar (Photo 20:8 shows its splice).

Make up the trailing edge with its spliced joints flat on the building board. Once the glue is hard, lift it and glue it into the ribs. Laminate the leading edge round the rib ends, one layer at a time. When hard bevel-cut their inner ends to the wheel well profile and add the W19/20/21 leading edges.

Form the wheel wells with gussets W24/25/26 (photo 20:7) and wrap $^1/_{16}$" vertical grain liners inside.

■ To operate the retract gear you will need to have air tubes leading to each end of both of the gear cylinders. Pipes can develop leaks so make provision for changing them without having to do major surgery on the finished wing. I threaded large diameter drinking straws from the wheel wells to the flap servo cavities (photo 20:9). the tubes can be pushed through any time.

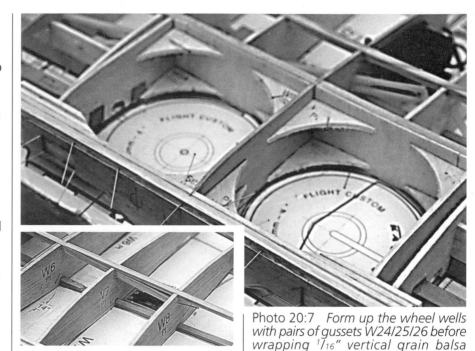

Photo 20:7 *Form up the wheel wells with pairs of gussets W24/25/26 before wrapping $^1/_{16}$" vertical grain balsa round the inside, reaching from the building board up to the sheet line.*

Photo 20:8 *The upper inside spar faces against W5 and the outer is spliced on.*

Photo 20:9 *Drinking straws added.*

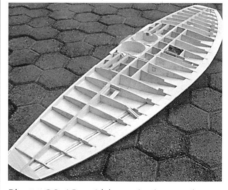

Photo 20:10 *Although the ailerons are cut out later, insert all the riblets and topside spars before sheeting the top surfaces. In fact, think through the steps and do everything you can now.*

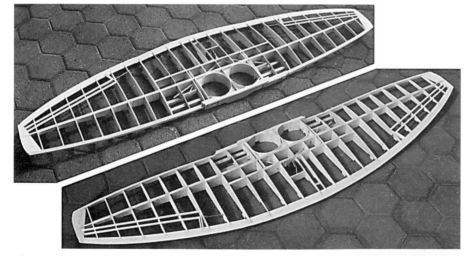

Photo 20:11 – 12 *Sand off the leading and trailing edges before covering.*

Wing spar webbing, aileron riblets, topside spars, servo trays and so on are added, then sand off for a good sheeting fit.

■ Sheet the leading edge topside between W3 and W5 first. Add W3B riblets, then continue sheeting the topsides.

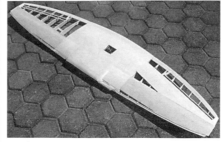

Photo 20:14 *I fitted plank at a time and edge-jointed as I went.*

Photo 20:13 *Although these photos show the wing free of the building board, always fix it down firmly before doing any major work like sheeting the topsides.*

The importance of holding the wing rigidly in place during major work is an expensive lesson to learn when you discover you have a permanent and irreparable twist glued in place!

Invert the wing and let in the lower aileron spars. Make up the channel to carry your servo leads along into the centre section. Again, you need to be able to install or replace a servo without major wiring difficulties. Complete the wing sheeting.

■ I glassed the surface of the whole prototype wing using 0.7oz cloth and epoxy resin diluted 70%/30% with acetone. Work this out to the thinnest possible coat. Saw out the ailerons, capping their leading edges and the wing cutouts. Test fit with the hinge pins and shape the aileron leading edges to get adequate downward movement (say ³/₄").

Photo 20:15   *See how the lower aileron spars are let into the wing ribs and the channel to carry the leads from the servo housings to the centre section access opening has been formed.*

The ailerons are left in as an integral part of the wing right through construction and basic surfacing. This makes sure they remain correctly aligned and retain their proper shape. Just make sure you mark their exact position so you know where to make the cuts!
While cutting them out be gentle as you saw through the brass hinge tubes (later you file the tube ends smooth and insert small washers when you slide in the hinge pins).

You will see from the ailerons' under-cut shape that upward movement is not restricted, but carefully round the lower leading edges to get the necessary downward movement.

Photos 20:16 to 19   *Once the ailerons are sawn free, their leading edges are capped. The hinge pins are inserted and the aileron movement is adjusted by shaping the aileron leading edge to allow about a ³/₄" downward movement.*

Photos 20:20 to 22   *In preparation for the Spitfire detailing, experiments were made on this model with panel marking. Several layers of tape are aligned against panel edges drawn on the wing. Against these edges a weak epoxy/balloon bog is carefully trowelled out. In all, the prototype used about 1cc of epoxy and plenty of balloons so the additional weight was very little (but remember, it all adds up!). When it has set hard, remove the tape and sand out any edges you don't want to show. I think the end result is quite impressive and, if I have time, will probably do the same with the Spitfire.*

186

Practice

■ The engine cowling:

Here we go into fibreglass a little deeper. We make an accurate mould then glass up the cowling (note: Photos 20:23 to 34 are from a small Sea Fury I built years ago).

Essentially we make a blade that's a half-profile of the cowling shape. We revolve this on a tube which we have fixed inside a suitable dam (plastic bowl, flowerpot or small bucket). We swing it round to shape builder's grade plaster of Paris that we gradually add until we have a complete inside-out mould of the cowling. To this we add a resist so fibreglass resin wont stick to it. Then we lay up our fibreglass.

This model won't be nose heavy so we can afford to build up a good thickness of glass.

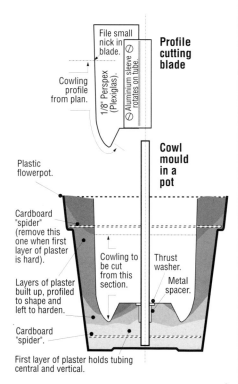

When it has cured we remove it from the mould (you'll probably have to break it off), trim off both ends and the job is done!

Just follow the photos and you can't go far wrong. Remember, take your time and don't panic when you think things are getting out of control.

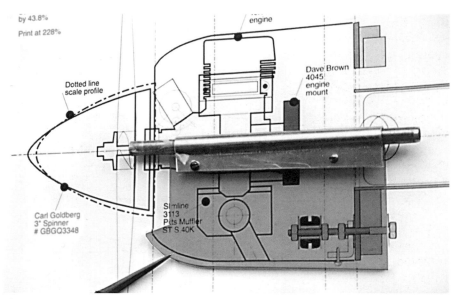

Photo 20:23   *Using say ¹/₈″ Perspex and some aluminium sheet, wrap the aluminium over a sample tube (that's the same size as you use inside the mould) and fix it to the Perspex to give it a bearing surface. Lay the tube on the centreline of the plan and cut the half-profile of the cowling, leaving plenty of overhang at both ends.*

Photo 20:24   *Make a cardboard 'spider' to hold the top end of the tube in the right place and set the bottom end into a good dollop of plaster.*

Photo 20:25   *When the plaster is set drop a spacer over the tube, then a washer. Test fit the blade down on the washer and see there's clearance.*

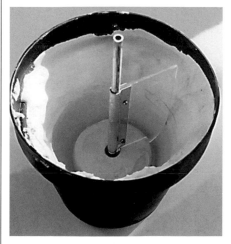

Photo 20:26   *Mix a smallish amount of plaster, add it to the mould and work it round, cleaning the blade regularly. After a few mixes it looks like this.*

Photo 20:27   *As you get near the top it's best to add a retaining ring of cardboard so you can tip the mould to build up the sides all the way.*

AIRCRAFT WORKSHOP: Learn to make models that FLY

187

Sea Fury, sheet 4: fuselage

Scale = 25%   Enlarge to 400% and check size against ruler.

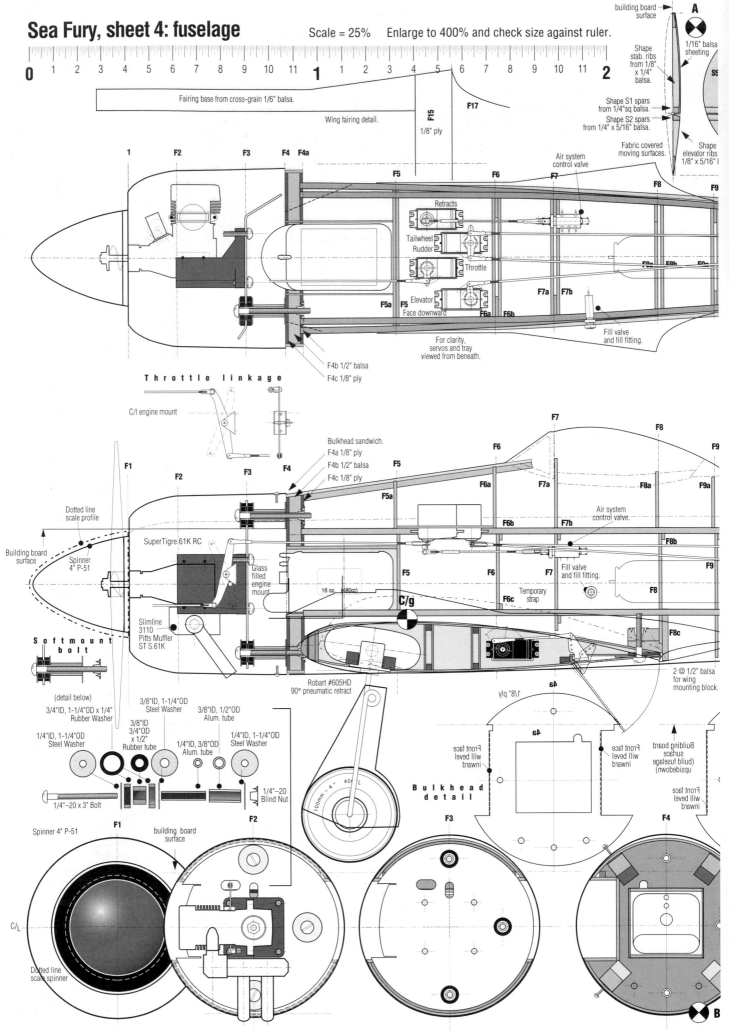

Fairing base from cross-grain 1/6" balsa.

Wing fairing detail.

building board surface

1/16" balsa sheeting

Shape stab. ribs from 1/8" x 1/4" balsa.

Shape S1 spars from 1/4"sq balsa.

Shape S2 spars from 1/4" x 5/16" balsa.

Shape elevator ribs 1/8" x 5/16"

Fabric covered moving surfaces.

F15   F17   1/8" ply

Retracts
Tailwheel
Rudder
Throttle
Elevator
Face downward

Air system control valve

For clarity, servos and tray viewed from beneath.

Fill valve and fill fitting.

F4b 1/2" balsa
F4c 1/8" ply

Throttle linkage

C/l engine mount

Bulkhead sandwich.
F4a 1/8" ply
F4b 1/2" balsa
F4c 1/8" ply

Dotted line scale profile

Spinner 4" P-51

Building board surface

SuperTigre 61K RC

Glass filled engine mount

Slimline 3110 Pitts Muffler ST S.61K

Softmount bolt

16 oz.   (480cc)

C/g

Air system control valve.

Fill valve and fill fitting.

Temporary strap

Robart #605HD 90° pneumatic retract

2 @ 1/2" balsa for wing mounting block.

(detail below)

3/4"ID, 1-1/4"OD x 1/4" Rubber Washer

3/8"ID, 1-1/4"OD Steel Washer

3/8"ID, 1/2"OD Alum. tube

1/4"ID, 1-1/4"OD Steel Washer

3/8"ID 3/4"OD x 1/2" Rubber tube

1/4"ID, 3/8"OD Alum. tube

1/4"ID, 1-1/4"OD Steel Washer

1/4"–20 Blind Nut

1/4"–20 x 3" Bolt

Front face will bevel inward

Front face will bevel inward

1/8" ply

Bulkhead detail

Building board surface (build fuselage upsidedown)

Front face will bevel inward

Spinner 4" P-51

building board surface

F1

F2

F3

F4

C/L

Dotted line scale spinner

188

AIRCRAFT WORKSHOP: Learn to make models that FLY

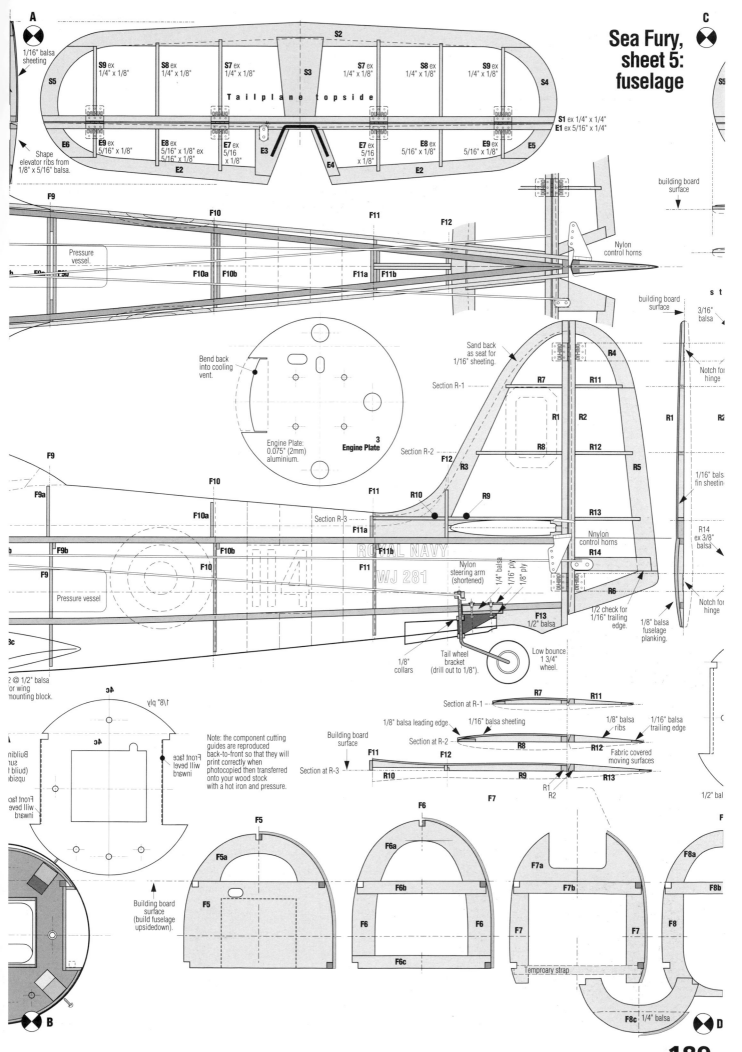

S2

S9 ex
1/4" x 1/8"   S8 ex
1/4" x 1/8"   S7 ex
1/4" x 1/8"   S3   S7 ex
1/4" x 1/8"   S8 ex
1/4" x 1/8"   S9 ex
1/4" x 1/8"

S5   S4

T a i l p l a n e   t o p s i d e

Shape
elevator ribs from
1/8" x 5/16" balsa.

S1 ex 1/4" x 1/4"
E1 ex 5/16" x 1/4"

E6   E9 ex
5/16" x 1/8"   E8 ex
5/16" x 1/8" ex   E7 ex
5/16
x 1/8"   E3   E7 ex
5/16
x 1/8"   E8 ex
5/16" x 1/8"   E9 ex
5/16" x 1/8"   E5

E2   E4   E2

F9

F10   F11   F12

building board
surface

Pressure
vessel.

F10a   F10b   F11a   F11b

Nylon
control horns

building board
surface

s   t

3/16"
balsa

Bend back
into cooling
vent.

Sand back
as seat for
1/16" sheeting.

R4

Section R-1   R7   R11

Notch for
hinge

F9

F9a

Section R-2   F12   R3   R1   R2

R8   R12

R1   R2

Engine Plate:
0.075" (2mm)
aluminium.   3
Engine Plate

R5

1/16" balsa
fin sheeting

F9   F10   F11   R10   R9

Section R-3   R13   1/16" balsa
fin sheeting

F10a   F11a   Nnylon
control horns

F9b   F11b   R14   R14
ex 3/8"
balsa

ROYAL NAVY
WJ 281

Pressure vessel   F10b   F10   F11   Nylon
steering arm
(shortened)   1/4" balsa
1/16" ply
1/8" ply   R6   1/2 check for
1/16" trailing
edge.   1/8" balsa
fuselage
planking.   Notch for
hinge

F9

3c   F13
1/2" balsa

1/8"
collars   Tail wheel
bracket
(drill out to 1/8").   Low bounce
1 3/4"
wheel.

2 @ 1/2" balsa
or wing
mounting block.

4c   1/8" ply   Section at R-1   R7   R11

Note: the component cutting
guides are reproduced
back-to-front so that they will
print correctly when
photocopied then transferred
onto your wood stock
with a hot iron and pressure.   1/8" balsa leading edge   1/16" balsa sheeting   1/8" balsa
ribs   1/16" balsa
trailing edge

4c   Building board
surface   Section at R-2   R8   R12   Fabric covered
moving surfaces

Front face
will bevel
inward   F11   F12   Section at R-3   R10   R9   R1
R2   R13

Front face
will bevel
inward   F6   F7   1/2" bal

F5

F5a   F6a   F7a   F8a

Building board
surface
(build fuselage
upsidedown).   F5   F5a   F6b   F7b   F8b

F5   F6   F6   F7   F8

F6c   Temporary strap   F7   F8

B   F8c 1/4" balsa   D

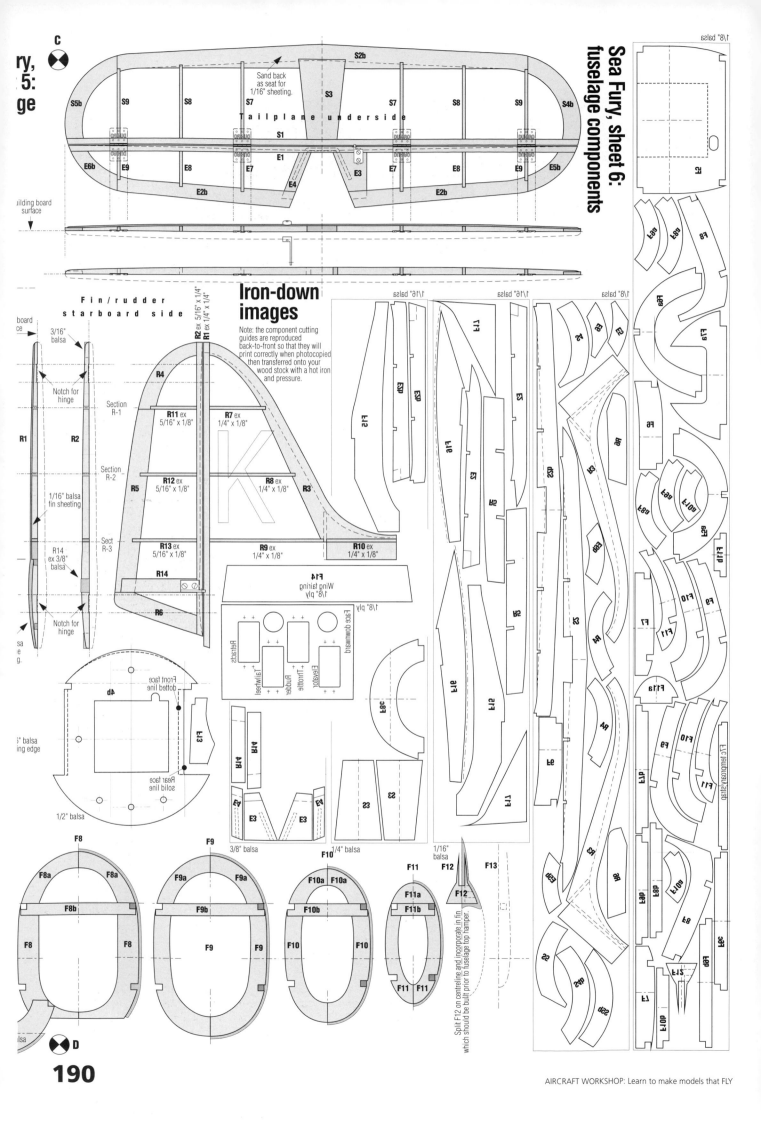

Iron-down images

Note: the component cutting guides are reproduced back-to-front so that they will print correctly when photocopied then transferred onto your wood stock with a hot iron and pressure.

Tailplane underside

Sand back as seat for 1/16" sheeting.

Fin/rudder starboard side

Photo 20:28 *By now the sides will look nice and smooth, and there should be a tiny scribed line showing where the back edge of the cowling will lie.*

There's a way of greatly increasing strength of the casting without adding a lot of extra weight. After a couple of layers of say 4 oz woven rovings (applied in small pieces) put in a layer of ⅛" soft balsa planks running front-to-back and cover them with a final layer of cloth. The result is incredibly strong. Just remember to seal with resin the edges of any final cutouts so this wood layer can't absorb fuel.

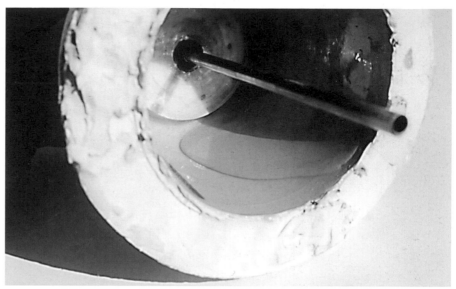

Photo 20:29 *Dry the plaster thoroughly (this takes a lot of time). Varnish the surface and paint with a resist (PVA resist). Once it has dried, I also smear out a thin coating of Vaseline. Work in a nice warm room. Mix some epoxy resin, pour it in and revolve the mould continuously. As the resin thickens, it builds up a coating over the mould. Keep working until it stops flowing.*

Photo 20:30 *When the coating gets rubber-like, start glassing up using smallish pieces of say 4 oz cloth. Ram small offcuts down into the resin that loads up at the bottom end and try to keep the glass content high relative to the resin.*

Photo 20:31 *Add balsa strips. These should be tapered at both ends, the lower ends to fit the curve of the cowling and the upper ends to fair out well before the back line of the cowl. Otherwise you could have wood appear when you trim off the trailing edge of the cowling. Now give it a final coat of resin and cloth.*

Photo 20:32 *Remove from the mould and wash thoroughly to get rid of any traces of Vaseline or resist that still clings to the casting.*

Photo 20:33 *A keyhole saw, hacksaw holder handle or even bare hacksaw blade will let you get in round the front to remove overhangs.*

Photo 20:34 *The scriber mark on the original blade should have marked the mould. This will have been transferred to the casting as your cutting guide.*

Practice

Photo 20:35 *The throttle linkage crank is bracketed to the engine mount before the linkage to the throttle arm is connected and adjusted for full travel.*

■ The engine module:

It is much easier to complete the engine installation and firewall fitting before you start building the fuselage.

So we can use a Pitts-style muffler and keep everything inside the cowling, the engine is mounted flat, head to starboard. This puts the throttle in a bad position, so we use a crank and linkage to get it back up and away from the fuel tank (photo 20:35).

Make up the firewall ply/balsa/ply epoxy sandwich, aluminium mounting plate and soft mounts (photo 20:36), leaving the mounts long at this time so you can adjust them back for a good fit to the spinner/cowling setup (different brands of spinner have different backplate thicknesses).

Assemble the module and compare measurements with the cowling requirements. Adjust the soft mount tube lengths for the correct forward/aft engine position. Mark up the cowling for its cutouts and test fit it. Add the cowling mounting blocks, align, drill and fit the cowling.

Remove the firewall and set the rest of the gear aside until later.

Why?

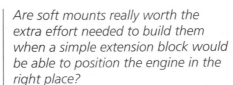

Are soft mounts really worth the extra effort needed to build them when a simple extension block would be able to position the engine in the right place?

Because

Soft mounts protect your aircraft in a number of ways. They can reduce the amount of vibration that the engine sends to the electrical components, although you should still suspend them in rubber. There are also all the mechanical parts like linkages, hinges, screws and control surfaces that vibration can loosen or wear out. Soft mounts can also help to reduce damage from a crash. In this case the aluminium mounting plate should bend long before any engine parts or before the firewall gets displaced. We have yet to find out!

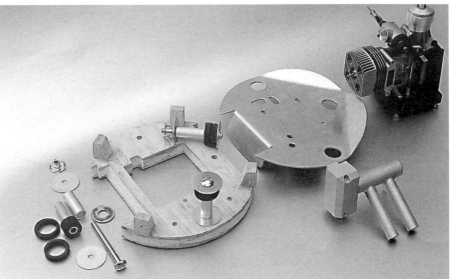

Photo 20:36   *The firewall sandwich, soft mounts, mounting plate and exhaust are all set up before fuselage construction begins. The throttle linkage is mounted on the engine mount and the throttle arm is connected to it.*

Photo 20:37   *The engine module is assembled to check for correct alignment and length.*

Photo 20:38 *All cowling apertures can be cut and checked for position, clearance and size. Seal the edges of all cutouts to prevent fuel from getting into the laminates.*

192

Practice

↓

■ Building the fuselage:

Make up the fuselage formers but don't join any 'a' sections to their lower parts. Just set them aside.

Assemble the building board flat, with the wedges removed. Mount the fuselage plan view (looking down) square along the board so the aft face of the firewall is flush with the end of the board.

■ Clamp down the upper fuselage longerons, tapered to fit at the rudder post, and add the formers F5 to F11. Assemble the fuel tank box through the firewall and back to fit neatly against F5 when the firewall is in its final position. Square up and glue. Add the lower longerons and proceed in the usual way.

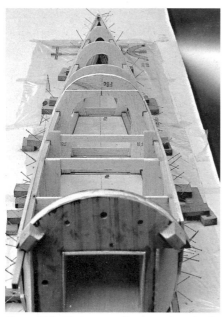

Photo 20:42 *Leave off when the planks reach the line of the second longerons, then attend to the tailwheel.*

Plank up the sides, leaving off the first plank to clear the clamps and making sure you are leaving access to the clamp screws.

■ Now watch the sequence of things. If your tailwheel is going to be fully enclosed it is necessary right away to make up and fit the mount, bracket and steering linkage. In photos 20:43 and 44 see how this is done with a little assembly which slides into the 'Vee' of the lower longerons.

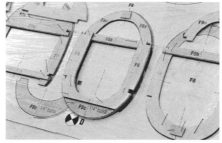

Photo 20:39 *Make up the fuselage formers, adding the 'b' braces but keeping the topsides separate for assembly later.*

Photo 20:40 *Build the fuselage upside-down over the plan with the firewall hanging off the end. After you have tapered the longerons for a good fit at the rudder post, begin building by clamping the upper longerons to the board. Add the formers to them. Now fit the lower longerons.*

Photo 20:43 *The steering arm is aligned and firmly fixed to the shaft. Attach a pushrod before you slide the assembly into place.*

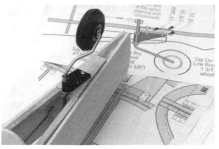

Photo 20:44 *When the assembly is correctly positioned, and you are sure there are clearances for the steering arm, glue it into position.*

Because

↓

You leave the upper section 'a' formers aside meantime because, in building the fuselage upside-down, you need a flat datum line. This is the line at the top of the upper longeron. Everything is set square to this surface. Because, for strength, the firewall incorporates the topside shape it is necessary to drop it over the end of the building board. This doesn't leave you much to hold it by. I use the fuel tank box to support, position and keep the firewall square to the longerons while building up the planking.

Photo 20:41 *Build up the sides, plank-about to each side, leaving the first space free of the longeron clamps. Be sure all clamp screws are outboard enough to be easily removed later.*

While it's not a very sensible practice to bury critical bearings and couplings behind permanent planking, the tail wheel steering on this design seems to justify it. But it does mean you must be extra vigilant to see that bends are right, set screws are tight and fixed with a lock solution. Linkages must be properly retained. Now is the time to make sure everything is free to move correctly, with sufficient clearance and no binding – don't wait until it's buried and out of reach.

It's also a good idea to keep a note of exactly how you have arranged everything. If at some time in the future you must undertake surgery, it's nice to know just where to make that first critical cut.

Practice

■ To fit the wing, we remove the fuselage from the board, turn it at right angles and clamp it down again. Now the ends of the board are out to the sides, letting you make accurate measurements from it as far out as the wingtips.

Shape and fit the wing mounting block per the plan. Place a ⅛" packer on the mounting block and lower the wing into position. When it's correctly seated and the tips are an equal distance from the building board, check that any side planking of the fuselage clears the wing topside by ⅟₁₆" front to back. Trim to achieve this. With the wing dead square, the tips locked down equally, and tape keeping it rigid, drill out the two ⅜" dowel holes. These go through the firewall and right into the wing wheel wells (use a piece of dowel to fill the first hole before you drill the second). Remove the wing and fit rounded end dowels in the firewall and glue. Plank the underside and test fit the wing to maintain the ⅟₁₆" clearance needed from the sides.

■ Proceed to fit out the fuselage with servos, snakes (including one for the Rx aerial), air control valve and air tank. It will never be easier than now – I know because I left it a little later and was sorry!

Photo 20:48 *Plank the underside and then add the topside formers.*

■ Continue planking down the sides to the centreline and onto the underside tail block. Add the topside formers and complete the fuselage planking, but leave a square cutout where the tailplane will be located. Take out to a well-aired area and sand smooth.

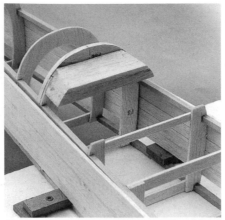

Photo 20:45 *The wing mounting block gets built in before the underside planking stage.*

Photo 20:47 *Install the servos, pushrods, snakes, and the basic air gear as soon as you have the fuselage sides planked.*

Photo 20:49 *The last of the side planking was left off until now to allow the fuselage to be clamped down.*

Photo 20:50 *I left it to this stage before installing the gear and found it a real fiddle.*

Because

Using the building board instead of a bench top lets you move the whole work from place to place, and in this case gives you all round access.

Photo 20:46 *Align the wing accurately and drill the dowel holes. Temporarily add a dowel into the first hole while you drill the second.*

The clearance you are providing above the wing topside will be used when you create the wing fairings. Meantime let's concentrate on getting a nicely faired fuselage line without having to work round other complicated shapes. Do take care when you are handling this fuselage from now on. It rolls round easily and it wouldn't be difficult to have it roll off the building board.

If you're sanding it on a hard work surface, rest the downside on an old cushion so you don't put bruises and dents in the opposite side from the one you're working on. In some ways it's best to stand it on its nose and work downwards. This also lets you revolve it to observe shadows (hollows) and highlights (bumps).

194

■ The fuselage will never be an easier shape to cover than right now, so go ahead and skin the whole surface with a light coat of 0.7 oz fibreglass cloth wetted out with 70/30 resin/acetone.

■ Make up the tail surfaces against the plan flat on the building board. These are made in paired half shells split through their centrelines to keep them

Photo 20:51 *Complete the upper side planking but leave a gap near the cockpit centre so you can still see the exact position of the formers and centreline reference.*

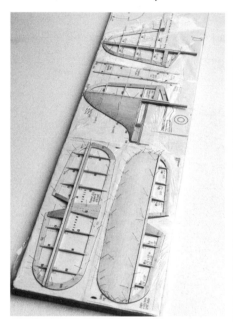

Photo 20:52 *The fin, rudder, tailplane and elevators are all split construction, and are planked and sanded in the flat.*

Photo 20:53 *Join the halves together with epoxy and tape until cured. Note that the elevator halves incorporate a piano wire stiffener within the joint.*

Photo 20:54 *Fix the fin with its rudder post onto the fuselage at the same time as the tailplane and elevator assembly. Add scrap balsa filler blocks to complete the fairing.*

true. They are only brought together after they are sheeted and the glue is hard. When the elevator shells are glued together they should enclose the piano wire stiffener which bridges the port and starboard panels. Mark the exact position of this stiffener so it doesn't foul the screws when you add the elevator control horn.

Tissue and dope the fin and tailplane. Cover the rudder and elevator with SIG Coverall and dope finish. Set the rudder aside meantime but hinge the elevator permanently on the tailplane. Fit the fin/rudder post and the tailplane assembly to the fuselage as one unit. Apply filler blocks to fair the tail surfaces to the fuselage, and finish with as little filler as necessary to obtain a clean fairing.

Why not build the fin into the fuselage at the beginning instead of adding it on at this late stage?

The most frequent disabling accident I see at the flying field is the aircraft that noses over and fractures the fin at the fuselage line.
If the fin can be reinforced with a rudder post that extends right down to the base of the fuselage it will be far stronger and should easily survive this sort of minor incident.
So, the design problem is to provide a full depth rudder post when, at the same time, we have a one-piece tailplane with a one-piece elevator which pivots ahead of the rudder post. There are two obvious solutions: either an enlarged slot ahead of the tailplane so the whole assembly can slide in sideways, then back into position; or lower the fin down onto the tailplane assembly during construction – like we do on this design.

Practice

■ The wing fairing is to be constructed with the wing mounted on the fuselage. Here's how:

To prevent the two from sticking together we use a layer of cling film. Glue the 1/8" ply F14 to the wing mounting block and when set, accurately mount the wing and drill out the two bolt holes. Remove the wing, drill out the holes in the fuselage to take the blind nuts, and fit them. Reassemble with the wing after covering its centre section with cling film. Add the two F17 fairings behind F14. Now, forward of F17, slide the 1/16" cross-grain balsa fairing between the wing and fuselage sides, and pin it down onto the wing. Add F15 and F16 to both sides of the fuselage, fitting them down neatly against the cross-grain balsa fairing. Glue. From scrap 1/8" balsa make two triangular gussets and fix as shown (photo 20:55).

From 1/16" balsa shape a fillet covering panel to bridge from the wing line to F16, and bevel its back edges for a good fit. Glue and pin down into the natural twisting curve of the fairing.

■ While the wing is attached, tip everything upside-down and build a fairing onto the underside of the wing. This matches up to the fuselage joint, extending it forward but finishing it to clear the flap.

■ Using as little filler as possible, complete the fuselage by filling any blemishes, improving joints, sharpening edges and defining panels. Later, you can detail to whatever level you want to achieve. In addition to the plans supplied, you can get a wealth of information from studying either an actual aircraft which may exist in your area, or from published photos. This can include join lines, filler caps, vent pipes and all manner of access hatches and so on. Meantime, you are only preparing the foundation for these details to be added.

Why?

Fairings are hard to make. What's their purpose?

Because

Wind tunnel tests have shown that at the junction of two different bodies such as where the wing meets the fuselage, there's usually a lot of turbulence generated. This translates into drag. Fairings can help reduce this turbulence.

Photo 20:55 *Glue the 1/8" ply F14 to the wing mounting block. Protect the wing with cling film, then fit the wing in position. Build up the wing fairings with the F17 panels and cross-grain 1/16" forward panels. Add the F15 and F16 profiles and then bridge each with a corner gusset as shown above.*

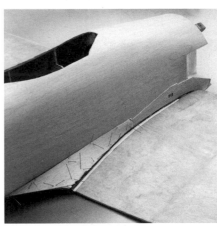

Photo 20:56 *Using 1/16" balsa, curve, shape and fit along the fairing. Pin and glue.*

Photo 20:57 *With epoxy/balloon bog, work up the detail while you blend the fuselage fit up to the cowling.*

196

Practice

■ The clear-view canopy:

There are vacuum frames and special ovens to form commercial products. However, with a minimum of gear you can still make a very respectable object. The method I used to make the prototype's canopy involved a nice piece of wood for the 'plug', some medium density fibre board (mdf), broom handle dowel, screws, and the kitchen oven. My friendly plastics fabricator sold me some 1.5mm polyethylene PETG (Sheffield's "Vivak") clear sheeting (many other materials could have been used).

Photos 1 through 8 show the procedure. The plastic is clamped between two frames, heated until soft, then pushed down over the plug and held there until cool. Heating the plastic is the tricky bit. I find it best to pre-heat the oven to 160° C then turn off the heat. I put the clamped plastic in at 150°C and leave it until it sags, take it out and bring it down smartly over the plug.

After fitting out the cockpit, fix the canopy in place and detailed the frame later.

Photocopy panels at actual size

Sea Fury, sheet 7: cockpit canopy and instrument panel

Scale = 25% Enlarge to 400% and check size against ruler

Clearview canopy moulding plug carved from solid fine-grain wood and sanded to final finish. See suggested moulding method.

Panels laminated with photocopy of instruments sandwiched between balsa and ply, with holes cut to allow instruments to show through. Ply painted matt black. Panel and sub panel finished separately, then sub panel superimposed last.

1/16" Balsa — Panel — Sub panel

Photocopy on paper

1/16" ply

Finished assembly then fixed at angle to former F6.

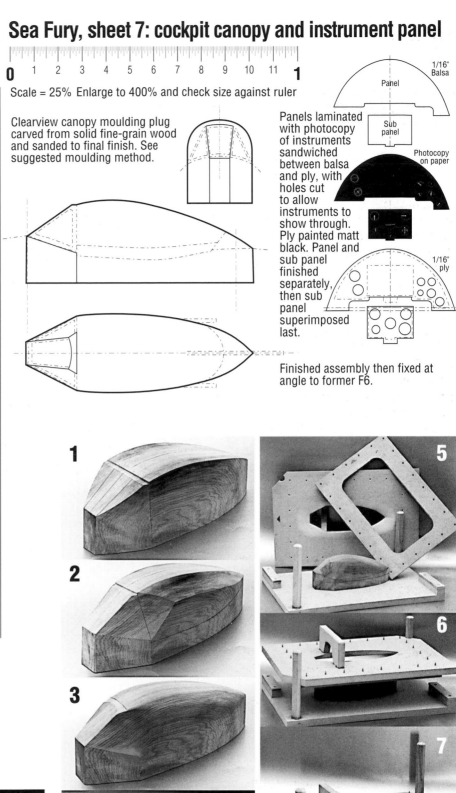

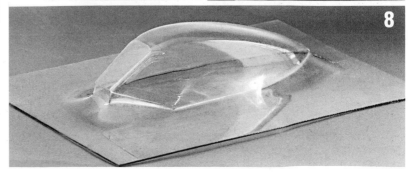

Practice

■ The pilot and cockpit:

Again, this is something you can make for yourself. Advantages over off-the-shelf pilots is that you can make the suitable type to the exact scale size, at less cost. Enlarging sheet 8 by 200%, cut out the enlarged profiles and match them up on adjacent sides of a block of EPS. Following the photos 9 through 14, you'll see the basic steps of cutting the profiles, carving the shape, adding detail with filler (epoxy bog in this case) and painting. Make up the seat and headrest from balsa or EPS. Fit out the cockpit, clean and glue the canopy to the fuselage, with, say Wilhold R/C-56).

Sea Fury, sheet 8: pilot

Scale = 50% Enlarge to 200% and check size against ruler

A six foot pilot would stand just 9" tall against this 1/7.7 scale model. This correct scale dummy pilot emphasises just how massive this piece of machinery really is. Similarly, a dummy of the wrong scale immediately destroys the proper impression.

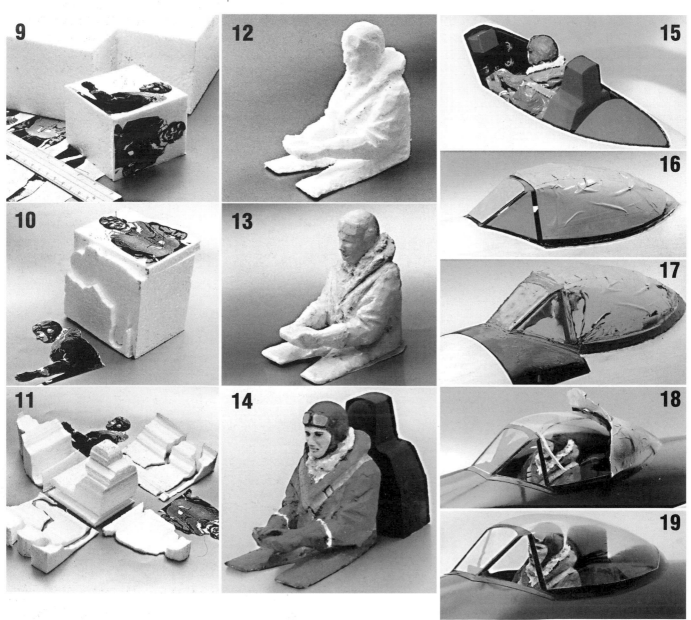

Practice	*Why?*	Because

■ Photos 16 through 19 show a way of applying frames to the canopy. I use several layers of signwriter's tape to make a thick mask, then appy blue-dyed epoxy bog to build up the frame. I leave the masking in place until I have spray paint the fuselage then strip off the mask taking care not to scratch the canopy in the process.

■ **Finishing:**

My model is spray-painted with automotive lacquer. This includes detail up to the invasion stripes. I use photocopy guides over signwriter's tape, and carefully cut out the Royal Navy roundels, squadron numbers and writing. You add as much detail as you want. I use electrical shielding tape behind the exhaust outlets. It looks like the stainless heat shield panels of the real thing.

Photo 20:58 *Detail (or the lack of it) is often the difference between your model looking like the full-size thing or a small, unconvincing imitation.*

When you describe building up the frame on the canopy, you slipped in that little mention of 'blue-dyed epoxy bog'. Why use dyed bog when we're going to paint it anyway?

Yes! Don't forget the canopy is transparent. Use natural-colour epoxy bog and that's what you'll see when you look through the canopy to the inside of the opposite side. So, dye it dark blue.

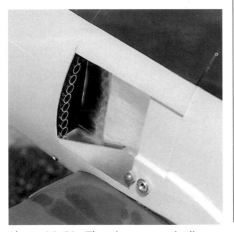

Photo 20:60 *The air pressure indicator and filler valve are tucked away, but readily accessible.*

Exhaust stacks are cut from old aluminium arrow shafts epoxied into the cowling cutouts. These give a touch of authenticity to ¾ aft views.

Wheel well covers are cut from aluminium litho printing plate. They are held from rotating on the undercarriage legs by screwing them to ⅛" aluminium straps behind the wheels; and are stitched to the leg at the top using florist's wire. The tailwheel doors are also litho plate, folded to grip the fuselage opening, and glued in place.

Photo 20:61 *Litho plate aluminium is ideal material for wheel well covers.*

Photo 20:59 *Even the servo access hatches can be folded up from litho plate. I used a few dabs of clear silicone gel to hold them in place.*

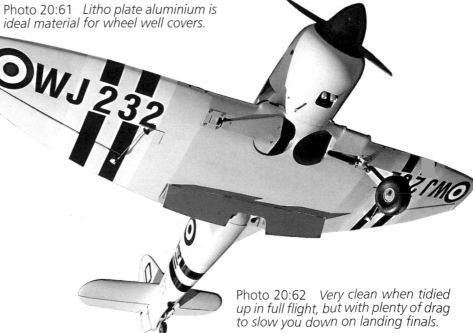

Photo 20:62 *Very clean when tidied up in full flight, but with plenty of drag to slow you down on landing finals.*

Practice

⬇

■ Test flight:

Before you do anything else, tune your engine to perform faultlessly during that first flight.

Check that all servo throws are in the right direction and that they travel the appropriate amount without binding. See they return to a true neutral. Note: neutral on the elevator can be misleading. The elevator has a pronounced taper. When checking for neutral trim, sight in from the end of the tailplane, not straight down.

Check the retract system and ensure there is no binding (I had one wheel lockup and was forced to belly-land (no damage).

The takeoff run is normal. Open the throttle progressively and any swing easily controlled. Hold her on the ground until you have plenty of flying speed. Control is powerful and fairly sensitive.

Why?

⬇

Why the emphasis on engine reliability at this stage?

A. Rivers

Photo 20:63   *Some models seem to take on a little magic when you see them in full flight. This is one.*

Because

⬇

Sure, engine reliability is important for all flights, but with a new plane that you've yet to get the feel of, reliability is vital. And, since it's probably a new engine in your new plane, it's wise practice to become familiar with how it behaves long before you get it 20 feet in the air in a hard, semi-controlled climb!

As loss of flying speed is probably the greatest hazard faced in a maiden flight, recovery from an engine cut on takeoff means you must pitch the nose down and fly straight ahead. And on most flying fields, you're going to have to fly into hostile territory. Alternatively, try to turn back without sufficient

A. Rivers

Photo 20:64   Alastair Rivers captured this maiden flight series which nicely shows off the Fury's clean lines and very stable attitude.

height, and speed will drop off and you'll probably fly straight into the ground. Enough doom. Off you go and enjoy some awesome flying!

Photo 20:65   *Like so many other warbird models, there would be good argument for building a full scale, 5-bladed Sea Fury propeller for static display of this model. In fact, the flying prop is a very long way from representing the real thing.*

200

Chapter 21: Researching Spitfire F.XIVE SM832

Photo © John M. Dibbs/The Plane Picture Company

Photo 21:1 *Spitfire F.XIVE SM832, arguably the most impressive WW II warbird flying today. Stationed at Duxford as part of The Fighter Collection, the author researched this aircraft in 1996. Since then it has passed into the hands of Christophe Jacquard of the Flying Legends and at the time of writing, is based at Dijon-Darois airfield, Bourgogne.*

Practice

Let's plan to build a serious replica of some wonderful aeroplane. To start with this involves some equally serious research.

What make, model, then individual aircraft is it to be?

For the purposes of this book, if the work we do is going to help the majority of modellers, it must be a very popular plane. This suggests a warbird, probably a Spitfire, Mustang or Fw 190. In the next breath, it should be unusual enough to stand out from the crowd to justify all the

Why?

Research . . . why research? Doesn't the plan give you all the information you need?

Photo 21:2 *The smell of paint and an air of great expectation. In two day's time there's the big display and you can feel the excitement building up all round you.*

Because

There's no point in trying to make a scale replica of an individual plane until we are sure we have access to enough reference material to do the job properly. The more you model, the more you'll discover the need for detail and information, which isn't shown on the plan. Finding out more could mean going to see the actual plane (if it still exists) or it could be that there is enough published material for us to work from. Either way, the more serious you are about making a fine model, the more important it is that you find out all you can about your plane.

Supermarine Spitfire F.XIVE

79" (88$^1/_2$") scale model aircraft
for 6-channel radio control and
2 cu in (32.5cc) 2-stroke engines
From 'AIRCRAFT WORKSHOP:
Learn to make models that FLY'
by Kelvin Shacklock ©
Model scale: 1/5 size of original

Specifications:	Spitfire SM 832 YBA	1/5 scale Model
Wingspan: SM 832	32' 7"	79"*
(elliptical wingtip)	(36' 10")	(88$^1/_2$")
Length overall:	32' 8"	79$^1/_2$"
Wing area SM832:	231 sq ft	9.2 sq ft
(elliptical wingtip):	244 sq ft	9.7 sq ft
Weight:	8,500 lb	20 lb
Wing loading SM832:	36.8 lb sq ft	34 oz sq ft
(elliptical wingtip):	34.8 lb sq ft	33 oz sq ft
Power:	Griffon	2 cu in
	60° 12 cylinder	2-stroke
	2375 hp	glow
Max speed:	439 mph at	
	24,500 ft	

* Note: the scale model wingspan has been increased by 1/2"
to bring the clipped model up to 2 metre ruling.

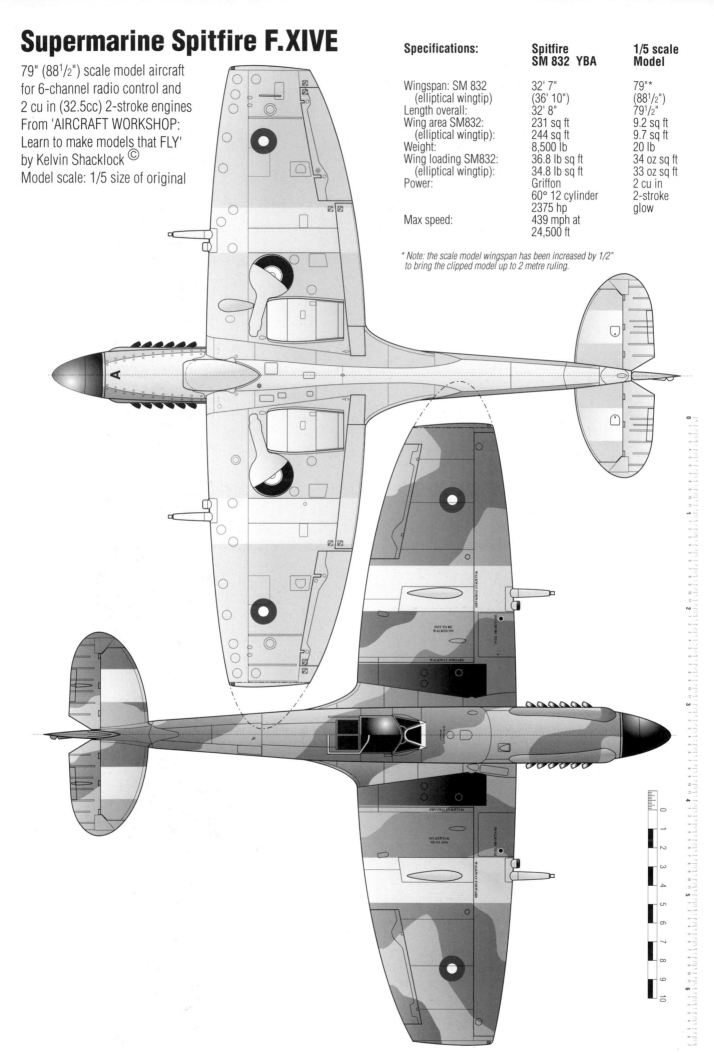

202

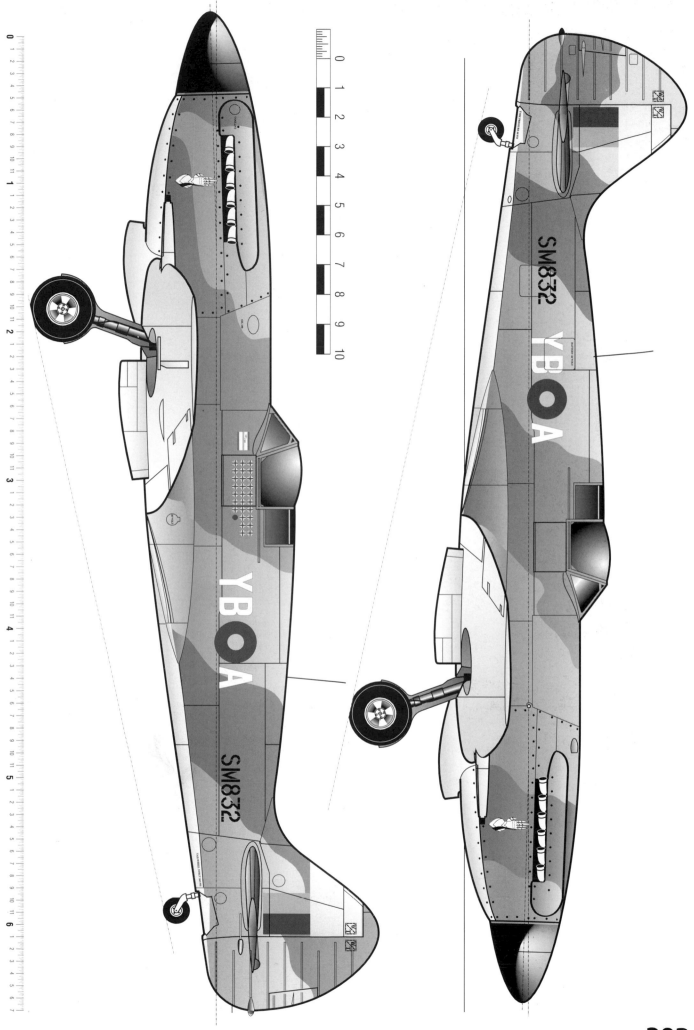

research. If we settle on a Spitfire we have many different Marks to choose from. There's the famous 'French Grey' prototype K5054 through tropical variants, photo reconnaissance, clipped or high altitude, Merlin or Griffon – and of course, the radical Mk 21s and 22s. Modelling a Spitfire would continue our theme of Mitchell, Schneider Cup, Battle of Britain and the Spit we started back in chapter one. So Spitfire it is.

While there were as many opinions on what was the best Spitfire version built during WW II as there were pilots to fly them,

Photo 21:3 *Small, light and agile is not the impression you get when you walk round the sharp end. This is pure power. Even so, where are we going to hide our engine?*

Photo 21:4 *A modeller's delight: stitched fabric covering on the control surfaces, worked aluminium panelling, hinges, pushrods, trim tabs, rivets, joints and fairings. Now we begin to see why 2-dimensional drawings can't convey the wealth of detail that's here.*

Advice from Sqn Ldr (Ginger) Lacey, OC 17 Sqn to his pilots converting to Spitfire F.XIVEs:
"Do not attempt a loop with anything less than 4000ft reading on the altimeter".
This tells us something of the weight, speed and momentum of the XIV with its 2000 hp and a 'do not exceed' speed of 470 mph. We'd be wise to anticipate that our model will also require a bit more sky than we might be used to.

The late Jeffrey Quill, famous Spitfire test pilot, in his book *'Spitfire, A Test Pilot's Story'* rates the Mk XIV as "the best of all the fighter variants of the Spitfire".

many modellers today would agree that the Rolls Royce Griffon-powered Mk XIV is about as potent looking as a Spitfire can get. And, to the modeller, appearance can be the prime consideration because, unlike the designers of the full-size Marks, he can modify the performance of virtually any version by adjusting all-up weight, relative power and control throws, etc.

To research the XIV, the reading begins. Evidently almost 1,000 Spitfire XIVs were manufactured during 1944–45 and served with the RAF until 1955. Their's was an air superiority period calling for exceptional straight-line speed which saw them used to great effect in mid-1944 against the V-1

Photo 21:5 *We have talked about Frise ailerons which drop their leading edge into the airflow to induce turn into the bank – see how far Mitchell takes this design theory!*

204

Practice

Photo 21:6 *Details of wheels and legs.*

flying bomb. All FR.XIVs (fighter reconnaissance) and some F.XIVs (fighter) versions had rear-view fuselages. For a Spitfire model surely the high-back is a must, so we now know what we are looking for — an F.XIVE high-back. Does one exist today? Yes, Spitfire SM832, a high-back, clipped 'E' wing, Mk XIV of the Fighter Collection, Imperial War Museum, Duxford Airfield, Cambs, UK.

Many Griffon Spitfires were deployed in the Far East during the last year of the war. 17 Sqd which had been fighting in the Burma campaign received F.XIVEs in mid-1945. TFC's F.XIVE has been prepared in these South East Asia Command markings, and represents a Spitfire flown by Battle of Britain ace, Sqn Ldr (Ginger) Lacey, OC 17 Sqn. while serving in Malaya in 1945. In this presentation the XIV looks very individual. Just the ticket.

How about research material? TRF's Spitfire SM832 is featured in many excellent aeronautical publications.* Combining this photographic reference with the wealth of superb technical drawings available for all Marks, a reasonably accurate set of computer 3-views is prepared. However, there are the inevitable gaps–what does this line of

Why?

Can just anyone go in and walk round these hangars?

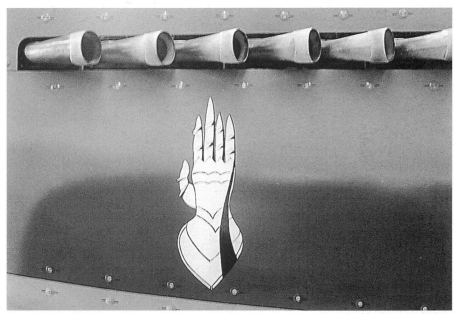

Photo 21:7 *The gauntlet on this port side is one exhaust stack forward of that on the starboard side shown in photo 21:3. Even allowing for the stacks being slightly staggered, this is a detail scale competition judges might pick. You need eagle eyes!*

Photo 21:8 *A very tricky signwriting job — the white squadron letters are outlined with a very fine black line.*

Photo 21:9 *Stencilled serial number presents less of a challenge.*

Because

As a great example of a 'living' aircraft museum, Duxford encourages visitors to enjoy the aircraft from as close as is practical. However, for much of the display this means keeping to roped walkways which may or may not run close to a particular aircraft you may be studying. If you are really interested and can show evidence of a genuine need, approach the staff to see if you can get special permission to go closer. But remember, don't touch!

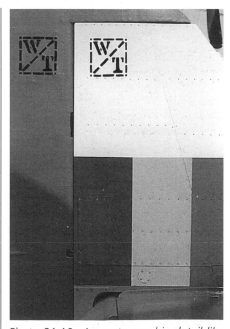

Photo 21:10 *Accurate graphic detail like this is hard to pick up from most general photographs. Here it has been enhanced.*

writing say? Is the other side the same as this side? How does the camouflage finish on that trailing edge? Eventually, everything which can be achieved from desk research is complete and it is time to make a 12,000 mile journey to check out the real thing.

Arriving at Duxford during the final run-up to the Flying Legends Airshow is hardly the most tactful approach, but TFC's Chief Engineer Pete Rushen and his team are more than cooperative and soon I am alongside SM832 adjusting drawings, photographing details and checking out text. This is when all the preparation really pays off. In a couple of hours all the details

Photo 21:11 to 13 *Although not SM832's cockpit, these details will help fill the gap. Plastic model kits and excellent magazine articles can add to your understanding.*

Photo 21:12 *If the model is to have an opening canopy be prepared for some intricate crafting!*

are noted, reference photos are taken and it's time to enjoy the rest of Duxford.

SM832 is a truly beautifully prepared aircraft which returned to The Fighter Collection at Duxford in 1989 where it was restored to flying condition. Restorers: Tim Roustsis and Clive Denny (Historic Flying Ltd, at Audley End Airfield). As a plane for us to replicate she is a beauty, combining aggression with elegance, hairy brute power with finesse and has an individual personality which stands out amongst many superb Spitfires.

Typical Mk XIV Specifications:

Power:–
  Griffon 65, 66 or 67
  60° V 12 cylinder
  Capacity 2,240 cu in (36.7 ltr)
  6" bore x 6.6" stroke
  2-stage supercharged
  65/66 –2,035 hp. (4.51:1 reduction gear)
  67   –2,375 hp. (5.10:1 reduction)

Propeller:
  5-bladed constant-speed
  Rotol airscrew

Dimensions:–
Span:
  Clipped wing   32' 7"
  Standard wing   36' 10"
Length: 32' 8"
Height: 12' 8"
Wing area:
  Clipped wing   231 sq ft
  Standard wing   244 sq ft
Weight: (maximum) 8500 lbs
Wing loading:
  Clipped wing   36.8 lbs sq ft
  Standard wing   34.8 lbs sq ft

Armament:–
'E' wing   2 x 20mm canon
              2 x 0.5" machine guns

Performance:–
Max speed:
  'S' gearing   439 mph at 24,500'
  'M' gearing   404 mph at 11,000'
Stalling speed at 8,375 lbs:
  clean   85 mph
  gear and flaps down   75 mph
Maximum permissible speed:
                               470 mph
Ceiling: 43,000 ft

206

Chapter 22: 1/5 scale replica Spitfire SM832

Photo 22:1 *Even at third glance, the model's a very convincing replica of the real thing. In basic outline, the major concession to smaller scale is the extended tail span. Rather than simply enlarging it in the conventional manner, this design substitutes the larger Mk 21 and 22 tailplane and elevator for the standard MkXIV version. Enthusiasts who don't appreciate the clipped wing can slip on elliptical tips.*

If you have worked your way successfully to this chapter your experience makes you a thoroughly competent aeromodeller. From here on you don't need me telling you how to do it. Rather, in this chapter, come on into my workshop and look over my shoulder. Question some of the reasons why I happen to do things my way. You'll have your own ideas and by now, your own ways of doing things. However, if you're going to follow this design, note the plan sheets are highly detailed and need a lot of enlargement (some 400% and some 500%). Photocopying and tiling from individual A4 pages would be a major exercise in itself. Rather, I strongly recommend that you write to the publishers and purchase full size drawings.

In flying a model of this size there's even more need to be responsible for the safety of others. Make sure it's your first priority. If the situation is inadequate, or if you're in doubt, don't. Building a big model like this, with a 2 metre-plus wingspan, 32cc engine and the need for a lot of custom components, is no cheap exercise. However, the rewards are also big. Provided you go in with your eyes open and take your time, you will experience one of the sport's ultimate building achievements. So, if you're ready, take a deep breath, come on in and we'll get started.

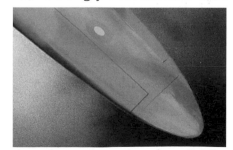

Photo 22:2 *If your love for a Spitfire depends upon those classic elliptical wingtips, don't worry, they're in the plan!*

Practice	*Why?*	Because

In the previous projects I have begun with the easy bits and left the harder parts to last. This was because you were improving your skills as you went along. Now I'm getting right on with the toughies because if we can't handle these, the whole project could be in question and now's the time to find out before we've invested too much time and money.

As it happens, this also means I'm starting right at the front with the propeller spinner. I have not found anything suitable locally so I'm making my own. Of course, you could be lucky or be less particular about its exact shape and use an off-the-shelf substitute.

■ The Spinner:

From 1/4" aluminium I'm turning up the backplate to the exact cross-section shown on page 211 with the outer edge sloped to the finished spinner profile. Note the slightly tapered 1/8" x 1/8" groove round the outer edge. The back of the plate is recessed for the engine drive dog to reduce weight (holes for the pins of the ST3250 dog will be drilled later).

The fibreglass shell is formed in much the same way as the cowling for the Sea Fury except the top edge, instead of being cut off later, is finished in the mould to give a rough fit into the groove in the backplate (see top of page 211). After a few layers of glass I am setting in the little turned aluminium insert, as shown in the detail drawing, then continuing the glassing. The insert is what holds the spinner shell against the back plate, so make sure it's well glassed in.

When the shell is cured, I break off the mould and set up the assembled spinner using a bolt from the back of the plate as a substitute for the engine shaft. With the plateback on the lathe I check it for true. I can now

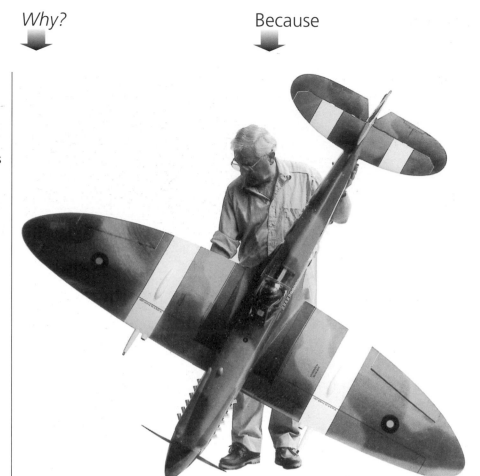

Photo 22:3 *Although not huge by today's standards, 1/5 scale gives a full 88 1/2" span, big enough to impress most of us. Bigger than this, storage and transport can become a a major issue.*

This sounds really complicated. Can you explain it in more detail?

Photo 22:4 *The huge spinner gives the Griffon Spitfire that particularly aggressive line. I was not prepared to settle for anything less, so had to make my own. You may have more luck.*

When it's finished, how do you balance the spinner assembly?

Right. The backplate does two jobs. It aligns the spinner shell, but it also provides a safety rim to reduce the risk of the fibreglass shell flying apart by centrifugal force. Even so, never let anyone stand in line with the propeller arc of this, or any other revving model plane engine. Tightening the central mounting bolt pulls the shell firmly into the retaining groove in the backplate. As the mounting bolt is tightened quite firmly, it needs a really good grip on the shell, so during the moulding process, I set in a sort of countersunk washer at the front of the shell to give it this solidarity.

So far I have been avoiding this problem. I plan to set up a pair of pivots, one which will centre on the backplate and the other on the countersunk insert. I'll hold the shell into the backplate with a smear of silicone sealant.

disassemble the spinner without removing the plate. To get a really positive fit between the plate and shell I smear epoxy bog into the groove, press the shell home and tighten the assembly screw, checking for true as I go. Naturally I had coated the plate with parting agent, paying particular attention to the groove area. Once cured, I spin the lathe and finish off the fibreglass surface ready for painting.

■ Exhaust manifold:

I do want the smoke and fumes to come from the scale exhaust stacks, so the problem is to pipe the hot gasses evenly into both sides and, at the same time, allow for metal expansion without producing any undue stress points. I'm not too concerned about noise. My solution is to make a small manifold that is mounted rigid to the engine and couple it to each exhaust with

Photo 22:9 *Still in the jig, the exhaust manifold after the first welding session.*

flexible silicone rubber tube. Since the scale manifolds are quite substantial structures, I am using them as an integral part of the engine soft-mount. They can be rigidly fixed to the engine and flexibly mounted to the firewall at the other end.

Being no expert at welding, I am jigging the structure with medium density fibreboard and taking it off for a welding session. Later I'll make the stubs and jig them in a similar way. Meantime I can go on with the fuselage.

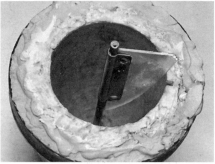

Photo 22:5 *It's just like moulding the Fury cowling except for the overhanging lip.*

Photo 22:7 *The cast lip of the fibreglass shell fits roughly into the groove in the backplate. After applying plenty of parting agent I cover the lip with epoxy bog, ram the shell into the groove and tighten it down, leaving it to set.*

Photo 22:10 *The exhaust manifold hanging on the fuselage during initial fitting.*

Photo 22:6 *The only way I can remove the mould from the casting is by breaking it.*

Photo 22:8 *Now the fibreglass shell fits very accurately into the backplate and I can spin the whole assembly in the lathe to clean up any small blemishes.*

Photo 22:11 *The exhaust manifold as it will look with stacks and plumbing, all then soft-mounted into the fuselage.*

Scale = 25% Enlarge to 400% and check.

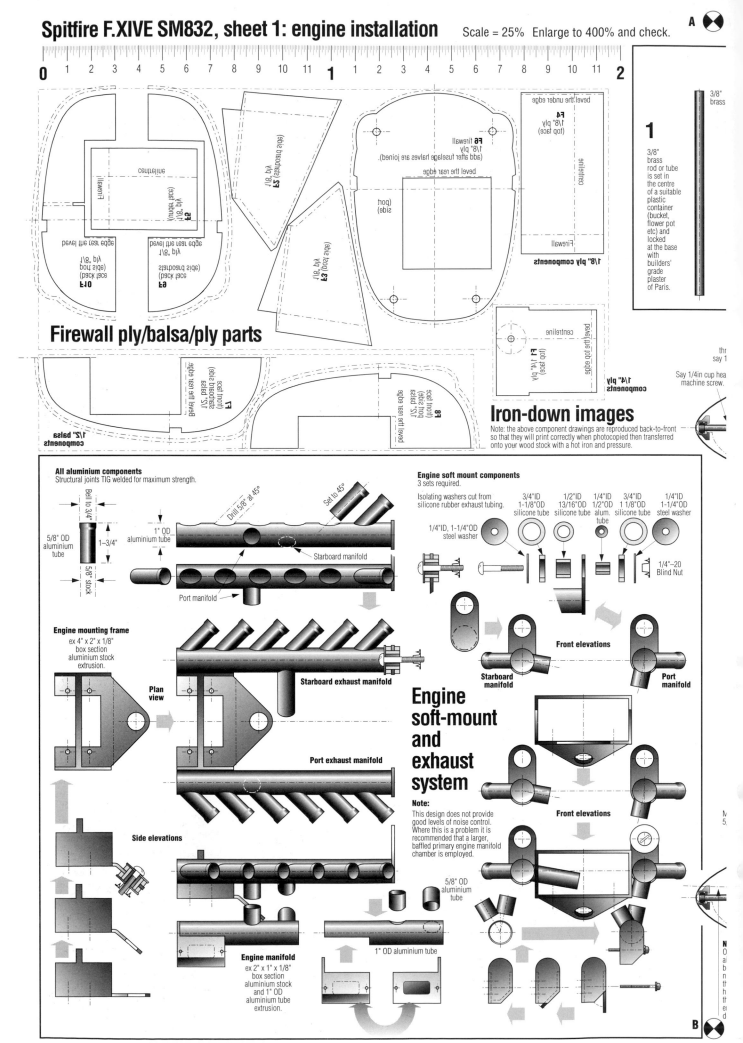

Propeller spinner mould making

2

3/8"
brass tube/rod

1/8" sheet aluminium wrapped round the brass rod and bolted to 1/8" Perspex profile blade. Tighten until smooth rotation is achieved.

Add a brass washer for the blade to rotate against.

3

Progressively add mixes of plaster while rotating the blade to form the mould walls. Lift out the blade and clean after each plaster batch has been added. Finish smooth.

4

After the wall is finished up to the notched mark on the blade shape the return on the top of the blade.

5

Once the plaster is absolutely dry form the rim in the same way as before but now use epoxy bog. You will not be able to remove the blade until the rim is finished and has set hard. Only then cut a 1/4" slot in the rim to lift out the blade.

6

Liberally coat the mould and the central rod with a release agent, then lay up a fibreglass body using say 2" squares of firstly a fine woven cloth (0.7 oz) then heavier (2 oz). Add a layer of carbon fibre then a heavier cloth. Now fit the insert.

7

Continue glassing to build up a wall of about 1/8" thick and finish with a fine cloth. Set aside to cure. Later break away the mould and gently drive out the rod.

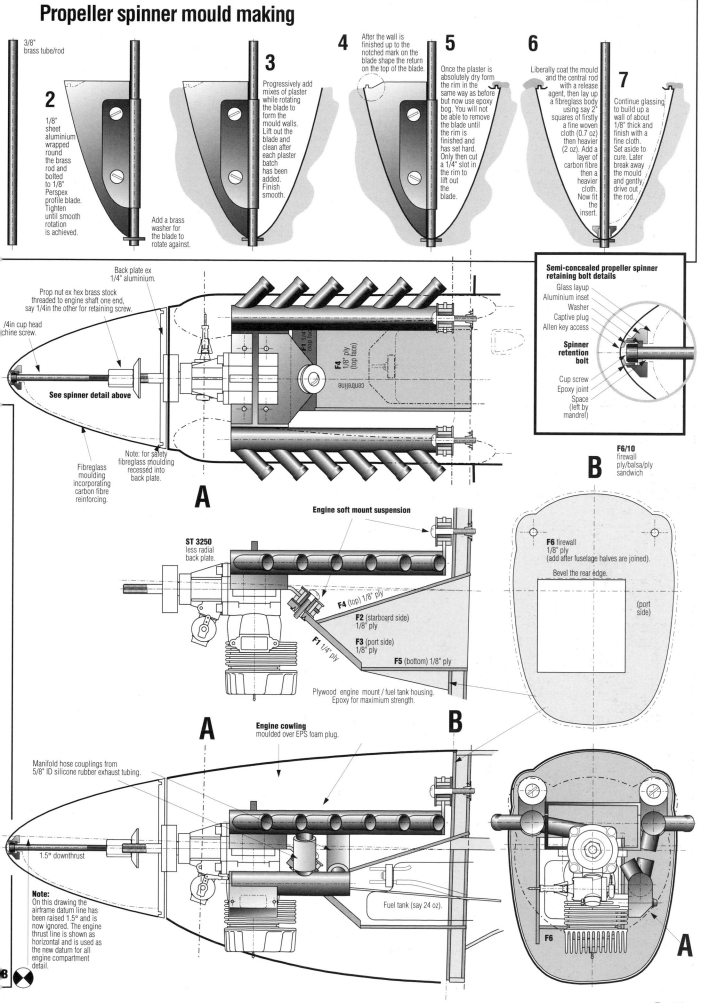

Back plate ex 1/4" aluminium.

Prop nut ex hex brass stock threaded to engine shaft one end, say 1/4in the other for retaining screw.

/4in cup head chine screw.

See spinner detail above

Fibreglass moulding incorporating carbon fibre reinforcing.

Note: for safety fibreglass moulding recessed into back plate.

F1 1/4" (top face)

F4 1/8" ply (top face)

centreline

A

Semi-concealed propeller spinner retaining bolt details

Glass layup
Aluminium inset
Washer
Captive plug
Allen key access

Spinner retention bolt

Cup screw
Epoxy joint
Space (left by mandrel)

Engine soft mount suspension

ST 3250 less radial back plate.

F4 (top) 1/8" ply

F2 (starboard side) 1/8" ply

F1 1/4" ply

F3 (port side) 1/8" ply

F5 (bottom) 1/8" ply

Plywood engine mount / fuel tank housing. Epoxy for maximum strength.

B

F6/10 firewall ply/balsa/ply sandwich

F6 firewall 1/8" ply (add after fuselage halves are joined).

Bevel the rear edge.

(port side)

A

B

Engine cowling moulded over EPS foam plug.

Manifold hose couplings from 5/8" ID silicone rubber exhaust tubing.

1.5° downthrust

Note:
On this drawing the airframe datum line has been raised 1.5° and is now ignored. The engine thrust line is shown as horizontal and is used as the new datum for all engine compartment detail.

Fuel tank (say 24 oz)

F6

A

A

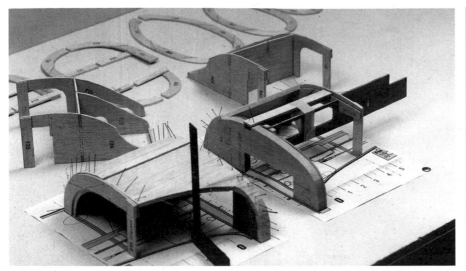

Photo 22:12 *The matched pair of shells which will form the front section of the fuselage.*

There is one serious consideration to allow for when building by this technique. That is, to make sure your shells are built to exactly matching profiles. This is more difficult as I am using a 'tiled' plan made up from individual A4 sheets joined together. The check I run is to tape one plan with its face to a glass door, then superimpose the other plan with its face toward me. The light through the door then lets me see that everything lines up on both plans.

■ The fuselage:

I want to learn something from every model I make. This time I try building the fuselage in two halves joined on the centreline.

The scale cowling carries way behind the model's firewall, with the front section of the fuselage designed so the cowling goes right over it. It's made first, in two halves (photo 22:12) which can be test-fitted together by bolting them to F6, the 3-ply firewall former (photo 22:13). Split apart again, they then get built into their fuselage shells (photo 22:14). The fuselage formers are set up on the plan and, instead of using longerons, I begin planking in the

Photo 22:13 *When the forward section shells are temporarily bolted to the firewall former I check for alignment and fit. Note the recessed strip in their sides which will allow the cowling shells to overlap along the join line and finish flush against each other.*

Later, when I finally join the matched shells I make quite certain that the centreline is straight, and that the rudder post is vertical to the centreline on the firewall. Otherwise I would end up with a twist or bend that would be a permanent feature of my plane!

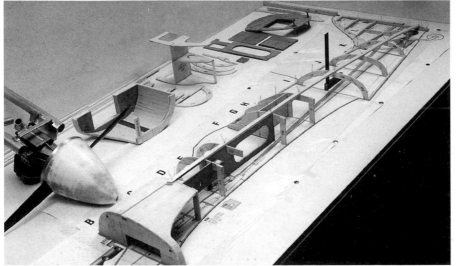

Photo 22:14 *There are no fuselage longerons. Instead, the ³/₁₆" planking serves the same purpose with the first plank being the central one. As I go, I true all the formers up to this plank, then add planks downward, one above and one below until the shell is fully formed.*

212

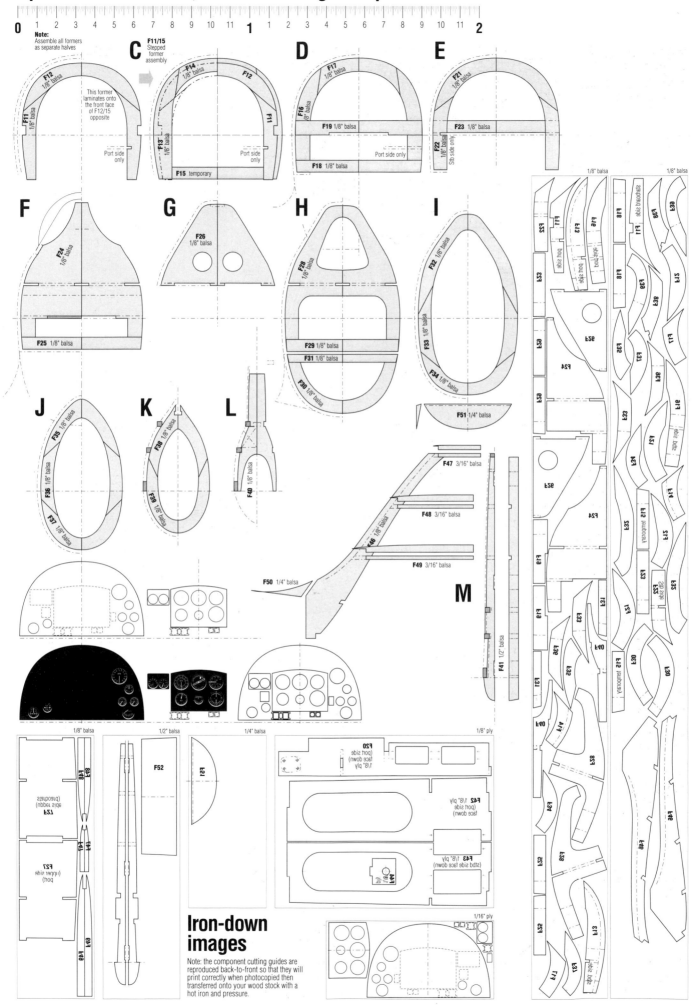

Note: Assemble all formers as separate halves

Iron-down images

Note: the component cutting guides are reproduced back-to-front so that they will print correctly when photocopied then transferred onto your wood stock with a hot iron and pressure.

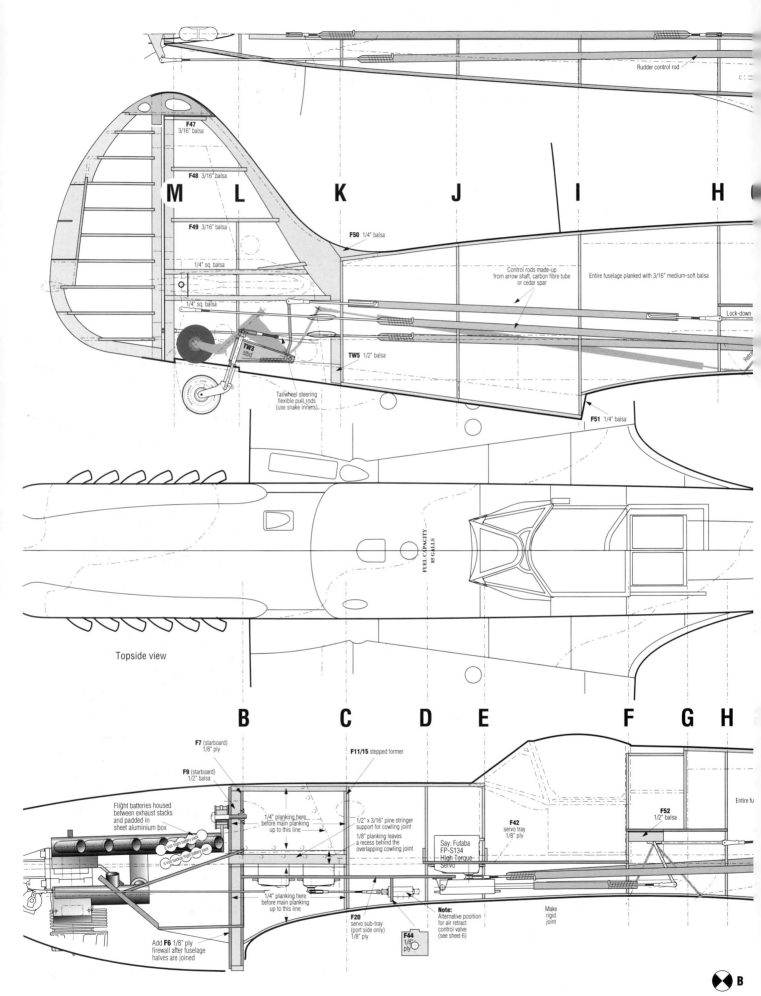

F47 3/16" balsa

F48 3/16" balsa

F49 3/16" balsa

1/4" sq. balsa

1/4" sq. balsa

M   L   K   J   I   H

F50 1/4" balsa

Control rods made-up from arrow shaft, carbon fibre tube or cedar spar

Entire fuselage planked with 3/16" medium-soft balsa

Rudder control rod

Lock-down

TW3 stbd

TW5 1/2" balsa

Tailwheel steering flexible pull rods (use snake inners)

F51 1/4" balsa

FUEL CAPACITY 85 GALLS

Topside view

B   C   D   E   F   G   H

F7 (starboard) 1/8" ply

F9 (starboard) 1/2" balsa

F11/15 stepped former

Flight batteries housed between exhaust stacks and padded in sheet aluminium box

1/4" planking here before main planking up to this line

1/2" x 3/16" pine stringer support for cowling joint

1/8" planking leaves a recess behind the overlapping cowling joint

F42 servo tray 1/8" ply

Say: Futaba FP-S134 High Torque Servo

F52 1/2" balsa

Entire fu

1/4" planking here before main planking up to this line

F20 servo sub-tray (port side only) 1/8" ply

Note: Alternative position for air retract control valve (see sheet 6)

F44 1/8" ply

Make rigid joint

Add **F6** 1/8" ply firewall after fuselage halves are joined

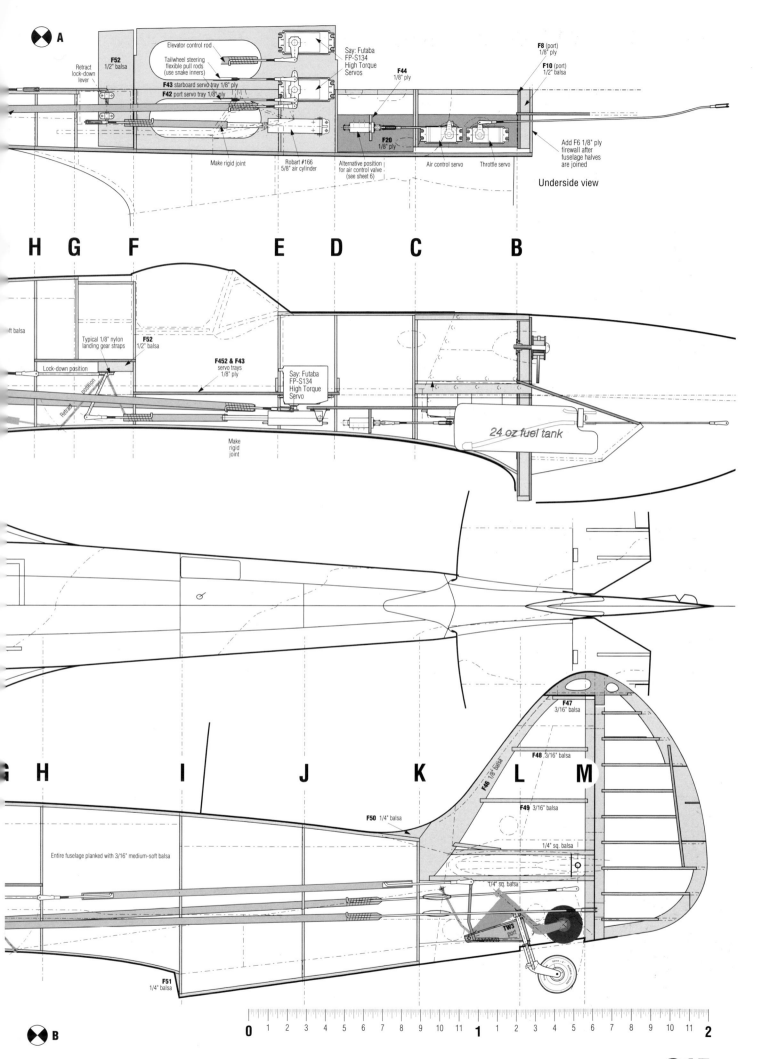

A

Retract
lock-down
lever

F52
1/2" balsa

Elevator control rod

Tailwheel steering
flexible pull rods
(use snake inners)

F43 starboard servo tray 1/8" ply
F42 port servo tray 1/8" ply

Say: Futaba
FP-S134
High Torque
Servos

F44
1/8" ply

F8 (port)
1/8" ply
F10 (port)
1/2" balsa

F20
1/8" ply

Make rigid joint

Robart #166
5/8" air cylinder

Alternative position
for air control valve
(see sheet 6)

Air control servo   Throttle servo

Add F6 1/8" ply
firewall after
fuselage halves
are joined

Underside view

H   G   F   E   D   C   B

ft balsa

Typical 1/8" nylon
landing gear straps

Lock-down position

Retract position

F52
1/2" balsa

F452 & F43
servo trays
1/8" ply

Say: Futaba
FP-S134
High Torque
Servo

Make
rigid
joint

24 oz fuel tank

G   H   I   J   K   L   M

F47
3/16" balsa

F48 3/16" balsa

F46 1/8" balsa

F50 1/4" balsa

F49 3/16" balsa

1/4" sq. balsa

Entire fuselage planked with 3/16" medium-soft balsa

1/4" sq. balsa

TW3
port

F51
1/4" balsa

B

0 1 2 3 4 5 6 7 8 9 10 11 1 1 2 3 4 5 6 7 8 9 10 11 2

conventional way, but start with a central plank that lies on the thrust line.

The expected advantage of the split construction really pays off as the fitting-out progresses. I treat one side as the master into which most of the almost finished components are fixed.

■ Retracting tailwheel:

Unlike early Spitfire models, the XIV has a full retracting tailwheel.

The design challenge is to make this wheel steer the model on the ground but, because space in the fuselage is so limited, have it remain centred while it is retracted. Skip ahead and study photos 22:19 and 20 to see how this is done.

I designed a double-tapered ply torsion box for the swing arm which carries the horizontal retract pivot tube at the front and the vertical tailwheel shaft tube, aft. The retract lever is wired and epoxied into the torsion box before the top is glued on. It's strong, rigid and light.

For a scale appearance the tailwheel fork is welded up in aluminium and shaped. This is then grub-screwed to its shaft which has a double-sided control horn silver-soldered to the top end.

This entire assembly is now slung inside the housing made from the former TW5 and ply sides TW6, and is temporarily fitted into the port fuselage shell. The two flexible pull rods are coupled to the steering servo so that they are tight when the tailwheel is down, but slack as soon as it begins to retract.

So that the tailwheel locks in the down position the air cylinder is coupled via a lever arrangement which rotates into an over-centre position. This is coupled to the retract lever by a light but rigid

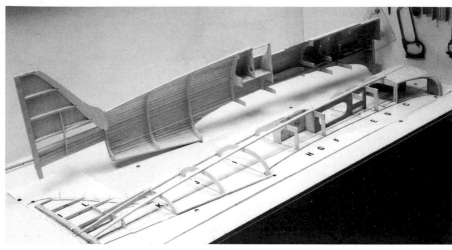

Photo 22:15 *Building the fuselage in two shells gives us unique access to mount, finish and adjust the complicated workings mechanisms like the retracting tailwheel.*

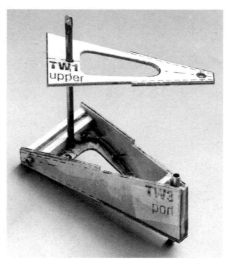

Photo 22:16 *The tailwheel swing arm is made up as a double-tapered torsion box with brass tubes epoxied into each end as bearings for the retract and steering rods. Then the retract lever is wired in and glued.*

Photo 22:18 *So that the tailwheel will not sag into the fuselage when the air pressure is lost, the retract mechanism features a mechanical lockdown which requires the air ram to move toward the retract position before the tailwheel can be pushed up.*

It may seem like overkill to engineer such a complex mechanism just for a tailwheel but, from my experience, it only takes a couple of near ground loops to over stress some of the most basic tailwheels, and I want this one to be as near trouble-free as I know how.

Photo 22:17 *The tailwheel steering and retract mechanism is made up of three subassemblies: the tailwheel, its fork, steering rod and control horns; the swing arm box including the retract lever; and the housing which carries all these parts, ready for gluing into the fuselage. This happens prior to joining the fuselage shells together. Even then, access is provided to let the subassemblies come out for servicing or repair without surgery on the finished model.*

Spitfire F.XIVe SM832, sheet 4: retracting tailwheel

Scale = 25%   Enlarge to 400% and check.

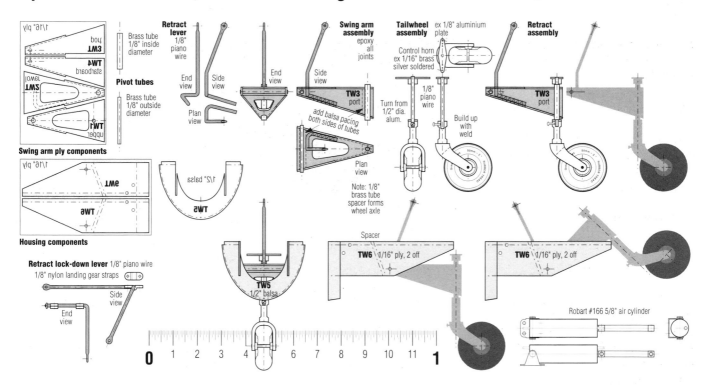

Swing arm ply components

Housing components

Retract lock-down lever 1/8" piano wire

1/8" nylon landing gear straps

Robart #166 5/8" air cylinder

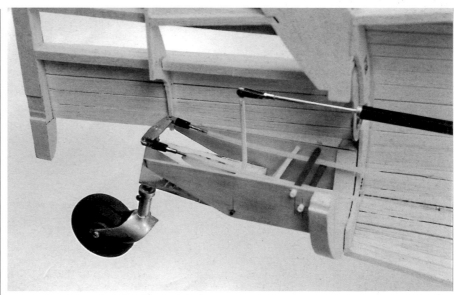

Practice

pushrod which holds it down until the air cylinder is physically driven in the opposite direction.
This feature is particularly helpful when you are setting up your plane at the field or even on the workbench.

Now is the time to test for movement and clearance, so I temporarily fit the fuselage shells together and activate both the steering and retract functions. On the prototype I find I must shave a little from the forward edge of the rudderpost to clear the tyre. Otherwise it's a neat action.

Photo 22:20 *Assuming you don't hit the retract switch while applying full rudder, the retract mechanism swings the tailwheel neatly up into its recess, letting the steering pull rods go slack. Now the rudder function has no effect upon the tailwheel.*

Why?

You're getting more technical than I want to go on my plane. Can't I make it a bit more simple?

Photo 22:19 *The tailwheel assembly fixes into one of the fuselage shells so the control gear can be set up and generally adjusted before the two shells are brought together and glued.*

Because

Absolutely! Forget the retract function and you can set up a very straightforward steering tailwheel just like the D.H.71. The same goes for much of this model.

Conversely, if you'd like to make a more complicated model with more realism, why not research a bit more and add in your fresh information.

Photo 22:21 *Before the shells are finally brought together and glued, all servos and control gear are fitted, the aerial tube is carried through to the rudder post outlet, the tailwheel assembly is in place, the cockpit is painted out and the completed instrument panel is mounted (into one side). The photo shows the pilot and canopy resting in place, but not fixed at this stage.*

■ Fitting out:

The elevator control horn is silver-soldered to the 'U' brace and set into a pivot plate on one shell. The opposite pivot plate will be added after the shells are joined.

At this stage I paint out the cockpit, fit the instrument panel, primary servos and their pushrods. I also epoxy the firewall former F6 onto the front of one of the shells, checking that the other shell will align against it.

■ Joining the shells:

This is the exciting bit. After checking that the halves will come together reasonably accurately, I epoxy all the joining edges and surfaces. The second shell is positioned and clamped against former F6. With masking tape I make a simple bandage to bind the shells just ahead of the fin, and *I sight the centreline, looking to see the line is straight and the fin is vertical.* I ease, squeeze, slide and push to adjust the line, then begin pinning the halves together as I go. When everything's snug I put it aside.

■ Tailwheel shroud:

Here I am using yet another method for moulding fibreglass.

Photo 22:22 *Fuselage skinning is cut back to provide a landing for the fibreglass shroud.*

Photo 22:23 *Litho plate is wrapped over the opening and taped down hard.*

Photo 22:24 *Plaster of Paris is dribbled on and built up to about 1/2" thick.*

Photo 22:25 *The tape is cut away and the mould is painted with resist.*

Photo 22:26 *The moulded fibreglass shroud is trimmed, fitted and painted.*

218

Notice the fuselage has been skinned to provide a shallow recess that the shroud fits into (photo 22:22). Now, hard against the outer fuselage surface I wrap a piece of thin aluminium litho plate (photo 22:23). You'll see I reinforce the edges lengthwise by bending up a small lip. Without removing the fixing tape I now dribble builder's Plaster of Paris onto the aluminium and, as it hardens, keep adding more until it's built up to about ½" thick (photo 22:24). It hardens quickly and I slit the tape to remove the finished mould (photo 22:25). Now a quick coat of PVA parting material and I glass up the shroud in the usual way. It is trimmed to fit, and then I gradually open out the hole to allow the wheel to be lowered without touching anywhere.

■ Completing the fuselage:

There are a few finishing touches to do now before I glass over the fuselage.

The engine mount/fuel tank housing is epoxied up and precisely aligned through the firewall.

I also tidy up the edges of the shells while making a flat seat for the wing centre to fit against. First I fit , glue and pin a ¹/₁₆" strip fore and aft along both sides. Then, when that's hard, I laminate another layer of ¹/₁₆" and use bulldog clips to clamp it in place while the glue hardens (photo 22:27).

There's a mounting block to set across the aft end and former F51 to glue in place and I'm ready.

I check the weight of the basic fuselage and it's 3 lb 4½ oz.

After glassing with 0.7 oz cloth and using as little diluted (30% acetone) resin as possible, I find I've added 3¾ oz, a weight penalty I'm happy with on a model of this size.

What are the advantages of this technique and where would I use this method instead of others?

How do you plan to hold the shroud in place when the plane is finally assembled?

It's ideal for making curved inspection hatches, straight turtle-backs and other simple-curve components that are normally made from say, aluminium sheet. Fibreglass has the advantage that it's easier to rework and is more forgiving of minor accidents, either during the building stage or in use. You'll find it's very difficult to remove small dents or creases from sheet metal.

Because it's a perfect fit, it is under no strains or stresses and can be easily held with some sort of removable adhesive. I'll use clear silicone sealer. You could use very small screws but they can become sloppy after just a few openings.

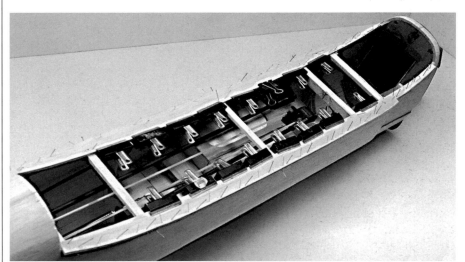

Photo 22:27 *The fuselage edges are trimmed and a broad seating is laminated on.*

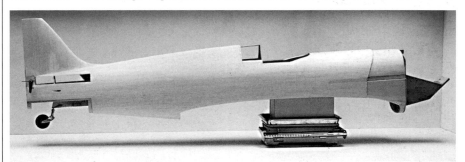

Photo 22:28 *Before glassing, the fuselage weighs in at 3 lb 4¹/₂ oz.*

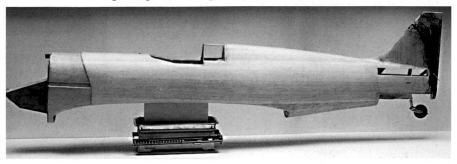

Photo 22:29 *After glassing it's 3 lb 8¹/₄ oz, a 3³/₄ oz weight gain.*

Practice

■ Engine cowling:

There are two distinct considerations in setting up to mould the cowling. Firstly, with the inverted engine I've designed the upper cowl to remain in place while the lower part is removed. Consequently, the upper cowl has a recessed strip, both ahead and behind the exhaust cutout, where the lower cowl overlaps and is screwed down to form a flush joint.

The second is to mould a ply ring into the front of the cowling. To secure it in the right place as the cowling is being built, a plywood disk representing the back of the spinner, is bolted onto the engine shaft and temporarily screwed to the ring.

Here's the process: I turn up a ply disk that serves as the back of the spinner, plus ⅛" extended aft, so it becomes slightly larger than the actual backplate. The back of the disk is recessed so that as I bolt it to the engine shaft it sits the same ⅛" aft of where the spinner would rest. Now, the back face of this disk becomes the mould for the front end of the cowling, and will leave a ⅛" clearance between the finished cowling and spinner. I cover the back face of this disk with plenty of resin resist.

From similar ply I make a ring which is about ¼" smaller than the disk and screw it against the back of the ply disk. This becomes part of the cowling when I glass over the foam plug. Once it's firm against the disk, I make a couple of cuts through the ring to allow the lower cowl to incorporate part of the ring into its moulding (see photo 22:36).

You'll see from photos 22:30–32 how I build up the foam plug and plaster it fair through to the fuselage recess. I cover the mould (photo 22.33) with PVA paint, then resist, keeping both off the ply ring where I need it to stick.

Photo 22:30 *The disk fixed to the engine shaft is used to keep the mould aligned.*

Photo 22:31 *The foam mould is built up to represent the final shape, less about ³/₃₂".*

Photo 22:32 *The shape is faired with stopping compound (Selleys' Rapidfilla).*

Photo 22:33 *Painted (PVA) and liberally coated with resist, especially the fuselage!*

Photo 22:34 *Glassed up, wrapped with cling film and bound against the mould.*

Photo 22:35 *The upper casting filled and shaped, removed, trimmed and replaced.*

Because

A lot of this sort of modelling comes down to using your skills as a sculptor. While we must know the desired cross section, in this case established by the firewall former F6, the circular spinner, section A and the elevation shown on sheet 1, it seems we each make slightly different interpretations. The photos in chapter 21 and any others you can refer to will help you to get it right. Just make sure you are referring to a Griffon Spitfire because its sections are quite different from the Merlin cowling.

To keep the cowling relatively light you will notice in some of the photos that I am building up the filler (to be removed after the casting has been made) on the section aft of the firewall until just before the cowling/fuselage join. Conversely, I am recessing the upper area for the central retaining screw as reinforcement. These are typical of the refinements you will choose to incorporate almost automatically as you go along, but to describe each one as it comes up would require a much bigger book than we have here.

Photo 22:36 *A couple of nice-looking cowlings parts, detailed and painted.*

220

■ **Pilot, cockpit and canopy:**

This time I use a commercial pilot, a J. Perkins 1/5 scale Spitfire bust and paint it with acrylic. Rather than just sitting there like a dummy, this chap has his head turned slightly and I am mounting him at a further angle so he looks reasonably 'animated'.

Other cockpit detail I add includes a headrest, control column (even though this pilot has no hands to hold it) and my symbolic version of a reflector gun sight.

The canopy I'm using is from a friend's mould and does not include the aft glasswork so I mould this in the same way I made the tailwheel shroud. However, instead of filling the mould with fibreglass, I heat clear acrylic and press that into the mould (photos 22.38 and 39).

Now the cockpit gets a really good spring cleaning to remove every trace of dust, and the canopy is glued in place with Wilhold R/C-56. Once it's hard it gets the dyed epoxy bog window frame treatment (as on page 198), finishing with a paint spray of green base coat along with the surrounding fuselage. The masking is removed and some little blemishes are touched up.

Photo 22:37 *The pilot's paint job gradually fades into darker colours toward its base.*

Photo 22:39 *Last chance to tidy up in the cockpit before the canopy is sealed down onto the fuselage.*

You don't include the reflector gun sight in the plan. What reference should I use?

While I heartily approve of blanked-off cockpits, especially where everything is disguised by a canopy, it really bugs me to see a pilot bust 'cut off at the waist' as we see so often, particularly on a lot of ARF kits. Sometimes no attempt is made to give the impression that the pilot is sitting in a hollow cockpit. My solution is to paint black everything I don't want seen. Areas I do colour are blended to black the further they get down toward the false bottom of the cockpit. This way it just gets too dark to see that the realism actually stops short of the truth.

Photo 22:38 *I needed to form the aft canopy as it was not part of the moulding that was available to me. Like the tailwheel shroud, I made an aluminium mould.*

Sorry, but I don't want to mislead you. My version is just a quick shot at what I generally remember they look like. Since I don't want to delay the

Photo 22:40 *I mask the bullet proof screen and sliding canopy with its tracks, and build up the frames with expoy bog. But, until the fuselage is painted, I only remove the masking from the detail that fits against the fuselage.*

Photo 22:41 *The finished canopy looks remarkably realistic once the detailed paint job is completed.*

■ **The tail feathers:**

There's nothing too unusual in the way I go about building and fitting the rudder, stabiliser and elevator.

model I'm going ahead without looking for an authentic reference. If you have the time I suggest there are quite a few cockpit drawings and photos which will help you make a more authentic version than mine.

Spitfire F.XIVE SM832, sheet 5: tail surfaces

Scale = 20% Enlarge to 500% and check against ruler.

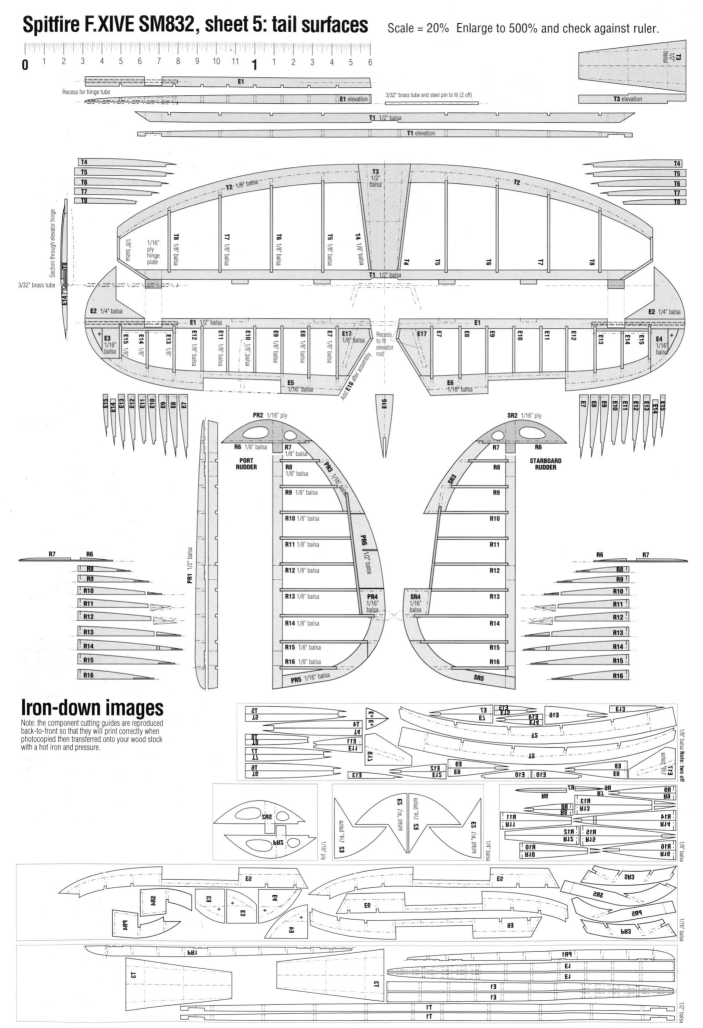

Iron-down images

Note: the component cutting guides are reproduced back-to-front so that they will print correctly when photocopied then transferred onto your wood stock with a hot iron and pressure.

Practice

Photo 22:42 *The outer elevator hinges are built from brass tube with steel rods inserted from the ends of the elevators. The inner hinges are dummy.*

Perhaps the hinging of the elevator needs explanation. A little like the aileron hinges, the elevator hinge is built with a single brass tube epoxied right through from tip, through the stabiliser hinge block and back into the elevator. When the epoxy has cured, I cut the brass tube on both sides of the stabiliser hinge with a fine fretsaw blade. A thin steel rod now slides in from the tip to provide the pivot.

■ The wing centre section:

This model is designed to come apart more than usual. The wing is too large to keep as one piece. As a split-wing, instead of making the centre section part of the fuselage, this one is separate and is used as a major access way into the central workings of the plane. In normal use it remains fixed to the fuselage and the outer wing panels plug into it.

In building the centre section I also make and fit the adjoining wing panel parts. This ensures the panels will fit accurately when they get built. Consequently, wing ribs W1, W2 and W3 are included in the centre section parts list. These are made up as one sub-assembly while C12 and C13 are joined as a second. Using short register dowels (photo 22:44), they are matched and pressed together. This fitting represents the eventual join between the centre section and the outer wing panel. I add the blind nut NOW.

Why?

Why did you finished the canopy detail even before you started building these tail surfaces?

Photo 22:43 *The rudder control horn is fabricated from circuit board and epoxied in during construction.*

Am I seeing straight or is the rudder trim tab offset in both directions, to starboard above and port below?

Photo 22:44 *Register dowels press through matching ¹/₄" holes in the two sub-assemblies which come together and will form the join between the centre section and the outer wing panel.*

Why worry about this join at such an early stage of the construction?

Because

Actually, this is a problem which comes about as I try to simplify the description. Rather than keep saying "now put that aside and we'll come back to it later" I describe the process through to its conclusion. In fact, once I seal the canopy to the fuselage I leave off and proceed to make and fit the tail surfaces. It's only when the whole assembly is ready for painting that I mask up the canopy and fill the frames.

Your sight's alright. Yes, the tab is split about half way up and each half is offset in opposite directions. I assume this is to counter buffeting or rudder 'flutter' which may be encountered at the very high speed that this Mark can achieve. Models can also experience control surface flutter. This is usually caused by sloppy control linkages, loose hinges and so on. If you hear your model make a strange humming noise, slow it down and land so you can check out the cause.

Photo 22:45 *The register pins are replaced by finished dowel pins. Temporary square spar blocks press into the spar slots to help keep everything correctly aligned.*

It's far easier to match up dowel holes and other aligned openings when you can hold the individual parts together than if you wait until they are locked into a full assembly. In this case I clamped the sub-assemblies together and drilled all the openings through both at the same time so they have to fit.

Spitfire F.XIVE SM832, sheet 6: wing centre section

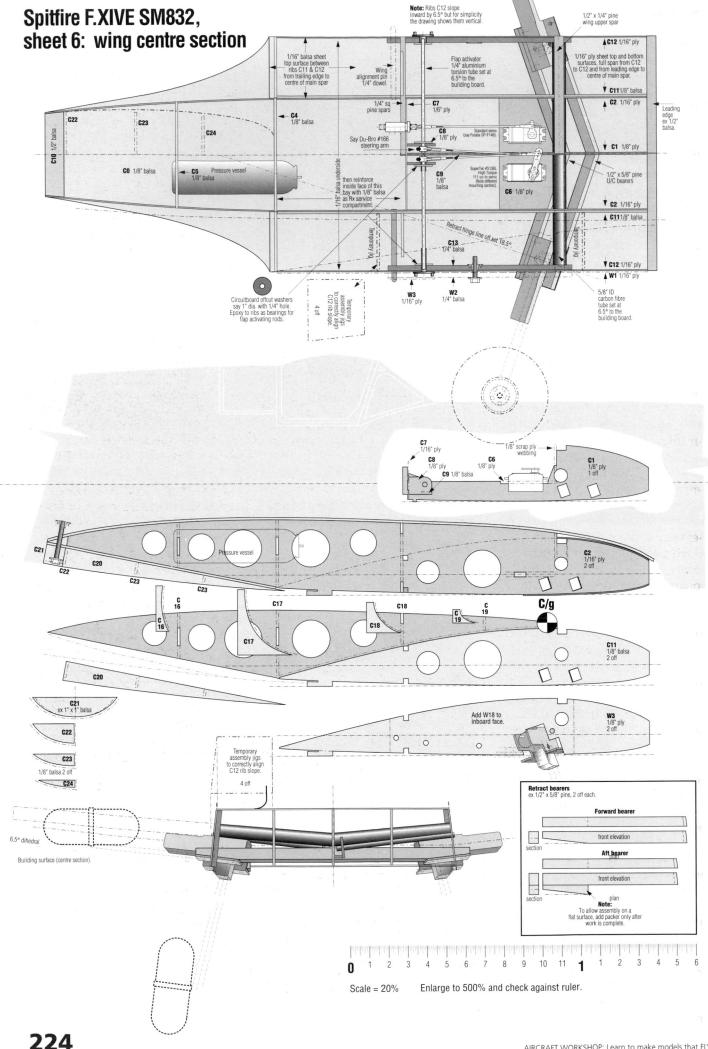

Note: Ribs C12 slope inward by 6.5° but for simplicity the drawing shows them vertical.

1/16" balsa sheet top surface between ribs C11 & C12 from trailing edge to centre of main spar

Flap activator 1/4" aluminium torsion tube set at 6.5° to the building board.

1/2" x 1/4" pine wing upper spar

1/16" ply sheet top and bottom surfaces, full span from C12 to C12 and from leading edge to centre of main spar.

Wing alignment pin 1/4" dowel

C4 1/8" balsa

C7 1/6" ply

1/4" sq pine spars

C8 1/8" ply

Say Du-Bro #166 steering arm

Standard servo (say Futaba SP-F148).

C9 1/8" balsa

SuperTec #S136L High Torque 111 oz-in servo (Note different mounting centres).

C6 1/8" ply

C22
C23
C24

C10 1/2" balsa

C0 1/8" balsa

C5 Pressure vessel 1/8" balsa

then reinforce inside face of this bay with 1/8" balsa as 'Rx service compartment'.

C12 1/16" ply

C11 1/8" balsa

C2 1/16" ply

Leading edge ex 1/2" balsa.

C1 1/8" ply

1/2" x 5/8" pine U/C bearers

C2 1/16" ply

C11 1/8" balsa

Retract hinge line off-set 18.5°

C13 1/4" balsa

C12 1/16" ply

W1 1/16" ply

Circuitboard offcut washers say 1" dia. with 1/4" hole. Epoxy to ribs as bearings for flap activating rods.

Temporary assembly jigs to correctly align C12 rib slope. 4 off

W3 1/16" ply

W2 1/4" balsa

5/8" ID carbon fibre tube set at 6.5° to the building board.

C7 1/16" ply

1/8" scrap ply webbing

C8 1/8" ply

C6 1/8" ply

C9 1/8" balsa

C1 1/8" ply 1 off

C21

C22
C20

Pressure vessel

C23
C23

C2 1/16" ply 2 off

C 16
C17
C18
C 19
C 19

C/g

C16
C17
C18

C11 1/8" balsa 2 off

C20

C21 ex 1" x 1" balsa

C22

C23

1/8" balsa 2 off

C24

Add W18 to inboard face.

W3 1/8" ply 2 off

Temporary assembly jigs to correctly align C12 rib slope. 4 off

6.5° dihedral

Building surface (centre section).

Retract bearers ex 1/2" x 5/8" pine, 2 off each.

Forward bearer

front elevation

section

Aft bearer

front elevation

section

plan

Note: To allow assembly on a flat surface, add packer only after work is complete.

Scale = 20%   Enlarge to 500% and check against ruler.

Practice

Assembly of the centre section proceeds as usual. I begin right in the centre by fitting C6 and C7 to C1, and work my way out after laminating C2 to C11 (all laminated parts are epoxied).

Photo 22:46 *All laminations have been made and assembly begins from the centre.*

Once the leading edge, spars and former C4 are in place I thread the full length carbon fibre tubes in until they match within rib C1, and epoxy them in place. I don't cut them off at the wing joint because I want to assemble the outer wing panels onto the tube while it is accurately held by the centre section.

Next come the retract bearers which take quite a bit of fitting before I am satisfied enough to epoxy them in place. Now's a good time to web round the carbon fibre tube to strengthen this vital area. I keep going as you can see in the photos, then begin fitting the centre section to the fuselage.

I dowel the leading edge to the firewall and seat the trailing edge to the fuselage at C10. The fairing must match the fuselage skin, so I now shape the upper edge to give $\frac{1}{8}$" clearance from the fuselage. This gives me space to cap the centre section along the join line.

The wing mounting bolt is set in place and I have the centre section finally fitting. With a sharp pencil I scribe the fuselage surface down onto the centre section capping, then pull it apart. I mark $\frac{1}{16}$" inside the line on the capping, then trim the capping back to the new line. It's now ready for the fairing formers and their $\frac{1}{16}$" planking.

Why?

When I look at the photos your ribs appear to have lots more and larger holes than shown on the plan. What gives?

Photo 22:47 *The key elements are complete ready for sheeting the wing stubs.*

Just tell me again what you mean about that carbon fibre tube being left at full length meantime.

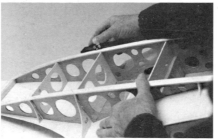

Photo 22:50 *Cutting the capping back to $\frac{1}{16}$" inside the fuselage skin line.*

Because

I don't think I ever really follow a plan to the last line, even my own. As I go along on this model I poke a few lightening holes in wherever I think they will reduce weight without sacrificing too much strength. I think that's a bit different from providing a plan where everything is cut to the bone. For instance, I don't know the quality or weight of the wood another modeller might select, and this could compromise safety if the line is too finely drawn.

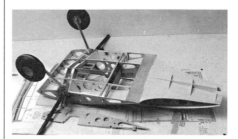

Photo 22:48 *The underside formers are in place. Now for the underside sheeting.*

In the finished model there will be four pieces of tubing, one for each side of the centre section and one inside each outer wing panel. To being with I am not separating the centre section tube from the wing panel tube. Left as one piece it sticks out from the centre section. Later I will build the wing panel over this part of the tube but won't glue it to any part of the tube. Once the panel

Photo 22:49 *With the centre section fully fitted to the fuselage with wing dowels at the front and a wing bolt at the rear, I provide a full $\frac{1}{8}$" clearance right along the join line.*

is fully framed and it fits nicely up against the centre section join, I'll cut the tube off flush with the centre section and epoxy the offcut into the wing panel. This ensures an absolutely precise fit.

Spitfire F.XIVE SM832, sheet 7: wing/centre section components

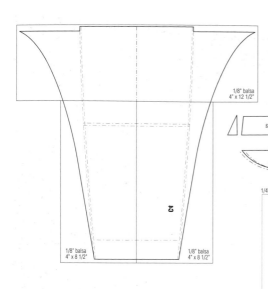

The fairing planking is a new challenge because, not only is the wood much thinner than on any of the previous models, but it is also set in a reverse curve.

Photo 22:51 *Planking the fairings calls for the next level of care and attention. Narrow planks and plenty of them is the key.*

I take particular care to get the planks to the right shape and, being an inside curve, I bevel the edges inward to the top. As they are glued in, I work the edges together to make sure the new

Photo 22:52 *The finished centre section module is just another Spitfire component full of those beautiful Mitchell curves.*

plank aligns against the previous one along its full length.
It all works well and soon the whole module is being glassed, filled and painted.

Iron-down images

Note: the component cutting guides are reproduced back-to-front so that they will print correctly when photocopied then transferred onto your wood stock with a hot iron and pressure.

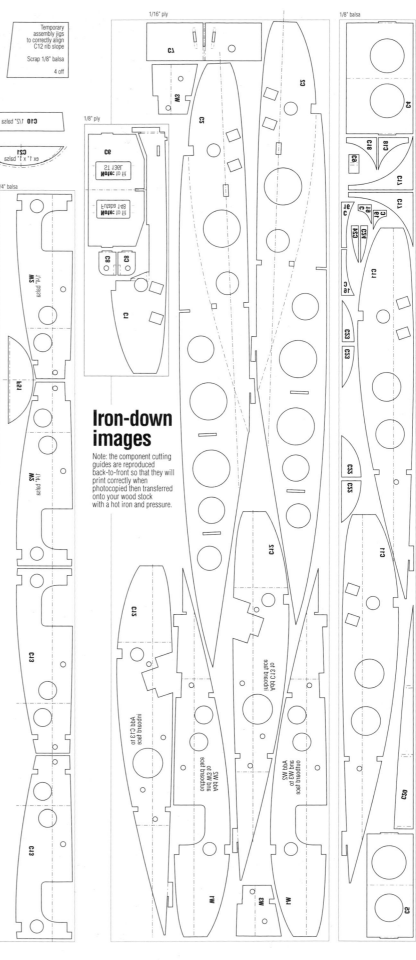

226

■ The outer wing panels:

There's a sequence to building most wings, and this one's no exception. I start with all the cut out components and make up two paper tubes. These are just copy paper spiral-wrapped over a ⁵⁄₈″ dowel and bound at about 1″ intervals with very narrow tape. I then take them outside and wet them inside and out with cyano. Once hard, they make great servo lead ducts.

Assembly starts with the lower spar clamped down on the plan and the paper tube threaded

Photo 22:54 *Typical of apertures in the wing sheeting, the servo access on the underside of the wing is framed up to sheeting level.*

through ribs W7 to W10 (photo 22:53). Now I take the centre section and cover the adjoining face with cling film. Next I slide ribs W1, W4, W5 and W6 onto the carbon fibre tube and position it with the join exactly aligned on the plan. Now I'm away and build up the wing as usual.

When the frame is complete and one side of the webbing is in place I take it off the board to work on the detail. I cut servo openings, block above and below the carbon fibre tube (before webbing the other side), wall the wheel wells, trim the paper tubes and so on.

The cutaways for the undercarriage legs need framing (very hard to show on the plan but see photo 22:57 and you'll see how I am doing it) and any openings which will show in the sheeting are backed up with struts at this stage.

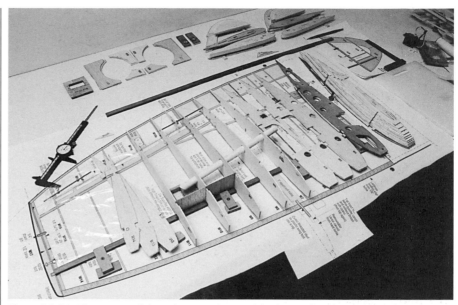

Photo 22:53 *First stage of the wing panel assembly shows the servo tray and supporting webbing with the servo lead duct threaded through ribs W7 to W10.*

When you bring the centre section down onto the plan how do you know how much to pack it up to give the wing the right amount of dihedral?

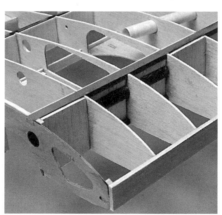

Photo 22:55 *When the carbon fibre tube is cut off and epoxied in the wing it is packed above and below, then webbed.*

The holes for the carbon fibre tube through ribs W1, W4, W5 and W6 are carefully drawn in the right place to set the angle. As soon as I clamp down these wing ribs into their correct position you'll see that the centre section is raised and held rigidly in place.

Just while I think of it, notice I have carved a strip out of my building board along the line of the join. This is to allow for the ¹⁄₁₆″ sheeting on the bottom of the centre section. Otherwise it would stop the centre section and wing panel ribs from matching properly (see the top right of sheet 8, front view of wing joint). Remember, the wing has yet to be sheeted.

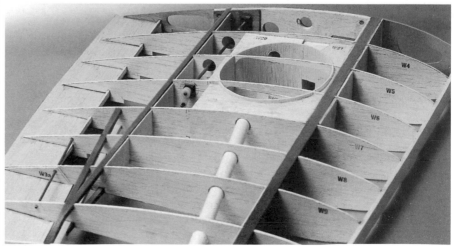

Photo 22:56 *The top side of the wing looks about ready for sheeting. Ignore the flap control gear which is shown here. I am just testing the system.*

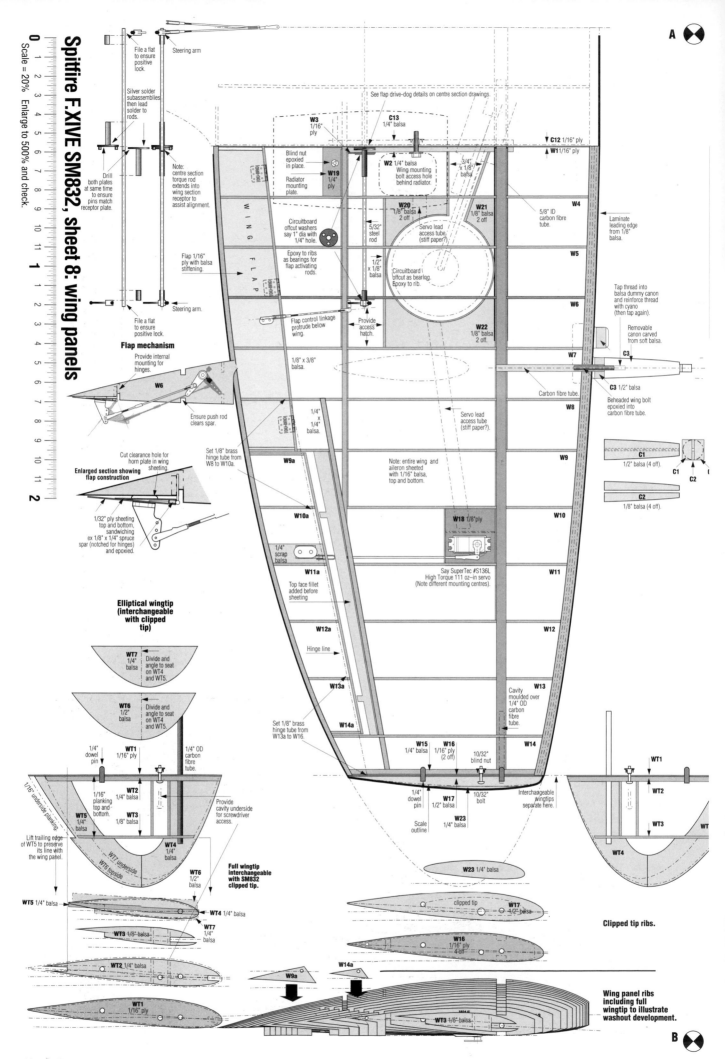

Spitfire F.XIVE SM832, sheet 8: wing panels

Scale = 20% Enlarge to 500% and check.

A

Flap mechanism

File a flat to ensure positive lock.

Steering arm

Silver solder subassemblies then lead solder to rods.

Drill both plates at same time to ensure pins match receptor plate.

Note: centre section torque rod extends into wing section receptor to assist alignment.

File a flat to ensure positive lock.

Steering arm.

Provide internal mounting for hinges.

W6

Ensure push rod clears spar.

Enlarged section showing flap construction

Cut clearance hole for horn plate in wing sheeting.

1/32" ply sheeting top and bottom, sandwiching ex 1/8" x 1/4" spruce spar (notched for hinges) and epoxied.

Elliptical wingtip (interchangeable with clipped tip)

WT7 1/4" balsa — Divide and angle to seat on WT4 and WT5.

WT6 1/2" balsa — Divide and angle to seat on WT4 and WT5.

1/4" dowel pin

WT1 1/16" ply

1/4" OD carbon fibre tube.

1/16" planking top and bottom.

WT2 1/4" balsa

WT5 1/4" balsa

WT3 1/8" balsa

Provide cavity underside for screwdriver access.

WT4 1/4" balsa

Lift trailing edge of WT5 to preserve its line with the wing panel.

1/16" underside planking.

WT7 underside
WT6 topside

WT5 1/4" balsa

WT4 1/4" balsa

WT6 1/2" balsa

WT7 1/4" balsa

WT3 1/8" balsa

Full wingtip interchangeable with SM832 clipped tip.

WT2 1/4" balsa

WT1 1/16" ply

See flap drive-dog details on centre section drawings.

W3 1/16" ply

C13 1/4" balsa

C12 1/16" ply
W1 1/16" ply

Blind nut epoxied in place.

W19 1/4" ply

Radiator mounting plate.

W2 1/4" balsa Wing mounting bolt access hole behind radiator.

3/4" x 1/8" balsa

Circuitboard offcut washers say 1" dia with 1/4" hole.

W20 1/8" balsa 2 off

W21 1/8" balsa 2 off

5/8" ID carbon fibre tube.

W4

Laminate leading edge from 1/8" balsa.

Epoxy to ribs as bearings for flap activating rods.

5/32" steel rod

1/2" x 1/8" balsa

Servo lead access tube (stiff paper?)

Circuitboard offcut as bearing. Epoxy to rib.

W5

W6

Tap thread into balsa dummy canon and reinforce thread with cyano (then tap again).

Flap control linkage protrude below wing.

W22 1/8" balsa 2 off.

W7

C3

Removable canon carved from soft balsa.

Provide access hatch.

Carbon fibre tube.

C3 1/2" balsa

Beheaded wing bolt epoxied into carbon fibre tube.

1/8" x 3/8" balsa.

W8

1/4" x 1/4" balsa.

Servo lead access tube (stiff paper?).

W9

C1

C1 1/2" balsa (4 off).

C2

W9a

Note: entire wing and aileron sheeted with 1/16" balsa, top and bottom.

C2 1/8" balsa (4 off).

Set 1/8" brass hinge tube from W8 to W10a.

W10a

W18 1/8" ply

W10

1/4" scrap balsa

W11a

Top face fillet added before sheeting

Say SuperTec #S136L High Torque 111 oz–in servo (Note different mounting centres).

W11

Hinge line

W12a

W12

Hinge line

W13a

W13

Cavity moulded over 1/4" OD carbon fibre tube.

Set 1/8" brass hinge tube from W13a to W16.

W14a

W14

W15 1/4" balsa

W16 1/16" ply (2 off)

10/32" blind nut

Interchangeable wingtips separate here.

1/4" dowel pin

W17 1/2" balsa

10/32" bolt

Scale outline

W23 1/4" balsa

WT1

WT2

WT3

WT4

W23 1/4" balsa

clipped tip

W17 1/2" balsa

Clipped tip ribs.

W16 1/16" ply 4 off

W9a

W14a

WT3 1/8" balsa

Wing panel ribs including full wingtip to illustrate washout development.

W16

B

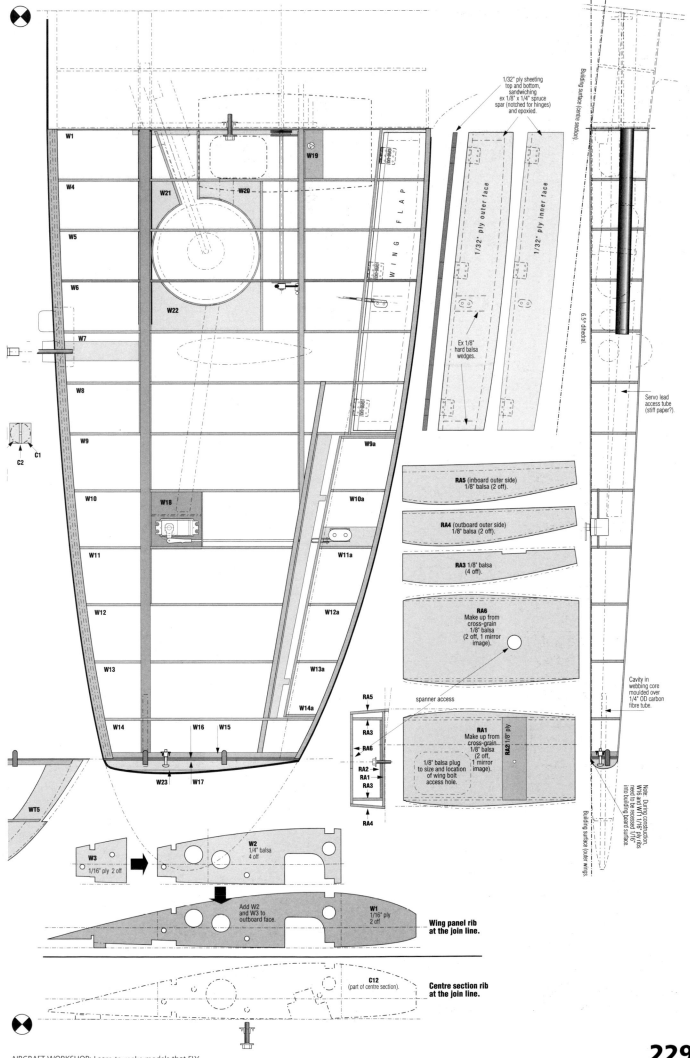

1/32" ply sheeting top and bottom, sandwiching ex 1/8" x 1/4" spruce spar (notched for hinges) and epoxied.

W1

W19

W4

W21

W20

W5

W6

W22

W7

W8

W9

W9a

W10

W18

W10a

W11

W11a

W12

W12a

W13

W13a

W14a

W14

W16

W15

W23

W17

WT5

C1

C2

WING FLAP

Building surface (centre section).

6.5° dihedral.

1/32" ply outer face

1/32" ply inner face

Ex 1/8" hard balsa wedges.

Servo lead access tube (stiff paper?).

RA5 (inboard outer side) 1/8" balsa (2 off).

RA4 (outboard outer side) 1/8" balsa (2 off).

RA3 1/8" balsa (4 off).

RA6 Make up from cross-grain 1/8" balsa (2 off, 1 mirror image).

spanner access

RA5

RA3

RA6

RA2 1/8" ply

RA1 Make up from cross-grain 1/8" balsa (2 off, 1 mirror image).

RA2

RA1

RA3

RA4

1/8" balsa plug to size and location of wing bolt access hole.

Cavity in webbing core moulded over 1/4" OD carbon fibre tube.

Building surface (outer wings).

Note: During construction, W16 and W1 1/16" ply ribs need to be recessed 1/16" into building board surface.

W3 1/16" ply 2 off

W2 1/4" balsa 4 off

Add W2 and W3 to outboard face.

W1 1/16" ply 2 off

Wing panel rib at the join line.

C12 (part of centre section).

Centre section rib at the join line.

Spitfire F.XIVE SM832, sheet 9: wing components

Scale = 20%   Enlarge to 500% and check against ruler.

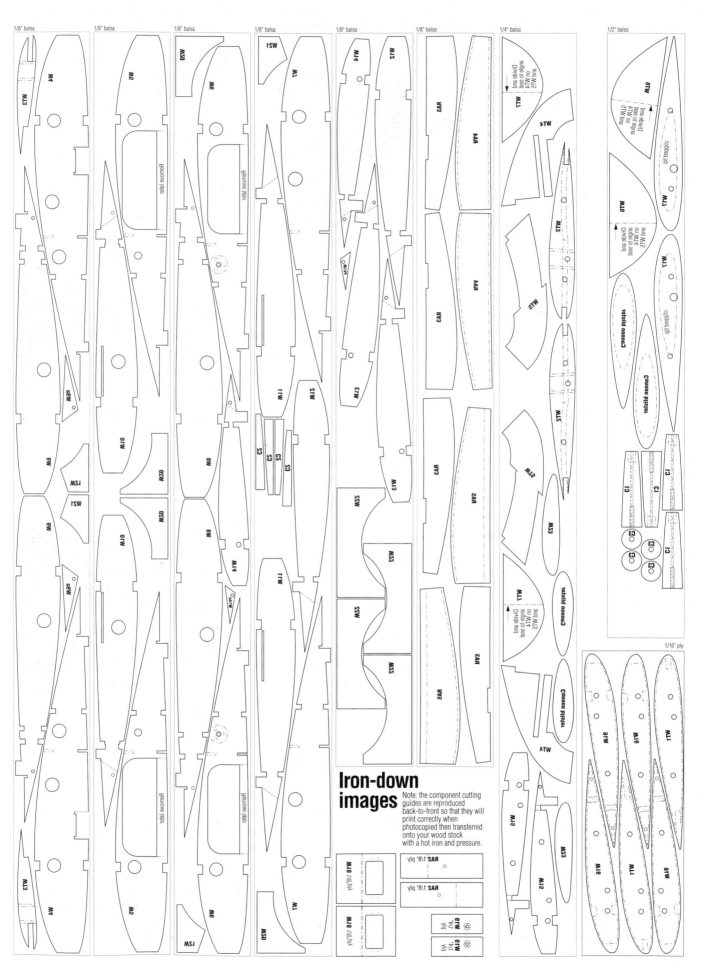

Iron-down images

Note: the component cutting guides are reproduced back-to-front so that they will print correctly when photocopied then transferred onto your wood stock with a hot iron and pressure.

■ I want to be able to interchange clipped tips with elliptical, so, having pre-drilled all the appropriate ribs I make up the tip assemblies per the plan (photo 22:58). The full tip is supported by a ¼" OD carbon fibre tube, so I make provision for it to slide into the wing and be held inside the webbing. I add the blind nut inside the wing and make provision for access to the bolt through the underside of the tip. Both sets of tips are put aside and I'll shape them when the wing is finished.

■ Now I start the sheeting, first just the forward panel underside. When it's set I turn the wing and sheet the upper-forward panel. In this case I hold the wing down hard on the building board, especially as the glue hardens. This makes sure the 'D' section torsion box (ref page 45 – Willy Messerschmitt) sets without any unwanted twist. From here on, the wing panel becomes a fairly rigid structure and the serious fitting out begins.

■ **Flaps and their gear:**

Although there are two separate flaps, one on each panel, this setup has them both operating from a single servo. The idea being that no servo-related problem can give the model one up, one down. However, it does involve me in a bit of 'bush engineering'. Sheet 8 shows how the servo rotates a shaft out of each side of the centre section. At the end of each shaft there's a drive dog with a central locator and two drive pins. Slide a wing panel into place, and the pins fit into holes in the drive plate on the end of flap operating shaft in the wing. Presto, the flap's connected.

In setting it up I am particularly careful to see there's no slack in the shaft bearings (cyano hardened holes in the ply) and there's no end play when the dog is engaged in the drive plate.

The plan doesn't appear to give much guide to shaping the elliptical tip. Is it straightforward?

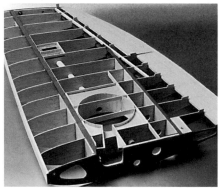

Photo 22:57 *The underside is about ready for its forward section sheeting (note I don't remove the temporary wheel well ribs until after the wing is sheeted).*

Photo 22:59 *The wing is held down flat while the 'D' section torsion tube is completed.*

I don't know that I would go to the trouble of making the linkage that goes with one-servo operation. What's the risk of something going wrong when using two servos?

You'll find it's really not too difficult. Final rib WT3 is quite a good guide but I am leaving it to last so the lines of the wing are very obvious and I will just follow them right out to the end of the tip. Even so, I will keep an eye of the washout and see it develops in the way it is drawn on the rib pattern at the bottom of sheet 8. Where WT4 joins WT5 you'll see there's quite a discrepancy in the way they lie. This is intended and it explains why WT6 and WT7 are to be cut on the line shown.

Photo 22:58 *Sliding in on a carbon tube, the elliptical tip is supported from deep inside the wing spar.*

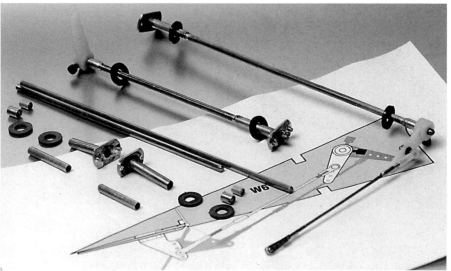

Photo 22:60 *The flap activating linkage looks more difficult than it is. I make it using a fine metal-cutting saw, my sanding wheel, drill, files and a heating flame.*

No arguments needed. Risk management in models is one of those very personal assessments and without hard data to prove a point, we're all guessing.

Separate flaps mean they can be built more lightly than one-piece flaps like on the Sea Fury. Also, they can be operated by a control horn placed near each of their centres, further reducing their tendency to twist. Even so, they must be fairly stiff. I am using two sheets of $^1/_{16}$" ply, the upper one feathered at the trailing edge and both separated by a very thin balsa frame. Epoxied together, they form a stiff torsion tube. Hinges are incorporated in the sandwich.

I feed the overhanging hinge flaps straight up into the wing and sandwich them against the flap opening spar and some scrap balsa packers. Naturally, all hinge flaps are pinned as well as glued.

■ Completing the wings:

I install, adjust and check out the flap mechanism, test tighten the wing bolts through into the centre section (framing the access holes after I see exactly how large they must be for my tightening method), and look over everything before sheeting the wing panels with $^1/_{16}$" balsa, top and bottom.

The ailerons are sheeted and cut from the wing then have $^1/_4$" leading edges added and shaped. Their hinge pins are test-fitted and I check the aileron clearances through their full movement.

■ Always conscious of weight vs strength, I choose to glass over the sheeting. Using 0.7oz cloth and diluted epoxy (30% acetone) I do one side at a time, but before the resin goes off, I stretch cling film over the surface and smooth out any air bubbles. This leaves a remarkably smooth surface and virtually eliminates the need to add filler (photo 22:65). The weight of each bare wing panel before glassing — 1 lb 5 oz, after glassing — 1 lb 7$^1/_2$ oz. Result, 5 ozs extra, but no filler and no sealer. It's a big plane so that's OK by me.

Photo 22:61 *The challenge is to build a lightweight flap that resists twisting and bending.*

Why use two sheets of $^1/_{16}$" instead of just one of $^1/_8$" ply?

The result is actually quite different. Using two thin sheets which can be separated, even at one edge, you have produced a tube (of triangular shape). This is in effect a torsion tube just like the wing's 'D' section tube.

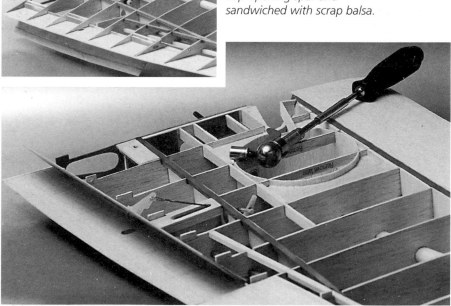

Photo 22:62
The flap hinges are brought up and secured against the flap opening spar and sandwiched with scrap balsa.

Photo 22:63 *With the flaps and their mechanism installed, I make provision for access to tighten each wing bolt, in my case an angle drive wrench but it could be say an Allen key.*

Photo 22:64 *After sheeting the wing, I continue with finishing the ailerons and cutting them free of the wing panels*

It's probably not a good idea to rationalise each bit of weight I add. It's just too easy to apply this sort of thinking to any number of little additions and before I know it I have built a brick. Remember, light is good, light flies better, light even has less momentum to damage itself when there's a sudden stop.

232

Practice

■ Detailing:

There are quite a few scale details to be added.

■ There's the canon. I take the heads off two ¼" wing bolts and epoxy them into ¼" ID carbon fibre tubes. The tubes slide into drilled holes in the leading edge of the wing and extend back onto the main spar webbing. I add thick 1" balsa washers to the protruding tubes and build up the fairings. The canon, turned from soft balsa, are threaded to take the bolts (I reinforce the threads with cyano), and they are done.

The canon blisters are carved from soft balsa, finished and filled, before gluing them in position.

■ Now, the radiators. These are designed to bolt on under the wings. They take one bolt each and are held in location by register blocks which fit neatly into the holes I made to access the wing mounting bolts. So in effect, the radiators become covers at the same time. I don't glass over the surface of the radiators because I want them to stay fairly weak. That way, they can be wiped off without tearing great chunks out of the wings.

■ The air and electrical installation is fairly straight-forward.

Since air is required in the fuselage to operate the tailwheel ram, it's no extra complication to mount the pressure indicator in the fuselage, too. I choose to put it in the scale position of the main fuel filler on the real thing (just ahead of the canopy). Here, it looks realistic and is easy to see prior to takeoff.

■ On to the paint job. Accurate camouflage painting calls for soft edges between the two topside colours. I get out the compressor and airbrush for this job.

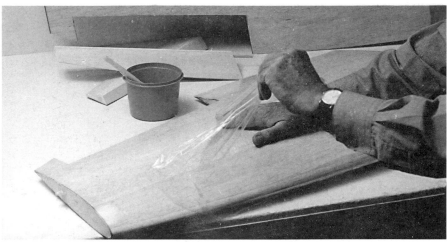

Photo 22:65   *I reinforce the balsa with 0.7oz glass and 70%–30% resin/acetone but, to reduce the weight of filler, stretch cling wrap over the wet resin and squeeze out any air bubbles. The finish is glassy and needs next to no filling. A light sanding is enough.*

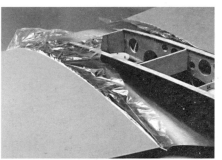

Photo 22:66 *Once again, I use the epoxy bog and cling film to get a really accurate fit between wing panel and centre section.*

Photo 22:67 *The pneumatics and electrics are shared between the centre section of the wing and fuselage. This gives great access to everything without crowding.*

Photo 22:68 *The canon are removable for easy transport. They are lightly built from very soft balsa, so that if they are knocked, they break off instead of being ripped bodily from the wings.*

Photo 22:69 *The radiators make effective covers for the wing-mounting access holes under the wings. They, too, are lightly built so that in the event of an emergency wheels-up landing, they are sacrificed rather than the under surface of the wing.*

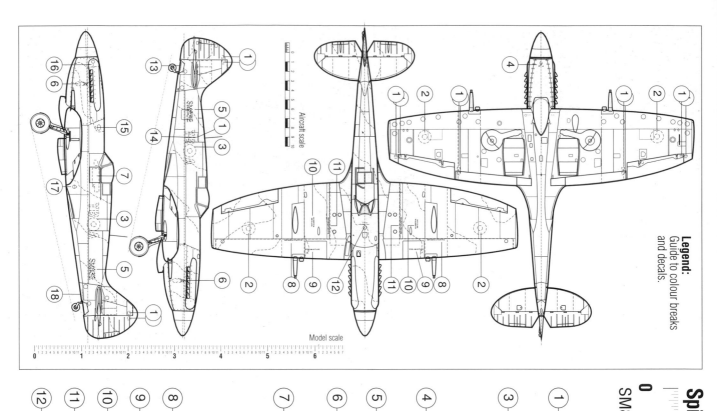

Legend: Guide to colour breaks and decals.

Aircraft scale

Model scale

Spitfire F.XIVE SM832, sheet 10: decals

SM832 in the colours of Sqn Ldr "Ginger" Lacey, OC 17 Sqn.

Scale = 50%   Enlarge to 200% and check size against ruler.

①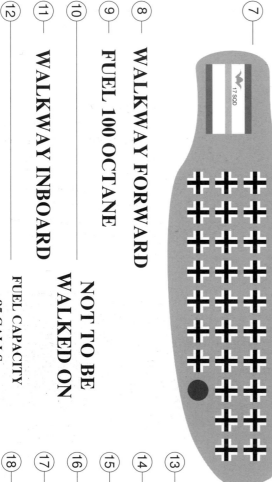

③ **A**

②

④ **YB**

⑤ **SM832**

⑥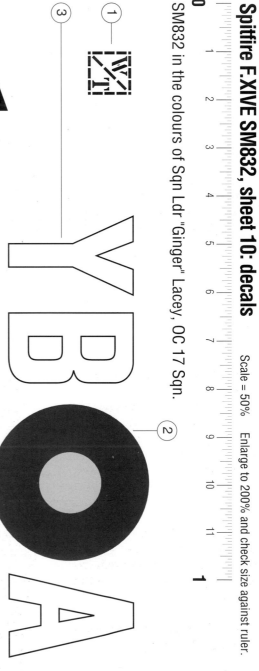

A

⑦ 17 SQD

⑧ WALKWAY FORWARD

⑨ FUEL 100 OCTANE

⑩ NOT TO BE WALKED ON

⑪ WALKWAY INBOARD

⑫ FUEL CAPACITY 85 GALLS

⑬ TYRE PRESSURE 60 PSI

⑭ BATTERY 24 VOLT

⑮ OIL 100

⑯ COOLANT

⑰ 24 VOLT

⑱ TAILWHEEL STRUT 265 PSI

234

Photo 22:70 *Allowing a certain degree of artist's license for the setting, it's hard to pick this is not the real thing setting off on dawn patrol. Fabric-covered control surfaces with trim tabs, cockpit and pilot detail plus the convincing exhaust stack all add to the impression.*

Practice

Detail is completed and now it's time for the final photo sessions before the test flying programme commences.

Photo 22:71 *Low angle views are my favourite for this model.*

Contrary to my general belief that we should do all our own maiden test flying, in this case there's even more than the model at stake. There's a publishing deadline and little leeway for things which could go wrong, so I put my nerves to one side and turn to the most experienced, large warbird pilot I know to handle the flying. I concentrate on photographing the event.

Warwick Blackman's comments after the first flight – "All trims neutral, almost no pitch from lowering the flaps . . . she flies beautifully."

Grateful thanks to Warwick for a fine piece of flying.

Why?

Why do you feel you should do your own test flying? I would have thought it best to let someone who has less emotional involvement take over the job.

Because

It is important that you have someone else go over your plane to check out everything. A second pair of eyes are invaluable. However, unless you are really nervous (as distinct from a little apprehensive), the thrill of sending your model off into unknown territory is a vital part of your piloting experience. Don't be too quick to pass it by.

Chapter 23: Where to from here?

Photo 23:1 *Graham Smithson's F16 is not just at the aerodynamic sharp end, for Graham has also built his own 12 lb thrust turbojet unit that provides the power (see photo 23.2). He is one of his country's model jet pioneer builders, starting out with a 4 lb thrust unit utilising a plywood centrifugal compressor. How quickly the scene is changing.*

We are seldom short of ideas for our next project, but it is often our modelling friends who inspire us to put those ideas into practice. Here we take just a few minutes to see what others are achieving. Some people, in what is virtually my back yard, are doing some very exciting modelling.

■ Naturally, speed is the first attraction to the eye, and there's little more spectacular than the

It sounds as if you live in a particularly active modelling area with a lot of very skilled radio fliers?

Photo 23:3 *Gas turbine performance is now in the big league and modern jet planes call for relatively advanced pilot skills, quick reaction time and well developed coordination.*

gas turbine. Many modellers see this as a totally practical proposition. Advances in aeromodel jet propulsion are happening with astonishing speed

Photo 23:2 *Commercial jet units are still quite expensive but some savings can be made if you have the necessary engineering skills and facilities to make your own.*

The skills that modellers everywhere bring to bear on the sport continue to astound me. It seems that whenever you move into a new location you discover another group of enthusiasts who are pushing the boundaries in some particular, and often unique way. It could be in aerial video filming, float flying, aerobatic competition, giant multi-engine modelling, and so on. Sometimes the differences are emphasised by local topography or weather patterns,

236

Photos 23:4 *Those magnificent birdmen flew some of the most extraordinary aerial contraptions and they can make equally extraordinary models. Alastair Rivers (my right hand action camera man) built this elegant Taube example and it was my turn to record the maiden flight.*

sometimes by the enthusiasm of one or two leaders in the field. All are valuable to the sport.

and there are commercial units which are now almost taken for granted. This field has also provided very interesting challenges, particularly for those with an engineering background and with access to some machine tools. They have been able to build and develop their own experimental engines, and with considerable success.

■ At the opposite end of the spectrum, slow flight has a whole range of attractions, too.

Modelling very early aircraft raises the stakes yet again. Some designs were based on a fairly loose understanding of aerodynamics and the model replica may have some unexpected characteristics to challenge the flier. Sometimes flight notes of the full-size aircraft are available and it is interesting to discover that your model has inherited the quirks of the breed.

■ Large, slow, scale models often call for highly coordinated control inputs before the model will manoeuvre in a convincing pattern. It's a case of practice, practice and more practice. The reward is that great feeling you get when you control a big beast through a really clean routine.

How can anyone put this much time into a model, then send it off into the sky and hope it will survive?

I think this is where we get the big adrenaline rush. With no risk, there's no thrill. Big risks give big thrills!

Photo 23:5 *Graham Wilcox has built an enviable reputation for large scale, authentic detail and realistic flight. Three examples from his 1/3 scale hangar leave us all in awe.*

Photo 23:6 *Big models have the chance to present truly authentic flight behaviour. Graham's big Stearman thunders down the runway and lifts gently on the air in preparation for another aerobatic routine that would convince the most sceptical.*

Practice ⬇	*Why?* ⬇	Because ⬇

Photo 23:7 *John Varley is an avid warbird modeller who's prepared to accept the challenge of multi-engine flying with his modified and armed version of a Brian Taylor PR 16 Mosquito. Multi engine models are probably more challenging than the real thing because when you lose a model's engine things can happen very quickly!*

While I, at times, envy the pilots who appear to have no nerves at all, I do wonder if they get to enjoy the highs that I experience at the end of a really challenging effort. Perhaps they are just better at hiding their feelings.

■ Multi-engine models are for those who have developed an understanding of their engines and how to operate them with almost absolute reliably. Without that skill, electric power would be a safer multi-engined approach.

What's your big point about engine management and multi-engined models?

There are critical phases in a normal flight envelope when uneven thrust or at worst, a total engine-out on one side, is the end-of-story.

■ The ducted fan alternative to gas turbine also calls for good engine know-how. To be efficient, the fan needs to rotate at very high revs. When piston-engines work in this speed-range they are very near the limit of the technology, and a small error in management can produce a large repair bill. On the other hand, in competent hands they are awesome.

What problems do the fan jet engines present to the inexperienced?

Photo 23:8 *George Reid built this very successful ducted fan Douglas Skyhawk.*

Photo 23:9 *Warwick Blackman's ducted fan Panther uses a lot of sky in a very short time. Jet pilots pay attention to the flight-path, keeping the mind well ahead of the plane.*

This whole ultra-high-speed area is best approached with the help of experienced fliers who can guide you round the traps.

The most common cause of engine fault, in flight, is a lean fuel mixture. With our engines relying upon the fuel to carry the lubricant, insufficient fuel also means insufficient lubricant. When a high-performance, boosted and tuned engine that is peaking in the high twenties runs short of lubricant it's in big trouble. The result is usually a calamitous seizure that leaves you in some financial trouble.

It would seem wise to gain experience with high-end engines and tuned pipes in propeller-driven models before venturing too far down the ducted fan flight line.

238

■ By nature, most modellers are also experimenters. And at model size, we can venture into the 'will-it-won't-it' world without mortgaging the house on a hair-brained hunch.

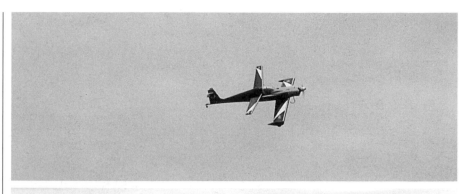

Photo 23:10 *This rather unconventional arrangement is a scale Pushy Cat, a Mike Peckham scratch-build.*

We can also experiment with models of full-size experimental aircraft, and so stay within the scale modelling boundaries. There are many examples such as the modern Rutan 'Quickie' or ancient Mignet 'flying flea' to challenge our aerodynamic understanding.

■ The craftsmen amongst us can really get into it, producing replicas of early aircraft which are accurate down to the smallest construction detail.

Photos 23:11 *Mike Peckham, still feeling a trifle bored with the conventional, decided to scratch design a canard Quickie II. The result is this foam-Kevlar, 8lb, 50" span, beauty that flies fast and true. It's powered by an OS 61 with tuned pipe. What's next Mike?*

Where do you get the detailed drawings you'd need for a project like this?

That's a good question. Peter Hewson's 1/4 scale Sopwith Pup shown here, is a Mike Reeves design.

Photo 23:12 *Peter Hewson's amazing Sopwith Pup before covering. Peter added a further dimension to modelling when he built his model while studying the rebuild at the RNZAF hangar, Wigram, of a full-size replica (which had crashed at Old Warden in 1986).*

Photos 23:13 *Peter's Sopwith Pup with the Wigram Replica. Which one is it that's shown flying? You guess.*

What a delight it is to see these works of art lift into the air, clatter round the circuit and eventually drift back to the grass.

Mike has an international reputation for producing many excellent WWI model designs and can supply much scale information and many fittings.

Photo 23:14 *Getting bigger means dearer, more complicated, but also, more fun!*

■ Others are attracted to the flamboyant colours, noise and aerobatic antics of the stunt planes – the Pitts Specials, Sukhois, Extras and Zlins. Always a test of flying ability, and a real challenge to fly a realistic routine.

■ How about putting four 0.90 cu in engines in sync and lifting off with a Herc, B-29 or Lancaster? Modellers are doing these things, and with great success. Just remember, if you're building this big you certainly need official large model oversight during the building process.

This is starting to get really serious. Where do you folk get the time to put this amount of effort into your modelling?

Photo 23:15 *Big helps aerobatic models to perform more to true scale. Even at 1/3 scale this Christen Eagle is still just under 7ft span – even so, it's a lot of aeroplane and needs plenty of horsepower to put it though its full routine. This model has a 70cc chainsaw engine converted to glow plug. Don't under estimate the cost of a flamboyant colour job like this. The masking alone cost as much as some models!*

Remember, it doesn't happen overnight. Most of these modellers have been at it for many years and work as time permits.

The art is to keep the hobby at an appropriate level relative to your other commitments. You'll do yourself, your family and employment no favours if you let it get out of hand.

I have found model building absorbing, challenging and rewarding. It makes winter evenings interesting and productive. Then, when the sun comes up on a lovely morning, what could be better than to head out into the country to meet some friends and fly some planes?

If this book has helped you to share a part of this enjoyment, then I'm satisfied.

Photos 23:16 *Ron Loader doesn't muck about. If he wants big, he builds big. This 110lb Hercules C130 has a 15' wingspan, the fuselage is 14" diameter and the rudder stands 3'6" off the ground. It incorporates 14 servos, 2 motor units (flaps and loading conveyor), landing light, taxi light and prop lights. Power is from 4 x OS 90s with tuned pipes. Wow.*

Summary of Contents

Subject	**Learn about**	Try it yourself

■ **Before we begin:**
An introduction to people who make and fly models, the models we will make and the experience this building and flying will give to you

Who the book is written for
Why it is written this way
How to get the most from it
What we are going to do
Why we will do it this way
What you will need to do it

You supply the enthusiasm then decide how to use the book and the information it gives
Take it step at a time at your own pace learning what you need to know as you progress

Pages 4 – 7

■ **Chapter 1: Our first 'chuckie'**
We model a simple hand-thrown glider made in the shape of a Spitfire then fly it to understand how and why it works

Materials and tools to start with, marking up, cutting out, assembling, then experiencing some simple rules of flight

Set up your work area
Begin to work with balsa wood
Get it right with jigs
Fly the model
Understand what it is doing
Meet the dreaded 'stall'
Study some of the causes

Pages 8 – 15

■ **Chapter 2: Designing your first 'chuckie'**
We look at pictures and plans of aircraft, put the plan on wood and turn it into a glider that flies

Choosing a 3-view, enlarging it –
*   by photocopier*
*   by scaling*
*   by grid plotting*
Making construction drawings
Building it to fly efficiently

Design a model yourself and discover it's not really 'magic'
Change the size of drawings with dividers, rule, calculator or grids
Test some basic rules of flight
See what works, what doesn't

Pages 16 – 29

■ **Chapter 3: Glider with control surfaces**
Now we build a bigger model with curved wing sections and with control surfaces so we can see what effect they have on how the model flies

How control surfaces work
How to make them and use them
Introducing wing 'camber'

Build a bigger Spitfire glider
Build a better glider
Make it more complicated
Build a cambered wing
Watch control surfaces at work
Try different settings
Try out a 'bungee' takeoff

Pages 30 – 37

■ **Chapter 4: Piper J-3 Cub building exercise**
Make a 36" rubber powered model of this famous plane
Though not intended to be a high performance flier, it is especially designed to include the basic building techniques you will need later

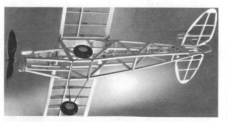
Fundamental construction methods
Accurate glue joints, wing twist,
fitting out and tissue covering

Start working with balsa struts to make up a properly shaped fuselage, ribs for the wing shaping, wire undercarriage legs, 'turn' wheels, install a simple rubber 'engine' and cover the model with tissue

Pages 38 – 56

|
| --- | --- | --- |

Subject ⬇	*Learn about* ⬇	Try it yourself ⬇

■ **Chapter 11: Adding the engine for a MkIII**
Choosing the engine then installing it in the Micro T

Engines that are available
Advantages and disadvantages of some common types
How 2-stroke engines work
Mounting our engine and its associated gear
How to make sure it's safe

Get to know the brands
Choose an appropriate type
Fit out your Micro T
Check that you've got it right
The care to take before you start your new engine

Pages 101 – 104

■ **Chapter 12: Managing the engine**
We look at your flight box and ground support gear
Engine starting and tuning
First powered flight

What you need to start the engine
Safety precautions and starting
How to adjust the carburettor
How to plan your first flight
What to prepare for in flight
How to care for your engines

Check the servo linkage, fuel, fuel supply and ignition
Accept help to start with
Decide what you intend doing
Visualise the flight
Anticipate what might happen

Pages 105 – 107

■ **Chapter 13: Now the MkIV gets wheels**
There's more to aircraft undercarriages than some realise. We discuss design, taxiing, takeoff and landing

Fitting wheels
Setting up the steering
Theory of ground resistance, straight-line stability, rotation on takeoff and landing
Ground handling techniques

Pages 108 – 110

■ **Chapter 14: The Micro T – MkV photo plane**
Here's a neat little camera pod we make which straps on to your Micro T in place of the cockpit canopy – comes off and it's a MkIV again. The pusher propeller makes this an ideal photo plane.

When you progress to greater things don't retire your Micro T, convert it to photography by adding a camera pod
Follow the plan for a standard 'throw-away' camera or adapt it to take a compact with auto-wind
Learn to visualise the camera angles
Smile, it's easy

Pages 111 – 114

■ **Chapter 15: Looking at full-size aircraft**
We study some aeronautical history with milestones of achievement, look at some well known planes and discuss characteristics which tell us about their performance

Learning to identify clues about the age and purpose of aircraft you see
Seeing performance features
Studying aircraft history
Knowing where to go see them
Knowing what they achieved
Why they were successful
In effect, becoming an informed follower of aviation matters

Visit your local library
Attend air shows, go to air museums
Know your local aircraft
Analyse aircraft design

Pages 115 – 120

Subject ⬇	*Learn about* ⬇	Try it yourself ⬇
■ **Chapter 16: Modelling a full-size aircraft** We look at real aircraft to find aerodynamic and structural characteristics that would make a good model	*Scale models need 'originals'* *What to look for in an original* *Knowing your limitations* *Knowibg where to get plans, etc* *How to plan within your budget*	Develop an eye for aircraft Take time to study them thoroughly Begin within your skill level Investigate plan sources Work out what it will cost **Pages 121 – 123**
■ **Chapter 17: Let's build a sports-scale plane** Charles Lindberg's "Spirit of St.Louis" has the right configuration and, with minor mods, makes a fine flier to help improve your technique		Plot an accurate aerofoil Modify a design to improve its handling. Use more standard building methods. Practice 'taildragger' takeoffs then try crosswind takeoffs and landings – just the plane on which to extend your flying skills. **Pages 124 – 143**
■ **Chapter 18: Building a 1/4 scale D.H.71** Being just 67½" span, this Golden Age racer from de Havilland provides an exciting intro-level to 1/4 scale modelling	*Another form of fuselage crutch* *Twin box spar wing with torsion box leading edge* *4-stroke engines and soft-mounts* *Moulding a fibreglass cowling* *Using heat shrink fabric, dope and paint finishing*	 **Pages 144 – 165**
■ **Chapter 19: Sport kit to Schneider racer** For light distraction take we a simple sport kit and convert it to into an entry-level seaplane Schneider look-alike that hurtles round the lake	*Improvising from an existing design* *Another form of aileron differential* *The principles of flying off water* 	Relax and build a very easy airframe Follow straightforward instructions to form the floats, (either hot-wire or bandsaw) then skin them with fibreglass Set up the plane for land to test then add the floats and go float flying! **Pages 166 – 177**
■ **Chapter 20: Building a 60" Hawker Sea Fury** Time to get serious and tackle a 6-channel, 0.60 2-stroke bird with all the feathers and a searing performance 	*A complex semi-elliptical wing* *Planking a full fuselage* *Moulding a fibreglass radial cowling* *Moulding an ABS canopy* *Installing an air system and retracts* *Setting up flaps and how they work* *Test flying*	You have learned to build an accurate wing, now make a complex one Plank an entire fuselage and then glass it smooth Make a mould for a round cowling then cast it in fibreglass Vacuum-form the cockpit canopy Fit retracts and set up the flaps **Pages 178 – 200**

Subject	Learn about	Try it yourself

Subject

Learn about

Try it yourself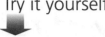

■ **Chapter 21: Researching Spitfire F.XIVE SM832**
This machine is considered by many as the greatest surviving example of the Spitfire line
We visit Duxford to research the fine detail

Decide to use the material supplied here with the plans in chapter 22 and build SM832 or make a different Griffon Spitfire based upon another example you can access
Alternatively, use this technique to research some other aircraft you want to build

Pages 201 – 206

■ **Chapter 22: 1/5 scale replica Spitfire SM832**
Come into the workshop while we build a 79" (clipped) or 88¹/₂" span, 32cc powered scale model based on research of TFC's SM832

Split fuselage construction technique
Building a propeller spinner
Scale exhaust systems
Retracting tailwheels
Canopy and cockpit detail
Camouflage paint jobs

Use all the special skills you have learned in the previous chapters
Work with aluminium tubing for an authentic exhaust system
Make a custom propeller spinner
Use an airbrush for camouflage painting techniques

Pages 207 – 235

■ **Chapter 23: Where to from here?**
The possibilities for extending your interest in the field of aeromodelling are almost limitless
We consider a few

Gas turbines really work
Vintage scale construction
Ducted fan instead of a propeller
Multi-engine aircraft
Large scale models
Scale aerobatics
Giant scale

Pages 236 – 240

■ **Documents**
A collection of reference papers useful to the aeromodeller
Scale effect
Conversion tables

Knowing exactly what is meant by various terms
Understanding why a model can't fly exactly like the full-size plane
Carving large wooden propellers
Converting imperial to metric, knots to mph and so on

When you're stuck for the meaning of an unfamiliar word it's quick to flick to the 'glossary' at the back
Refer to alternative wiring systems
Calculate your model's accurate scale
Get the pilot's size right and so on

Pages 241 – 263

■ **Full-size plans: Ordering**
Full-size plans for the models described in this publication are available for purchase direct from the publishers.
This section catalogues what is available and how to order

All the plans you need to build the models shown in the book are provided at a reduced size to fit the pages. While there are instructions on how to enlarge them back to full-size using an enlarging photocopier, you may prefer full-size originals

You may want to use all your precious building time making planes instead of enlarging plans so consider ordering a set of full-size drawings that are immediately ready to work on, especially for the more complicated models

Page 264

Glossary of terms

Glossary of terms

3-views Usually line drawings, showing the subject from three angles (front, side and top) although frequently five views are given plus some cross-sections.

Aerofoil The cross-section of an aerodynamic body such as an aircraft wing.

Aileron The moveable control surface of a wing designed to control roll.

Balloons (filler) Microscopic hollow glass spheres supplied as a powder which is mixed with epoxy to produce a lightweight filler.

Bellcrank A pivoting plate having two arms, normally set 90° apart, used to change the direction of a linkage.

Blind nut Sometimes also known as a spike nut, intended for fixing to a wooden surface to avoid the need for a spanner.

Chamfer The tapered face of an angle cut.

Chicken stick A solid shaft held in the hand and used to flick-start an engine.

Chord The longitudinal measurement, parallel to the centreline, made over an aerofoil.

Chuckie A small (usually sheet balsa) hand-launched glider which is thrown into the air.

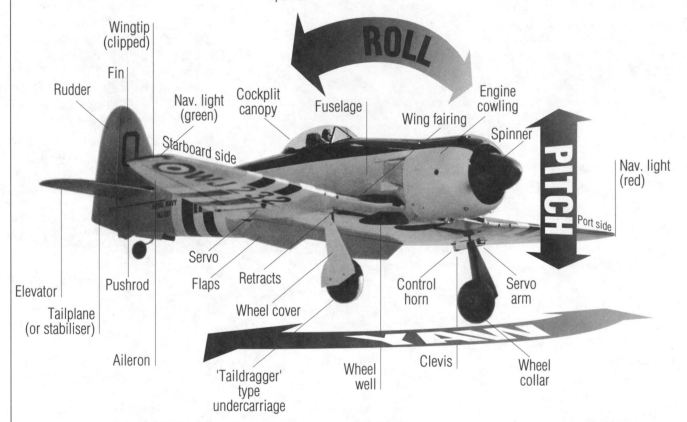

Wingtip (clipped) · Fin · Rudder · Nav. light (green) · Cockplit canopy · Fuselage · Wing fairing · Engine cowling · Spinner · ROLL · PITCH · Nav. light (red) · Port side · Starboard side · Servo · Pushrod · Flaps · Retracts · Control horn · Servo arm · Elevator · Tailplane (or stabiliser) · Wheel cover · Aileron · 'Taildragger' type undercarriage · Wheel well · Clevis · Wheel collar

Aliphatic resin A water-based waterproof, lightweight adhesive, relatively low-cost and used as a primary glue in aeromodelling.

Angle of attack The angle at which a lifting body is inclined above its line of motion, relative to the air in which it is travelling.

ARF The description used for a kit model which is supplied in an 'almost-ready-to-fly' state. Finishing time is minimal.

Ballast Non-functional weight which is added to adjust the balance point of a model.

Bog Filler, in our case an epoxy/balloon mixture, used to fill unwanted cavities.

C of G Centre of gravity, the point of balance normally specified for stable flight.

Camber The imaginary centreline of a curved aerofoil.

Carbon fibre A reinforcing filament used in the place of glass fibre in an epoxy resin.

Centre section Usually used to describe the centre part of a wing inboard of dihedral.

Clevis The device used to pivot a linkage rod end onto a control arm.

Clunk In a fuel tank, the weighted intake which ensures the pick-up pipe follows the fuel as the aircraft changes attitude.

Control surface A moveable section of an aerofoil which alters its lift to produce a change of direction.

Crutch One of the side frames making up a conventional fuselage structure.

Cyanoacrylate (CA) A fast-acting glue available in a number of consistencies: thin to penetrate, thick to gap-fill.

246

Datum line The plotting line from which all appropriate measurements are made.

Dihedral The upward angle that wingtips are raised from the base datum line.

Dope The general name used to describe cellulose solutions used to shrink and or fill covering surfaces.

Doubler Used to reinforce an area, either as a second strut or layer of sheeting.

Dowel A round-section wooden stick used to align components.

Elevons On deltas and canards where the elevator and aileron functions are mixed into the same control surfaces.

EPS Expanded polystyrene foam.

Fibreglass In our case, glass filaments (woven cloth–rovings, or chopped strand) suspended in epoxy resin.

Finals The last turn onto the line of the runway during the landing procedure.

Firewall Usually the first fixed former of a fuselage, but the solid former to which the engine support is mounted.

Flare In the landing procedure, used to describe the gradual pitching up of the nose just prior to touchdown.

Flaperons Some designs incorporate the ability to lower both ailerons at once to simulate the effect of flaps.

Flaps Control surfaces on the inner wing which can be lowered to increase the camber and provide braking effect.

Former A cross-section profile member of a fuselage which supports the outer longitudinal members.

Freeflight An uncontrolled, untethered flight relying upon inbuilt stability.

Fuselage The body section of an aircraft.

Ground loop A ground manoeuvre where an aircraft swings wildly from its intended path and ends facing the opposite direction.

Horn An arm fixed to a control surface to which a pushrod can be attached.

Jig A building aid used to hold components in their correct position during assembly.

Laminate Where two or more pieces are joined face-to-face.

Linkage The mechanism used to transfer movement from a servo to a control horn.

Longeron A construction member lying fore and aft along a fuselage.

Pitch The rise or fall of the nose of an aircraft from the line of travel.

Port The left-hand side (when viewed from behind, looking forward). Remember, 'red', 'left', 'port', all the shorter words.

Prototype The original from which others are produced (sometimes used to refer to the full-size aircraft from which a model is made – but more correctly to refer to the original model).

Pushrod The device used to link the rotating action of a servo arm through to a remote control arm.

Razor saw A very fine-toothed saw with no offset on the teeth, but with a sharpened edge like a knife.

Rib capping Applied to the edge of a rib to provide lateral reinforcing and increased surface area for the covering.

Rib stitching Fabric-covering on full-size aircraft is stitched down against the framing, creating a surface pattern.

ROG Rise-off-ground is the term used to describe a model capable of taking off without assistance (as opposed to hand launching).

Roll The change in an aircraft's attitude round the longitudinal axis.

Rudder The moving control surface pivoted from the vertical fin.

Rudder post The stationary spar at the aft edge of the vertical fin from which a rudder is hinged.

Rx The radio receiver.

Scratch Making without the help of a plan (scratch design) or a kit (scratch built).

Sheeting Wooden sheet surfacing covering an open framework.

Snake A flexible tube containing a flexible pushrod used for control linkage.

Spacer A construction member lying across a fuselage between two crutches.

Spar A construction member lying along the span of a wing.

Starboard The right-hand side (when viewed from behind, looking forward). Remember, 'green', 'right', 'starboard', all the longer words.

Tailplane The stationary part of a horizontal tail surface from which the elevator is hinged (sometimes referred to as a stabiliser).

Thermal Air which, because of its warmth, is rising relative to the cooler surrounding air.

Torque rod An alternative to a pushrod mechanism where rotation of one end of a rod imparts movement at the other.

Torsion tube A construction feature designed to resist twisting moments.

Trim Control trim usually refers to the slide adjustment on a transmitter used to modify a neutral control position.

Turtleback A raised section on the fuselage behind the cockpit, usually non-structural.

Tx The radio transmitter.

V tail A configuration where rudder and elevator functions are incorporated in two diagonal surfaces.

Webbing Structural panels linking two spars to impart additional strength.

Wing loading The weight imposed per unit of area of a wing.

Wing rib The name for an aerofoil-shaped former within a wing.

Yaw The swing to the side of the line of travel by the nose of an aircraft.

Measuring wing area and wing loading

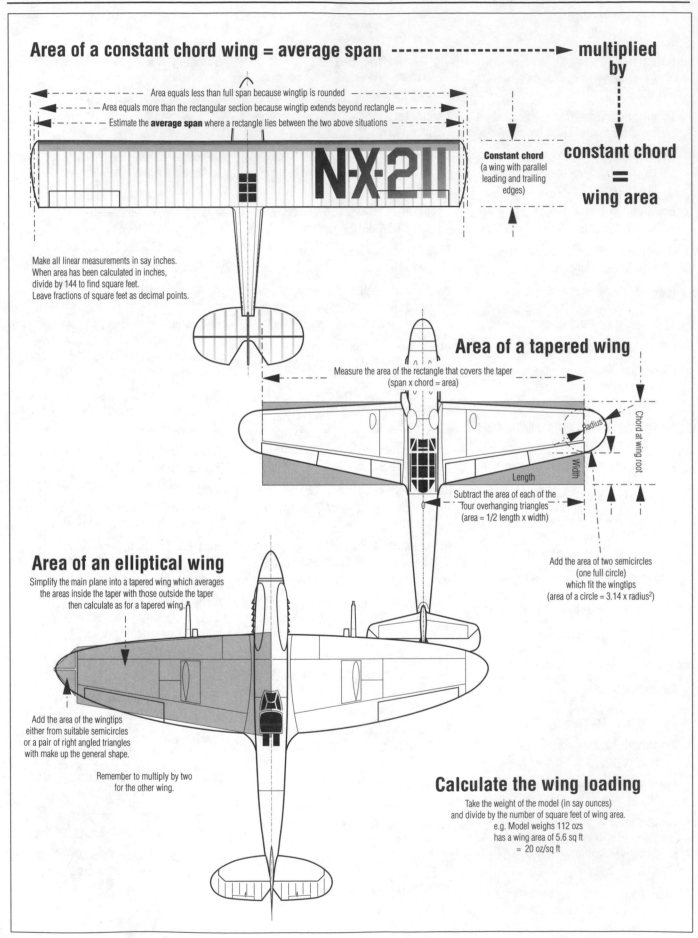

Area of a constant chord wing = average span - ► **multiplied by**

← - - - - - - - - Area equals less than full span because wingtip is rounded - - - - - - - - →

←- - - - - Area equals more than the rectangular section because wingtip extends beyond rectangle - - - - →

←- - - - Estimate the **average span** where a rectangle lies between the two above situations - - - →

N-X-211

Constant chord
(a wing with parallel
leading and trailing
edges)

constant chord
=
wing area

Make all linear measurements in say inches.
When area has been calculated in inches,
divide by 144 to find square feet.
Leave fractions of square feet as decimal points.

Area of a tapered wing

Measure the area of the rectangle that covers the taper
(span x chord = area)

Radius

Chord at wing root

Width

Length

Subtract the area of each of the
four overhanging triangles
(area = 1/2 length x width)

Add the area of two semicircles
(one full circle)
which fit the wingtips
(area of a circle = 3.14 x radius^2)

Area of an elliptical wing

Simplify the main plane into a tapered wing which averages
the areas inside the taper with those outside the taper
then calculate as for a tapered wing.

Add the area of the wingtips
either from suitable semicircles
or a pair of right angled triangles
with make up the general shape.

Remember to multiply by two
for the other wing.

Calculate the wing loading

Take the weight of the model (in say ounces)
and divide by the number of square feet of wing area.
e.g. Model weighs 112 ozs
has a wing area of 5.6 sq ft
= 20 oz/sq ft

Calculating the scale of a model aircraft

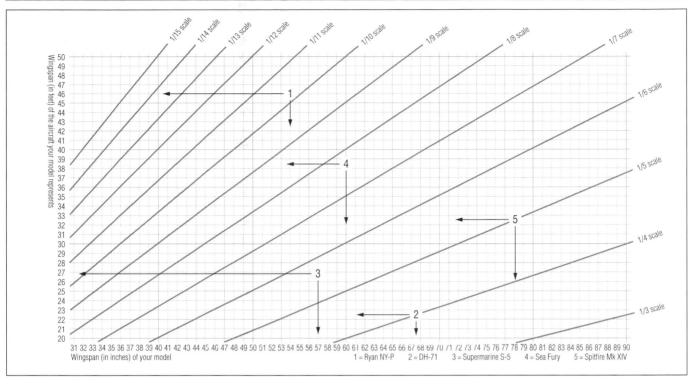

Wingspan (in feet) of the aircraft your model represents

Wingspan (in inches) of your model

1 = Ryan NY-P   2 = DH-71   3 = Supermarine S-5   4 = Sea Fury   5 = Spitfire Mk XIV

To find the scale speed for a model, first we need to know the model's scale. We can easily calculate this mathematically by dividing the wing span of the full size plane (say in inches) by the wing span of the model (in inches). The Spitfire has a 391" span, the model has a 78" span. 78 goes into 391 five times so the scale is ¹/₅. Alternatively, the above chart gives us a quick reference without the bother of maths.

Now divide the maximum speed of the full size aircraft by the scale of the model to find the maximum scale speed. The table opposite gives us a quick reference, again without the maths.

The longer we model, the more we appreciate the need to reduce the relative weight of our models. And, this is the one way to achieve slower, more realistic flight.

While it is seldom possible to slow a model to an actual scale flying speed, it does set us an objective well worth aiming for.

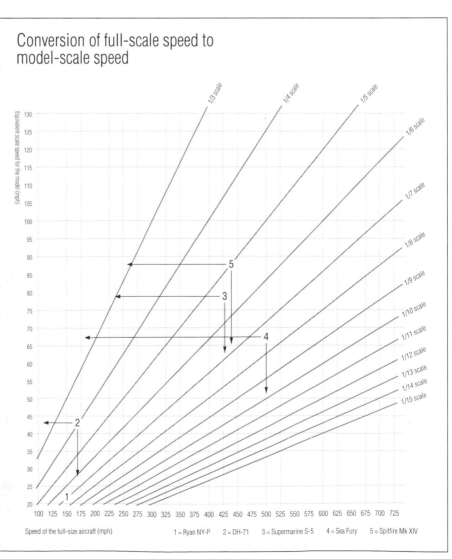

Conversion of full-scale speed to model-scale speed

Equivalent scale speed for the model (mph)

Speed of the full-size aircraft (mph)

1 = Ryan NY-P   2 = DH-71   3 = Supermarine S-5   4 = Sea Fury   5 = Spitfire Mk XIV

Effects of size on weight and strength

As model makers, we have little concept of the forces that are applied to full-size aircraft, or the complexity of designing airframes capable of surviving their influence.

Size actually has a huge effect upon the structural strength of a construction. Imagine a giant, five times our size, bending down and picking up a Spitfire by its middle; standing it on one wingtip to adjust the undercarriage; or tipping it on its back to clean off some gluck. The plane would be destroyed. Yet, the materials it's made from are far stronger than the flimsy balsa we use in building a $^1/_5$ scale model of the same plane. Somehow our models get away with all this rough handling while the bigger aircraft can't. Well, why don't the big boys build their planes the same way we do? We could enlarge one of our models, scale stick-by-stick, and it would turn out to be so weak and so heavy it would (or should) never fly. Why?

There's no high maths needed to understand the most basic laws of physics which explain much.

When we halve the size of say, a piece of wood, we don't half its weight and strength. It's half as deep, but now it's also half as wide. The cross-section has become $^1/_4$ of the area, so it now has only $^1/_4$ the strength. However, it's also only half as long so its cubic volume, or weight, is now just $^1/_8$ of the original piece of wood. The end result is much lighter but, relative to its new weight, twice as strong component – just what we want!

This explains why we don't need the rocket scientist background to set about designing our small-scale models. But remember, the bigger we build, the more we need to know about structures and stresses.

Our models are generally overbuilt, especially from an aerodynamic point-of-view. A very large part of the strength we expect is there to provide for robust ground handling, carrying and storage. We don't expect our models to disintegrate and scatter along the runway if we mis-judge a landing approach or if a gust gets under a wingtip. But the lesson should be that the smaller we build, the lighter we can afford to make our structures. Like so many perverse aspects of our sport, the better pilots we become, the lighter we can afford to build our planes, and these will fly better because they have a lower wing loading. Unfair isn't it?

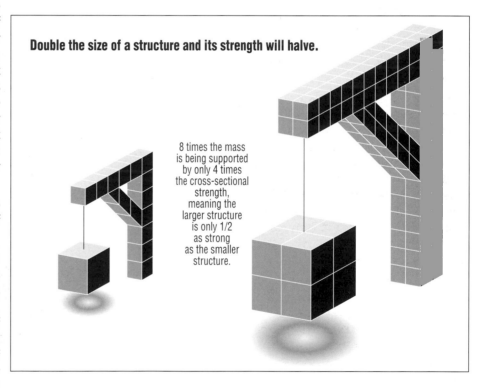

Double the size of a body and the mass increases eight times.

Original size — Double the length (multiplied) = Four times the area (squared) = 8 times the volume (cubed)

2 x length — 2 x width — 2 x depth

Enlarging say 1/10 scale model to 1/5 scale. = Twice the wing span = Four times the wing area = 8 times the mass (would result in twice the wing loading of the original 1/10 scale model).

Double the size of a structure and its strength will halve.

8 times the mass is being supported by only 4 times the cross-sectional strength, meaning the larger structure is only 1/2 as strong as the smaller structure.

Summary:

When we halve the size of a model and scale all the construction dimensions, we reduce its wing area to $^1/_4$ and reduce its weight to $^1/_8$. It will have twice the strength and half the wing loading.

Conversely, if we double the size of a model and its construction details, we will quadruple its wing area and increase its weight eight times. It will have half the strength and twice the wing loading.

250

Effects of scale speed on wing loading

Ever wondered why, say a full-size Spitfire Mk XIV can weigh 8,000lb, have a wing loading of over 34lb/sq ft and still fly, while we must look for loadings of around 1lb/sq ft?

The primary reason comes down to flying speed. While the full-size plane might be flying at 300mph, for the model to look realistic, say at $1/5$ scale, it should be going at about 60mph ($1/5$ of the speed).

But here's the rub: instead of dividing the lift by 5 ($1/5$ scale), we need to divide it by the square of the scale, that is 25 (lift increases by velocity^2). Suddenly that 34.5lb/sq ft wing loading of the full-size plane becomes 1.38lb/sq ft for our model!

When we translate the wing loading into comparable aircraft weights we need to multiply the wing loading by the sq ft of wing available. The full-size aircraft has 230sq ft x 34.5lb/sq ft wing loading, equalling about 8000lbs all up weight. The $1/5$ scale model has 9sq ft x 1.38lb/sq ft loading for an all up weight of just 12.5lb. Although far from impossible, that's quite a big challenge.

Now do the sums for say, a $1/10$ scale 40" span Spitfire and, to achieve a similar ratio, the model would have to have a wing loading of say 0.4lb/sq ft and weigh under 1lb!

This exercise serves to demonstrate that when we talk of a certain wing loading as being high (or low), it is vital to take into account the relative scale of the model we are discussing and the speed at which we expect it to fly. The larger the scale the higher the acceptable loading – and that increase is dramatic.

It also emphasises that, once again, the smaller we build, the more difficult it is to reproduce realistic flight.

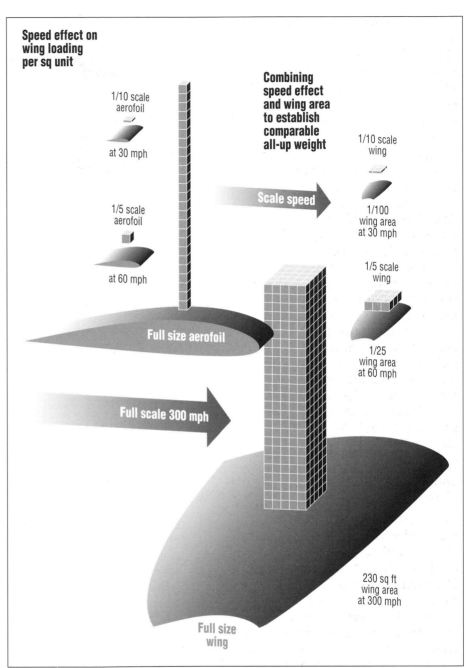

Speed effect on wing loading per sq unit

1/10 scale aerofoil
at 30 mph

1/5 scale aerofoil
at 60 mph

Full size aerofoil

Full scale 300 mph

Combining speed effect and wing area to establish comparable all-up weight

Scale speed

1/10 scale wing
1/100 wing area at 30 mph

1/5 scale wing
1/25 wing area at 60 mph

230 sq ft wing area at 300 mph

Full size wing

Scale:	Full size	1/5 scale	1/10 scale
Scale speed (mph):	300.00	60.00	30.00
Wing loading (lb/sq ft):	34.10	**1.36**	**0.34**
Wingspan (ft):	32.58	6.52	3.26
Average chord (ft):	7.20	1.44	0.72
Wing area (sq ft):	234.58	9.38	2.35
Weight (lb):	8000.00	**12.80**	**0.80**

* Read: *Model Aircraft Aerodynamics* by Martin Simons (1999, Nexus Special Interests) and *The Simple Science of Flight* by Henk Tennekes (1992, the MIT Press, Cambridge, Massachusetts).

Effects of speed on realistic flight

There are two reasons why it is physically impossible for a small-scale model to accurately reproduce the flight of a full-size aircraft. Both reasons involve the apparent speed of the model – too fast in flight and too fast in reaction to changes of direction.

Watch a Spitfire make a low pass. Count off the seconds as it lines up with the runway, comes down to the deck, streaks past, pulls up into a roll then a vertical bank and into the upwind leg. Try the same timing even with a ⅕ scale model and it will be past and out of sight before it's time to even begin the roll. What's going on?

Firstly, the model is unlikely to be flying at scale speed. If a Mk XIV could fly by at 400mph the ⅕ scale model should pass at only 80mph and a ¹/₁₀ scale model at just 40mph.

Let's imagine our models are able to perform well at these low speeds and consider the other problem, momentum. This is the force we feel when we go round a corner. The faster we travel, the greater the force we feel as we change direction. The corner we can go round comfortably at 40mph can be unpleasant at 60 and impossible at 80 so we end up going straight out of the turn. By doubling the speed, we have not just doubled the momentum, we have squared it, so the force is four time as great.

Aircraft counter momentum by banking the wings so their lift can be used to counteract the force. The faster the speed, the greater the force so the steeper the wings must be banked and the longer it will take to complete the turn.

Without going into all the maths, the diagram at the right shows that reducing speed down to scale dramatically reduces momentum. The slower the model the easier it can change direction, far in excess of the indicated scale turn.

Summary:

The more we try to slow our models to scale speed, the less realistic the flight path. It seems we can't win.

The most practical compromise appears to be to fly models slowly, keep manoeuvres long and lazy, use and as much sky as we can.

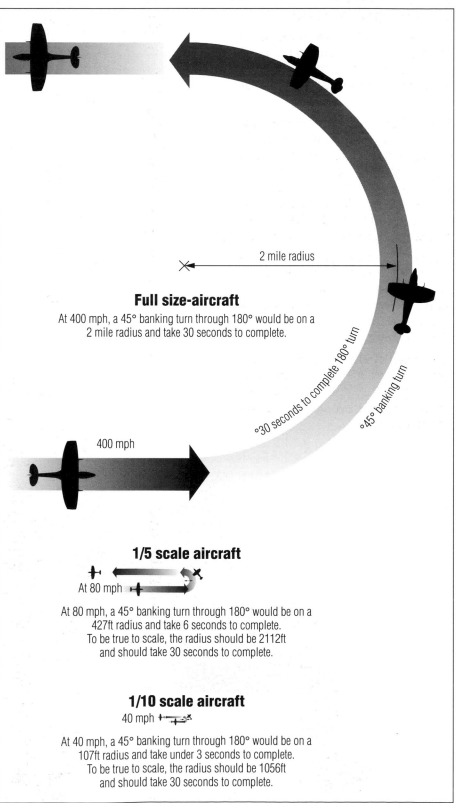

2 mile radius

Full size-aircraft
At 400 mph, a 45° banking turn through 180° would be on a 2 mile radius and take 30 seconds to complete.

30 seconds to complete 180° turn

45° banking turn

400 mph

1/5 scale aircraft
At 80 mph

At 80 mph, a 45° banking turn through 180° would be on a 427ft radius and take 6 seconds to complete.
To be true to scale, the radius should be 2112ft and should take 30 seconds to complete.

1/10 scale aircraft
40 mph

At 40 mph, a 45° banking turn through 180° would be on a 107ft radius and take under 3 seconds to complete.
To be true to scale, the radius should be 1056ft and should take 30 seconds to complete.

252

Calculating the scale for dummy pilots

The size of the pilot in our scale aircraft says as much about realism as almost any other visual clue. And, the wrong size dummy can be the quickest give-away. It's worth getting it right. Here's how.

Let's take the life size of our pilot as say 5'10" or 70" tall. On this basis our ¹/₅ scale pilot, such as we use in the Spitfire, should be ¹/₅ of 70" or 14" tall.

The difficulty is that we seldom deal with a standing dummy pilot. What we need is another size reference. Bust height will vary according to where the particular manufacturer has chosen to make the cut, so head height is probably the best alternative measurement we can go by.

From chin to crown, a human head measures about ¹/₇ of a person's overall height, making our 5'10" pilot's head 10" high. On this basis our ¹/₅ scale head should measure about 2″ high.

Now calculate the size of the head which is correct for your model by dividing 10" by the scale number or, to avoid the maths, use the above table.

Scale of model	Overall standing	Seated (half height)	Head only
1/3	23"	11¹/₂"	3³/₈"
1/4	17¹/₂"	8³/₄"	2¹/₂"
1/5	14"	7"	2"
1/6	11¹/₂"	5³/₄"	1⁵/₈"
1/7	10"	5"	1³/₈"
1/8	8³/₄"	4³/₈"	1¹/₄"
1/9	7³/₄"	3⁷/₈"	1¹/₈"
1/10	7"	3¹/₂"	1"
1/11	6¹/₄"	3¹/₈"	⁷/₈"
1/12	5³/₄"	2⁷/₈"	¹³/₁₆"
1/13	5¹/₄"	2⁵/₈"	³/₄"
1/14	5"	2¹/₂"	¹¹/₁₆"
1/15	4¹/₂"	2¹/₄"	⁵/₈"
1/16	4¹/₄"	2¹/₈"	⁹/₁₆"

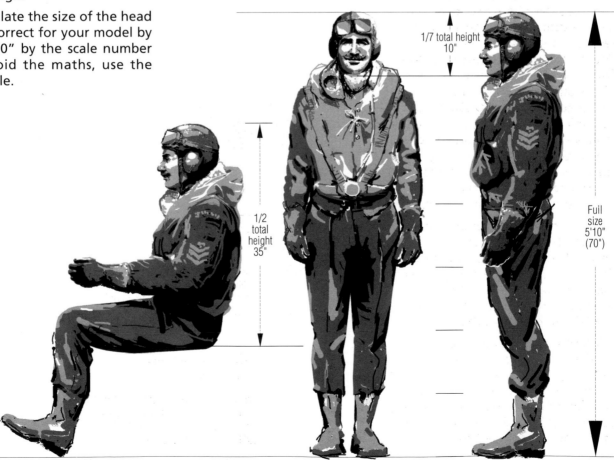

1/7 total height 10"

1/2 total height 35"

Full size 5'10" (70")

Circuit backup

As the weight and value of models go up, there is increasing need for incorporating backup systems to protect them from equipment failure.

One of the most common causes of such failure is loss of continuity of the power supply into the receiver.

This can be caused by insufficient amperage from the battery pack (either low-charge or downright failure), unreliable contacts in the power switch, dirty or slack contactors in the plug connection to the Rx or a wiring break.

Beyond simply, good management of your charging and maintenance regime, there are several methods of reducing the risk of failures.

The most simple answer is to provide duplicate systems. The schematic wiring diagrams below and opposite show two methods of setting up a more reliable power supply to a model's radio receiver.

Rx double harness system

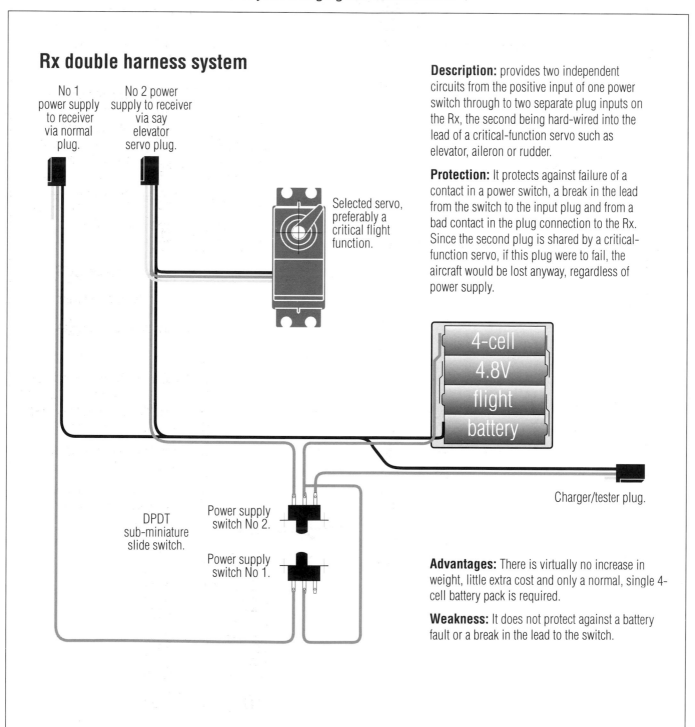

No 1 power supply to receiver via normal plug.

No 2 power supply to receiver via say elevator servo plug.

Selected servo, preferably a critical flight function.

4-cell 4.8V flight battery

Charger/tester plug.

DPDT sub-miniature slide switch.

Power supply switch No 2.

Power supply switch No 1.

Description: provides two independent circuits from the positive input of one power switch through to two separate plug inputs on the Rx, the second being hard-wired into the lead of a critical-function servo such as elevator, aileron or rudder.

Protection: It protects against failure of a contact in a power switch, a break in the lead from the switch to the input plug and from a bad contact in the plug connection to the Rx. Since the second plug is shared by a critical-function servo, if this plug were to fail, the aircraft would be lost anyway, regardless of power supply.

Advantages: There is virtually no increase in weight, little extra cost and only a normal, single 4-cell battery pack is required.

Weakness: It does not protect against a battery fault or a break in the lead to the switch.

Battery backup

Rx double battery backup system

No 1 power supply to receiver via normal plug.

No 2 power supply to receiver via say elevator servo plug.

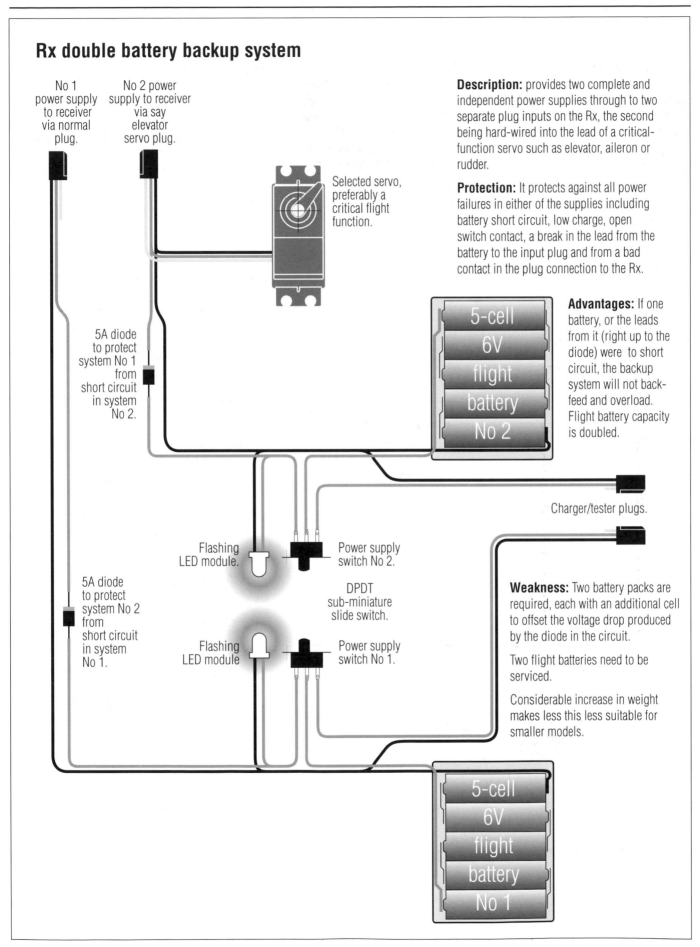

Selected servo, preferably a critical flight function.

5A diode to protect system No 1 from short circuit in system No 2.

5A diode to protect system No 2 from short circuit in system No 1.

5-cell 6V flight battery No 2

Charger/tester plugs.

Flashing LED module.

Power supply switch No 2.

DPDT sub-miniature slide switch.

Flashing LED module

Power supply switch No 1.

5-cell 6V flight battery No 1

Description: provides two complete and independent power supplies through to two separate plug inputs on the Rx, the second being hard-wired into the lead of a critical-function servo such as elevator, aileron or rudder.

Protection: It protects against all power failures in either of the supplies including battery short circuit, low charge, open switch contact, a break in the lead from the battery to the input plug and from a bad contact in the plug connection to the Rx.

Advantages: If one battery, or the leads from it (right up to the diode) were to short circuit, the backup system will not back-feed and overload. Flight battery capacity is doubled.

Weakness: Two battery packs are required, each with an additional cell to offset the voltage drop produced by the diode in the circuit.

Two flight batteries need to be serviced.

Considerable increase in weight makes less this less suitable for smaller models.

Hand-carving propellers

Big propellers are not always available in the size, pitch and price that you want. So, what's the option? We are modellers, so we can make our own.

Hand carving propellers used to be an integral part of powered aircraft modelling – 9" diameter by 11" pitch toothpicks for trusty Eta 29s and McCoy Redheads! We all did it (with varying degrees of success) and didn't even dream of today's machine-carved wood or moulded glass/carbon marvels.

It's a dying skill because who would choose to spend hours making what can be bought for a few dollars? However, big model props, special pushers, small diameter 'paddles', and even display props for large-scale models, are often a different matter. Rather than be stuck, when the time comes, refer to these pages. While it's not as hard as you may think to produce a good, workable prop, getting one to look, feel and be just right is about the most demanding and satisfying carving task you'll ever do.

The secret is in preparing a special 'blank' that is such a shape that the twist is almost built in before you start actually carving. Use only first-class materials.

The plan opposite shows the overall size of the basic block (either solid or laminated from flats). The centred prop shaft hole is drilled first, then the profile shape is cut downward. Balance. Accurately mark the taper on the sides and chamfer across the blank. Balance. You now have a squared-off block ready for carving. Cut away the back face, flat from trailing edge to the pitch line. Finish and balance. Carve the front face to produce a nice aerofoil. Finish and balance.

Well done.

Big models do bring added complications, not least being the propellers that drag them. This 70cc converted chain saw engine can swing a 24" x 12" prop; not the sort of thing you pick up off the shelf at the corner hobby shop. This example was carved from an epoxy-laminated blank made from $^3/_{16}$" red beech planks and finished with polyurethane. Note the tips are painted 'day-glow' red for safety, no small concern on props of this size!

While we should always give every attention to safety regardless of size, be aware that bigger means more dangerous. When you compare the 24" x 12" carved propeller with a typical commercial 12" x 8" plastic model as shown on the left, you can see we're not fooling. Never use your hand to swing-start the engine. Never try to reach round the propeller to adjust the needle or remove the plug lead. Secure the prop and its spinner to make sure they stay there. Have a helper hold your plane and be sure he (or she) is ready for the engine to start, and sometimes, backwards. Spectators must stay back and out of the propeller arc. With basic safety precautions and common sense, you can relax and enjoy the thrill of big planes.

Propeller plan

With enlargement this plan can produce the following propellers:

Enlargement	Size			
100%	= 10" dia	x	5"	pitch
110%	= 11" dia	x	5$\frac{1}{2}$"	pitch
120%	= 12" dia	x	6"	pitch
130%	= 13" dia	x	6$\frac{1}{2}$"	pitch
140%	= 14" dia	x	7"	pitch
150%	= 15" dia	x	7$\frac{1}{2}$"	pitch
160%	= 16" dia	x	8"	pitch
170%	= 17" dia	x	8$\frac{1}{2}$"	pitch
180%	= 18" dia	x	9"	pitch
190%	= 19" dia	x	9$\frac{1}{2}$"	pitch
200%	= 20" dia	x	10"	pitch
210%	= 21" dia	x	10$\frac{1}{2}$"	pitch
220%	= 22" dia	x	11"	pitch
230%	= 23" dia	x	11$\frac{1}{2}$"	pitch
240%	= 24" dia	x	12"	pitch

Pitch can be increased or decreased by varying the thickness of the wooden blank. Thicken the blank to increase pitch.

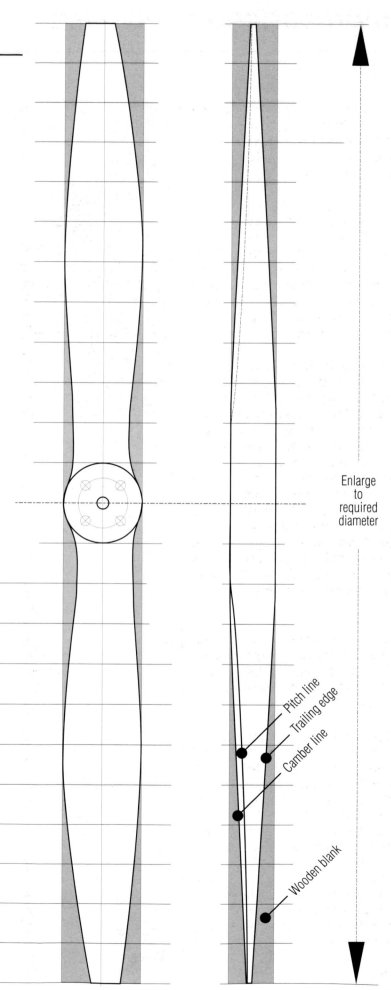

Enlarge to required diameter

Pitch line
Trailing edge
Camber line
Wooden blank

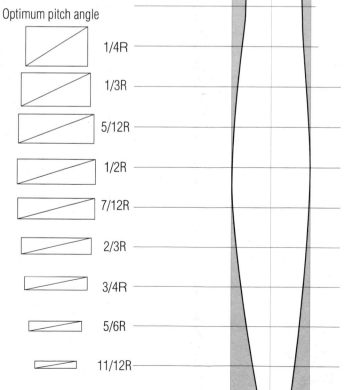

Optimum pitch angle

1/4R
1/3R
5/12R
1/2R
7/12R
2/3R
3/4R
5/6R
11/12R
1R

British Standard Colours BS381C

Your local automotive paint supplier can usually prepare accurate colours.

Colour name	Alt. name	Period	Code
Aircraft Black	Night Black	65-	642
Aircraft Blue	—	65-	108
Aircraft Grey	—	65-	693
Aircraft Grey	—	65-	283
Anchusa	—	65-	109
Arctic Blue	—	65-	112
Aurora	—	65-	447
Azo Orange	—	65-	593
Azure Blue	—	65-	104
Beech Brown	—	65-	490
Beige	—	65-	388
Biscuit	—	65-	369
Bold Yellow	—	92-	363
Brilliant Green	—	65-	221
Camouflage Red	—	65-	435
Canary Yellow	—	65-	309
Champagne	—	65-	386
Chocolate	—	65-	451
Crimson	—	65-	540
Cypress Green	—	65-	277
Dark Admiralty	—	65-	632
Dark Blue Grey	—	65-	695
Dark Brown	—	65-	412
Dark Camouflage	—	65-	436
Dark Crimson	—	65-	452
Dark Earth	—	65-	450
Dark Green	—	94-	241
Dark Green	—	65-	641
Dark Sea Grey	—	65-	638
Dark Weatherworn	—	65-	677
Deep Bronze	—	65-	224
Deep Brunswick	—	65-	227
Deep Buff	—	65-	360
Deep Cream	—	65-	353
Deep Indian Red	—	65-	448
Deep Orange	—	65-	591
Deep Saxe Blue	—	65-	113
Dove Grey	—	65-	694
Eau de Nil	—	65-	216
Extra Dark Sea	—	65-	640
Forest Green	—	65-	282
French Blue	—	65-	166
French Grey	—	65-	630
Golden Brown	—	65-	414
Golden Yellow	—	65-	356
Grass Green	—	65-	218
Gulf Red	—	65-	473
Imperial Brown	—	65-	415
Lead	—	65-	635
Leaf Brown	—	65-	489
Lemon	—	65-	355
Light Admiralty	—	65-	697
Light Aircraft	—	65-	627
Light Biscuit	—	65-	385
Light Bronze	—	65-	222
Light Brown	—	65-	410
Light Brunswick	—	65-	225
Light Buff	—	65-	358
Light French B	—	65-	175
Light Olive Green	—	65-	278
Light Orange	—	65-	557
Light Purple	—	65-	449
Light Salmon	—	65-	442
Light Slate Grey	—	65-	639
Light Stone	—	65-	361
Light Straw	—	65-	384
Light Violet	—	65-	797
Light Weatherworn	—	65-	676
Lincoln Green	—	65-	276
Manilla	—	65-	367
Maroon	—	65-	541
Medium Sea Green	—	65-	637
Mid Brunswick	—	65-	226
Middle Bronze	—	65-	223
Middle Brown	—	65-	411
Middle Buff	—	65-	359
Middle Graphite	—	65-	671
Middle Stone	—	65-	362
Nato Green	—	65-	285
Nut Brown	—	65-	413
Olive Drab	—	65-	298
Olive Green	—	65-	220
Opaline Green	—	65-	275
Orange Brown	—	65-	439
Oriental Blue	—	65-	174
Oxford Blue	—	65-	105
PRU Blue	—	65-	636
Pacific Blue	—	65-	107
Pale Cream	—	65-	352
Peacock Blue	—	65-	103
Poppy Red	—	65-	536
Portland Stone	—	65-	364
Post Office Red	—	65-	538
Primrose	—	82-	310
Primrose Jasmine	—	65-	354
Quaker Grey	—	65-	629
RAF Blue Grey	—	65-	633
Rail Blue	—	65-	114
Rail Red	—	89-	08442/5
Red Post Service	—	65-	539
Red Oxide	—	65-	446
Rich Cream	—	65-	366
Roundel Blue	—	65-	110
Royal Blue	—	65-	106
Ruby	—	65-	542
Sage Green	—	65-	219
Salmon Pink	—	65-	443
Sea Green	—	65-	217
Service Brown	—	65-	499
Shell Pink	—	65-	453
Signal Red	—	65-	537
Silver Grey	—	65-	628
Sky	—	65-	210
Sky Blue	—	65-	111
Sky Blue	—	65-	101
Slate	—	65-	634
Smoke Grey	—	65-	692
Steel Furniture	—	65-	279
Sunshine	—	65-	387
Terra Cotta	—	65-	444
Traffic Blue	—	65-	169
Traffic Green	—	65-	267
Traffic Red	—	65-	570
Traffic Yellow	—	65-	368
Turquoise Blue	—	65-	102
Vellum	—	65-	365
Venetian Red	—	65-	445
Verdigris Green	—	65-	280
Very Dark Drab	—	65-	437
Violet	—	65-	796
Viridian Emerald Gr.	—	65-	228

Pre-flight check list

Previous day

Airframe
- [ ] Flex wing for damaged spars
- [ ] Flex tail surface joints for weakness
- [ ] Test engine mounting and firewall
- [ ] Inspect covering for tightness and tears
- [ ] Test that all hinges are secure
- [ ] Inspect all clevis retainers
- [ ] Ensure servo mountings are secure

Engine
- [ ] Mounting lock nuts tight
- [ ] Muffler is secure
- [ ] Propeller is undamaged
- [ ] Propeller/spinner secure
- [ ] Check fuel tubes for leaks
- [ ] Check fuel 'clunk' in position
- [ ] Check throttle linkage movement

Radio
- [ ] Receiver padded but secure
- [ ] Battery pack padded but secure
- [ ] Rx plugs firm and secure
- [ ] Switch snap-action OK
- [ ] Rx now switched off
- [ ] Rx placed on charge
- [ ] Tx placed on charge

Flight box
- [ ] Fuel filtered and container full
- [ ] Starter battery charged
- [ ] Glow driver charged
- [ ] Spare glow plug
- [ ] Appropriate tools
- [ ] Cleaning liquid
- [ ] Cleaning cloth

At the field

Tx
- [ ] Switch still off
- [ ] Aerial installed
- [ ] Placed in pound

Airframe
- [ ] Check for transport damage
- [ ] Assemble and check
- [ ] See Rx

Rx
- [ ] Switch still off
- [ ] Aerial correctly deployed
- [ ] Servo plugs correctly inserted

Fuel
- [ ] Fuel up avoiding dirt

Preparing to fly

Tx
- [ ] Claim frequency peg
- [ ] Check frequency peg matches your Tx
- [ ] Check model memory (if appropriate)
- [ ] Check all switches and trim tabs
- [ ] Extend aerial about 6" only
- [ ] Shut the throttle stick and switch on

Rx
- [ ] Switch on
- [ ] Test control surface throws
- [ ] Stand behind model, facing forward and ensure each aileron rises to 'meet the stick'

Startup
- [ ] Secure the model
- [ ] Set throttle to $\frac{1}{4}$ open
- [ ] Choke and turn over by hand
- [ ] Apply glow plug power
- [ ] Apply starter
- [ ] Allow idle to settle then remove power

Range check
- [ ] Check Tx aerial only 6" up
- [ ] Walk away in line with Rx aerial
- [ ] Go about 50* paces
- [ ] Point Tx aerial at the model
- [ ] Ensure model responds to all control inputs

After all checks are satisfactory, fully extend the Tx aerial and proceed to the flight line for approval to move onto the runway for takeoff.

When your flight is ended, switch off your model, then your transmitter and place it in the pound so the frequency peg is available to the next user.

*This distance will vary slightly from day-to-day, depending upon environmental conditions.

Model details

Name

Builder

Description

Specifications:

Wingspan _____

Length _____

Wing area _____

Weight _____

Wing loading _____

C/G % chord _____

Fuel capacity _____

Source

☐ Scratch design
☐ Scratch build
☐ Kit
☐ ARF
☐ 2nd hand
☐ Other _____

Type

☐ Scale
☐ Semi-scale
☐ Dream scale
☐ Sport
☐ Pattern
☐ Pylon
☐ Other _____

Power

☐ Glow
☐ Petrol
☐ Fan
☐ Turbine
☐ Electric
☐ Glider
☐ Other _____

Gear	New	Used	Age
Engine	☐	☐	_____
Rx	☐	☐	_____
Aileron servo	☐	☐	_____
Elevator servo	☐	☐	_____
Throttle servo	☐	☐	_____
Rudder servo	☐	☐	_____
U/c servo	☐	☐	_____

History:

Purchased _____
Started _____
Build time _____
Build cost _____
Completed _____
1st flight _____
Other _____

Flight Log

Date			Location	Total flights		Total duration		Fuel consumed		Rx Voltage		Comments, equipment changes, reminders, notable events, requiring attention, etc.	Maintenance checks
Day	Month	Year		For the day	For the model	For the day	For the model	On the day	Over all	Start of flying	End of flying		Airframe / Propeller / Engine mount / All pushrods / All clevises / All hinges / Wheel collars / Wing mounts

(subsequent pages)

Flight Log

| Date | | | Location | Total flights | | Total duration | | Fuel consumed | | Rx Voltage | | Comments, equipment changes, reminders, notable events, requiring attention, etc. | Maintenance checks | | | | | | | | | |
Day	Month	Year		For the day	For the model	For the day	For the model	On the day	Over all	Start of flying	End of flying		Airframe	Propeller	Engine mount	All pushrods	All clevises	All hinges	Wheel collars	Wing mounts

Conversion tables

Linear conversion between imperial/metric
(Note: not to scale)

Decimal conversion of imperial fractions

	imperial		metric
Fractions of an inch	Simple decimal equivalent	Accurate decimal equivalent	Metric equivalent
1/64"	0.02	0.015625	0.4 mm
1/32"	0.03	0.03125	0.8 mm
3/64"	0.05	0.046875	1.2 mm
1/16"	0.06	0.0625	1.6 mm
5/64"	0.08	0.078125	2.0 mm
3/32"	0.09	0.09375	2.4 mm
7/64"	0.11	0.109375	2.8 mm
1/8"	0.13	0.125	3.2 mm
9/64"	0.14	0.140625	3.6 mm
5/32"	0.16	0.15625	4.0 mm
11/64"	0.17	0.171875	4.4 mm
3/16"	0.19	0.1875	4.8 mm
13/64"	0.20	0.203125	5.2 mm
7/32"	0.22	0.21875	5.6 mm
15/64"	0.23	0.234375	6.0 mm
1/4"	0.25	0.25	6.4 mm
17/64"	0.27	0.265625	6.7 mm
9/32"	0.28	0.28125	7.1 mm
19/64"	0.30	0.296875	7.5 mm
5/16"	0.31	0.3125	7.9 mm
21/64"	0.33	0.328125	8.3 mm
11/32"	0.34	0.34375	8.7 mm
23/64"	0.36	0.359375	9.1 mm
3/8"	0.38	0.375	9.5 mm
25/64"	0.39	0.390625	9.9 mm
13/32"	0.41	0.40625	10.3 mm
27/64"	0.42	0.421875	10.7 mm
7/16"	0.44	0.4375	11.1 mm
29/64"	0.45	0.453125	11.5 mm
15/32"	0.47	0.46875	11.9 mm
31/64"	0.48	0.484375	12.3 mm
1/2"	0.50	0.5	12.7 mm
33/64"	0.52	0.515625	13.1 mm
17/32"	0.53	0.53125	13.5 mm
35/64"	0.55	0.546875	13.9 mm
9/16"	0.56	0.5625	14.3 mm
37/64"	0.58	0.578125	14.7 mm
19/32"	0.59	0.59375	15.1 mm
39/64"	0.61	0.609375	15.5 mm
5/8"	0.63	0.625	15.9 mm
41/64"	0.64	0.640625	16.3 mm
21/32"	0.66	0.65625	16.7 mm
43/64"	0.67	0.671875	17.1 mm
11/16"	0.69	0.6875	17.5 mm
45/64"	0.70	0.703125	17.9 mm
23/32"	0.72	0.71875	18.3 mm
47/64"	0.73	0.734375	18.7 mm
3/4"	0.75	0.75	19.1 mm
49/64"	0.77	0.765625	19.4 mm
25/32"	0.78	0.78125	19.8 mm
51/64"	0.80	0.796875	20.2 mm
13/16"	0.81	0.8125	20.6 mm
53/64"	0.83	0.828125	21.0 mm
27/32"	0.84	0.84375	21.4 mm
55/64"	0.86	0.859375	21.8 mm
7/8"	0.88	0.875	22.2 mm
57/64"	0.89	0.890625	22.6 mm
29/32"	0.91	0.90625	23.0 mm
59/64"	0.92	0.921875	23.4 mm
15/16"	0.94	0.9375	23.8 mm
61/64"	0.95	0.953125	24.2 mm
31/32"	0.97	0.96875	24.6 mm
63/64"	0.98	0.984375	25.0 mm
1"	1.00	1	25.4 mm

Speed conversion between imperial / metric / nautical

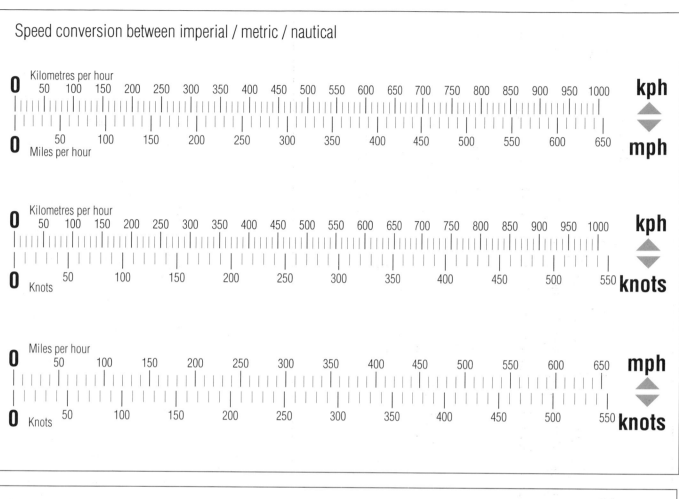

Volume conversion between litres and millilitres / pints and fluid ounces

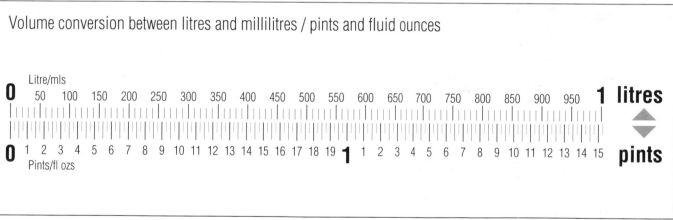

Weight conversion between kilograms and grams / pounds and ounces

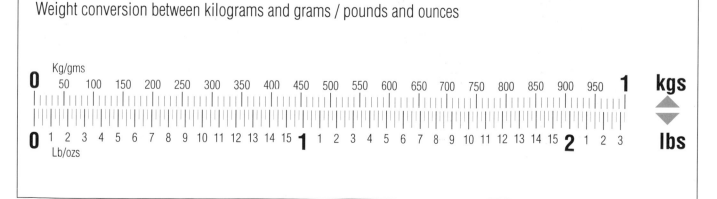

Full-size plans

The advantages of purchasing full-size plans are twofold. Naturally, it is easier than enlarging pages from the book, but also, the large plans are able to be periodically upgraded in light of further flying experience with the prototype models.

Piper J-3 Cub, 36" wingspan, semi-scale, rubber powered model aircraft (see page 39)
bundled with
Supermarine Spitfire Mk 12-B, 24¹/₂" wingspan, control surface glider (see page 31) .... Catalogue No.AM1881

Micro T trainer, MkI to MkV models, lightweight progressive trainer, 60" wingspan for 4-channel radio control and 0.25 to 0.35 cu in 2-stroke engines
(see page 63) .... Catalogue No.RC1883

Ryan NYP 'Spirit of St.Louis', 54" wingspan scale model aircraft for 4-channel radio control and 0.25 cu in 2-stroke engines (see page 125) .... Catalogue No.RC1884

De Havilland D.H.71 'Tiger Moth', 67¹/₂" wingspan, ¹/₄ scale model aircraft for 4-channel radio control and 0.70 cu in 4-stroke or 0.50 cu in 2-stroke engines
(see page 145) .... Catalogue No.RC1885

Supermarine S-5, fun-scale, 57" wingspan, float plane model for 0.45 to 0.50 cu in, 2-stroke engines
(see page 145) .... Catalogue No.RC1886

Hawker Sea Fury, 60" wingspan, scale model aircraft for 6-channel radio control and 0.90 cu in 4-stroke or 0.60/0.90 cu in 2-stroke engines
(see page 179) .... Catalogue No.RC1887

Supermarine Spitfire F.XIVE, 79" (88¹/₂") ¹/₅ scale model aircraft for 6-channel radio control and 2 cu in (32.5cc) 2-stroke engines (see page 202) .... Catalogue No.RC1888

Write: Nexus Plan Service, Nexus House, Swanley, Kent BR8 8HU, United Kingdom.
Telephone: +44 01322 660070
International Fax: +44 01322 667633